Living Water, Sealing Spirit

D1456897

Readings on Christian Initiation

edited by Maxwell E. Johnson

Living Water, Sealing Spirit

Readings on Christian Initiation

Maxwell E. Johnson
Aidan Kavanagh
Georg Kretschmar
Adela Yarbro Collins
Gabriele Winkler
Paul F. Bradshaw
Jean Laporte
Joseph L. Levesque
Frank C. Quinn
Paul Turner
Laurence H. Stookey
Eugene L. Brand
Bryan D. Spinks
Paul F. X. Covino
Mark Searle

A PUEBLO BOOK

The Liturgical Press   Collegeville, Minnesota

A Pueblo Book published by The Liturgical Press

Design by Frank Kacmarcik, Obl.S.B.

Library of Congress Cataloging-in-Publication Data

Living water, sealing spirit : readings on Christian initiation / Paul
   F. Bradshaw . . . [et al.] ; edited by Maxwell E. Johnson.
      p.   cm.
   ''A Pueblo book.''
   Includes bibliographical references and index.
   ISBN 0-8146-6140-8
      1. Initiation rites—Religious aspects—Christianity—History.
   2. Initiation rites—Religious aspects—Catholic Church.
   3. Catholic Church—Liturgy—History.   4. Catholic Church—Liturgy.
   I. Bradshaw, Paul F.   II. Johnson, Maxwell E., 1952-   .
   BV873.I54L58   1995
   265'.1—dc20   94-23990
                                                                      CIP

Contents

v

The Contributors

PAUL F. BRADSHAW is professor of Liturgy at the University of Notre Dame.

EUGENE L. BRAND, former project director for the Lutheran Book of Worship (1978), directs the Office of Ecumencial Affairs of the Lutheran World Federation.

ADELA YARBRO COLLINS is professor of New Testament in the Divinity School at the University of Chicago.

PAUL F. X. COVINO, former associate director of the Georgetown Center for Liturgy, Spirituality and the Arts, Washington, D.C., is a liturgical consultant from Upton, Massachusetts.

MAXWELL E. JOHNSON is assistant professor of liturgy in the school of theology, St. John's University, Collegeville, Minnesota.

AIDAN KAVANAGH is professor of liturgics in the Divinity School at Yale University.

GEORG KRETSCHMAR is vicarious bishop of the Lutheran Church in Riga, Latvia.

JEAN LAPORTE is associate professor of theology (emeritus) at the University of Notre Dame.

JOSEPH L. LEVESQUE is provincial superior of the Vincentians in Philadelphia.

FRANK C. QUINN is professor of theology at Aquinas Institute of Theology, St. Louis.

MARK SEARLE (+ 1992) was associate professor of liturgy at the University of Notre Dame.

BRYAN D. SPINKS is chaplain to the Chapel at Churchill College, Cambridge, England.

LAURENCE H. STOOKEY is professor of theology at Wesley Theological Seminary in Washington, D.C.

PAUL TURNER is pastor of St. John Francis Regis Parish, Kansas City, Missouri.

GABRIELE WINKLER is professor of Liturgiewissenschaft at the University of Tübingen.

Introduction

The late Geoffrey Cuming (+ 1989) concluded his brief 1981 survey of contemporary liturgical scholarship on the Eucharist by saying that "the time has come to rewrite the textbooks."[1] While Cuming was concerned therein specifically with the development of the eucharistic prayer, his remark is certainly applicable to the rites of Christian initiation as well. Indeed, it was once common to think that there was a single normative and universal pattern for baptism, "confirmation," and first communion in Christian antiquity, a pattern reflected in the catechumenate and the prebaptismal, baptismal, and postbaptismal rites of Western — i.e., North African and Roman — Christianity (e.g., the second-century *De baptismo* of Tertullian and the (presumably) third-century *Apostolic Tradition* ascribed to Hippolytus of Rome). Any variations from this pattern discerned within other liturgical traditions — and there are many — were treated by scholars as departures or deviations from this norm.

Thanks to more recent research, however, the interpretation of the origins and development of Christian initiation has changed considerably. Instead of claiming that there was a common initiatory pattern and that it should serve as a norm for judging the rites of various Christian liturgical traditions, the modern study of these rites, to borrow a phrase from Anglican liturgiologist Paul Bradshaw, is "a study in diversity." It is a study which is now coming to recognize that the differences in ritual structure, specific

[1] Geoffrey Cuming, "The Early Eucharistic Liturgies in Recent Research," in B. Spinks (ed.), *The Sacrifice of Praise* (Rome 1981) 69.

detail, prayer content, and theology within the various rites are significant differences, which indicate that from the beginning the Christian liturgical tradition was itself multi-layered, multi-form, and multi-liturgical. A pattern normative for one church is not necessarily normative for others in widely different cultural, linguistic, theological, and ecclesiological contexts. Differences need not equal deviations from a norm. "To emphasize what is common and to ignore what is distinctive of individual churches — or worse still to force that evidence to fit some preconceived notion of a normative pattern — is seriously to distort our understanding of primitive Christian practice, and to lay a false foundation for the modern revision of initiation rites."[2]

This collection of twenty essays from various scholarly periodicals and books may thus be viewed as a first step toward the rewriting of a textbook on the history and theology of the rites of Christian initiation. These particular essays have been chosen either because they offer significant challenges to traditional assumptions and underscore that diversified approach noted above, because they provide clear summaries and analyses of the rites themselves, or because they suggest questions about the origins or meaning of these rites which are yet to be fully resolved. They are presented here not in the chronological order of their original publication dates but in the order in which they might be used in seminary or graduate-level courses on the historical development and theological interpretation of Christian initiation.

The first two essays, Aidan Kavanagh's "Christian Initiation in Post-Conciliar Catholicism: A Brief Report," and Georg Kretschmar's "Recent Research on Christian Initiation" are intended to be read as introductions to the whole topic of Christian initiation and to the kinds of issues that the other essays in this volume will address. Kavanagh's critical reflections on the current Roman rites — the *Ordo Initiationis Christianae Adultorum* (1972), the *Ordo Baptismi Parvulorum* (1969), the *Ordo Confirmationis* (1971), and the *Ordo Admissionis valide iam Baptizatorum* (1972) — strongly argue that, while it is the unified rite for adults which is to be viewed as normative

---

[2] Paul F. Bradshaw, *The Search for the Origins of Christian Worship* (London/New York 1992) 183–84.

for Roman Catholic initiatory theology, current Roman initiatory practice actually affirms and places in tension two different visions of Christian initiation and, hence, two different ecclesiologies, two different ways of being Church in today's "post-Christendom" world: one (adult) which is ancient and paschal-oriented, and another (infant) which is medieval and "socio-personal" in orientation.

If Kavanagh is concerned with contemporary questions still needing to be addressed and resolved, Kretschmar's focus is on the origins and development of the rites themselves. Originally presented at the 1977 meeting of Societas Liturgica and appearing in print the same year, Kretschmar's "Recent Research on Christian Initiation" represents a major turning point in the history of initiation scholarship. Instead of repeating previous attempts at harmonizing the diverse patterns discerned in Christian antiquity into a single normative or classic shape, Kretschmar challenges this traditional approach altogether by taking this ancient diversity seriously. The so-called "Golden Age" of the fourth and fifth centuries, according to him, has been shown by more recent scholarship to be a time of "radical change" and the "classic" three-fold pattern — baptism, consignation (handlaying and/or anointing), and communion in this order — stands at the *end* and not at the beginning of initiatory development, at least in the Christian East as the Church came to adapt itself to the demands brought about by its new post-Constantinian context. While Western Christianity might be able to claim that its three-fold pattern is ancient, "traceable indeed back into apostolic times," Kretschmar concludes that a "plurality of possibilities is itself apostolic" and suggests on this basis that one ritual pattern should never be regarded as common or normative for all the churches of the ancient world.

The next six essays are all concerned with various aspects regarding initiation in the New Testament and patristic period through the fourth and fifth centuries. Adela Yarbro Collins' "The Origin of Christian Baptism" is a compelling study of baptism in the New Testament. Against the traditional assumptions that Christian baptism, having its immediate origins in the baptismal activity of John the Baptist, was based either on Essene practice at Qumran or on that of Jewish proselyte baptism, Collins suggests that its ultimate origins are to be located in the ritual washings of Leviticus (15:5-13) and in the ethical and eschatological ablution imagery and symbolic action of the Old Testament prophetic tradition (e.g., Isaiah 1:16-17 and Ezekiel 36:25-28). Highly intriguing is her conclusion that the Johannine three-fold claim of Jesus himself baptizing others (John 3:22, 26; 4:1) is to be taken as historically accurate and, as such, provides an important connecting link between the baptism of John and that of early Christianity.

While scholarship had long recognized the presence of a prebaptismal anointing and the absence of postbaptismal rites in the early Syrian tradition, and had proposed various theories to account for this,[3] it is Gabriele Winkler's "The Original Meaning of the Prebaptismal Anointing and its Implications," together with her extended and more detailed study *Das armenische Initiationsrituale*,[4] which is now viewed as the standard and authoritative work on the subject. According to Winkler, the earliest Armenian and Syrian sources indicate that their original interpretation of baptism was that it was a pneumatic ritual of rebirth related both to Jesus' own baptism in the Jordan and the Johannine theology of new birth through water and the Holy Spirit in John 3. The high point of this ritual was the prebaptismal anointing — originally of the head only in a manner similar to the anointing of kings and priests in the Old Testament — understood not in an exorcistic manner at all but as the assimilation of the baptismal candidate by the Holy Spirit to the messianic and priestly kingship of Christ. Only in the fourth century did all of this change in the Syrian Christian East with the introduction of a pneumatic postbaptismal anointing, a reinterpretation of baptism as death and resurrection in Christ along the lines of Romans 6, and a concomitant revision of the prebaptismal anointing(s) as exorcistic, purificatory, and preparatory for the immersion and consequent gift of the Holy Spirit.

What Winkler does for the early Syrian shape of initiation Paul Bradshaw's "Baptismal Practice in the Alexandrian Tradition: Eastern or Western?" does for the early Egyptian tradition. Against

---

[3] For a succint summary of previous scholarship see Ibid., 163ff.

[4] Orientalia Christiana Analecta 217 (Rome 1982).

the widely-held assumption that the early Alexandrian tradition was essentially Western (i.e., Roman) in ritual structure and content, Bradshaw argues that its character is better viewed as neither "Eastern" nor "Western" but as "Alexandrian." Its indigenous post-Epiphany forty-day baptismal season points to its uniqueness in relation to both East and West, while the great importance attached to the prebaptismal anointing — along with the introduction of a postbaptismal anointing in this rite only in the fourth century — suggests a relationship with early Syrian practice.

The relationship between sin and baptism in the West has been dominated by an Augustinian theology of the transmission of original sin from Adam. Jean Laporte's "Models from Philo in Origen's Teaching on Original Sin" provides a different view of that relationship again from the perspective of the early Alexandrian tradition, as that tradition is reflected in the theology of its most influential theologian. This important essay not only challenges much of previous scholarship on Origen in general. It also underscores Origen's typological understanding of baptism as the crossing of the Jordan under Joshua/Jesus and concludes that Origen did not view Adam as the historical *cause* and *source* of the transmission of sin but as one symbol among many of the universality of the sinful human condition.

Along with the acceptance of a primitive and common normative structure for Christian initiation has also been the assumption that the early Church always celebrated the rites of initiation at Easter. My own contribution to this collection, "From Three Weeks to Forty Days: Baptismal Preparation and the Origins of Lent," surveys a variety of liturgical sources in both East and West and suggests, with the exception of Egypt, that underlying Lent in many Christian traditions was a three-week baptismal preparation period with no original connection to any particular designated baptismal day. This three-week period became part of Lent only after Nicea when Lent itself developed from the merger between a period of paschal preparation and the forty-day post-Epiphany fast of Alexandria. Paul Bradshaw's " 'Diem baptismo sollemniorem': Initiation and Easter in Christian Antiquity" takes this argument a step further. Bradshaw notes the lack of references to a preference for paschal baptism outside of North Africa and Rome in early

Christianity until the fourth century, as well as indications that baptisms did indeed take place on other days even within the fourth century. He concludes that baptism at Easter was "never the normative *practice* in Christian antiquity that many have assumed." At most it was "an experiment that survived for less than fifty years."

There is probably no more difficult or controverted issue in the study of Christian initiation than that of the origins and meaning of confirmation and to whether the term "confirmation" itself refers to an episcopal imposition of hands or to the anointing of the newly baptized. While the Apostolic Constitution of Paul VI, *Divinae consortium naturae* (1971), defines confirmation as the anointing with chrism in order to effect the seal of the Holy Spirit, this issue is far from resolved today. Some, in fact, would see this definition as indicating the "Byzantinization" of a uniquely Roman liturgical rite. Along with Winkler's "The Original Meaning of the Prebaptismal Anointing," which has been summarized above, the next five essays are all concerned with problems in the history and interpretation of this particular rite, a rite which still may be defined as being "in search of a meaning."

It is hard to overestimate the importance of the *Apostolic Tradition,* ascribed to Hippolytus of Rome, for the development of Christian initiation in the Roman Rite or for contemporary liturgical renewal in many Western churches today. Aidan Kavanagh's intriguing study of confirmation in this early and influential document, "Confirmation: A Suggestion from Structure,"[5] argues that what eventually became the (Roman) rite of confirmation has its origins in the structural unit of prayer and imposition of hands by the bishop, the *missa* or rite of dismissal which generally concluded a variety of ancient liturgical acts in different churches and geographical areas. Only later was this *missa*, occurring after baptism and presbyteral anointing as the "dismissal" from the bath to the table in the *Apostolic Tradition,* later reinterpreted in the Roman West as an invocation and bestowal of the Holy Spirit.

Joseph Levesque's "The Theology of the Postbaptismal Rites of

[5] Kavanagh has expanded this essay into a book length treatment of the topic in his *Confirmation: Origins and Reform* (New York 1988).

xvi

the Seventh and Eighth Century Gallican Church" is a lengthy and in-depth study of the postbaptismal rites of the major Gallican liturgical documents. While these non-Roman Western medieval liturgical sources do not contain a structural parallel to confirmation in the Roman Rite, that is, an episcopal imposition of hands and second anointing, Levesque concludes that they are, nevertheless, to be interpreted as expressing an equivalent theology of full and complete initiation by water and the Holy Spirit.

Independently of Levesque, Gabriele Winkler's analysis of the same sources in her "Confirmation or Chrismation? A Study in Comparative Liturgy" argues that these Gallican documents actually show signs of early Syrian characteristics. Such signs include a strong Johannine rebirth theology, rather than the baptismal death and resurrection theme of Romans 6, and references to the gift of the Holy Spirit associated with the prebaptismal anointing. Highly suggestive is her reinterpretation of the phrases *una benedictio* and *in confirmatione* in the second canon of the Council of Orange (November 8, 441) as references not to an episcopal imposition of hands but to the postbaptismal anointing itself. The *one* postbaptismal anointing was not to be repeated by the bishop *in confirmatione* (understood as a juridical process of episcopal ratification of the presbyter's ministry) but to be supplied by the bishop if it had been omitted by the presbyter.

A different view is presented by Frank Quinn's "Confirmation Reconsidered: Rite and Meaning." In this detailed analysis of both Roman and non-Roman Western sources, Quinn argues that it is to the episcopal handlaying, not to the anointing, that the term confirmation originally referred and that this imposition had as its referent the invocation and gift of the Holy Spirit. Following the work of Thomas Marsh,[6] Quinn concludes that the origins of what became the separate rites of baptism and confirmation in the West are to be located within the practice of water baptism and (pneumatic) hand laying already described in the Acts of the Apostles. To this primitive practice was later added: (1) an anointing between the water rite and handlaying; and (2) still later, and only

[6] Thomas Marsh, *Gift and Community: Baptism and Confirmation* (Wilmington 1984).

at Rome, another anointing after this imposition. In his opinion, therefore, the reference to *in confirmatione* in canon two of the Council of Orange was to the episcopal imposition of hands and not to the anointing at all.

To conclude this section on confirmation, Paul Turner's excellent and critical review of Kavanagh's *missa* thesis, "The Origins of Confirmation: An Analysis of Kavanagh's Hypothesis," as well as Kavanagh's response to Turner are presented. While Turner is genuinely appreciative of Kavanagh's overall approach, he analyzes the evidence for the *missa* structure in a number of liturgical sources and questions whether the structural unit of the episcopal liturgical act in the *Apostolic Tradition* is actually a *missa*. An entrance of the newly baptized into the assembly, he notes, is an odd place for a "dismissal" to be located. Alternatively, he conjectures that this unit "may have been the first public gesture of ratification for the bishop and the faithful who did not witness the pouring of water." In his grateful response to Turner, Kavanagh notes that, whether this unit is called a *missa* or an imposition of hands, the "liturgical elements peculiarly associated with bishops" in Christian antiquity — prayer and handlaying at dismissals — are present in this unit of the *Apostolic Tradition*. It is this ritual structure and act, this *lex supplicandi*, which is later theologically pneumaticized into "confirmation" in the Roman West.

The next four essays deal with different aspects of the contemporary reform of initiation rites in various Christian churches. Aidan Kavanagh, in his "Unfinished and Unbegun Revisited," draws out the implications for catechesis, theology, and especially ordination and ministry in the current Roman Rite of Christian Initiation of Adults, implications yet to be fully realized. Laurence Stookey's "Three New Initiation Rites" surveys and analyzes the proposed initiation rites of the American Episcopal, United Methodist, and North American Lutheran churches, noting that these rites — which, since Stookey's work was first published in 1977, have now, with some changes, been officially incorporated into the worship books of these three traditions — display a great commonality of structure, content, and theology and underscore the centrality of baptism in and for the Christian life. Eugene Brand's "New Rites of Initiation and their Implications: in the Lutheran

Churches" summarizes the various proposals for new initiation rites throughout world Lutheranism, drawing special attention to Scandinavia, Germany, and North America. He expresses the hope that the "restoration" of handlaying and chrismation to baptism in the North American rite may be a "harbinger of things to come." And Bryan Spinks' "Vivid Signs of the Gift of the Spirit" analyzes and evaluates the act and significance of anointing and handlaying in ten contemporary English language liturgies from the perspective of the 1982 Lima document of the World Council of Churches, *Baptism, Eucharist and Ministry.* Of particular importance is Spinks' insight that in relation to both handlaying and anointing in these rites confusion reigns and the various "signs" associated with the Spirit are not yet all that "vivid."

The concluding three essays in this volume are all concerned with questions related to the initiation of infants. Paul F. X. Covino's "The Postconciliar Infant Baptism Debate in the American Catholic Church" is an extremely important summary of the key arguments or "schools" in the American Catholic debate from 1965 to 1980 over the advisability of infant baptism. Especially with the publication of the unified Roman Rites of Christian Initiation of Adults (1972) reconsideration of the place and role of infant baptism in the whole initiatory process was and remains mandatory. From a Lutheran perspective, Eugene Brand's "Baptism and Communion of Infants: A Lutheran View" presents cogent sacramental and ecclesiological arguments for the inclusion of baptized infants in the Church's Eucharist. While writing for Lutherans in particular, a church which still "precludes" the communion of infants without a firm theological rationale, Brand's arguments have much wider ecumenical implications, implications which are yet to be realized other than in the American Episcopal Church, where, at least in some dioceses, infant communion is reaching the status of a norm. Finally, Mark Searle's "Infant Baptism Reconsidered" provides a brief history of infant initiation and offers a brilliant defense of its continuation in the Church "less as a problem to be grappled with than as an opportunity to be grasped." Indeed, the name of Mark Searle (+ 1992) has been synonymous with concerns related to infant initiation in the American Catholic Church[7]

[7] See his *Christening: The Making of Christians* (Collegeville 1980).

as well as, through his numerous ecumenical students, in other communions. It is thus highly fitting that he should have the last word on the subject in this collection.

While other editors would have undoubtedly chosen different essays for a volume such as this, it is hoped that these particular articles will be a valuable supplement for use with other general studies of the initiation rites and with collections of primary liturgical texts such as E. C. Whitaker's *Documents of the Baptismal Liturgy*[8] and T. Finn's recent two-volume *Early Christian Baptism and the Catechumenate*.[9] It is further hoped that what R. Kevin Seasoltz's excellent collection of essays *Living Bread, Saving Cup: Readings on the Eucharist*[10] has done for the contemporary study and teaching of the Eucharist in making readily available and easily accessible the work of several scholars, *Living Water, Sealing Spirit: Readings on Christian Initiation* will do for the study and teaching of the rites of Christian initiation.

Maxwell E. Johnson
School of Theology
Saint John's University
Collegeville, Minnesota

---

[8] London 1970.
[9] Collegeville 1992.
[10] Collegeville 1982, 1987.

Aidan Kavanagh

1. Christian Initiation in Post-Conciliar Roman Catholicism: A Brief Report

THE "ORDO INITIATIONIS CHRISTIANAE ADULTORUM"
I am asked to report what I think are some implications of the
new initiation rites in the Roman Catholic Church. Since these
rites affect the whole sweep of initiatory polity — including not
only the sacraments of baptism and confirmation for both children
and adults, but also the matters of pre-evangelization, evangelization, catechesis, and post-baptismal mystagogy — my task is obviously an impossible one. To accomplish anything worthwhile, I
shall have to synthesize the data drastically and comment only on
those things that strike me as having major implications for future
thought and practice regarding who a Christian is. I shall thus discuss not the rites in detail but the whole range of reformed
Roman initiatory polity from the vantage point of what appears to
me as the central norm of that polity, namely, the new *Ordo
Initiationis Christianae Adultorum* (1972).

This is my first synthetic reduction. It is at the same time what I
think is the most fundamental implication of the Roman reforms,
if not the most obvious. Among all the reformed initiatory rites —
the *Ordo Baptismi Parvulorum* (1969), the *Ordo Confirmationis* (1971),
the *Ordo Admissionis valide iam Baptizatorum, etc.* (1972), and the
various permutations of these rites for pastoral reasons — it is
clear that the rite of initiation of adults is the one that gives
shape, articulation, and fundamental meaning to all the other rites
which constitute the Roman initiatory economy. If this be true,
then it represents a crucial restoration in the way Roman Catholics
think about sacramental reality. Rather than regarding sacraments

as separate entities, each containing its own exclusive meaning for theological exploitation, the *Ordo Initiationis Christianae Adultorum* presumes that all the initiatory rites form one closely articulated whole which, in turn, relates intimately with all the other non-initiatory sacraments and rites. Not only does this mean that infant baptism must be seen anew (perhaps as a legitimate abnormality out of which too much should not be made in theory and practice), but that confirmation as well must be revalued in a more rigorously baptismal context — the same context from which it gradually became separated in the West prior to the scholastic period.[1]

TWO UNDERSTANDINGS OF INITIATION
No doubt the reappraisal of infant baptism is the more emotion-laden practice of the two in the general consciousness of the Church. But relating confirmation to baptism is perhaps the more theologically fertile issue of the two since, as the *Ordo Initiationis* says:

"Hac conexione significantur unitas mysterii paschalis, necessitudo inter missionem Filii et effusionem Spiritus Sancti coniunctioque sacramentorum, quibus utraque persona divina cum Patre baptizatis advenit."[2]

---

[1] Alexander Schmemann, *Of Water and the Spirit*, (New York) 76–77, is simply wrong when he implies that the separation of confirmation from baptism in the Roman Church was caused by scholastic theories on grace. While some of these theories were used to explain the separation, the latter had already occurred quite prior to the scholastic period. In fact, scholastic theologians were doing precisely what Schmemann says all theologians should do, namely, explain the liturgy as tradition delivers it. The problem with this is that it ignores a hermeneutic of liturgical tradition, leaving the theologian at the mercy of the forms received. Conventionalisms as well as relatively recent innovations thus are indistinguishable from "tradition." This afflicted scholastic theologians without doubt: it continues to afflict Orthodox theologians to this day.

[2] "By this connection is signified the unity of the paschal mystery, the necessity that obtains between the mission of the Son and the pouring out of the Holy Spirit, and the joint relationship of the sacraments [of baptism and confirmation] by which each divine Person comes with the Father upon the baptized" (*OICA*, para. 34). I offer here my own translation since that of the

If the theology expressed here is to be taken seriously for what it says, then it is inevitable that the continued separation of baptism in infancy from confirmation at a later period must be reviewed. The alternative will be to sustain two quite different sets of meanings, catecheses, and ritual forms for confirmation. The first will be that for adults, who are baptized and confirmed within the same service even if the bishop is absent: the ethos of this ritual form of confirmation is splendidly baptismal, paschal, and trinitarian. The second will be that for children and adolescents who were already baptized years previously: the ethos of this ritual form of confirmation has more to do with its marking an educational or life-crisis point in the development of the recipients by episcopal presidency at the event.

In other words, the Roman Rite now finds itself affirming in practice *two* initiatory theories and practices that have successively held sway in its history: the first is antique and paschal, the second medieval and sociopersonal in emphasis (*ad robur*). The first presupposes the presence of adult converts in local churches, yet these are rare in most places. (In 1976 less than one in eleven baptisms were of an adult in my country — 80,000 versus almost 900,000). The second presupposes a sustained Catholic birthrate and functioning forms of religious education such as the parochial school.

But the implications of these contrasts go far beyond sacramenal practice in the narrow sense. Both sets of initiatory theories and practices now embraced by the Roman Rite rest upon rather different views of the Church and its situation in the world. If, as in the medieval period in the West, the Church could reasonably presume to be correlative with the society of which it was largely the author, then it could and did expect that evangelization and catechesis would be done on many levels throughout a society based on Christian assumptions. The Church itself, in such a situation, could direct its attention toward keeping the foci of social-political power reasonably Christian in order that preaching and exhortation to more devout piety within the Church might

---

International Committee on English in the Liturgy subtly weakens the sense of the Latin original.

function freely. This medieval polity was, to put it another way, directed not so much at strategic conversion to the faith as at tactical conversions within the faith to lives of greater piety and more intense devotion, as exhibited in the many religious orders and pious lay movements. Thus the ancient baptismal catechumenate never died: it was rather transferred into religious houses, becoming the novitiate and, later, a seminary education. By the same token, religious vows and priestly ordination took on much of the aura once possessed by baptism — a development that has returned to haunt us in the demand of women for priestly ordination, a demand often based on baptism's creating a Christian proletariat while holy orders creates something called "first-class citizenship" in the Church. In this one detects a sacramental theology *ad robur* taken to not illogical extremes.

On the other hand, the more antique set of initiatory theories and practices dates back to a period prior to the emergence of medieval "Christendom," when the correlation of Church and civil society either did not exist or was only just beginning. The baptismal writings surviving from this period — witness Tertullian, Cyril of Jerusalem, Chrysostom, Ambrose, and Augustine — all attest presumptions about evangelization and catechesis that at best infrequently envisage these being done in whole or part by the society at large. Nor do they regard Christian initiation as a therapeutic social event nor the Church as a state function. I should say that this set of initiatory theories and practices reflects a view of the Church in society that more closely resembles the facts of our own day than does the first, despite the difficulty many modern Christians experience in coming to terms with these facts.

Be that as it may, the juxtaposition of two distinct sets of initiatory theories and practices within the present Roman Rite cannot but affect them both. My own opinion is that the juxtaposition is healthy since it reflects the reality of our present position, but that, granted the accuracy of our being a Church in a post-Christendom world, the antique polity will eventually prevail in modified form over the medieval.

This means, I think, that the days of baptism in infancy and confirmation in adolescence as our norm are numbered; that the days of evangelization by initiating youths into "appropriate" civil structures are numbered; that the days of catechizing solely in school classrooms are numbered; that the days in which we regard a man's or woman's entry into novitiate or seminary as their "entry into the Church" are numbered; that the days of our practical equation of Church and civil society are over.

I may be wrong about all this, but I do not think so. For as I have travelled my own hemisphere speaking with a variety of Christian groups, I find recurring quite across denominational lines a growing concern for Christian identity as individuals and as churches. The questions "Who am I as a Christian?" and "Who are we as a Church?" must be regarded as initiatory questions if Tertullian was right when he said *Fiunt non nascuntur Christiani*. The answers begin in the "making" of Christians — from the first stirrings of belief, through the catechumenate (a catechumen is a type of Christian already endowed with sacramental rights to Christian marriage, the liturgy of the Word, and Christian burial), to the united sacramental process of baptism-confirmation-eucharist which constitutes the assembly of the *fideles*, and beyond that into the continuing conversion which is ecclesial life together. The Roman rites view all this, both in whole and in each of its parts, as a sustained and closely articulated process rather than as a series of separate and discrete events. It is a

". . . transitus, secum trahens progressivam sensus et morum immutationem, cum suis socialibus consectariis manifestus fieri et tempore . . . paulatim evolvi debet."[3]

---

[3] ". . . transition that brings with it a progressive change in outlook and style of life which should become evident by a gradual evolution over a period of time" (OICA, 19:12, quoting the decree on missions, *Ad Gentes*, of the Second Vatican Council, para. 13). Referring primarily to the time of the catechumenate, the principle stated nonetheless applies to the whole process of initiation and of the rest of ecclesial life as well.

Here we may see something of the sense of "economic dynamism" restored to a sacramental theology *ad robur*. This implies
that no single sacrament by itself discloses its root-meaning in iso-
lation from those that precede and succeed it within the continuing conversion that is ecclesial life. Concretely put, conversion
leading into baptism-confirmation can now more fertilely be seen
as the compound way in which the eucharist begins, and the eucharist can be seen as the mode in which that compound way is
sustained in the Church's annual round of life, especially through
Lent and in the paschal vigil. Among other things, this perspective throws new light upon how penance, for example, might be
more adequately grasped in theory and employed in pastoral practice: rather less as an ecclesiastical technique for alleviating guilt
similar to that of psychological analysis; rather more as an act of
worship by which baptismal conversion in faith is strengthened
and eucharistic communion in faith is sustained. For the sacrament of reconciliation is not primarily about guilt: it is about a life
of faith shared — as, indeed, are all the sacraments.

SOME DIFFICULTIES

I cannot emphasize too strongly my belief that in the restored
Roman initiation polity lie the germs of a vastly revitalized
sacramental theology and pastoral practice. At the same time I
would be less than honest if I did not express my equally strong
belief that the radical traditionalism of the documents is perhaps
an Achilles' heel. By this I mean that, to have their salutary effects, the rites must be transferred from the printed texts into the
lives of our churches. These churches, their clergy and people, are
at present generally about as prepared to regard adult initiation as
normative as they are ready for the Parousia. Nor are they prepared for the evangelical tasks that are necessary to produce,
under God's grace, adult candidates for initiation. Even less do
we possess the catechetical insights and structures necessary to
form an adult catechumen's burgeoning personal faith adequately
into that mature ecclesial faith the documents describe so splendidly as requisite for sacramental initiation. Religious educators in
my country find it difficult to understand that catechesis is conversion therapy of a definite sacramental and ecclesial kind. What

now dominates the field is much purely personal counselling on one hand and much formal religious education in school classrooms on the other. Neither of these is the catechesis of which I understand tradition or the Roman documents to speak.

To make a long matter short, the restored Roman initiation polity is, if truth be told, a major intimidation to many local churches because it is rightly perceived by those who study the documents to be explosive of the conventional patterns of church life. Most priests are horrified at the thought of dismissing catechumens from the Sunday eucharist, no matter how powerful a non-verbal catechesis this might be for the faithful on the grand dignity of their own baptism. Most bishops are quite incapable of viewing confirmation, along with ordinations and blessing chrism, as anything other than "their" sacrament. They perceive catechesis to be catechetics, and turn the matter over to their diocesan school board. And it has really never yet occurred, either to clergy or people in general, that a non-baptized catechumen of whatever age is not a pagan in some danger of hell should death transpire before the waters are poured. As long as this last assumption prevails, infant baptism will remain in place as our *de facto* initiatory norm, despite the affirmations of tradition and the recent Council that a catechumen is already in a degree of true communion with Christ in his Church.[4]

Because of these and other easily perceptible difficulties in the restored initiation polity, most clergy regard its implementation as problematic if not impossible. They are right. For what the Roman documents contain are not merely specific changes in liturgical rubrics, but a restored and unified vision of the Church. One might describe it as a concentric ecclesiology locked together by the sacramental discipline of faith shared on all levels, rather than as a pyramidal ecclesiology of juridical delegation of power that rests upon the base of a baptized proletariat.

---

[4] See, for example, the dogmatic constitution on the Church, *Lumen Gentium*, of the Second Vatican Council, para. 14; the decree on missions, *Ad Gentes*, para. 13–14. Also Hippolytus' *Apostolic Tradition* 19:2 (G. Dix, *The Apostolic Tradition*, London ²1968, 30), concerning the salvation of a catechumen who suffers death before baptism.

Woven throughout the restored polity is a concept of "orthodoxy" as "right worship," a concept of the law of worship founding the law of faith (*lex orandi legem statuat credendi*), a concept of faith as a life lived in common under the law of the Gospel, a concept of the Church as a communion in faith and as a commonwealth of discipline — a ministry of reconciliation. Scholars talk of these things as ideals: the Roman documents on initiation make them a norm that all must secure to some degree in practice.

Here is both the rub and the promise. One may turn an altar around and leave *reform* at that. But one cannot set an adult catechumenate in motion without becoming necessarily involved with *renewal* in the ways a local church lives its faith from top to bottom. For members of an adult catechumenate must be secured through evangelization; they must be formed to maturity in ecclesial faith through catechesis both prior to baptism and after it; and there must be something to initiate them into that will be correlative to the expectations built up in them throughout their whole initiatory process. This last means a community of lively faith in Jesus Christ dead, risen, and present actually among his People. In this area, when one change occurs, all changes. Few are able to bear the rub, but all desire the promise howsoever inchoately.

THE NEED FOR PUBLICITY

This brings me to the last major implication of restored Roman initiatory polity I shall be able to mention here. It is the inevitable need for more and better expository publicity for the new rites, especially for those that deal with the Christian initiation of adults. To date there has been rather a dearth of commentary about this on both sides of the Atlantic. Perhaps this is understandable because these rites appeared almost at the end of a decade of reform in the Roman liturgy. For this reason the *Ordo Initiationis Christianae Adultorum* strikes me as being the most mature piece of liturgical reform to have issued from the Second Vatican Council, and the most portentous by far for both theological reflection and pastoral practice in the future. Yet several factors seem to have militated against its being seen for what I think it is, in addition to the difficulties inherent in it sketched above.

One of these factors is that by the time it appeared in 1972 people were weary of reforms. So much had been only partly absorbed already over the previous decade that the new *Ordo* fell on ears deafened and hearts hardened by previous stresses.

Another factor seems to have been a peculiar Roman Catholic, shall one say, lack of interest in baptism. A review of monographic literature on baptism for the thirty years preceding 1972 will, I think, show few significant titles on the matter by Roman Catholics (one naturally thinks of A. Stenzel, B. Neunheuser, T. Maertens, and some others).[5] There was no issue to evoke such publications, and even when the Holy Office felt compelled to reiterate in 1958 the discipline of *quamprimum* baptism of infants, its *monitum* evoked only sporadic comment and little literature. (The Second Vatican Council was summoned the following year.) The fact is that baptismal issues and literature were being produced during this period by non-Roman Catholics (one thinks of the Dix-Lampe-Thornton debate on confirmation in the Church of England and the Barth-Cullmann confrontation over infant baptism in the continental Protestant Churches of the late 1940's and early 1950's). The conclusion is inescapable that Roman Catholic interest lay with the eucharist and, to a lesser extent, with penance: Protestants were concerned with baptism and all that.

A third factor is that, while this situation is now changing, it has only just begun to do so. In my own country, no Roman Catholic scholar produced anything on baptism even approaching a worthwhile monographic scope until Hugh Riley's *Christian Initiation*, done as a dissertation at Regensburg in 1971 and published in Washington in 1974.[6] Not until 1974 was a public assembly held on Christian Initiation under Roman Catholic auspices in my country, at the University of Notre Dame.[7] But we still have yet to see

[5] A. Stenzel, *Die Taufe: eine genetische Erklärung der Taufliturgie* (Innsbruck 1958); B. Neunheuser, *Taufe und Firmung* (Freiburg i.B., 1964); T. Maertens, *Histoire et pastorale du rituel du catéchuménat et du baptême* (Bruges 1962).

[6] H. Riley, *Christian Initiation: A Comparative Study of the Interpretation of the Baptismal Liturgy in the Mystagogical Writings of Cyril . . . Chrysostom . . . Mopsuestia and Ambrose . . .* (Washington 1974) xxxiii–481.

[7] The papers appeared in *Made, not Born: New Perspectives on Christian Initiation and the Catechumenate*, ed. Murphy Center for Liturgical Research (Notre Dame 1976) ix–183.

the matter of baptismal theory and practice addressed by any of our official episcopal meetings, our theological societies, or our quasi-official liaison committees on ecumenical relations. The silence from these groups is loud, yet they proceed to treat matters of Church discipline, Christian ethics, the sex of the minister, and the union of the churches east and west on the basis of baptismal presumptions about Christian identity that are largely as unexamined as they are merely conventional. This bodes ill, I think, for discipline, ethics, ministry, and ecumenical growth in both theory and practice. For all these matters arise out of who Christians are and how they live their lives in faith together. This is a baptismal question that cannot be too long ignored if the Church is to remain faithful.

I shall take confidence that the restored Roman rites of Christian Initiation have begun to come alive when I read a treatise in Christian ethics that begins with baptism into Christ; when I see episcopal meetings deciding on Church discipline from a baptismal perspective; when I partake in ecumenical discussions that begin not with Luther or Cranmer or Calvin or Trent, but with baptism; when I am lectured on ministry in terms not of modern sexual roles but of baptism; when I can worship in a parish that consummates its corporate life through Lent at the paschal vigil, gathered around the font where all new life begins.

In the meantime, there is much work to be done.

Georg Kretschmar

2. Recent Research on Christian Initiation

THE QUEST FOR THE PRIMITIVE STRUCTURE

When Duns Scotus, the first of the great Franciscan teachers of the island of Britain, whose path led him to the Continent and who found his grave in what we now know as Germany, characterized theology as *cognitio* or *scientia practica*, his definition was certainly not based on the modern conventional distinction between theory and practice. He means nonetheless that theological knowledge enjoys a practical significance and is a determinative factor in human action.[1] This is particularly true and relevant where liturgiology is concerned. Even contributions to historical research, especially the far-reaching theories, are in most cases intended to clear up some contemporary problem, to explain, justify or alter the Church's practice of worship, or at least to deepen the theology of worship. It would be easy to exemplify this from many of the recent studies on the history of the baptismal liturgy.

I should prefer, then, not to present the "recent research on Christian initiation" against the background of a settled body of questions and achieved results (as may be found in typical surveys of the subject from former days) but to begin directly with a controversy which seems to me to have a distinctively English flavour

---

[1] Duns Scotus died in Cologne in 1308. On his definition of theology cf. Reinhold Seeberg, *Lehrbuch der Dogmengeschichte* III (⁴1930) ⁵1953, 647f.; Étienne Gilson, *Jean Duns Scot (1952)*, German trans. as *Johannes Duns Scotus: Einführung in die Gruntgedanken seiner Lehre* (Düsseldorf 1959) 679ff. On its antecedents see Ulrich Köpf, *Die Anfänge der theologischen Wissenschafts-theorie im 13. Jahrhundert* (Tübingen 1974). The second English Franciscan to enter what is now Germany was William of Ockham, d. 1347 in Munich.

and which has proved to be exceptionally fruitful in its effects on the course of research. In my own experience also it was this controversy which about thirty years ago aroused my interest in the history of baptism.

I refer to the attempt by a number of scholars of Anglo-Catholic conviction such as Gregory Dix and Lionel S. Thornton to prove that, according to the faith of the New Testament and the fathers, the seal of the Spirit, the gift of the Spirit to the baptized, is essentially linked with the imposition of hands — and so, in contemporary terms, with episcopal confirmation.[2] This last implication may be put too pointedly, but at its heart this approach contains an impressive concept of the total history of Christian initiation which throws up a whole series of problems for research to tackle. It is to this stimulus that we owe even the fine and helpful collections of sources and descriptive material by J. D. C. Fisher on baptism in the medieval West and in the Reformation period,[3] the volume on the Middle Ages bears the revealing sub-title: "a study of the disintegration of the primitive rite of initiation." The unity of water-baptism, imposition of hands and first communion which that expression assumed to be the norm did undeniably fall asunder in the West in the Middle Ages. It was by contrast preserved in the Orthodox and other oriental rites, a point now clearly and forcefully emphasized by theologians of those churches.[4] At this point at least it becomes clear that the view we summed up so

[2] Gregory Dix, *The Theology of Confirmation in relation to Baptism* (London 1946); L. S. Thornton, *Confirmation: its place in the Baptismal Mystery* (London 1954). On the controversy and the events leading up to it see Lampe (as in n. 5), vii–xiv.

[3] J. D. C. Fisher, *Christian Initiation: Baptism in the Medieval West. A Study in the disintegration of the primitive rite of initiation* (Alcuin Club Collections XLVII) London 1965 and also *Christian Initiation: Some early reformed rites of Baptism and Confirmation and other contemporary documents* (Alcuin Club Collections 51) London 1970.

[4] E.g. Paul Verghese, "Relation between Baptism, 'Confirmation' and the Eucharist in the Syrian Orthodox Church" in *Studia Liturgica* IV (1965), 81–93; Euangelos Theodorou, "Die Einheit der Initiationsmysterien in der orthodoxen Kirche" in H. Auf der Maur and B. Kleinheyer, eds., *Zeichen des Glaubens: B. Fischer zunt 60. Geburtstag* (Einsiedeln and Feiburg 1972) 315–8; Alexander Schmemann, *Of water and the Spirit* (New York 1976, London 1976).

briefly above, first developed within a specifically Anglican controversy, is capable of having ecumenical significance. On the simplest level, the issue of the participation of baptized children in Holy Communion is at present a lively topic of debate in many churches. To sum up this thesis briefly for the purposes of this discussion: There exists an original normative structure of Christian initiation (or, we may simply say, of baptism, for that is the original name of the whole act of initiation) consisting of immersion, imposition of hands and Eucharist, each of which elements has its peculiar and distinctive spiritual significance. This order is apostolic. The clearest evidence is in the Church Order of Hippolytus (c. 200) and the baptismal catecheses of the fourth and fifth centuries.

We may contrast another conception of the matter: in his thorough and learned work[5] on early Christian baptism in 1951, G. W. H. Lampe made a well-known attempt to show that the disintegration of the New Testament doctrine of the seal of the Holy Spirit began as early as the second century. For him "baptism" — at least in the New Testament period — denotes not a complex rite but simply the immersion. The link between the imposition of hands and the impartation of the Spirit is secondary, and anointings are typically Gnostic. The controversy often hinges upon details and concentrates upon the lexicology of "seal"; here Lampe is at his most convincing. For us, however, the important point is that for Lampe too there exists an original and normative structure, i.e., the immersion, the "baptism of Christ," the effectual sign of the application of Christ's saving work to the believer (p. 57), which includes the fulness of the Spirit. What Dix and his supporters see as the classical age has in Lampe's eyes the marks of a fatal confusion as to the relationship between baptism and the Spirit. The medieval and Reformation period must then be regarded as a time which helped to rectify this confusion — but this is a thesis beyond the stated subject of the book.

For completeness' sake let us mention as the third theory the admirable concise presentation[6] of the history of baptism and con-

[5] G. W. H. Lampe, *The Seal of the Spirit: a study in the doctrine of Baptism and Confirmation in the New Testament and the Fathers* (London 1951).

[6] Burkhard Neunheuser, *Taufe und Firmung* (M. Schmaus, J. R. Geiselmann

firmation by Burkhard Neunheuser (1956). For him too the age of the great fathers of the fourth and fifth centuries is the "epoch in which the theology of baptism flourished with strongest and most mature growth" (p. 71). "The basic structure of the administration of baptism is . . . the subject of a far-reaching agreement in the most important Churches of East and West alike at the close of the patristic period. It is not hard to recognize that in this very matter, even in liturgical families of differing character, a shared and unitive faith has been given the liturgical expression which its nature demands" (p. 73). The central act is a simple baptismal bath in water. The baptismal bath and anointing with chrism or laying on of hands are joined as closely as possible in a single act which leads into the Eucharist. Nonetheless, the two are clearly distinguished. Liturgical procedure and theological interpretation co-exist however in a state of mild tension. At all events, that status of confirmation as a sacrament in its own right was not fully recognized in the West until later (pp. 101ff.). With all due respect to the fathers, it is then impossible to discover in one given epoch the universally normative model of Christian initiation.

It is obvious that each of these bodies of theory has its own rela-tionship with dogmatic considerations; but they also reflect a par-ticular stage in research work. How does a change in the situation of research affect a difference in our over-all picture — or pictures?

THE GOLDEN AGE OF THE CHURCH FATHERS
Let us start with the great age of Church fathers of the fourth and fifth to sixth centuries. It is no novelty to observe that this period saw the formation of the rites of the Middle Ages and of the pres-ent; but this view has been confirmed by a series of monographs, in the case of the Roman rite by the splendid and now almost

---

and A. Grillmeier, eds., *Handbuch der Dogmengeschichte*, Bd IV, fasc. 2) Freiburg [and see English trans. *Baptism and Confirmation*, New York and London, Herder, 1964: Tr.]. Supplementary matter in the same author's "Erwägungen zur ältesten Taufliturgie" in P. Granfield and J. A. Jungmann, eds., *Kyriakon: Festschrift J. Quasten* (Münster 1970, ²1974) 702–23. An equally suitable choice would have been A. Stenzel (see n. 7). The subject receives a more comprehensive treatment in Neunheuser's work.

classical study[7] of Alois Stenzel (1958), for some of the eastern liturgical traditions by myself, in extremely condensed form.[8] There have since become available the painstaking studies[9] by Sebastian Brock of Syriac formularies on the basis of hitherto neglected manuscripts. These studies close the gaps in our knowledge between the catecheses of the fourth century and the ritual books and standard editions of modern days, based on much later manuscripts. We may add a reference to the dissertation by Gabriele Winkler[10] on baptism in Armenia, soon to appear in print. T. C. Akeley's investigation into the Spanish-Vizigothic baptismal rite, in its cautious conclusions, portrays the independent traditions of a national Church which set at naught entirely the usual Western pattern — for example, in that the functions of presbyter and bishop in baptism were not distinguished, so that no signs can be found in the period investigated of consignation receiving an independent liturgical status, which marks a difference from the events in the Frankish kingdom.

The importance of peculiar geographical factors is of course comparable with the nature of the sources available: a series of ancient liturgical books of Spanish provenance have been preserved, which have long attracted the attention of students to this province.[11] Quite different reasons account for Syrian tradition becoming a specially important field of research. It is becoming

[7] Alois Stenzel, *Die Taufe. Eine genetische Erklärung der Taufliturgie* (Innsbruck 1958).

[8] *Die Geschichte des Taufgottesdienstes in der alten Kirche* in K. F. Müller and W. Blankenburg, eds., *Leiturgia: Handbuch des evangelischen Gottesdienstes,* Bd V: *Der Taufgottesdienst* (Kassel 1970) 1–348, written in 1963/4; cited in these notes as *Taufgottesdienst*. I am referring here especially to 280–96.

[9] Sebastian Brock, "Studies in the early history of the Syrian Orthodox Baptismal Liturgy" in J.T.S., N.S. 23 (1972) 16–64 and "The consecration of the water in the oldest manuscripts of the Syrian Orthodox Baptismal Liturgy" in Or. Chr. Per. 37 (1971).

[10] Gabriele Winkler, *Das Armenische Initiationsrituale* (dissertation for the degree of Doctor of Philosophy, Munich 1977).

[11] T. C. Akeley, *Christian Initiation in Spain c. 300–1100* (London 1967). On this subject cf. J. Krinke, "Der spanische Taufritus im frühen Mittelalter" in *Gesammelte Aufsätze zur Kulturgeschichte Spaniens* (= Span. Forsch. der Görresgesellschaft, I/9) Münster 1954, 33–116.

increasingly clear how many liturgical developments in the Church at large owe their inspiration to this area. In the period we are now concerned with, Antioch and Jerusalem rose to the rank of liturgical centres, the rays of whose influence streamed both east and west; in the case of initiation rites, later traditions both West Syrian and Byzantine look back to the uses of the city on the Orontes. Above all, the publication (as long as twenty years ago) by Antoine Wenger[12] of previously unknown baptismal catecheses of John Chrysostom made it possible to see the history of the baptismal liturgy in this city much more clearly. The monographs of Thomas M. Finn (1967) on Chrysostom and the wide-ranging comparison of the fourth-century baptismal catecheses from Jerusalem, Antioch, Mopsuestia and Milan by Hugh M. Riley[13] in 1974 have provided an extensive foundation for and confirmation of Wenger's initial observations. In particular it can now be claimed as an assured result that in Antioch John Chrysostom knew no anointing or imposition of hands as a post-baptismal rite, and that the baptismal bath was followed immediately by the assumption of the new garment, the baptismal kiss[14] and the baptismal Eucharist.

[12] *Jean Chrysostome: Huit catéchèses baptismales inédites. Introd., texte crit., trad. et notes* de Antoine Wenger (= S.C. 50) Paris 1958. Wenger drew attention also to another series which had indeed been published but in an edition extremely hard to find: A. Papadopoulos-Kerameus, *Varia Graeca Sacra = Sbornik greceskikh bogoslovskikh tekstov IV–XV vecov* (St. Petersburg 1909) 154–183. An English version of all extant catecheses is to be found in P. Harkins, *St. John Chrysostom: Baptismal Instructions* (= A.C.W. 31), Westminster and London 1963.

[13] Thomas M. Finn, *The Liturgy of Baptism in the Baptismal Instructions of St. John Chrysostom* (= The Catholic University of America, *Studies in Christian Antiquity* 15), Washington 1967; Hugh M. Riley, *Christian Initiation: a comparative study in the interpretation of the Baptismal Liturgy in the mystagogical writings of Cyril of Jerusalem, John Chrysostom, Theodore of Mopsuestia and Ambrose of Milan* (same series, 17, Washington 1974). [and cf. E. Yarnold, *The Awe-Inspiring Rites of Initiation: Baptismal Homilies of the Fourth Century*, Slough, England, ²1973: Tr.]

[14] On the distinctive character of the baptismal kiss as opposed to that of other examples of the sacred kiss, see also now Klaus Thraede, "Ursprünge und Formen des 'heiligen Kusses' im frühen Christentum" in JbAC 11/12 (1968/9), 124–180.

This discovery was in itself nothing sensational. It had long been known that in Syria, especially in Eastern Syria (but not in Jerusalem) an anointing or imposition of hands before the baptismal bath bore the significance of the "sign" and of the gift of the Holy Spirit. Third century evidence to this effect was known, and as long ago as 1947 T. W. Manson had drawn attention to the suggestion that the order in which the gift of the Spirit preceded the baptismal bath might be traced back into the New Testament.[15] Even earlier authors were obliged to wrestle with the unusual Syrian custom and offered diverse explanations for it; as a rule it was regarded merely as an idiosyncratic tradition worthy of no more than a passing mention. However, shortly before Wenger's set of baptismal catecheses came to light Bernard Botte had already succeeded in giving a clear outline of the history of baptism in Syria.[16] It was nonetheless only at this stage that the significance of this peculair tradition received more widespread attention, and it became clear that this tradition originally enjoyed a wider currency, in Cappadocia and Armenia and also, as I believe, in Egypt.[17]

What does this mean for our present question? With regard to Antioch in particular we must agree that in the light of present liturgiological research the epoch from the fourth to the sixth century cannot be called the classical period in the sense that a settled structure of the baptismal liturgy can be traced in it. On the contrary, these were generations of radical change. John Chrysostom found no post-baptismal rite of anointing in the tradition he inherited, and obviously did not feel that anything was missing. The pre-baptismal anointing which he inherited was in his days (I shall return to this) divided into an anointing of the forehead on Good Friday, called the "seal," and the anointing of the whole body immediately before the baptismal bath. He differs however from the third-century texts already mentioned in interpreting neither of

[15] T. W. Manson, "Entry into Membership of the Early Church" in J.T.S., 48 (1947), 25–32; and see also Wolfgang Nauck, *Die Tradition und der Charakter des ersten Johannesbriefes* (= W.U.N.T. 3) Tübingen 1957, 147ff.

[16] Bernard Botte, "Le baptême dans l'église syrienne" in O.S. 1, 1956, 137–155.

[17] *Taufgottesdienst*, 133ff., 210ff.

these acts as the impartation of the Spirit — the candidate received the Spirit in the baptismal bath itself, and in this connection John alludes to the laying on of the baptizing minister's hand at the immersion of the candidate.[18] Nonetheless, the liturgical tradition springing from Antioch retained even into later periods the reference to the gift of the Holy Spirit in the prayers at the prebaptismal anointings, as Sebastian Brock has shown.[19] Soon after John Chrysostom Antioch too must have adopted the post-baptismal anointing, presumably from Jerusalem, but with a formula that speaks of the "impress and perfection of the grace of the Holy Spirit."[20] However, Theodore of Mopsuestia and the *Apostolic Constitutions* show clearly that as far as the adoption of a post-baptismal anointing in the satellite areas of Antioch is concerned, we are dealing with something more than an importation from Jerusalem.[21] It would not be hard to list further important alterations in the rite of baptism at Antioch between the fourth and the sixth centuries, as for example the already mentioned excision of the renunciation and the *syntaxis* and the transfer of this service for the profession of faith to Good Friday,[22] although on Antiochene assumptions this must have been counted among the central rites of initiation. Such novelties are naturally no cause for astonishment. The second half of the fourth century was the period of a mass accession to the Church. Sheer practicality made necessary alterations to the structure of Mass and baptism alike. In the disputes about dogma and Church government even the ortho-

[18] Ed. Wenger, 138 and 148.

[19] Studies, 29–40.

[20] Brock, Studies, 33, 38f. What was later to be the classical formula of the West Syrian rites calls the oil of anointing "the holy *myron* of Christ (who is) God." This is reminiscent of Ps.-Dionysius. But the christological interpretation of the oil corresponds also to the mystagogic catecheses of Jerusalem origin.

[21] These are, of course, acquainted with a post-baptismal anointing already, but with an unspecified formula. On the subject of Ap. Const. see also Georg Wagner, "Zur Herkunft der Apostolischen Konstitutionen" in *Mélanges liturgiques . . . B. Botte* (Louvain 1972), 525–537; his examination of the eucharistic prayers confirms the long-held suspicion of the author's heterodox position.

[22] First noticed by Wenger; I have tried to develop this in *Taufgottesdienst*, 181ff.

dox members of the circle of Meletios, John Chrysostom being of their number, were not shy of liturgical innovations.[23] To master the great inrush it became usual, presumably in all the larger cities of the East, to administer the separate initiatory acts in separate rooms, with different ministers officiating, and with a separation of men and women dictated by considerations of seemliness. When, then, at the end of the period under discussion infant baptism established itself as the only procedure in normal cases, yet further new arrangements were pressingly needed. Whatever may be the truth about the antiquity, origin and relative meanings of the three central elements of Christian initiation, baptismal bath, consignation and communion, in Antioch at least this three-fold pattern occurs not at the beginning of a development but at its end.

Events followed the same course in other areas originally unacquainted with any post-baptismal signation, such as Eastern Syria and the already mentioned provinces of Cappadocia, Armenia and Egypt, although we cannot identify the precise moment of the reform. The motives for it must have been compelling; what exactly they were is a matter for conjecture. A factor in some cases may have been dependence on hierarchical centres of the desire for ecumenical uniformity, but in the last analysis the reasons must have been theological — the obvious resort to scriptural models such as the Synoptic accounts of the baptism of Jesus, which explicitly depict the Spirit descending upon the Lord in the form of a dove after he had come up from the water (a piece of information directly adduced by the Jerusalem catecheses as well as by Theodore of Mopsuestia), and above all the account of the relationships within the Trinity which came to prevail after 381 and in which it is the Spirit who brings all things to completion. Be that however as it may, we may validly apply to the history of the baptismal liturgy an observation indisputably true in the case of eucharistic worship: common patterns of rite shared by different regions of the Church are by no means always a sign of great

[23] See also my observations in the article "Abendmahlsfeier — I: Alte Kirche," in TRE Bd I (1977), 229–278; on the origin of the Liturgy of St. John Chrysostom, 264.

antiquity, for they may be the result of a conformity introduced later in the wake of new theological insights.[24]

This enables us to see clearly the manifold divergences in fourth-century rites when we look further afield than Antioch. Jerusalem and Antioch differ with regard to the post-baptismal anointing, but both have a baptismal formula to be uttered by the minister at the moment of the baptismal bath (in this matter I work from the assumption that the issue of the basic structure of the Jerusalem baptismal rites is independent of the question of the extant series of mystagogical catecheses being from the pen of Bishop Cyril or of his successor John; but the preacher's style of theological argument does seem to me to be more consistent with a later date, towards the end of the century.[25]

Ambrose in Milan, to take another case, shows every sign of being anything but the guardian and spokesman of an ancient and settled local tradition; liturgical reforms were in his view part of the task of rebuilding his Church after the "Arian" bishop Auxentius. He, like Jerusalem, is certainly familiar with a post-baptismal rite which conveys the Spirit, but it is the laying-on of the bishop's hand, not an anointing. On the other hand, baptismal questions addressed to the candidate are still in use and a baptismal formula is unknown. Further: the Milanese writer ascribes a major theological dignity to the foot-washing between the baptismal bath and the consignation, a thought for which I know of no analogy in the East and which was also opposed in the West (e.g. by Augustine). An approach toward distinguishing the vital moments in baptism, the washing in water and the consignation, is to be seen in Ambrose, but not in the Eastern fathers. I have mentioned here only three centres from which baptismal catecheses are extant. A fuller picture would be provided by the inclusion of Rome, Alexandria, Carthage and Spain. There is indeed a

---

[24] Examples, see ibid., 243–246.

[25] Last discussed by A. Piédagnel, *Cyrille de Jérusalem: Catéchèses mystagogiques* (S.C. 126), Paris 1966. For the rest, I may refer, with regard to these catecheses and to this liturgical tradition in general, to the out-of-the-way but excellent bibliography of Ch. Renoux, *Hierosolymitana* I in *Eleona* (four-monthly periodical of the "Friends of Eleona"), Toulouse 1974–1977. *Hierosolymitana* II began with the number for July 1977.

host of shared motifs (as is shown with particular skill in Riley's work) and it is possible to speak of common basic elements; but in the matter of the essential rites at the core of the action, that we are looking for, the diversity is greater than we have hitherto been willing to admit.

This observation does not deny the greatness of the period — quite the reverse. Respect for the fathers can only increase as we watch them coming to terms with divergent liturgical traditions, making them their own and interpreting them on the basis of Scripture. Admittedly theologies differ between Antioch, Jerusalem and Alexandria, between Augustine and Ambrose,[26] but it is this very same theological preoccupation with the right understanding of baptism, making special use of Rom. 6, found in the baptismal catecheses of this century, and the readiness to come to grips in liturgical arrangements with the new situation which had developed everywhere in the Empire, that are largely responsible for the impression of vigorous unity given by these catecheses. Burkhard Neunheuser had after all chosen his words advisedly when, thinking of these fathers, he wrote of a flowering of theology, for such it was.

It is abundantly clear that this state of research, if I have presented it correctly, cannot simply be aligned with either of the two theories we mentioned at the outset. The question of the unity of baptism in the multiplicity of traditions cannot be answered, in the case of the fourth century, either with any assertion of the faithful preservation of an ancient arrangement or by any theory of a confused decline from an apostolic truth long since lost in

---

[26] Recent important new contributions on our subject which I have noted: Th. Camelot, "Note sur la théologie baptismale des catéchèses attribuées à Saint Cyrille de Jérusalem" in *Kyriakon: Festschrift J. Quasten* (as in n. 6), 725–729; Hans-Werner Müsing, *Augustins Lehre von der Taufe* (dissertation for the degree of Doctor of Theology, Hamburg 1969); V. Grossi, *La liturgia battesimale in S. Agostino* (Stud. Ephem. "Augustinianum" 7), Rome 1970. The controversy over the authorship of *De Sacramentis* has not stood still. In Klaus Gamber's view these catecheses are to be ascribed to Nicetas of Remesiana — see his *Die Autorschaft von De Sacramentis (Studia patristica et liturgica 1)*, Regensburg 1964, and also *Niceta von Remesiana: Instructio ad Competentes (Textus patristici et liturgici 1)*, Regensburg 1964.

darkness. The theology of the fourth century fathers seems to me a good example of a determined reaffirmation of the Gospel of Christ in the midst of a totally altered situation, with new questions demanding solution. But then where does this leave us with the problem of the origin of the variety of liturgical traditions and the unity of baptism as a rite? We must pursue this matter back into the Ante-Nicene period.

THE ANTE-NICENE PERIOD

The state of research on the ante-Nicene period is marked less by comprehensive theories than by specialized studies into the principal sources, monographs on particular rites and above all a new appreciation of the period as an entity. Nonetheless, we have a short account of the history of baptism in the first four centuries from André Benoit, and Carl Andresen has plenty to say about Christian initiation in his fascinating book on the early Christian churches.[27]

With regard to the baptismal orders preserved from these centuries there remain many differences of opinion, both about the *Didache* and the *Apostolic Tradition of Hippolytus*. That in the baptismal passages of the Teaching of the Twelve Apostles we are confronted by a very ancient set of Christian ritual instructions from the beginning of the second century is as far as I know undisputed.[28] Not even the voluminous and learned studies of Jean Michel Hanssens have in my judgement solved the riddle of the origin of Hippolytus, the Greek-speaking teacher in Rome. In the baptismal liturgy in particular I can see no original link with Alexandria:[29] this does not affect the fact that Hippolytus' Church Order later found its way to Egypt. It is more important that we

---

[27] A. Benoit-B. Bobrinskoy-F. Coudreau, *Baptême Sacrement d'unité* (Tours 1971), 13–84; Carl Andresen, *Die Kirchen der alten Christenheit* (Stuttgart 1971).

[28] Cf. now Willy Rordorf, "Le baptême selon la Didaché" in *Mélanges liturgiques . . . B. Botte* (as in n. 21), 499–510.

[29] Johannes Michael (Jean Michel) Hanssens, *La liturgie d'Hippolyte* (Rome 1959, ²1965), id., *Documents et études* (Rome 1970). My view has been formed in attempts to illuminate the earliest Alexandrian tradition — see *Taufgottesdienst* 210ff. The agreements between Hippolytus and oriental traditions point rather to Jerusalem.

have learned not to differentiate the two Church Orders by saying that one is "archaic" and the other "the result of extended development," but first and foremost to see them in the setting of very different traditions and Church structures. The *Apostolic Tradition* of Hippolytus is written for an urban neighbourhood community, comparable with the Pauline communities of the Mediterranean sea-board, but now equipped with a bishop and a relatively elaborate body of clergy. For the *Didache* the introduction of localized offices is a thing of the recent past (cf. 15.1f.). It is composed for the situation of a Christian community scattered here and there in villages and under the spiritual guidance of wandering charismatics. This might be thought of as an extension of the church structure assumed by the Gospel of Matthew.[30] That would also fit Northern Syria as the putative country of origin.

It is conventional to describe the special flavour of the *Didache* by calling the traditions preserved in it "Jewish-Christian" — not applying this to the book itself, for this is explicitly addressed to Gentiles and assumed the separation of Church and Synagogue. It is well known that Jean Daniélou[31] has singled out Jewish Christianity as the vehicle of an independent Christian tradition and has thereby encouraged us to devote serious theological attention and more intense research to Jewish Christianity, at least. Nonetheless, some terminological problems immediately appear in this subject which reflect certain obscurities as to matters of fact. Traditionally, the Jewish Christians were understood to be, according to the division of labour between Peter and Paul in Gal. 2, Christians who retained their position in the Jewish national community and held to the Torah. By this definition the adherents of the traditions which Daniélou calls Jewish-Christian were as a rule Gentile Christians. It is not enough to talk of the survival of Jewish-

[30] See now Eduard Schweizer, *Matthäus und seine Gemeinde* (SBS 71), Stuttgart 1974; see also my own "Ein Beitrag zur Frage nach dem Ursprung frühchristlicher Askese" (1964), now in K. S. Frank, ed., *Askese und Mönchtum in der alten Kirche* (Wege der Forschung CCCCIX, Darmstadt 1975), 129–180.

[31] Especially influential was Jean Daniélou, *Théologie du Judéo-Christianisme* (*Histoire des doctrines chrétiennes avant Nicée*, I) Tournai 1958; for further relevant works, see the bibliography in *Judéo-Christianisme: vol. offert au Card. J. Daniélou* (Rech. Sc. Rel. 60, 1972, 1–320), 11–18.

Christian traditions in Gentile-Christian communities, for we have learned to acknowledge more and more the importance of the Jewish roots of all early forms of Christianity. The "Church structure" of the *Didache* reflects the situation existing in Palestine and Syria; the Pauline community, as a social phenomenon, continues the life-style of Greek-speaking Jewry in the western Diaspora, which too existed in the great cities in the form of self-contained congregations. Instead of "Jewish Christianity" in Daniélou's sense, I prefer to speak of "Syrian-Palestinian tradition."[32] It seems to me to be an assured result of research that East Syrian, Aramaic-speaking Christianity owes its origin to a mission based in Palestine. This is the unanimous result of the work of Arthur Vööbus, Gilles Quispel, A.F.J. Klijn, Helmut Köster and other scholars, the most recent example being the fine book by Robert Murray, *Symbols of Church and Kingdom*, published in 1975.[33]

From this area of Eastern Syria come the apocryphal *Acts of Thomas*, which, together with few other sources represent our most important evidence for a third-century tradition of administration of baptism beside those in the *Didache* and Hippolytus. Here too we must look to the special, indeed peculiar Church structure. These Acts are not written from the point of view of communities in the course of formation (like the *Didache*) but from that of wandering charismatic ascetics who model themselves on the Apostles, the glorification of whose miraculous deeds is the burden of the apocryphal Acts.[34]

The marked differences between these three types of baptism in the second and third centuries are public knowledge. In the

---

[32] For discussion of Daniélou's thesis, see *Aspects du Judéo-Christianisme: Colloque de Strasbourg 1964* (Paris 1965). My position is there more fully argued with special reference to liturgiology, 113–136.

[33] Arthur Vööbus, *History of Asceticism in the Syrian Orient*, I (Louvain 1958); Gilles Quispel, *Makarius, das Thomasevangelium und das Lied van der Perle* (= SNT XV, Leiden 1967); A. F. J. Klijn, *Edessa die Stadt des Apostels Thomas. Das älteste Christentum in Syrien* (Neukirchen 1965); Helmut Köster and James M. Robinson, *Entwicklungslinien durch die Welt des frühen Christentums* (Tübingen 1971); Robert Murray, *Symbols of Church and Kingdom. A Study in Early Syrian Tradition* (Cambridge 1975).

[34] And see my *Beiträge zur Geschichte der frühchristlichen Askese* (as in n. 30).

Didache we read only of baptism (by immersion or by infusion), with no mention of any pre- or post-baptismal rite, except for fasting before baptism. Nothing is said of what is given in baptism: Did. 7 refers neither to the Spirit nor to the forgiveness of sins; an interpolated sentence in 9.5 mentions baptism as at most a precondition for admission to communion. It is obviously assumed that the minister of baptism utters a triadic baptismal formula during the baptism. The Church Order of Hippolytus is familiar with anointings which frame the baptismal bath, but the most important post-baptismal act is an imposition of hands by the bishop (linked with an anointing of the forehead) which has something to do with the gift of the Spirit, or, more exactly, confers the charisma which strengthens the Christian for service. In the Syriac *Acts of Thomas* the baptismal bath is preceded by an anointing with oil which is obviously to be understood as a conferring of the Spirit; the ruaḥ is called down upon the oil and water in lengthy epicleses expressed in mystifyingly oblique and figurative language. In all three traditions the abiding influence of Jewish ideas and ritual principles can be traced.[35] Before we bring these observations together with our quest for the origin of the diversity of early Christian baptismal traditions, however, this picture must be enlarged.

There exist a number of investigations, conducted in recent years, into individual rites of the baptismal service and explaining their history. Among such rites are the anointings, always a special problem for the liturgist. Particular mention must be made of the book by L. C. Mitchell; additional material is supplied by the studies of Emil Joseph Lengeling, and we must refer again here to the dissertation by Gabriele Winkler. Some of Sebastian Brock's discoveries have already been mentioned.[36] It is undeniable, and indeed not denied, that since the second century at the latest

[35] On the Syriac *Acts of Thomas* cf. the commentary by A. F. J. Klijn (SNT V) Leiden 1962; other texts, as in nn. 46 and 47.

[36] Leonel C. Mitchell, *Baptismal Anointing* (Alcuin Club Collections XLVIII) London 1966; Emil Joseph Lengeling, "Vom Sinn der präbaptismalen Salbung" in *Mélanges liturgiques* . . . *B. Botte* (as in n. 21), 327–357. On Brock see n. 9.

anointings of the most diverse kinds and bearing the most widely differing interpretations have made an entry into the baptismal liturgy. The fact that this sort of thing first comes to our notice in Gnostic texts is, in our present state of knowledge, not specially significant, since clearly the Gnostic teachers were hardly at all liturgically creative, but rather saw their business as the reinterpretation of existing rites — I shall however return to this topic.

Even if we succeed in classifying the miscellaneous anointings which turn up in later liturgical orders according to their various characters (in many cases no longer understood by those who had inherited their use), and settle their mutual historical relationships, we are still left with the question of their origin. In the Syrian-Palestinian tradition the pre-baptismal oil-rite in the Syriac *Acts of Thomas* (and rather similarly in the Syriac *Didascalia*) was originally the one and only anointing; in the *Didascalia* it was a total anointing starting with an unction of the head, and no doubt this held good in the case of the *Acts of Thomas*. How the later four anointings of the West Syrian rites grew out of this has been explained by Brock; the main points have already been mentioned in this survey. As we have said, Hippolytus' *Apostolic Tradition* is already familiar with three anointings with two different oils, a total anointing before and after the baptismal bath and an anointing of the forehead at the episcopal laying-on of hands. At the same period Tertullian was familiar with only one post-baptismal total anointing, preceding the imposition of hands.[37] For the purposes of interpretation the same categories are everywhere available, to a large degree, but they are applied to different rites. E.g., the anointing corresponds to the hallowing of kings and priests in the Old Testament (applied to the pre-baptismal anointing of the head in the *Didascalia*, to the post-baptismal total anointing in Tertullian). It conveys the Spirit (Syria). It makes a Christian (applied to the pre-baptismal anointing in Syria, to the post-baptismal total anointing in Tertullian, and cf. Hippolytus). It has an exorcistic function (applied to the pre-baptismal total anointing in Hippolytus, but possibly also in the *Acts of Thomas*). It bestows the charisma on the baptized (applied to the post-baptismal anointing

[37] De bapt. 7; de res. carn. 8.3; adv. Marcionem I.14.3.

of the forehead in Hippolytus — but this last interpretation may be a fragment of the author's personal theology). To reduce this confusion to some sort of order, Eduard Stommel suggested in 1959 that the anointings could in general be derived from ancient bathing-customs, and E. J. Lengeling has recently supported this opinion.[38] In this view the secular usage of oiling oneself before and after bathing was retained by the Christians; these anointings had been patient of a more profound symbolic interpretation, for which people resorted to the Old Testament and other readily accessible circles of ideas. This is a striking hypothesis, but I cannot regard it as a universal solution, for it is not obvious that baptism was equated with the idea of a bath with cosmetic, hygienic or gymnastic associations. Baptism was always a cultic bath. We must agree therefore with Mitchell in looking for sacral oil-rites; but in the case of Judaism at least the results are disappointing. The comparison with the formal bathing-usages of antiquity would in any case explain only the total anointing before and after the baptismal bath, not an anointing of the forehead in connection with an imposition of hands. In that case at least I posit, not a symbolic up-grading of a secular custom but a conscious resort to principles of Old Testament ritual: baptism is the hallowing of kings and priests.[39] If such a view is justified, however, it becomes difficult to trace the anointings back to one original custom or one original meaning.

As long ago as 1960 Hans Kirsten devoted a commendable study to the baptismal renunciation.[40] He saw in it the theologically important counterpart to the baptismal confession. It is in such a guise that it appears in Tertullian and Hippolytus. Furthermore, in the meantime Hans Freiherr von Campenhausen has pointed out in lively style that the association of baptism with a formulated

---

[38] Eduard Stommel, "Christliche Taufriten und antike Badesitten" in JbAC 2 (1959), 5–14.

[39] Already pointed out by Mitchell, but chiefly in terms of typology. Royal anointing cannot be stressed at the expense of priestly anointing. Cf. *Taufgottesdienst*, 27–31.

[40] Hans Kirsten, *Die Taufabsage. Eine Untersuchung zur Gestalt und Geschichte der Taufe nach den altkirchlichen Taufliturgien* (Berlin 1960).

creed is by no means very early[41] — I would rather say, it was not universal. The Syrian tradition at its earliest stage lacks creed and renunciation. Where the baptismal questions are customary, the baptismal act may be preceded by a three-clause baptismal renunciation. Where a baptismal formula is presupposed, an association of *apotaxis* and *syntaxis* before baptism can be traced. The terms of the traditional formula of renunciation are directed at a disowning of the heathen gods and their worship. The formal scheme of renunciation-adhesion goes far back into Jewish tradition and corresponds, we may say, to the doctrine of the Two Ways. Here too a theory of a single origin leads us into difficulties, for we should have at least to assert that a custom originally native to one tradition only was later universally adopted for the sake of its theological value.

It was Franz Joseph Dölger who set the baptismal exorcisms in the context of the history of religion. Now Otto Böcher has sought, in his far-reaching two-volume investigation, to show that the setting of the origin of baptism altogether is a demonistic world-view.[42] As a general approach this is a certainly helpful, and turns our gaze in a more convincing direction than ancient bath-conventions, so far as the meaning of the baptismal bath is concerned. The significance of the discovery that Christ is stronger than all demons for early Christian faith and mission cannot be exaggerated. But I still have doubts as to Böcher's general theory, for he has not devoted much effort to tracing links with the baptismal exorcisms actually attested. I see as one of the key historical problems the fact that the exorcistic usages and miraculous deeds of the Christians were in large measure an inheritance from the activity of the Jewish exorcists, so highly regarded in antiquity, and often of course in competition with them. It is precisely in the Palestinian-Syrian setting that we find, from the Gospels onwards, the issue of domination over the powers of evil playing a major

[41] Hans Freiherr von Campenhausen, "Das Bekenntnis im Urchristentum" in Z.n.W., 63 (1972), 210–53.

[42] Franz Joseph Dölger, *Der Exorzismus im altchristlichen Taufritual* (Paderborn 1909); Otto Böcher, *Dämonenfurcht und Dämonenabwehr. Ein Beitrag zur Vorgeschichte der christlichen Taufe* (BWANT 5.F, Heft 10) Stuttgart 1970; same author, *Dämonismus und Taufe im Neuen Testament* (same series, Heft 16) Stuttgart 1972.

role. Yet it is here, in the Syrian tradition, that we at first hear nothing of baptismal exorcisms. This may be bound up with the already mentioned diversity of church situations: in the hellenistic West the congregations existed as a closed and separated society; baptism marked the change from one world, one society, to another. Here both renunciation and (especially after the development of the catechumenate) exorcism had an obvious place. In the Palestinian situation too it was a matter of deciding for Christ, but not of renouncing the God of Israel. Exorcisms are directed against involvement in a world possessed by demons, but that cannot be said of God's ancient people Israel in the same way that it could be applied to the Gentile world. In any case, we have another proven example of the distinction between different traditions going back into the earliest period, so that we cannot derive these traditions one from another, but yet they seem to have sprung from the same soil.

I have come across no corresponding monographs on the complex of problems surrounding the baptismal formula and baptismal questions and their relationship with the Jewish berakah, for example, nor on the hallowing of water and oil.[43] Probably, however, studies of this nature, very desirable as they are, would lead to the same questions. It may perhaps be left as an open question whether or not we are faced with a much greater diversity than we have yet realized in the oft-repeated contrast between Palestine and Syria and the Pauline mission-field. Further, it is not surprising that differing baptismal traditions correspond with different Christian groupings of the second and third and perhaps also of the first century. This has implications for the quest for the original form of baptism.

Our understanding of the complexity of nascent Christianity has often been put out of focus by an uncritical acceptance of the views of history and of the distinction between orthodoxy and heresy held by the great fathers of the late second century. This obscures the fact that the rallying of the Catholic Church around

[43] These questions are handled only fragmentarily in such older works as Hubert Scheidt, *Die Taufwasser-Weihegebete im Sinne vergleichender Liturgieforschung untersucht* (LQF 29) Münster 1935. Cf. Brock (as in n. 9).

the canon of the New Testament at this period, a novel phenomenon, was achieved only in the midst of vigorous disputes. Recent
discoveries of documents (particularly, but not exclusively, the
writings of the Gnostic library of Nag-Hammadi) afford us insights
into the wide spectrum of early Christian groups existing before
and outside the emergent Great Church, insights as yet by no
means fully appreciated. A great deal of work in the general and
religious history of the period remains to be done after the phi-
lologists have completed their task, already begun, of making
these texts available. It is becoming constantly more obvious that
these Christian groups belong within the broad stream of a
baptism-movement.

A new text concerned with Mani, not yet published in entirety,
has shown us that this Gnostic teacher sprung of the Parthian
royal family in Mesopotamia came, not from the Mandaeans, as
previously assumed, but from the unequivocally Jewish-Christian
sect of the Elchasaites.[44] In connection with Mani's departure from
these "baptists" we meet new information about their immersions
and their encratite theology. Böcher's thesis of the exorcistic meaning of rites of this sort is thereby confirmed. At the same time our
quest for the origin of the multiplicity of Christian baptismal traditions may come to be seen in a new light. Hegesippus already, as
is well known, recognized a connection between pre-Christian
Jewish sects and at least some of the — heretical — Christian
groups of his own day (Eusebius, h.e. IV.22.4f.). Is it also possible
to trace divergent baptismal uses among the Christians back to
pre-Christian traditions?

In the present state of research, one hesitates to give too cate-
gorical an answer. But we can see some signs of the way forward.
Thus, the Syrian sequence: impartation of the Spirit — immersion
finds its most convincing analogy in the regulation of the Qumran
community that purification by the Spirit was a prerequisite of cultic lustrations (I QS 3, 4ff.). This link was pointed out more than
twenty years ago by Wolfgang Nauck.[45] In addition, there is much

[44] A. Henrichs and L. Koenen: "Ein griechischer Mani-Codex (P. Colon.
inv. nr. 4780)" in *Zeitschrift für Papyrologie und Epigraphik* 5 (1970), Bonn,
97–216, esp. 133–160.
[45] Cf. n. 15.

to be said for the view (and this another long-held thesis) that the requirement in Did.7.1 that baptism be in ὕδωρ ζῶν (supported by other texts of oriental tradition) preserves material from the tradition of pre-Christian baptismal sects.[46] Rabbinic immersions were at all events permitted in cisterns as well. It was as long as 1947, however, that Willem Cornelis van Unnik drew attention to the fact that an actual set of ritual instructions for rabbinic immersions had been preserved in the baptismal order of *Apostolic Tradition*.[47]

These are not the latest fruits of research; but they may acquire new significance for current New Testament exegesis. There existed, beyond doubt, differing Jewish traditions as to immersions. Without taking the matter further, it seems to me a quite plausible hypothesis, from the point of view of present New Testament study, that particular groups which joined the primitive Christian community or were caught up by the early Christian mission, brought their own baptismal traditions with them — and that primitive Christianity was in itself in many respects a gathering of movements: the Twelve, bearers of the tradition of a sharing in the itinerant preaching and ministry of the Lord on earth, were joined in Jerusalem by James, called by the Lord risen from the dead, together with the family of Jesus. Other people who had known Jesus as preacher and miracle-worker will have found their way into the Church. The schism among the disciples of the Baptist over the decision for or against Jesus will have continued into this stage. All these groups will have been united by the proclamation of the resurrection of Christ, who now calls us, through his witnesses, to conversion and faith, faith in God's saving act in him, Jesus of Nazareth, as the dawn of the echatological fulfilment, which is already attested by the Spirit. Part of this message is the invitation to baptism. The "institution of baptism" is a dogmatic category for establishing the authority by which the

[46] The classic investigation comes from the pen of Theodor Klauser, *Taufet in lebendigem Wasser!* (1939) and now to be found in Theodor Klauser, *Gesammelte Arbeiten zur Liturgiegeschichte, Kirchengeschichte und christliche Archäologie* (JbAC, Ergänzungsband 3), Münster 1970, 177–183. However, Klauser supposes a practice customary throughout Judaism, which I do not regard as adequate.

[47] W. van Unnik, "Les cheveux défaits des femmes baptisées" in Vig. Chr., 1 1947), 77–100. This very rite can however also be traced in the baptistic sects.

Church baptizes. Historically, it was not a matter of instituting a new rite, but of stamping the new character of Christ's person and promise on the inherited procedure of Jewish baptism. This new authority and the supersession of the old dispensation will always have found liturgical expression, whether in the formula of praise uttered at baptism or in some other form. For Palestinians this would easily suggest a link with traditions of immersion-ritual which had been maintained before this supersession of normal Jewish rites, among such people as the men of Qumran. For the mission in the Diaspora, proselyte baptism may have become important. The gesture of the post-baptismal imposition of hands, ἐπίθεσις τῶν χειρῶν in Acts in baptism (19.6; 9.17; cf. 8.18) and in procedures akin to ordination (6.6; 13.3) is obviously not identical with, say, the rite of the imposition of the right hand known among the Mandaeans, and is also distinct from later layings-on of hands at baptism. It is reminiscent of the ''leaning'' with both hands in the rabbinic *semikah*,[48] which could be consistent with a charismatic understanding of the gift of the Spirit in *Acts*. The tendency of these authors and indeed of the rite itself seems to me to suffer from no lack of clarity. The issue is always the singling out of the special element distinguishing this Christ-baptism from Jewish immersions or even from the baptism of John. This can however be achieved by means of very diverse rites — so why not (as is still the case in the *Didache*) purely by means of the formula of benediction uttered at baptism?

These are more like hints than results. However, the present state of scholarly concern with the early history of Christian baptism makes it hard to go on speaking of a single original and therefore normative form of baptism. A similar judgement may also, in principle, be valid in the case of the Eucharist. At all events, the later liturgies of East and West take up different elements of the old Jewish table-ritual,[49] but in the case of the Lord's Supper a lasting norm was established by the reference back to

[48] Eduard Lohse, *Die Ordination im Spätjudentum und im Neuen Testament* (Göttingen and Berlin 1951); Georg Kretschmar, ''Die Ordination im frühen Christentum'' in *Freiburger Zeitschrift für Phil. und Theol.* 22 (1975), 35–69.

[49] On this and the following passages see TRE I (1977), 232–248.

the accounts of Jesus' last meal with the disciples "in the night before he was betrayed." In addition, between the second and the fourth centuries, from all the multifarious ways of celebrating the Eucharist there partly emerged, partly survived, a firm structure of the service, in which admittedly the meal is perpetuated only in a ceremonialized form, but which left its impress on all the great rites of the centuries to come. Things were different with baptism. In this case the divergent traditions were not brought into conformity with one another until a later stage, and were never entirely fused. Common ritual property is long restricted within a narrow compass, basically to the baptismal bath itself. Yet even for this diverse forms were possible, all the more because this baptismal bath itself never in the ancient Church underwent such a ceremonialization as had befallen the meal in the eucharistic service. This is not to deny that the individual baptismal orders respectively each display a ritual with its own internal structure, with the result that even supplementary ritual acts such as imposition of hands or anointing exercise the function of expressing the special character and fullness of Christian initiation. So, since we are dealing with the one Christian baptism, it is entirely possible to compare differing rites and to identify differing elements of the ritual in distinct traditions with one another, as e.g. the pre-baptismal anointing of the Syrians with the post-baptismal imposition of hands of the Latins. But this is not obvious from the rite as such, but from an overall understanding of baptism as a total phenomenon which is unfolded in differing baptismal orders. The unity of baptism, which is of course a ritual act, does not lie simply in the execution of a given ritual procedure but in Christ's saving work, bestowed upon the baptized by baptism by virtue of the Lord's institution and promise — from faith to faith.

As to the question which we have pursued through this article, the triadic pattern of baptismal bath / imposition of hands / Eucharist is a venerable Western tradition, traceable indeed back into apostolic times — but we have no right to regard it as the sole normative structure of Christian initiation. The plurality of possibilities is itself apostolic. On the other hand, however, there is no apostolic norm in a bare immersion, without accompanying rites (nor is it probable that any such thing ever existed) nor is a por-

trayal of the meaning of the gift given in baptism in a series of
ritual acts of itself a process of disintegration. The historian of
liturgy can never escape the tension involved in recognizing the
one Christ-baptism in widely differing baptismal orders.

Adela Yarbro Collins

3. The Origin of Christian Baptism

THE BAPTISM OF JOHN

Since the late nineteenth century, students of the New Testament have recognized that the history of early Christianity begins in an important sense with John the Baptist.[1] However much Jesus may have differed from John in lifestyle and teaching, the fact that he was baptized by John suggests that the Jesus movement had its roots in the activity of John. All four gospels begin the account of Jesus' public life with his baptism; the point is most vividly dramatized in Mark and is made explicit in Acts 1:21-22: the one to replace Judas among the Twelve had to be one who had been with them "beginning from the baptism of John until the day when [Jesus] was taken up from us."[2] I would suggest that Christian baptism also had its origin in the baptism performed by John.

In order to understand the origins of Christian baptism, therefore, it is important to understand the nature of the baptism performed by John. The primary sources for the reconstruction of the historical John the Baptist are the synoptic sayings source (Q) that is recoverable through a comparison of the gospels of Matthew and Luke, the four canonical gospels (Mark, Matthew, Luke and John), the book of the Acts of the Apostles, and Josephus.[3]

[1] See most recently Hendrikus Boers, *Who Was Jesus?*, San Francisco, forthcoming.

[2] Translations of passages from the New Testament are taken from the Revised Standard Version.

[3] Other, less reliable, sources are Justin Martyr, The Book or Protoevangelium of James (2nd century C.E.) and other infancy gospels dependent on it, Tertullian, Hippolytus, Origen, the Gospel of the Ebionites (whose tradition

Josephus discusses John the Baptist in book 18 of the *Antiquities of the Jews*. The most important part of the account is as follows:

". . . he was a good man and had exhorted the Jews to lead righteous lives, to practise justice towards their fellows and piety towards God, and so doing to join in baptism. In his view this was a necessary preliminary if baptism was to be acceptable to God. They must not employ it to gain pardon for whatever sins they committed, but as a consecration of the body implying that the soul was already thoroughly cleansed by right behaviour. When others too joined the crowds about him, because they were aroused to the highest degree by his sermons, Herod became alarmed. Eloquence that had so great an effect on mankind might lead to some form of sedition, for it looked as if they would be guided by John in everything that they did. Herod decided therefore that it would be much better to strike first and be rid of him before his work led to an uprising, than to wait for an upheaval, get involved in a difficult situation and see his mistake."[4]

This passage is authentic, since it displays no Christian tendencies and coheres with Josephus' usual content and style. Its reliability is qualified by Josephus' well known biases, namely, that he consistently avoided any mention of Jewish eschatology and that he attempted to present Jewish ideas and practices in as clear and rational a manner as possible and in Greco-Roman terms, often philosophical terms. The first bias is clearly at work here. In stark contrast to the Christian texts, Josephus makes no mention of John's orientation to the future.[5] The reasons given for Herod's

---

may go back to the second century) as cited by Epiphanius (4th century), the Gospel of Nicodemus or Acts of Pilate (4th or early 5th century), the Clementine Homilies and Recognitions (3rd century), the Mandaean literature (8th century), and the Slavonic manuscripts of Josephus' *Jewish War* (15–16th century). On the Christian apocryphal works, see E. Hennecke and W. Schneemelcher, *The New Testament Apocrypha*, 2 vols. (Philadelphia 1963 and 1965); on the Mandaean literature see Charles Scobie, *John the Baptist*, (Philadelphia 1964), 23–31.

[4] Josephus, *Ant.* 18. 116–119; translation cited is by Louis H. Feldman in *Josephus* (Cambridge, MA 1965), 9. 81, 83.

[5] Although Bo Reicke mentions the fact that the baptism of John was eschatological, he also minimizes this characteristic, in order to fit John and Jesus

execution of John may reveal indirectly the political effect of John's eschatological teaching. The second bias may be behind Josephus' emphasis that the ablution was not meant to be effective in itself. This emphasis could be a distortion meant to impress Josephus' enlightened and skeptical Gentile readers, his own importing into his understanding of John ideas foreign to John himself, or a rationalizing understanding of John's teaching that the ritual required appropriate preparation and disposition.

The passage from Acts that presents the baptism of John as the beginning of Jesus' public life has already been cited (1:21-22). The bias of the book of Acts on this issue comes through most clearly in its repeated contrast between the baptism of John with *water* and the baptism through Christ with *spirit*.[6] In a speech of Paul, Acts describes John as one who "preached a baptism of repentance to all the people of Israel" (13:24). This brief description is compatible with Josephus' account and is probably reliable. It is embedded, however, in a context which portrays John as the forerunner of Christ (Acts 13:23-25).

The idea that John consciously prepared the way for Jesus the Messiah is a typical Christian bias and is probably not historical. This Christian interpretation of the significance of John is present already in the oldest narrative gospel, Mark, in the announcement placed in John's mouth, "After me comes he who is mightier than I, the thong of whose sandals I am not worthy to stoop down and untie. I have baptized you with water; but he will baptize you with the Holy Spirit" (Mark 1:7-8). The gospel of Matthew minimizes the authority of John by having him demur at baptizing Jesus (Matt. 3:14). Luke refrains from describing the actual baptism of Jesus by John, presumably for a similar reason. In the gospel of John, the Baptist's role as the forerunner of Christ is elaborated and his inferiority to him is emphasized (John 1:6-8, 19-37, cf. 3:22-30, 4:1-3).[7]

---

into a theological framework of Law and Gospel ("The Historical Setting of John's Baptism" in E. P. Sanders, ed., *Jesus, the Gospels, and the Church: Essays in Honor of William R. Farmer* (Macon, GA 1987) 209-24.

[6] Acts 1:5, 11:16, 18:25, 19:1-7.

[7] See further Walter Wink, *John the Baptist in the Gospel Tradition* (Cambridge 1968).

The synoptic sayings source (Q), which is probably as old as and independent of Mark, also included a saying in which John identifies himself as a forerunner.[8] According to this form of the saying, the one who comes after John, the mightier one, will baptize not only with holy spirit, but also with fire. To this saying is added another: "His winnowing fork is in his hand, to clear his threshing floor, and to gather the wheat into his granary, but the chaff he will burn with unquenchable fire" (Luke 3:17; cf. Matt. 3:12).

Behind the Christian picture of John pointing ahead to Jesus the Messiah there may well be a historically accurate tradition that John presented himself as a forerunner. Rather than a human messiah, however, it is likely that John spoke of a direct divine intervention.[9] Support for this hypothesis lies in several considerations. The gospel of Mark (1:2-3) quotes Mal. 3:1 and Isa. 40:3 and implies that John the Baptist is the messenger spoken of and Jesus is the Lord who is coming. If John the Baptist alluded to Scriptures like these, he probably interpreted the Coming One as God, an interpretation which is closer to the original sense than the Christian reading. Jewish texts written relatively close to the time and place of John's activity make plausible the hypothesis that he used imagery of spirit and fire for the future activity of God. According to the Community Rule from Qumran:

"at the time of the visitation . . . God will then purify every deed of man with his truth; he will refine for himself the human frame by rooting out all spirit of falsehood from the bounds of his flesh. He will cleanse him of all wicked deeds with the *spirit* of holiness; like purifying waters he will shed upon him the *spirit* of truth. . . ."[10]

Book 4 of the Sibylline Oracles was composed by a Jewish writer around 80 C.E.[11] Its call for righteousness and its eschatological

[8] This saying has been preserved in Matt 3:11 and Luke 3:16.

[9] Albert Schweitzer argued that John the Baptist considered himself to be the forerunner of the forerunner, Elijah (*The Mysticism of Paul the Apostle* [New York 1931] 162-3, 231).

[10] Translation cited is by Geza Vermes, *The Dead Sea Scrolls in English*, 2nd edn. (New York 1975, 77); emphasis added.

[11] See John J. Collins, "The Sibylline Oracles" in J. H. Charlesworth (ed.), *The Old Testament Pseudepigrapha* (Garden City 1983), 1.381-82.

perspective are similar to the message of John the Baptist as it can be reconstructed from the accounts of Josephus, Acts, Mark, and Q. Divine punishment by fire plays an important role in this work. A climactic passage reads:

"But when faith in piety perishes from among men, and justice is hidden in the world, untrustworthy men, living for unholy deeds, will commit outrage, wicked and evil deeds.

"No one will take account of the pious, but they will even destroy them all, by foolishness, very infantile people, rejoicing in outrages and applying their hands to blood.

"Even then know that God is no longer benign but gnashing his teeth in wrath and destroying the entire race of men at once by a great conflagration.

"Ah, wretched mortals, change these things, and do not lead the great God to all sorts of anger, but abandon daggers and groanings, murders and outrages, and wash your whole bodies in perennial rivers.

"Stretch out your hands to heaven and ask forgiveness for your previous deeds and make propitiation for bitter impiety with words of praise; God will grant repentance and will not destroy. He will stop his wrath again if you all practice honourable piety in your hearts.

"But if you do not obey me, evil-minded ones, but love impiety, and receive all these things with evil ears, there will be fire throughout the whole world, and a very great sign with sword and trumpet at the rising of the sun."[12]

The Q-saying preserved in Matt. 3:11-12 and Luke 3:16-17, that describes metaphorically judgment to be executed by the Coming One with spirit and fire, may therefore be a Christian application to Jesus of a saying spoken by John with reference to divine judgment.

The question of the origin of the baptism of John has been disputed. One theory is that it was based on the ritual ablutions at Qumran. Some scholars have argued that the Qumran community required a ritual immersion connected with initiation into the com-

---

[12] *Sib. Or.* 4. 152–174; translation cited by John J. Collins, ibid., 388.

munity, i.e., a baptism.[13] One form of this hypothesis is based on a passage in the Community Rule declaring that any hypocritical member of the congregation could not be cleansed by any ablution (1QS 3:4-9).[14] The argument is that this text is in proximity with the description of the ceremony of entry into the covenant community (1:16–2:18) and that it precedes the instruction on the two spirits that may have been part of the instruction given to members about to be initiated. The problems with this view are that no immersion is mentioned as part of the ceremony and the ablutions referred to are the repeated ritual washings practised by the group. Another passage used to support this view is the remark that the men of falsehood shall not enter the water to partake of the pure meal of the saints, i.e., the members of the community.[15] This passage, however, more likely refers to the daily immersion of full members of the community before the main meal that was eaten in a state of ritual purity. The ablutions at Qumran then did not include an initiatory baptism. Rather, they were Levitical washings related to ritual purity.[16] Admission to the regular ablu-

---

[13] W. H. Brownlee, "John the Baptist in the New Light of Ancient Scrolls" in Krister Stendahl (ed.), *The Scrolls and the New Testament* (New York 1957); see J. Gnilka, "Die essenischen Tauchbäder und die Johannestaufe" in *Revue de Qumran* 3 (1961–62) 185–207 for a discussion of this issue and further bibliography.

[14] Otto Betz, "Die Proselytentaufe der Qumransekte und die Taufe im Neuen Testament" in *Revue de Qumran* 1 (1958) 213–34, especially 216–17.

[15] 1QS 5:7-15; the paraphrase given above is based on Vermes' translation, *The Dead Sea Scrolls in English*, 79; this is Brownlee's argument (see note 13).

[16] At some point, immersion became also a symbol of higher purification and consecration. See the remark that "None may enter the Temple Court for [an act of the Temple-] Service, even though he is clean, until he has immersed himself. On this day the High Priest five times immerses himself and ten times he sanctifies [his hands and his feet], each time, excepting this alone, in the Temple by the Parwah Chamber" in the Mishnaic tractate Yoma 3.3. "This day" is, of course, Yom Kippur (the translation cited is by Herbert Danby, *The Mishnah*, London 1933, 164). On this point, see L. Finkelstein, "The Institution of Baptism for Proselytes" in *The Journal of Biblical Literature* 52 (1933) 205–6. See also idem, "Some examples of the Maccabean Halaka" in *The Journal of Biblical Literature* 49 (1930) 37–8. This new understanding may have been operative already in the higher ablutions at Qumran.

tions and the meal symbolized the conviction that those admitted were pure and free of sin and were living in a holy manner and thus widely separated from sinful and impure people.

The baptism of John did have certain similarities to the ritual washings at Qumran: both involved withdrawal to the desert to await the Lord; both were linked to an ascetic lifestyle; both included total immersion in water; and both had an eschatological context. These features, however, were not unique to John and the community at Qumran.[17] The differences are at least equally striking; a priestly, exclusive community versus the activity of a prophetic, charismatic leader in a public situation;[18] a ritual practised at least once daily versus an apparently once and for all ritual; and a self-enacted ritual versus a ritual administered by John.

Proselyte Baptism. If the ritual washings at Qumran do not provide a credible context for the origin of the baptism of John, perhaps proselyte baptism provides the key. There are certain important similarities. Proselyte baptism is at least witnessed and may be understood as administered. It is a once and for all ritual understood as a sign of an inner transformation. If the practice of proselyte baptism is older than the time of John, his baptism may be understood as a reinterpretation of that ritual. For example, his intention may have been to signify that the whole Jewish people had become like the Gentiles; since they were apostates from the

[17] According to Acts 21:38 a charismatic leader called simply "the Egyptian" assembled a large following in the desert; Josephus calls him a false prophet and says that he led his followers from the desert to the Mount of Olives, proposing to take Jerusalem by force (*J. W.* 2.261–63; cf. *Ant.* 20. 169–70 where Josephus says that he promised to make the walls of the city collapse). Bannos, Josephus' teacher for three years, lived in the desert and practised frequent ablutions in cold water, by day and night; he was also ascetic, wearing only what the trees provided and eating only things which grew of themselves (Josephus, *Vita* 11). Eschatology was apparently widespread at this time (see, e.g., the Psalms of Solomon and the Assumption or Testament of Moses). Total immersion had long been practised by priests and other Jews for purification and at this time the ritual was becoming more common.

[18] On John the Baptist as a prophet, see Richard A. Horsley and John S. Hanson, *Bandits, Prophets, and Messiahs: Popular Movements at the Time of Jesus* (Minneapolis 1985) 175–81.

covenant, they too were unclean.[19] John's baptism thus meant a reentry into the covenant relationship or an initiation into an eschatological community, prepared for the visitation of the Lord.

If, however, proselyte baptism originated later than John, it cannot be the source of meaning of his baptism. The date of the origin of proselyte baptism has been much discussed. The issue is complex, because the notion and practice of proselyte baptism seem to have evolved gradually, rather than been instituted *de novo* at a particular point in time. The discussion has been confused because of a lack of clarity over what is being talked about. A major root of this confusion is the fact that, in the rabbinical writings, the noun *tebilah* is used in two ways: to mean the ordinary ritual bath and the immersion that was part of the initiation of proselytes. The problem is how to determine when the second meaning is present. If the notion and ritual of proselyte baptism evolved gradually, one must distinguish between the first ordinary ritual ablution of a convert to Judaism and an immersion that is part of an initiation ceremony. One important criterion is that proselyte baptism is present only when the ritual is administered or at least witnessed.

There have been three major theories in the literature about the origin of proselyte baptism. Gedalyahu Alon represents the position with the earliest date for the ritual. He has argued that the immersion of proselytes goes back to the early Second Temple period. The purpose was to remove the uncleanness of the Gentiles that derives from idols.[20]

The second major view, held by Israel Abrahams, H. H. Rowley, Joachim Jeremias, and Lawrence Schiffman, is that proselyte baptism was a widespread practice at least prior to John the Baptist.[21]

---

[19] J. Leipoldt and Robert Eisler argued along these lines; see the discussion in Scobie, *John the Baptist*, 101 and n. 1.

[20] Gedalyahu Alon, *Jews, Judaism and the Classical World* (Jerusalem 1977) 146-89.

[21] Israel Abrahams, *Studies in Pharisaism and the Gospel.* 1st series (Cambridge 1917 = New York 1967), 30-46; H. H. Rowley, "Jewish Proselyte Baptism and the Baptism of John" in *Hebrew Union College Annual* 15 (1940) 313-34; Joachim Jeremias, *Infant Baptism in the First Four Centuries* (Philadelphia 1960); Lawrence

Jeremias stated that the older Jewish view was that the priestly purity laws were not binding on Gentiles. Therefore, only circumcision was necessary for the proselyte. This view was still dominant in the second century B.C.E., as Judith 14:10 shows. When Achior joined the house of Israel, he was circumcised, but no mention is made of baptism. Jeremias suggested that the newer view arose in the first century B.C.E., namely, that all Gentile women were impure because they did not purify themselves after menstruation. Therefore, all Gentile men were also impure because of their contact with Gentile women. To support this hypothesis, Jeremias pointed to a text in the Testament of Levi, part of the patriarch's speech to his children, the beginning of the priestly line of the nation:

"with harlots and adulteresses will you be joined, and the daughters of the Gentiles shall you take to wife, *purifying them with unlawful purifications;* and your union shall be like unto Sodom and Gomorrah" (*T. Levi* 14:6).[22]

Jeremias also pointed to rabbinic texts in support of his view.[23]

In his treatment of the issue, Lawrence Schiffman admitted that there is no definite attestation of immersion for conversion before the early Yavnean period.[24] Nevertheless, he concluded that it is necessary to date the Jewish ritual prior to John the Baptist in order to explain his baptism and that of the early Christians.[25]

Schiffman, *Who Was a Jew?* (Hoboken, NJ 1985). T. F. Torrance also takes this position: "Proselyte Baptism" in *New Testament Studies* 1 (1954) 150–4.

[22] Jeremias, *Infant Baptism in the First Four Centuries*, 25–28; quotation is from 26; emphasis added. The emphasized phrase (*katharizontes autas katharismō paranomō* in the Greek manuscripts) was excluded from the critical edition by Robert Henry Charles (*The Greek Versions of the Testaments of the Twelve Patriarchs*, Oxford 1908 = Hildesheim 1960, 57) and thus from the translation by Howard C. Kee (*The Old Testament Pseudepigrapha*, 1. 793). The reading is present, however, in most of the older manuscripts and is included in the critical edition of M. de Jonge (*The Testaments of the Twelve Patriarchs: A Critical Edition of the Greek Text* (Leiden 1978) 42).

[23] Mishnah Pesahim 8.8 and Eduyoth 5.2; B. J. Pesahim 92a; Tosefta Pesahim 7.13.

[24] Schiffman, *Who Was a Jew?*, 29.

[25] Ibid., 26, 29.

The third major theory is that proselyte baptism developed in Judaism in the second half of the first century or in the second century C.E. Among those holding this position are Charles Scobie and S. Zeitlin.[26] The studies of A. Büchler have suggested to some that the immersion of proselytes was instituted in about 65 C.E. with the enactment of the eighteen decrees, one of which declared (for the first time) that Gentiles were intrinsically unclean. Büchler viewed this decree as a precautionary measure against Roman sodomy.[27] Scobie argued that the rabbinic texts regarding proselytes which are early have no explicit allusion to immersion as part of the initiation ceremony. The rabbinic texts which speak explicitly of such an immersion date to the late first or early second century C.E. He suggested that, after the destruction of the temple, the ritual of immersion could have risen in importance as the only available ritual for female proselytes.

All modern scholars who have addressed the subject agree that there is no proselyte baptism in the Jewish Tanakh, the Christian Old Testament. With regard to Alon's theory, it is possible that some proselytes observed ritual washings in the early Second Temple period. In some cases, the first ablution may have been thought to counteract impurity contracted by Gentile life. But there is no evidence that such ablutions, if they occurred, were "baptisms," since there is no reliable evidence that they were tied to an initiation rite, administered, or performed in the presence of witnesses.

Jeremias' appeal to the Testament of Levi does not demonstrate that proselyte baptism was instituted in the first century B.C.E. The Testaments of the Twelve Patriarchs is virtually impossible to date. It is not even certain that the document was originally Jewish, since its present form is Christian. Further the comment about

---

[26] Scobie, *John the Baptist*, 95–102; S. Zeitlin, "The Halaka in the Gospels and its Relation to the Jewish Law in the Time of Jesus" in *The Hebrew Union College Annual* 1 (1924) 357–63 and "A Note on Baptism for Proselytes" in *The Journal of Biblical Literature* 52 (1933) 78–9.

[27] A. Büchler, "The Levitical Impurity of the Gentile in Palestine Before the Year 70" in *The Jewish Quarterly Review* 17 (1926/27) 1–81; Schiffman, *Who Was A Jew?*, 26, 85 n. 44.

"purifying them with an unlawful purification" is not a certain allusion to proselyte baptism.

In the proselytizing of the Maccabean period, admission to Israel was always simply by circumcision, according to the evidence.[28] Furthermore, Philo often speaks of proselytes, but never mentions proselyte baptism. Josephus discusses the admission of proselytes, but mentions circumcision only. The rabbinic texts cited by Jeremias which relate to the Passover contain no indication that the immersion mentioned was part of a ceremony of initiation.[29]

The oldest clear reference to proselyte baptism is in the Babylonian Talmud, Yebamoth 46a. The relevant passage begins with the question of the status of children conceived by Jewish women from proselytes who had been circumcised but had not performed the required ablution. If the fathers were proper proselytes, the children were Jews, if the fathers were not proper proselytes, the fathers were idolators and the children bastards. In the course of the discussion, the opinions of Rabbi Eliezer ben Hyrcanus and Rabbi Joshua ben Hananiah are cited. These two rabbis apparently belonged to the second generation of the Tannaim, active from about 90 to 130 C.E.[30] Rabbi Eliezer is quoted as teaching that a proselyte who was circumcised but had not performed the prescribed ritual ablution was a proper proselyte. Rabbi Joshua is said to have taught that a proselyte who had performed the prescribed ablution but had not been circumcised was a proper proselyte. This tradition is evidence, at most, that around the end of the first and the beginning of the second century, proselyte baptism was beginning to be recognized as an essential part of the initiation into Judaism, but was not yet recognized as such by all authorities.[31]

A saying of Epictetus, preserved by Arrian, implies that baptism was an essential part of the process of conversion to Judaism.[32]

---

[28] Josephus, *Ant.* 13.257-58, 318-19.

[29] See the discussion by Scobie, *John the Baptist*, 98.

[30] Hermann L. Strack, *Introduction to the Talmud and Midrash* (New York 1969) 110–11.

[31] See the discussion in Scobie, *John the Baptist*, 99.

[32] Text, translation, and notes are given by Menahem Stern, *Greek and Latin Authors on Jews and Judaism* (Jerusalem 1976) 1.542-4.

Some scholars have argued that Epictetus is referring here to Christians and not to Jews.[33] Menahem Stern argues that the philosopher was indeed referring to Jews. Following Fergus Millar, he places this discourse at Nicopolis and dates it to about 108 C.E. Even if Stern is correct, this bit of evidence does not support the emergence of proselyte baptism before the end of the first or the beginning of the second century.

The Origin of John's Baptism. Schiffman's argument that proselyte baptism must be dated before John the Baptist in order to explain his baptism and that of the early Christians is unwarranted. Only two elements have a firm claim for consideration on the question of the origin of the baptism of John. Without these two elements, this baptism would be unintelligible. One of these is the tradition and practice of Levitical ablutions. This ritual is the ultimate source of the form of John's ritual which apparently involved total immersion in water. The other element is the prophetic-apocalyptic tradition.[34] One aspect of this tradition important for John's baptism was the expectation of a future, definitive intervention of God. Another significant aspect was the ethical use of ablution imagery. For example, Isaiah 1:16-17 exhorts the people:

"Wash yourselves, make yourselves clean;
remove the evil of your doings from before my eyes;
cease to do evil, learn to do good;
seek justice, correct oppression;
defend the fatherless, plead for the widow."[35]

In some texts, such as Ezekiel 36:25-28, ablution imagery was used both ethically and eschatologically. God's transformation of the people in the eschatological restoration was to involve a new spirit and a new heart. This new creation was to begin with a divine sprinkling of clean water upon the people to cleanse them

[33] Scobie, *John the Baptist*, 99 n. 2.

[34] Schweitzer believed that the prophetic tradition alone, along with John's eschatological orientation, was sufficient to explain the origin of John's baptism (*The Mysticism of Paul the Apostle*, 231–2).

[35] Translations from the Tanakh/Old Testament are according to the Revised Standard Version.

from their sins and acts of idolatry. The tradition of prophetic symbolic actions may have played a role. The baptism of John may have been intended to signify God's approach as purifier before the promised judgment and transformation. As has already been noted, ritual ablutions were growing in importance in John's time. This development is attested by the literature from Qumran, the traditions about the Pharisees and about meal-associates, and traditions about ascetic individuals, like Bannos, the teacher of Josephus. The tradition of the prophetic symbolic action and the growing importance of ritual ablutions were contributing factors in making John a baptizer rather than simply a preacher or oracular prophet.[36] The significance of John's baptism is best understood in terms of a prophetic reinterpretation of the sense of defilement in ethical terms and an apocalyptic expectation of judgment.

JESUS AND BAPTISM

One of the few strong points of consensus on the historical Jesus is that he was baptized by John. The fact that Jesus sought baptism by John is evidence that Jesus recognized the authority of John as an agent of God. The Synoptic tradition reflects that recognition on the part of Jesus, in spite of its subordination of John to Jesus.[37] Presumably, Jesus, by accepting the baptism of John, accepted its prophetic-eschatological significance. Many students of the New Testament conclude that Jesus' eschatology was more orientated to the present time of fulfilment than to the future consummation.[38]

The relationship between the activity of John and that of Jesus is portrayed differently in the Synoptics than in the gospel of John. According to Mark, Matthew, and Luke, Jesus' activity of teaching and healing began only after John was arrested.[39] There is no indi-

---

[36] John's activity of baptizing calls into question his identification as an "oracular prophet" rather than "action prophet" by Horsley and Hanson; see note 18 above.

[37] Matt 11:9-19// Luke 7:26-35; Mark 11:27-33// Matt 21:23-27// Luke 20:1-8; Matt 21:32.

[38] See, for example, Boers, *Who Was Jesus?*

[39] The point is explicit in Mark 1:14 and Matt 4:12-17; it is implicit in Luke 3:18-23.

cation in these gospels that either Jesus or his disciples baptized during the life of the historical Jesus.[40] The gospel of John describes Jesus' public activity as overlapping with John's.[41] It differs from the Synoptics also in stating (three times) that Jesus was baptizing many people.[42] These statements, however, are corrected, perhaps by a later hand, with a parenthetical remark that Jesus himself did not baptize, but only his disciples.[43]

Whether the Synoptics or John present the historically more reliable picture has been disputed. One theory is that the picture of the gospel of John is unreliable, because it is a literary composition reflecting rivalry between the followers of John the Baptist and those of Jesus at the time the gospel was written.[44] Another point of view is that the gospel of John is more accurate than the Synoptics on this point, because there is no plausible theological reason why the tradition that Jesus and his disciples once baptized would be invented. The practice of Christian baptism did not need such support. If there were followers of the Baptist around who rivalled the Christians for whom the gospel was written, the information that Jesus had imitated John would provide them with ammunition against the independence and authority of Jesus.[45] A further argument in favour of the reliability of the gospel of John is that the report of Jesus' baptizing creates a problem for the evangelist. In 1:33 Jesus was presented as the one who baptizes with holy spirit. But the description in chapters 3–4 does not imply that Jesus' baptism was different in kind from John's. According to 7:39, the spirit is given only after Jesus' "exaltation." The appropriate conclusion seems to be that the gospel of John is historically accurate on this point and that the authors of the other

---

[40] Baptizing is not one of the activities enjoined by Jesus on the disciples during his earthly life; see Mark 3:13-19, 6:7-13; Matt 10:1-15; Luke 9:1-6, 10:1-12. It is only after the resurrection, according to Matthew, that the command to baptize was given: 28:16-20.

[41] John 3:22-30, 4:1-3.

[42] John 3:22, 26; 4:1.

[43] John 4:2.

[44] Rudolf Bultmann, The Gospel of John: A Commentary (Philadelphia 1971) 167.

[45] Raymond E. Brown, The Gospel According to John (I–XII) (Garden City 1966) 155.

gospels were unaware of, or suppressed, the tradition that Jesus baptized.

If Jesus administered baptism of a kind similar to John's, one would expect continuity between the baptism of John and early Christian baptism. The discontinuity is as great as the continuity in the cases of the gospel of Matthew and the letters of Paul, but there is striking continuity between John's baptism and the baptism to which Peter invited the Jews assembled in Jerusalem on Pentecost according to the second chapter of Acts.

CHRISTIAN BAPTISM

The origin of Christian baptism has been disputed. The traditional view, of course, is that the practice of baptism in the early Church was the result of the command of the risen Lord as reported in the gospel of Matthew (28:16-20). There are problems with the assumption that this passage is authentic.[46] Even if the passage is assumed to be authentic, it is still necessary to place the command in a context, to ask what the early Christians understood themselves to be doing.

Students of the New Testament who assume that Jesus did not baptize have usually taken one of three basic positions. Some have hypothesized that the early Christians reverted to the baptism of John and reinterpreted it.[47] Others have argued that the metaphor of baptism in the spirit in the teaching of John gave rise to a baptismal ritual associated with the gift of the spirit. Many have taken the position that the early Church simply borrowed the ritual of proselyte baptism from the Jews. Another possibility is that there was an unbroken continuity from the baptism of John, through the baptism associated with the activity of Jesus, to the baptism practised by the early Christians. The first fundamental change occurred in the context of the Gentile mission under the increasing influence of Hellenistic culture.

Baptism in Acts 2. The assumption of unbroken continuity has two main advantages. It explains why the 120 or so persons re-

[46] G. R. Beasley-Murray, *Baptism in the New Testament* (London 1962 = 1972).
[47] This is the position taken by Schweitzer (*The Mysticism of Paul the Apostle*, 233–4).

ferred to in Acts 1:15 are not said to have undergone any particularly Christian baptismal ritual. It also explains why the basic function of baptism as reflected in Peter's Pentecost sermon is so similar to the baptism of John. New elements are added, but the starting point is the same.[48]

Peter calls for repentance, just as John is said to have done.[49] Peter indicates that the baptism is for the forgiveness of sins. The same association is made in Mark and Matthew.[50] Peter exhorts his Jewish audience, "Save yourselves from this crooked generation." Their response is to submit to baptism.[51] According to Matthew, going to John for baptism was a means of fleeing from "the wrath to come" (Matt. 3:7). The images of trees being cut down and thrown into the fire and of chaff being burned in unquenchable fire also point to a coming judgment.[52] Thus, on the most basic level, the meaning of the ritual of baptism in Acts 2 is similar to that of John the Baptist and to the ablutions called for in the fourth Sibylline Oracle: wrath is coming on this evil generation; members of this generation may be saved by repenting and receiving baptism; this baptism is a metaphorical cleansing so that the fire of judgment will, at worst, further refine and not destroy.[53]

There are two new elements in the function and meaning of baptism in Acts 2. One is that baptism occurs "in the name (*epi tō onomati*) of Jesus Christ," (v. 38). There has been a debate over the origin of this phrase. Albrecht Oepke, following A. Deissmann, argued that it has a Greek origin and that the phrase *eis to onoma*[54] was a technical term in commerce. The literal meaning was "to the account of."[55] Here the metaphorical meaning is that the person baptized belongs to Christ. Others argued that the phrase was

[48] This essential continuity was recognized by Schweitzer (*The Mysticism of Paul the Apostle*, 236).
[49] Cf. Acts 2:38 with Mark 1:4; Matt 3:2, 11.
[50] Cf. Acts 2:38 with Mark 1:4 and Matt 3:6.
[51] Acts 3:40-41.
[52] Matt 3:10, 12.
[53] Cf. I Cor 3:15.
[54] Cf. I Cor 1:13, 15; Matt 28:19.
[55] Albrecht Oepke, "Baptō, Baptizō" in *The Theological Dictionary of the New Testament* 1 (1964) 539 and n. 51.

Greek, but that its original provenance was magic. Abrahams and Jeremias argued for a Semitic origin.[56] They suggested that it expressed the intention of a cultic action. For example, in Gerim 1.7 it is said, "Whoever is not a proselyte in the name of heaven is no proselyte." In b. Yebamoth 45b and 47b it is said that slaves after becoming free are rebaptized in the name of freedom.

The variation in the wording of the phrase counts against Deissmann's thesis.[57] The variation could be explained by differing translations of a Semitic phrase. Whatever its origin, the meaning of the phrase in Acts 2:38 is to associate baptism with acceptance of the proclamation about Jesus. (The reception of baptism becomes an outward sign of faith in God through Jesus.) When John baptized, reception of that baptism implied acceptance of his message of the wrath to come and of repentance. It further implied the recognition that the will of God was manifest in the preaching of John. When Jesus and his disciples baptized, reception of that baptism implied acceptance of the proclamation about the nearness of the kingdom of God. It is also implied recognition that the will of God was manifest in the teaching of Jesus. After the crucifixion and the appearances of the risen Lord, the followers of Jesus did not have the same direct authority that John and Jesus had. Reception of baptism at their hands implied acceptance first of all that there was a need for repentance in the face of the wrath to come or in preparation for the full manifestation of the kingdom of God. It also implied the recognition that the will of God was manifest in the death of Jesus and that God had raised him from the dead. The ritual of baptism for John, and probably for Jesus, was primarily an individual matter, although it took place in the context of the covenant people of God. But among the early Christians, because of the link of baptism with acceptance of what God had done with Jesus, the ritual became an initiation rite into a community. Acceptance of the proclamation about Jesus meant joining a group whose *raison d'être* was faith in Jesus as the medi-

[56] Abrahams, *Studies in Pharisaism and the Gospels*; Jeremias, *Infant Baptism in the First Four Centuries*; cf. Billerbeck 1. 1054–55; 4. 744.

[57] In Acts 10:48 it is *en tō onomati*; in Acts 2:38, as noted above, it is *epi tō onomati*.

ator of salvation. The group was proselytizing, and the outsiders, those who refused to join, were those who did not accept Jesus' role as the primary mediator. Although the picture in Acts of the Christian community in Jerusalem is an idealized one, there is no reason to doubt that a new group identity formed early.

The other new element is the association of baptism with the gift of the Holy Spirit (Acts 2:38). In Acts 1:5 the prophecy of John the Baptist is alluded to, that the Coming One would baptize "with the Holy Spirit and with fire" (Luke 3:16). The metaphorical fulfilment of that prophecy, with regard to the 120 or so followers of Jesus, is narrated in the beginning of Acts 2. Thereafter, the ritual of baptism in the name of Jesus Christ is associated with the gift of the Holy Spirit. Peter's sermon, however, does not quote John the Baptist. Instead, there is a pesher-like interpretation and application of Joel 3:1-5 (2:28-32 in the RSV). The prophecy of Joel that God would pour out the divine spirit on all humankind is explicitly declared to be fulfilled in the reception of the spirit by the band of Jesus' followers. In the Biblical tradition, the spirit of God rested only on certain charismatic individuals and on those appointed to a particular office, such as kings, prophets, and judges. The Joel prophecy looked forward to the day when the gift of the spirit would be democratized. The early Christians claimed that the day had come. Not only free men, but slaves and women now receive the spirit of God. The letters of Paul give evidence for the early association of the gift of the spirit with baptism and for its universal character.[58]

Variety in Interpretation. The early Christian community had a somewhat different eschatological schema than John the Baptist. They understood themselves to be farther along the eschatological trajectory because one human being had already been raised from the dead. For those associated with the risen Christ, that event meant for them a proleptic resurrection from the dead. The implication for baptism is that, as an expression of faith, it transforms human nature and makes possible in the present the living of a supra-human life. But in Acts' account of Christian beginnings and baptism in that context, the operative symbol is still cleansing.

[58] I Cor 6:11, 12:13; Gal 3:27-29.

The basic, fundamental meaning of the ritual of baptism as a washing, a cleansing from sin, originated with John the Baptist and continued to be expressed in early Christian writings on into the second century. It is present, as we have seen, in Acts 2. It was presupposed by Paul.[59] It is expressed in Ephesians[60] and in the Shepherd of Hermas.[61]

Other interpretations arose and developed alongside the original one. The notion of baptism as God's seal on Christians, authorizing, ratifying them and guaranteeing their protection, occurs in Paul's letters[62] and in the deutero-Pauline letter to the Ephesians.[63] This interpretive image is also found in the Shepherd of Hermas.[64]

As was suggested earlier, Christian baptism early on developed connotations of an initiation ritual, initiation into the community of those who accepted Jesus as the Messiah, who believed that God had raised him from the dead. This sense is implied, as we have seen, by the phrase "in the name of Jesus Christ" in the account of Acts 2 (v. 38). It is also implied by the narrator's remark that "there were added that day about three thousand souls" (v. 41). The following comment, that "they devoted themselves to the apostles' teaching and fellowship, to the breaking of bread and the prayers" (v. 42), is an indication that "adding souls" does not refer only to a heavenly tally of the "saved" but to the growth of the Christian community. The notion of baptism as a ritual of initiation is implied also by Matt. 28:18-20. The command of the risen Lord associates baptism with "making disciples" and "teaching them to observe all that I have commanded you." Clearly one aspect of baptism here is initiation into the community of the disciples of Christ. The function of initiation is implicit in some of Paul's remarks on baptism also. In I Cor. 12:12-13, baptism is the means whereby Jews and Greeks, slaves and

---

[59] See I Cor 6:9-11; I Cor 15:29 presupposes that baptism is a kind of expiation for sin; cf. II Macc 12:39-45. See also the speech attributed to Paul in Acts 22, especially v. 16.

[60] Eph 5:25-27.

[61] Hermas, *Mandates* 4.3.1.

[62] II Cor 1:21-22; cf. Rom 4:11.

[63] Eph 1:13-14; 4:30.

[64] Hermas, *Similitudes* 9.16.1-4.

free people are joined into one body. Similarly, according to Gal. 3:26-29, baptism overcomes distinctions between Jews and Greeks, slaves and free, men and women, and makes them all one in Christ. By the time of the deutero-Pauline Colossians, baptism's character as a ritual of initiation can be taken for granted to the extent that it can be presented as a new circumcision, a circumcision made without hands (2:11).

Baptism as Death and Resurrection. Two sayings attributed to Jesus in the Synoptic tradition seem to use the word baptism metaphorically to mean death, especially the death of Jesus.[65] In these sayings, the operative symbol has shifted from cleansing that leads to a pure and holy life to death that leads to new life. These sayings are close to Paul's interpretation of baptism in Romans 6, one of the most important passages on baptism in the New Testament.

Since the publication of Richard Reitzenstein's *Die Hellenistischen Mysterienreligionen* in 1910, a debate has raged continually on the relation between Romans 6 and the Greco-Roman mystery-religions.[66] Reitzenstein argued that baptism had already been shaped by Hellenism in the pre-Pauline tradition. Paul did not therefore reinterpret baptism in the language of the mysteries. The similarity was already present. Paul himself, according to Reitzenstein, was familiar with the language of the mysteries. Thus his formulations of basic powerful images are informed by the mysteries and he borrowed particular terms from their traditional terminology.[67] Another leader of the history-of-religions school, Willhelm Bousset, argued in more detail that Christian faith and ritual were already Hellenized in the tradition that Paul received. He suggested that the process began in the Christian community of Antioch in Syria.[68] In the foreword to his book, Bousset

[65] Mark 10:38-39; Luke 12:50.
[66] The third edition was published in 1927; see now the English translation by J. E. Steely (Pittsburg 1978).
[67] J. H. Randall (*Hellenistic Ways of Deliverance and the Making of the Christian Synthesis,* New York 1970) and Joscelyn Godwin (*Mystery Religions in the Ancient World,* New York 1981) have also concluded that Paul was influenced by the mystery religions.
[68] Wilhelm Bousset, *Kyrios Christos: A History of the Belief in Christ from the Beginnings of Christianity to Irenaeus,* trans. J. E. Steely (Nashville 1970). Ernst

responded to the criticism that the Hellenistic texts cited by the historians of religion as analogues to Romans 6, for example, were later than the date of Romans by stressing that it was not a question of literary dependence. The history-of-religions school did not take the position that Paul had read the Corpus Hermeticum, or even Philo. Rather, they were concerned to show broad intellectual connections between certain forms of early Christianity and the Hellenistic mystery religions. They wanted to reconstruct and illustrate a form of piety that grew quite early in its own soil (the Hellenized ancient Near East) and later fused with the gospel of Christ. They did not assert that particular forms of Christian faith and ritual were dependent, for example, on the Mithraic cult, but that both made use of common, earlier ideas. Most of those who have denied that Paul was dependent on the mystery religions missed the point that the history-or-religions school was making.[69]

In Romans 6:1-14 the ritual of baptism is explicitly interpreted as a reenactment of the death and resurrection of Jesus in which the baptized person appropriates the significance of that death for him- or herself. In this understanding of the ritual, the experience of the Christian is firmly and vividly grounded in the story of the death and resurrection of Christ. These qualities of reenactment of a foundational story and the identification of the participant with the protagonist of the story are strikingly reminiscent of what is known about the initiation rituals of certain mystery religions, notably the Eleusinian mysteries and the Isis mysteries.[70]

Käsemann (Commentary on Romans, trans. G. W. Bromiley (Grand Rapids 1980), and Robert C. Tannehill (Dying and Rising with Christ, Berlin 1967) also conclude that Hellenization took place prior to Paul.

[69] Those who have argued against the influence of the mystery religions on Paul include Arthur Darby Nock, "Early Gentile Christianity and Its Hellinistic Background" in A. E. J. Rawlinson (ed.), Essays on the Trinity and Incarnation (London 1928) 51–156; idem, Early Gentile Christianity and Its Hellenistic Background (New York 1964) 109–45; Günter Wagner, Pauline Baptism and the Pagan Mysteries: The Problem of the Pauline Doctrine of Baptism in Romans VI.1-11, In the Light of Religio-Historical 'Parallels,' trans. J. P. Smith (Edinburgh 1967); and Ronald H. Nash, Christianity and the Hellenistic World (Grand Rapids 1984) 115–59.

[70] For the story or hieros logos of the Eleusinian mysteries, see the Homeric Hymn to Demeter. An English translation of this hymn, along with an in-

One of the distinctive features of Romans 6 is that Paul avoids saying "we have risen" with Christ; rather he speaks of "newness of life." The implication of Paul's restraint is that the transformation is not complete. There is still an apocalyptic expectation of a future, fuller transformation into a heavenly form of life. This expectation fits with Paul's use throughout the passage of the imperative alongside the indicative. "Newness of life" is a real, present possibility, both spiritually and ethically, but the actualizing of that possibility requires decision and commitment as well as grace.[71]

At some point, at least forty years after Paul's death, the notion of death and rebirth was also attached to proselyte baptism in Judaism. Two passages in the Babylonian Talmud mention the opinion that one who became a proselyte is like a child newly born.[72] The rebirth of the rabbinic proselyte baptism, unlike the Christian form, was not eschatological. No direct link to immortality was made. As Israel Abrahams put it, proselyte baptism did not ensure sinlessness nor the transformation of human character. Such, according to the rabbis, was not possible in the pre-messianic age.[73] The image of rebirth thus shows the gulf between life within and life outside the covenant people.

Christian and rabbinic baptism both have their ultimate roots in the ritual washings of Leviticus. Both came to function as rituals

---

troduction and bibliography, has been published by Marvin W. Meyer, *The Ancient Mysteries: A Sourcebook* (New York 1987) 17–30. For an account of an initiation into the mysteries of Isis, see Apulcius, *The Golden Ass,* Book 11. See also Plutarch's *On Isis and Osiris.* Meyer has included book 11 of the Golden Ass and selections from Plutarch's work (ibid., 176–93 and 160–72).

[71] Note that the author of Colossians does not hesitate to say that Christians have risen with Christ (2:12, 3:1). Baptism is also linked to the resurrection of Christ in 1 Peter 3:21. See also the related interpretation of baptism as rebirth in John 3:3-8 and Titus 3:5.

[72] Yebamoth 62a; Bekoroth 47a; see George F. Moore, *Judaism in the First Centuries of the Christian Era: The Age of the Tannaim* (Cambridge, MA 1927 = New York 1971) 1.334-5. See also Yebamoth 48b, M. Keritoth 8b, Tos. Shekalim 3:20, Gerim 2.5; Jeremias, *Infant Baptism,* 33 n. 8; Rowley, "Jewish Proselyte Baptism and the Baptism of John," 329.

[73] Abrahams, *Studies in Pharisaism and the Gospels,* 42; in support of his point, he cites Gen. Rab. 70.8, b. Qiddushin 30b, and Midr. Tanhuma, Mesora 17-18.

of initiation. The major difference is the relation of this ritual to eschatology. Both expect a fulfilment but the two communities place themselves on different sides of the turning point between the two ages.

Gabriele Winkler

4. The Original Meaning of the Prebaptismal Anointing and Its Implications

The great variety of anointings at baptism has led to considerable confusion over their respective meaning. Moreover, scholars have nearly unanimously accepted the fact that the prebaptismal anointing has a purificatory or even exorcistic purpose. Such an understanding is certainly true for the baptismal tradition in the West. Hippolytus (third century), for instance, makes this statement immediately after the renunciation: "And when he has said this let him anoint with the oil of exorcism, saying: 'Let all evil spirits depart far from thee.' "[1] Here we see that the anointing is strictly linked with the preceding rite of renunciation.

In the East, however, the prebaptismal anointing was not always associated with an apotropaic ritual. The Syrian rite of baptism, for example, knows of various anointings in connection with baptism — twice before and once after the baptism. Scholars were slow to accept the fact that the Syrian rite originally knew only one prebaptismal anointing, namely, the pouring of oil over the head, and that only at a later period in history was the whole body anointed.[2]

[1] See E. C. Whitaker, *Documents of the Baptismal Liturgy*, 2nd ed. (London 1970) 5.

[2] Even today, A. F. J. Klijn ("An Ancient Syriac Baptismal Liturgy in the Syriac Acts of John," *Novum Testamentum* 6 [1963] 227) and others suggest that originally the whole body and not the head was anointed. In a paper delivered at the Second Symposium of Syriac Studies held in Paris, I demonstrated the original structure of the Syriac rite of baptism, comparing the Syriac evidence with the oldest Armenian sources: Orientalia Christiana Analecta 205 (Rom 1976) 317–324.

Before we consider the reasons why the East adopted first an anointing of the whole body (before baptism) and, second, an anointing following baptism, it will be useful to outline briefly the sources we are going to look at and to analyze them carefully.

We can distinguish three main groups: those that refer incidentally to baptism; the commentaries and church orders; the baptismal *ordines*.

To the incidental references belong the so-called *Teaching of St Gregory*,[3] which forms part of the *Agathangeli Historia*;[4] the Syriac *Acts of Thomas* (third century) and *Acts of John* (fourth century);[5] and the fourth century writings of Aphraates[6] and Ephrem.[7] None of these sources refers to an anointing after baptism.

Among the commentaries, baptismal instructions and church orders, attention should be drawn to the *Didascalia*,[8] the *Apostolic Constitutions*,[9] the explanations of baptism attributed to Cyril of Jerusalem,[10] the commentary of Theodore of Mopsuestia,[11] and the baptismal instructions of John Chrysostom.[12]

[3] This Armenian document is now available in English: R. W. Thomson, *The Teaching of Saint Gregory: An Early Armenian Catechism. Translation and Commentary*. Harvard Armenian Texts and Studies 3 (Cambridge, Mass. 1970).

[4] See R. W. Thomson, *Agathangelos: History of the Armenians. Translation and Commentary* (New York 1976).

[5] See W. Wright, *Apocryphal Acts of the Apostles Edited from Syriac Manuscripts in the British Museum and Other Libraries*, 2 vols. (London/Edinburgh 1871). A. F. J. Klijn adopted the occasionally inexact translation of Wright in his new book, *The Acts of Thomas. Introduction, Text, Commentary* (Leiden 1962).

[6] See the excellent study by E. J. Duncan, *Baptism in the Demonstrations of Aphraates the Persian Sage*. Studies in Christian Antiquity 8 (Washington, D.C. 1945).

[7] See the edition and German translation of Ephrem's writings by E. Beck in various volumes of Corpus Scriptorum Christianorum Orientalium [CSCO] (Louvain).

[8] See R. H. Connolly, *Didascalia Apostolorum* (Oxford 1929).

[9] See F. X. Funk, *Didascalia et Constitutiones Apostolorum*, 2 vols. (Paderborn 1905; reprint, Turin 1964).

[10] See F. L. Cross, *St. Cyril of Jerusalem's Lectures on the Christian Sacraments: The Procatechesis and the Five Mystagogical Catecheses* (London 1951).

[11] See A. Mingana, *Commentary of Theodore of Mopsuestia on the Lord's Prayer and on the Sacraments of Baptism and the Eucharist*. Woodbrooke Studies 6 (Cambridge 1933).

[12] See P. W. Harkins, *St. John Chrysostom: Baptismal Instructions*. Ancient

From the great variety of baptismal *ordines,* I choose the Armenian ordo[13] because of its great antiquity (the oldest manuscripts, which I quote, belong to the ninth/tenth century; however, because of structural and other internal criteria the Armenian ritual has to be compared with the Syriac sources of the third to fifth centuries[14]). In a few instances a brief glance at the Orthodox West Syrian[15] and the East Syrian baptismal ordo[16] can complete the picture.

TERMS USED FOR THE OIL AND THE ANOINTING

One of the thorniest problems in the development of the rites of initiation is the historical evolution of the anointings in connection with baptism. In earlier studies various unproved hypotheses, inaccurate inferences and untenable conclusions about the original meaning of the various anointings have been suggested. Although L. L. Mitchell in his book on the anointings provides extensive documentation, the chapters on the Syriac evidence show considerable weakness.[17] If any progress on this highly controversial

---

Christian Writers 31 (Westminster, Md. 1963); A. Wenger, *Jean Chrysostome: Huit catéchèses baptismales inédites.* Sources chrétiennes 50 (Paris 1957).

[13] See the English translation of F. C. Conybeare, *Rituale Armenorum. Being the Administration of the Sacraments and the Breviary Rites of the Armenian Church together with the Greek Rites of Baptism and Epiphany Edited from the Oldest Mss.* (Oxford 1905). In my study, *Das armenische Initiationsrituale. Entwicklungsgeschichtliche und liturgievergleichende Untersuchung der Quellen des 3. bis 10. Jahrhunderts.* Orientalia Christiana Analecta 217 (Rome 1982), I edited the oldest manuscripts, with a complete *index verborum* and a German translation of the Armenian manuscript.

[14] See my study, n. 13 above.

[15] See *The Sacrament of Holy Baptism According to the Ancient Rite of the Syrian Orthodox Church of Antioch.* Translated from the original Syriac by Deacon Murad Saliba Barsom; edited and published by Metropolitan Mar Athanasius Yeshue Samuel. Syriac and English translation (Hackensack, N.J. 1974).

[16] See *The Liturgy of the Holy Apostles Adai and Mari Together with Two Additional Liturgies to Be Said on Certain Feasts and Other Days: And the Order of Baptism* (London: SPCK 1893).

[17] *Baptismal Anointing.* Alcuin Club Collections 48 (London 1966). For a critique of Mitchell's study, see the chapter, "Die Bedeutung der präbaptismalen Salbung im armenischen Text . . .," in my study, n. 13 above.

issue is to be achieved, rigorous attention must be paid to the various terms used for the oil and the anointings.

The Syriac and Armenian Terminology. It is striking that the oldest sources, of both Armenian and Syriac origin, never refer to the oil as *myron*, but invariably use "(olive) oil": *mešḥā* (Syriac); *iwl* (Armenian); [*elaion* = Greek]. This usage is found in the *Didascalia*,[18] the *Acts of Thomas*,[19] the *Acts of John*,[20] the writings of Aphraates,[21] Ephrem,[22] and Theodore of Mopsuestia.[23] All these Syriac sources use the term "(olive) oil" (*mešḥā*) or compounds like "oil of anointing" (*mešḥā da-mᶜšīḥūtā*). Unfortunately these terms have not always been translated as "(olive) oil," as they should have been, but by misleading terms such as *myron* or "chrism."

The earliest Armenian sources seem to have taken over the Syriac terminology. The oil is likewise called "oil of anointing" (*iwl awcowt'ean*),[24] and we also find the simple term "(olive) oil" (*iwl*) or "holy oil" (*iwl sowrb*), respectively, "all-holy oil" (*iwl amenasowrb*).[25]

Before turning to the Greek terms for the oil, we want to complete the picture with a brief glance at the terms for "anointing" in the Syriac documents. We have already mentioned that originally the Syriac Church probably knew of just one prebaptismal anointing, the anointing of the head. Besides this anointing of the head, gradually also an anointing of the whole body was introduced before baptism, and eventually an anointing after baptism.

The oldest Syriac sources of the third and fourth centuries regularly call the prebaptismal anointing of the head *rušmā* (sign,

[18] See ch. XVI.

[19] See chaps. 27 and 132.

[20] See ed. Wright, II, 40, 54.

[21] Aphraates talks of the fruit of the "splendid olive tree, wherein is the sign (*rušmā*) of the mystery of life, whereby Christians (*mᶜšīḥē*) and priests and kings and prophets are perfected"; see *Demonstratio* 23; ed. D. J. Parisot, *Aphraatis sapientis Persae demonstrationes* II. Patrologia Syriaca (Paris 1907) 10.

[22] See *De epiphania* III, responsorium, 1, 6.

[23] See Mingana, *Commentary of Theodore of Mopsuestia*, pp. 176, 179 (Syr.); the English translation ("chrism") is inexact, for "chrism" is not *mešḥā*.

[24] See *Agathangeli Historia*, no. 833. For a complete analysis, see my study, n. 13 above.

[25] See my study, n. 13 above.

mark),[26] whereas the term "seal" (ḥatmā) is normally reserved for the postbaptismal anointing that was introduced by the end of the fourth century. Great confusion was created by the inaccurate translation of rušmā as "seal" instead of "sign" or "mark." This misleading translation of the terms for "oil" and "anointing" occurs in all texts and studies dealing with this subject.[27]

We have seen that the prebaptismal anointing of the head was regularly called rušmā (sign, mark). The main term for the prebaptismal anointing of the body seems to have been m'šīḥūtā (anointing), whereas the postbaptismal anointing was normally referred to as ḥatmā (seal).[28]

The Greek Terminology. It is well known that the *Apostolic Constitutions* incorporated material from the *Didache* (first/second century) and from the *Didascalia* (third century). Therefore the *Apostolic Constitutions* consist of various layers that do not reflect the same age. Another feature of this document should be mentioned here: although the Constitutions belong to the Syrian church orders of the fourth century, they have come down to us in Greek.

In Books 3 and 7, which depend heavily upon the *Didache* and the *Didascalia*, and therefore belong to one of the oldest layers of

[26] See *Acts of Thomas*, chaps. 49–50 (In Klijn, *The Acts of Thomas*, and Whitaker, *Documents of the Baptismal Liturgy*, the translation "seal" is wrong, for "seal" does not translate rušmā.); Aphraates, *Demonstratio* 23 and *passim* (ed. Parisot, II, 9–10); Ephrem, *De virginitate* VII, 6 and *passim*. Occasionally "imprint" is also used.

[27] To name only a few recent ones: Mitchell, *Baptismal Anointing* 33, 42, and *passim*; Klijn, *The Acts of Thomas* 90 and *passim*; hence the confusion in his introduction (55): ". . . first of all [we] have to deal with the word 'seal' in these Acts . . .," identifying (correctly) "seal" with *sphragis*; but in the first place, "seal" does not translate rušmā (*signum*). In short, the *Acts of Thomas* never uses the term "seal" when referring to the anointing but rušmā (mark, sign). We find further incorrect translations in Whitaker, *Documents* 14 and *passim*; Th. M. Finn, *The Liturgy of Baptism in the Baptismal Instructions of St John Chrysostom*. Studies in Christian Antiquity 15 (Washington, D.C. 1967) 131.

[28] This distinction can be traced back to a certain extent even in the oldest Syriac manuscripts for baptism; see S. Brock, "Studies in the Early History of the Syrian Orthodox Baptismal Liturgy," *Journal of Theological Studies*, n.s. 28 (1972) 31–33.

the *Apostolic Constitutions,* the oil for the prebaptismal anointing is always referred to as "(olive) oil" (*elaion*) or "holy oil" (*hagion elaion*).[29] We have already met this term (with or without the attribute "holy") in our previous sources as one of the original terms for the oil.

With Chrysostom, however, and more importantly with Cyril of Jerusalem, we are faced with an entirely new terminology for the oil used for the prebaptismal anointing. Chrysostom refers to the oil either as *myron*[30] or as "spiritual oil" (*elaion pneumatikon*),[31] but occasionally he also uses "oil of gladness" (*elaion agalliaseōs*).[32] Cyril, who is known to have introduced other hitherto unknown practices,[33] says to the neophytes: "Ye were anointed with exorcised oil (*tō elaiō eporkistō*)."[34]

So far we have established the various terms that were used in the inner region of Syria (cf. *Acts of Thomas, Acts of John,* Aphraates, Ephrem); Armenia (*Agathangelos,* baptismal ordo); the Greek-speaking coastline of the western half of Syria and Palestine (Chrysostom, Cyril of Jerusalem).

In the oldest East Syrian and Armenian documents, the oil for the prebaptismal anointing is called "(olive) oil," or "(olive) oil of anointing" or "holy (olive) oil," never *myron.* (The oldest stratum of the *Apostolic Constitutions* follows this group in calling the prebaptismal oil "(olive) oil" or "holy (olive) oil.") This anointing before baptism is regularly called "mark" or "sign" (Syriac: *rušmā*) in the Syriac sources. When the Syriac Church eventually adopted an anointing after baptism, it was referred to as "seal" (*ḥatmā*).

The *Apostolic Constitutions,* which reflect the practices of the western half of Syria, are one of the first sources that refer to an

[29] See Book III, 17, 1 and VII, 22, 2. The oil for the prebaptismal anointing is called "oil" or "holy oil," whereas the oil used for the anointing after baptism is always called *myron;* see III, 16, 31; VII, 22, 2; 44, 2 (Whitaker, *Documents* 31, 32, 34, gives inexact translations).

[30] See Wenger, *Jean Chrysostome* 145–146. In contrast to Chrysostom, this term is reserved in the *Apostolic Constitutions* for the postbaptismal anointing (see previous note).

[31] See Finn, *Liturgy of Baptism* 121ff.

[32] Finn, 130, n. 49.

[33] See G. Dix, *The Shape of the Liturgy* 348ff.

[34] *Mystagogical Catecheses* 2, 3.

anointing after baptism. The oil used at the prebaptismal anointing is regularly called "(olive) oil" or "holy oil," whereas the oil that is applied after baptism is always designated as *myron*. With Chrysostom and Cyril of Jerusalem, the old term for the prebaptismal anointing is dropped entirely. Chrysostom takes the *myron*, which in the *Apostolic Constitutions* is restricted to designate the postbaptismal anointing, as a term for the prebaptismal anointing. Cyril goes even a step further in calling the prebaptismal oil "exorcised oil."

Does this change in terminology also reflect an alteration in the meaning of the prebaptismal anointing? And if we come to an affirmative conclusion, we have to ask: What caused this change? It is time now to look more closely at what the various writers say about the anointing(s) and at the main themes with which they associate the anointing.

CHANGE IN THE LEITMOTIV OF THE
PREBAPTISMAL ANOINTING

1. *The Main Theme in the Earliest Sources of Syria and Armenia.* In the *Acts of Thomas* we find five accounts of baptism. [1] Chapters 49–50 give a brief report of a baptism that took place in the river, followed by the Eucharist. This report is of no interest for the moment, since there is no detailed description of an anointing. [2] Chapters 25–27 and 132–133 mention only one anointing, namely, the pouring of the oil over the head before baptism. [3] Chapters 121 and 156–158 refer to two anointings before baptism: the anointing of the head and of the whole body. No indication, however, is found of any further anointing after baptism.

We give here the text of the first two reports that mention just one anointing which took place before baptism (quoted from Wright's edition).

Chapter 27	Chapter 132
[He] poured oil upon their heads, and said:	He cast oil upon their heads, and said:
Come, holy name of the Messiah, come, power of grace, which art from on high,	Glory to thee, (thou) beloved fruit! Glory to thee, (thou) name of the Messiah!

come, perfect mercy,
come, exalted gift,
come, sharer of the blessing,
come, revealer of the hidden
  mysteries . . .
come, messenger of reconciliation,
come, spirit of holiness
and purify their reins and hearts.

Glory to thee, (thou) hidden power that
dwellest in the Messiah![35]

In chapter 27 the cleansing aspect of the anointing is clearly stated, but attention should be drawn to the compiler's emphasis on associating the oil with the Messiah.

In the next two accounts the picture is slightly different. First of all, two anointings are indicated (of the head and of the whole body), although only for the anointing of the head is a prayer (or further explanation) given.

Chapter 121	Chapter 157
And he cast [the oil] upon the head of Mygdōnia and said:	And he cast [the oil] upon the head of . . . these, and said: In thy name, Jesus the Messiah, let it be to these persons for the remission of offences and sins, and for the destruction of the enemy,
Heal her of her old wounds,	and for the healing of their souls and their bodies.
and wash away from her her sores, and strengthen her weakness.	

As in the previous group, there is no postbaptismal anointing. It should not be overlooked that in the second group, just quoted, the theme changes slightly in comparison with the first two accounts (chaps. 27 and 132). Although the prayer (cf. ch. 157) is still addressed to Jesus *the Messiah*, the theme of the Messiah no longer plays any real role. The leitmotiv is clearly restricted to the healing aspect of the oil.

[35] I doubt whether the Syriac manuscript really gives ''Messiah'' (*mšiḥā*) and not rather ''(olive) oil'' (*mešḥā*). At any rate, the Syriac play on words cannot be rendered in any modern language.

Comparing these two groups, I came to the hypothetical conclusion that the *Acts of Thomas* consist of various layers, and that the second group (chaps. 121 and 157) belongs to a later stratum. This hypothesis is based on the following reasons.

We know that originally there was only one anointing, namely, the anointing of the head. The anointing of the whole body was introduced at a later stage. This anointing of the whole body, which took place after the anointing of the head, is first attested in the second group of the *Acts of Thomas*. It is of great interest that the Greek version of the Acts does not include this second anointing.[36]

If we look at the context of the first two reports, that is, chapters 27 and 132 (Klijn, pp. 77, 135), we note that there still was no special prayer for the blessing of the oil; the consecration of the oil is secondary. Like the anointing of the whole body, the blessing of the oil is mentioned for the first time in the second group of the *Acts of Thomas* (chaps. 121 and 157; Klijn, pp. 130, 149).

In my opinion, the most striking evidence, however, for assuming a later stratum for chapters 121 and 157 is indicated by the shift from the leitmotiv centered around the Messiah to the healing aspect of the anointing. This will become more obvious when we analyze the next sources.

In one of the oldest Syriac documents, the *Didascalia* (ch. XVI), the anointing is associated with the following leitmotiv: "As of old the priests and kings were anointed in Israel, do thou in like manner, with the imposition of hand, anoint the head of those who receive baptism." Here the anointing is linked with that of the Israelitic priest-king. The same connection is found in the *Apostolic Constitutions* (III, 16, 3-4). This text connects the anointing before baptism, moreover, with the New Testament (incorporating 1 Peter 2:9)[37] in the following manner: Through Christ, the Anointed (Messiah-King, *Christos* indicate just their different etymological provenance; the meaning is the same), the newly anointed, that is

---

[36] See Klijn, *The Acts of Thomas* 285.

[37] "You, however, are a chosen race, a royal priesthood, a holy nation. . . ."

the baptizandus,[38] becomes assimilated to the messianic priesthood and kingship of Christ.

In the Armenian baptismal ordo we find the following prayer, which also takes up 1 Peter 2:9: "Blessed are you, Lord our God, who has chosen you a people unto priesthood and kingship for a holy race and for a selected people, as you have already previously anointed priests and kings and prophets with such all-holy oil. . . ."[39]

The continuity between the priest-king of the Old Testament, the fulfillment of this kingship at the baptism of the Messiah in the Jordan, and the handing down of this reality to the apostles and the "children of the church" is especially stressed in the Armenian Teaching of St. Gregory: ". . . The horn of the oil [that is, the anointing of the priest-king in Israel] was the type of the anointing of Christ. . . . Thence also Aaron was anointed to the priesthood of the Lord . . . to anoint according to the same type. . . . (no. 432); . . . The mystery was preserved in the seed of Abraham . . . until John, priest, prophet and baptist . . . and he gave the priesthood, the anointing, the prophecy and the kingship to our Lord Jesus Christ (no. 433); . . . and Christ gave them to the apostles, and the apostles to the children of the church" (no. 469).[40]

Ephrem also stresses the close ties between the "christians" (the anointed) and the Messiah (the Anointed): "In symbol and truth Leviathan is trodden down by mortals: the baptized, like divers,

---

[38] It is interesting to note that the appellation christianos (Christian) still refers to Christos = the Anointed. In the eastern half of Syria, the Christians were originally called mᵉšiḥē (the anointed); see the careful study on that topic by S. Brock, "Some Aspects of Greek Words in Syriac," Synkretismus im syrisch-persischen Kulturgebiet. Bericht über ein Symposion in Reinhausen bei Göttingen in der Zeit vom 4. bis 8. Okt. 1971. Abhandlungen der Akademie der Wissenschaften in Göttingen 96 (Göttingen 1975).

[39] In my study, n. 13 above, I have shown that this prayer, which today is said at the blessing of the oil, originally belonged to the prebaptismal anointing.

[40] Thomson, The Teaching 94ff; see also the striking affinity in the apocryphal Testamenta XII Patriarcharum, cited in G. Kretschmar, Die Geschichte des Taufgottesdienstes in der alten Kirche. Leiturgia. Handbuch des evangelischen Gottesdienstes (Kassel 1970) 28–29.

strip and put on oil (*mešḥā*), as a symbol of Christ (*mᵉšiḥā*)."[41] In another hymn Ephrem not only makes an allusion to the priests and kings of the old covenant, but refers also to the gift of the Spirit bestowed on the baptizandus at this prebaptismal anointing: "This oil is a dear friend of the Holy Spirit; it serves Him, following Him like a disciple. With it the Spirit signs priests and anoints kings; for with the oil the Holy Spirit imprints His mark in His sheep. Like a signet ring whose impression is left on wax, so the hidden seal of the Spirit is imprinted by oil on the bodies of those who are anointed in baptism."[42]

The same association with the coming of the Spirit at the anointing before baptism is given in the *Apostolic Constitutions* (VII, 22, 2): "But thou shalt first anoint the person with holy oil; afterwards baptize him . . . that the anointing (*chrisma*)[43] may be a participation of the Holy Spirit." In Book III, 17, 1, this is again mentioned: "The oil [is given] instead of the Holy Spirit."[44]

All the texts I have quoted so far speak unambiguously at this point about the prebaptismal anointing. Why did the Syrians think of associating the anointing in Christian baptism with the anointing of the priest-kings and with the gift of the Spirit? The only possible answer that makes sense to me must be sought in the texts of the Old and New Testaments.

One simply cannot overlook the striking structural resemblance between the divine nomination of the priest-kings in the old covenant and the Christian prebaptismal anointing: the prophet instructs the newly appointed king before his anointing (see the catechetical instructions of the baptizandus); the prophet anoints the head of the king; in connection with the anointing, the Spirit descends upon the king.[45]

[41] *De fide* (hymns) 82, 10. The passage is quoted according to the English translation of S. Brock, *The Harp of the Spirit: Twelve Poems of Saint Ephrem. Introduction and Translation.* Studies Supplementary to *Sobornost* 4 (1975) 33.

[42] *De virginitate* VII, 6; Brock, *The Harp of the Spirit* 50. That this anointing precedes baptism is stated in verse 8.

[43] Whitaker, *Documents* 32, gives the inaccurate translation: "that the anointing with oil. . . ."

[44] For further references, for example in the documents of Cappadocia, see my study, n. 13 above.

[45] See the anointing of Saul and David in 1 Samuel 9:15ff; 16:1-13. Here is the

Other strong indications support this comparison. The kings of Israel were anointed with the "horn of oil." The Syriac Bible, called the *Pešiṭta*, gives: *qarnā d-mešḥa* (horn of oil).[46] We have already met the simple word for the oil, *mešḥā*, in all the old sources, whether of Syriac, Armenian or Greek origin. Furthermore, exactly the same combined term, that is "horn of oil," but also sometimes "horn of anointing" (*qarnā da-mᵉšīḥūtā*) has survived in East Syrian sources, for example in Ephrem and in a commentary on baptism by an anonymous writer of the ninth century.[47]

Besides the striking affinity in the terminology, another important feature should be mentioned here. We have already referred to the continuity that the Syrians and Armenians saw in the anointing of the priest-kings of the Old Testament and the anointing of Christ at his baptism in the Jordan. This is seen, for example, in the Armenian *Teaching of St. Gregory*: ". . . the mystery [of the anointing in the Old Testament] was preserved . . . until John, priest, prophet and baptist . . . and he gave the priesthood, the anointing, the prophecy and the kingship to our Lord Jesus Christ" (nos. 432, 433). Here it is implicitly stated that the anointing and kingship of the Old Testament were passed over to Jesus at his baptism by John.

The term "Christ" (Messiah = the Anointed) could be taken as an indirect indication of the anointing of Jesus. Yet no explicit reference to Christ's anointing at the Jordan is given in the first

---

description of Saul's anointing: "Then, from a flask he had with him. Samuel poured oil on Saul's head . . . and the Spirit of God rushed upon him" (1 Sam 10:1, 10; see also v. 6). And David's anointing: "Then Samuel, with the horn of oil in hand, anointed him in the midst of his brothers; and from that day on, the spirit of the Lord rushed upon David" (1 Sam 16:13). See E. Kutsch, *Salbung als Rechtsakt im Alten Testament und im alten Orient*. Beihefte zur Zeitschrift für die alttestamentliche Wissenschaft 87 (Berlin 1963) 52–63; G. Widengren, *Sakrales Königtum im Alten Testament und im Judentum* (Stuttgart 1955) 31ff; idem, *Religionsphänomenologie*, 2nd ed. (Berlin 1969) 228–229, 385.

[46] See, for example, 1 Samuel 16:13; 1 Kings 1:39.

[47] See Ephrem, *De epiphania* III, 6; *De virginitate* VII, 1; *Expositio* of an anonymous writer: tract. V, 5; ed. R. H. Connolly, *Anonymi auctoris expositio officiorum ecclesiae Georgio Arbelensi vulgo adscripta, accedit Abrahae bar Lipeh interpretatio officiorum* II. CSCO 76, t. 32 (Louvain 1953) 95.

three gospels. But in Acts 10:38 Jesus is presented as the one whom "God had anointed with the Holy Spirit and with power." And in Luke 4:18 Jesus, while reading the Scriptures to the Jews in the synagogue, applies Isaiah 61:1-2 to himself: "The Spirit of the Lord has been given to me, for he has anointed me."

From these indications in Scripture and in the early writings of Syria and Armenia, one can assume that the descent of the dove at Christ's baptism is the visible manifestation of the Spirit's presence, and that with the divine voice, "You are my Son, the Beloved; my favor rests on you," Jesus is anointed and invested as the Messiah-King.[48]

How closely the Syrians shaped their baptismal liturgy after Jesus' descent into the Jordan becomes evident through another passage of the *Didascalia* (ch. IX). In this short reference to baptism, the dignity of the bishop plays the predominant role: "through whom the Lord gave you the Holy Spirit . . . through whom you became sons of the light and through whom the Lord in baptism, by the imposition of the hand of the bishop, bore witness to each one of you, and uttered His holy voice, saying: 'Thou art my Son. I this day have begotten thee.' "

---

[48] See my forthcoming article on Jesus' baptism and the Christian rites of initiation as an enthronization ritual, in *Le Muséon*, and the interesting aspect E. O. James has pointed out in his book *Christian Myth and Ritual. A Historical Study*, 2nd ed. (Cleveland/New York 1965) 100–101: "Viewed in relation to the coronation ritual, the baptism of Christ, as recorded by the synoptists, is highly significant, since it contains most of the essential elements in the pattern. First there is the proclamation of the kingdom by the precursor, which is followed immediately by the ablution at the hands of John in preparation for the investiture as the Son of God. This was accomplished by a special anointing of the Holy Spirit from heaven with a visible manifestation of the divine presence in the form of a dove, just as in the Egyptian coronation the gods frequently appeared as some kind of creature in which they dwelt. Thus installed by God Himself as the Messiah-King, and 'begotten' again like an ancient monarch at his coronation, He betook Himself into the wilderness to undergo a period of seclusion and fasting from which He emerged victorious over the powers of evil. Having first received a spiritual renewal . . . after His struggles, immediately He proclaimed Himself the anointed Messiah [cf. Luke 4:18ff] or Christ, and gathered Himself followers to establish the kingdom." See also G. Widengren, *Religionsphänomenologie* 228–229, 385; *idem*, *Sakrales Königtum* 31ff.

In the last phrase, Psalm 2:7 is quoted. It is interesting to note that this quotation is also given as a variant reading of Luke's presentation of the heavenly voice at Christ's baptism (3:22). It is possible that this reading was the original one, which was eventually dropped because of its possible adoptionalistic connotation.[49]

From the *Didascalia* we can deduce that these words were said by the bishop as a formula while he laid his hand upon the head of the baptizandus. The gesture of laying on the hand was accompanied by another one, namely, the pouring of the oil over the head, which is not mentioned explicitly here but in chapter XVI of the *Didascalia*: ". . . with the imposition of hand anoint the head of those who receive baptism." But let us come back to the previous important statement in the *Didascalia* (ch. IX), including the variant reading in Luke 3:22 about being "begotten" at the rites of initiation. It is a common imagery among all Syriac writers to speak of baptism as a womb. Here the idea of rebirth is taken up as it is depicted in John 3:3-5: "I tell you most solemnly, unless a man is born from above, he cannot see the kingdom of God. . . . unless a man is born through water and the Spirit he cannot enter the kingdom of God."

To summarize, in the oldest Syriac documents, Christian baptism is shaped after Christ's baptism in the Jordan. As Jesus had received the anointing through the divine presence in the appearance of a dove, and was invested as the Messiah, so in Christian baptism every candidate is anointed and, in connection with this anointing, the gift of the Spirit is conferred. Therefore the main theme of this prebaptismal anointing is the entry into the eschatological kingship of the Messiah, being in the true sense of the word assimilated to the Messiah-King through this anointing.

Only with this discovery are we now able to explain [1] why the oldest Syriac and Armenian sources knew of just one anointing, namely, the pouring of the oil[50] over the head: At the anointing of

[49] See E. C. Ratcliff, "The Old Syrian Baptismal Tradition and Its Resettlement under the Influence of Jerusalem in the IV Century," in J. Vellian, *The Syrian Churches Series 6* (Kottayam 1973) 88–89.

[50] These sources mention explicitly that the oil was *poured* or *cast* over the head, for example, the *Acts of Thomas* (chaps. 27 and 132, 121 and 157) and

the priest-king of the Old Testament, the oil was poured over the head of the newly appointed king; [2] why the coming of the Spirit is associated with this anointing of the head: In connection with the anointing of the priest-king of Israel, the Spirit of the Lord came over the newly nominated king; [3] the deeper meaning of this Old Testament imagery: The anointing of the priest-king of the old covenant prefigured the anointing of the Messiah. Jesus is revealed as the Messiah-King at the Jordan through the descent of the Spirit in the appearance of a dove. What happened at the Jordan is dramatically reinvoked in the earliest Syriac documents.

It is also no longer puzzling why the anointing, and not the immersion in the water, forms the central part of baptism in the early Syriac sources (see, for example, the *Acts of Thomas*). The description of Christ's baptism culminates in the appearance of the dove and the divine voice. This event, and not the actual descent into the water, is emphasized by Matthew, Luke and Mark. Furthermore, in John (1:32-33) Jesus is explicitly depicted as the one who baptizes with the Spirit, in contrast to John's baptism with water: "John also declared: 'I saw the Spirit coming down on him from heaven like a dove and resting on him. . . . he who sent me to baptize with water had said to me, "The man on whom you see the Spirit come down and rest is the one who is going to baptize with the Holy Spirit."'"

In the process of ritualization, therefore, it was the anointing that became, in Syria, the first and only visible gesture for the central event at Christ's baptism: his revelation as the Messiah-King through the descent of the Spirit.

In the early Syriac and Armenian reports about baptism, we frequently find miraculous events connected with the mentioning of the oil or the anointing.[51] Beyond doubt, we have to interpret all the accounts about any *epiphaneia* or miracles in general in connection with the oil in the light of these findings.

Agathangelos (no. 833; see edition of Thomson, 368/389). The signing of the forehead with the sign of the cross seems to be the later form.

[51] See *Agathangelos*, no. 833, *Acts of Thomas*, chaps. 25-27 (Whitaker, *Documents* 14), and the *Acts of John* (ed. Wright, II, 39, 54).

This concept of shaping the baptismal liturgy after what had happened at the Jordan[52] certainly represents the oldest and most powerful stratum in Syria. Yet, already in those two accounts of the *Acts of Thomas* (chaps. 121 and 157, cited above), where for the first time a second prebaptismal anointing is introduced, another possible interpretation of the anointing makes its way. The anointing of the whole body, besides that of the head, prepares for the eventual oblivion of the earlier powerful ritual, and for the reinterpretation of the prebaptismal anointing about a hundred years later.

For the moment it is enough to know that the prebaptismal anointing lost its original impact as an independent, even central element within the whole ritual, and that this anointing became attached to the previous rites, namely, renunciation and exorcism. During Chrysostom's time, for instance, the reinterpretation of the anointing before baptism is already well underway. Hence he removes our leitmotiv from its original *Sitz im Leben* (that is, at the anointing) and transfers it, together with the gift of the Spirit, to the immersion into the water at baptism proper: ". . . in this manner you become also a king, a priest, and a prophet in the bath."[53] Yet, Chrysostom does not know of any anointing after baptism. At the time of Cyril of Jerusalem, however, or his successor John — at any rate toward the end of the fourth century — an anointing after baptism was adopted for the first time in the East. And now the conferring of the Spirit (which Chrysostom had moved to the immersion), with its association of the royal and sacerdotal anointing, is attached again to the anointing, but now it is the anointing after baptism: ". . . for what time Moses imparted to his brother the command of God, and made him Highpriest, after bathing in the water, he anointed him; and Aaron was called Christ [or Anointed], from the emblematical chrism

[52] Hence the designation of the baptismal font as "Jordan" (or "womb," according to John 3) in the Syriac writers and in their baptismal *ordines*.

[53] See Chrysostom, *In 2 Cor. 3:7*, quoted in F. Ysebeart, *Greek Baptismal Terminology: Its Origins and Early Development*. Graec. Chr. Primaeva 1 (Nijmegen 1962) 378; see also Finn, *The Liturgy of Baptism* 177ff. Traits of the old stratum are still present in the East and West Syrian liturgies for baptism. See my study, n. 13 above.

[chrisma]. So also the High-priest raising Solomon to the kingdom, anointed him after he had bathed in Gihon. To them, however, these things happened in a figure, but . . . ye were truly anointed by the Holy Ghost."[54]

Before we ask how these writers interpreted the anointing before baptism, and why an anointing after baptism was introduced at all, let us see if we can trace the leitmotiv even further.

The association of the anointing with the priest-kings of Israel is a universal phenomenon and not restricted to the Syriac Church, although it has without any doubt found its clearest expression in the Syrian communities. How widespread this leitmotiv with its specific meaning in the early Church was, has somehow escaped the attention of liturgical scholars. We find the three elements — baptismal anointing, gift of the Spirit, royal and sacerdotal anointing — also in the West. Here the anointing and the coming of the Spirit naturally took place after baptism, according to the Western tradition. We shall quote only Tertullian and Ambrose, bishop of Milan. Tertullian writes: ". . . we come up from the washing and are anointed with the blessed unction [benedicta unctione], following that ancient practice by which, ever since Aaron was anointed by Moses, there was a custom of anointing them for priesthood with oil out of a horn."[55] Ambrose, too, interprets the postbaptismal anointing as a sacerdotal and regal anointing, taking up the anointing of Aaron and connecting it with 1 Peter 2:9: "What is the people itself, if not a priestly people? To these it was said: 'But you are a chosen generation, a royal priesthood, a holy nation,' as the apostle Peter says. Everyone is anointed into the priesthood, into the kingdom."[56]

We have already met the quotation of 1 Peter 2:9 in the *Apostolic Constitutions* and in the Armenian baptismal ordo. Therefore we can assume that we are dealing here with a common stream of tradition. Beyond doubt its origin is in Syria, more precisely in the

[54] *Mystagogical Catecheses* 3, 6 (ed. Cross, 66).
[55] *De baptismo* 3, 7 (Whitaker, *Documents* 8).
[56] *De sacramentis* 4, 3. It is interesting to observe the slight shift in the reference to the Old Testament; here the emphasis is not on the messianic king but on his priesthood. This can also be seen in Cyril; see n. 54 above.

(gnostic) Judeo-Christian communities. The charismatic anointing, with its sudden epiphanic character before the immersion into the water and the lack of any cathartic or exorcistic connotations at this anointing, belongs to one of the earliest and most powerful traits of ritualization of baptism.

2. *The Prebaptismal Anointing as a Cathartic and Apotropaic Ritual in Syro-Palestine at the End of the Fourth Century.* In my forthcoming study on the Armenian rites of initiation, I show in detail that along the Greek-speaking coastline of the Mediterranean, in contrast to East Syria and Armenia, the preparatory rites of baptism developed into one of the most evolved and important parts of the whole baptismal liturgy. In the writings of Chrysostom, Theodore of Mopsuestia, and above all Cyril of Jerusalem, it is obvious that the confrontation with the demonic powers becomes one of the main issues in the homilies they addressed to the candidates for baptism. The preparation as a whole is viewed as a drama-like battle with Satan.[57] It did not take long before this battle was also reflected in the shaping of the ritual. The drama of warfare with the demons begins with the enrollment of the baptismal candidate and culminates in the daily exorcisms during his preparation. The process of cleansing became a predominant factor in the western half of Syria and Palestine. In the Syrian hinterland and the regions of Armenia, the necessity for a wholehearted conversion of the candidates naturally formed a basic theme as well, but the purificatory elements never became ritualized to such an extent as in fourth century Syro-Palestine. The ritualistic expression of the warfare being waged between the catechumen and Satan is reflected in the daily exorcisms. It is interesting to note that the ritualization of this inner conflict seems to be restricted to the coast areas of the Mediterranean, whereas in inner Syria and Armenia — in those regions which were cut off from the Roman Empire — these apotropaic rites never achieved any significant

---

[57] J. Daniélou, in *The Bible and the Liturgy* (Notre Dame 1966, 19–34) gives a good outline of this conflict situation. It is true that we find this basic confrontation also in East Syria, for instance, but it never became ritualized to such an extent. That is the salient point.

role.[58] In my research on the preparatory rites of baptism, I came to the conclusion that in the Persian and Armenian Churches these rites were never as fully developed as in Syro-Palestine, and that the apotropaic and cathartic elements did not prevail over the teaching of the faith in the regions outside the Roman Empire, in contrast to the big cities along the Mediterranean coast.

The view that the whole baptismal ritual can be regarded as a death of the previous life, culminating in the Pauline baptismal theology of dying and being buried with Christ — a very deep concept indeed — is a phenomenon alien to the early Syriac and Armenian writers. Baptism is always conceived of as a birth, and the baptismal water is seen as a womb, never as death or sepulcher or grave.[59] In the fourth century, however, the concept of baptism underwent considerable change, at least in the western half of Syria, including the south with its center, Jerusalem. With the continuously growing and expanding preparation, which lasted for several years — very often even to the deathbed, a fact that aroused more than one of the great figures of that epoch! — the purificatory elements were particularly emphasized and ritualized. Once the preparatory rites assumed a predominantly cathartic and exorcistic character, attaining at the same time the indispensable condition for the reception of the Spirit, it was unthinkable to maintain a prebaptismal anointing with which the gift of the Spirit was associated. Only when the catechumen was thoroughly cleansed and his sins washed away could the Spirit enter his heart. Hence an anointing after baptism was introduced, and the coming of the Spirit was now assigned to this anointing. The anointing before baptism lost its original meaning and became part of the apotropaic preparatory rites.

This is also reflected in the terminology for the oil. The clearest expression for the complete change of the prebaptismal anointing can be found in Cyril of Jerusalem. After removing their clothing, which is interpreted as the stripping of the old man, the catechumens are anointed with "exorcised oil (tō elaiō eporkistō) from top to foot."[60] It is obvious that the prebaptismal anointing is now at-

[58] See the full documentation in my study, n. 13 above.
[59] Ibid.
[60] Mystagogical Catecheses 2, 3.

tached to the exorcistic rites of preparation, and it seems that the apotropaic rites culminate in this anointing.

Let us listen how Cyril interprets baptism proper: "After these things, ye were led to the holy pool . . . as Christ was carried from the cross to the sepulchre which is before our eyes. . . . and [ye] descended three times into the water, and ascended again; here also covertly pointing by a figure at the three-days burial of Christ."[61] The baptismal font, once the womb (or Jordan) now becomes the sepulcher, and the immersion is now a symbolic gesture of Christ's burial in the earth.

The rites of initiation are no longer shaped after the event of the Jordan but follow closely Paul's doctrine of baptism (Rom 6): death to sin (ritualized in the preparatory rites), dying and being buried with Christ (ritualized in the immersion). Although Paul speaks also of the resurrection as the other part of the paschal mystery, the death mysticism at baptism plays the predominant role and in the fourth century this concept eventually became ritualized in the East.

Antioch in the fourth century reflects an intermediary stage between Jerusalem and the Syrian hinterland. Chrysostom, for example, who still does not know of any postbaptismal anointing, calls the oil "spiritual oil" (elaion pneumatikon), but also myron or "oil of gladness" (elaion agalliaseōs),[62] since it is a sign of the final victory over Satan.

In all the writings from the Eastern Church of the fourth century, mainly in those that stem from the Greek-speaking coastal regions of the eastern part of the Mediterranean, the anointing before baptism has changed into a purificatory and apotropaic, or at least prophylactic, ritual. Sometimes the old name for the oil is still maintained, for example in Theodore of Mopsuestia, but the concept of the prebaptismal anointing was irretrievably changed. The reason for this alteration lies, beyond any doubt, in the considerable change in the concept of baptism as a whole: the entire ritual assumed more and more a predominantly purificatory

[61] *Mystagogical Catecheses* 2, 4 (ed. Cross, 60).
[62] See nn. 30–32 above.

character.[63] From the fourth century onward the cathartic and apotropaic elements grew to such a proportion that one can, to some extent at least, speak of an estrangement of the original concept of baptism. Nearly every part of the ritual was reshaped with mainly exorcistic elements: besides the daily exorcisms of the catechumen, the oil was exorcised, the anointing assumed an exorcistic character, and even from the baptismal water, which once represented simply the Jordan, the demons were now expelled.

It is beyond the scope of this article to show how much of the original character of baptism as an actualization of Jesus' baptism in the Jordan is still maintained in the Eastern rites of initiation. Here I refer to my study on the Armenian ritual for baptism. The

[63] I do not believe that Ratcliff's theory (in "The Old Syrian Baptismal Tradition," n. 49 above) is really convincing. All the Eastern liturgies of baptism (with some caution this includes the East Syrian ritual) eventually adopted a postbaptismal anointing. Ratcliff supposes that this innovation was due to the influence of the baptismal liturgy of Jerusalem. Because of topographical reasons — the holy places at Jerusalem reminded people of Christ's Passion — the baptismal font was reinterpreted as the sepulcher of Christ. And since the liturgy of Jerusalem began to follow the sequence of the economy of salvation, an anointing after baptism, with the association of the gift of the Spirit, was adopted. From Jerusalem it eventually spread to other churches.

Nor can I accept Botte's hypothesis as fully satisfactory ("L'onction postbaptismale dans l'ancien Patriarcat d'Antioche," in *Miscellanea Liturgica in onore di Sua Eminenza Cardinale Giacomo Lercaro* 2 [Rome/Paris/New York 1967] 795–808). Botte linked the introduction of the postbaptismal anointing in the East with the acceptance of heretics. If someone outside orthodoxy who had been baptized in one of the heretical communities decided eventually to turn to orthodoxy, he was not rebaptized at this reception but only anointed. This led to the innovation of the postbaptismal anointing.

In my opinion, the reinterpretation of the rites of initiation, that is, mainly of the prebaptismal anointing and the baptism proper, was not brought about through any heterogeneous initiative, nor through "topographical" or "heretical impulses," but because of the inner change of dynamics within the ritual itself. Once baptism moved away from its original essence, being the *mimesis* of the event at the Jordan, and shifted at the same time toward a cathartic principle, it was inevitable that all rites that preceded baptism proper became subordinated to a process of thorough cleansing. The catharsis slowly became an indispensable condition for the coming of the Spirit. Consequently, only after intensive purification and the washing away of sins could the Spirit enter the heart of the baptized.

Armenian rite has preserved to a very large extent the archaic features of the third and fourth centuries.

CONCLUSION

In contrast to the West, where the rites that preceded baptism proper never seemed to have any connotation other than a purificatory one, these rites underwent considerable change in the East.

The crucial difference between the East and West springs from which aspect of the New Testament experience of baptism was taken as a basis for the ritualization of baptism in the growing early Church. In the process of ritualization, there was the possibility of stressing either the purificatory aspect, which was already present in the baptism of John the Baptist, or the charismatic elements, which obviously formed the central part of Jesus' descent into the Jordan. Furthermore, explicit reflection and different theological interpretation of the baptismal reality by the main figures of the New Testament played a considerable role. In John 3 this is depicted predominantly as birth event, whereas Romans 6 emphasizes the aspect of dying (to sin), and in the deepest possible reflection of the final aspect of dying, Paul assimilates man's death and dying to Christ's own death.

Whether the West never shaped the baptismal liturgy as a birth ritual but rather developed the cathartic elements right from the beginning remains to be seen. The East, in its earliest ritualization at least, followed closely the event at the Jordan, forming the rites of initiation basically as a birth into the eschatological reality. In the oldest Syriac sources the anointing before the immersion forms the central part of the whole ritual. The gesture of anointing is the ritualization of the entry into the messianic kingship of Christ (the Anointed), which is made known through the coming of the Spirit at this anointing. Let us listen once more to the prayer in the *Acts of Thomas* that is said at the anointing of the head: "Glory to thee, (thou) beloved fruit! Glory to thee, (thou) name of the Messiah! Glory to thee, (thou) hidden power that dwellest in the oil [*meshā*]."[64] At another point of the Acts, the prayer at the anoint-

---

[64] See chap. 132; also n. 35 above.

ing takes the form of an epiclesis: "Come, holy name of the Messiah . . . come, sharer of the blessing, come, revealer of the hidden mysteries . . . come, spirit of holiness . . ." (ch. 27).

In the fourth century, however, the development of the whole baptismal liturgy underwent considerable change, beginning along the coast of the eastern Mediterranean. Slowly the ritual moved through the growing dominance of the preparatory rites, with their emphasis on purification, toward a new interpretation of all rites that preceded baptism proper. The anointing before the immersion, which once formed the very center of the Syriac rites of initiation, became subordinated to the basic cleansing aspect of preparation, losing at the same time its original meaning as true initiation into the messianic kingship. The baptismal font, once seen as womb and also referred to as Jordan, changes now in West Syria and Palestine into sepulcher and grave; the immersion becomes the imitation of Christ's burial and resurrection.

The basic reason for this change is the increasing predominance of cathartic and apotropaic elements in the evolution of the entire baptismal ritual. Purification becomes the fundamental requirement for the coming of the Spirit. Therefore the anointing before baptism, with which the gift of the Spirit was once associated, had to be changed into a prophylactic or cathartic ritual. The descent of the Spirit remains connected with the anointing, but this anointing now follows after the washing away of sins.

The underlying shift from a ritual that once was viewed mainly as a birth event, in accordance with the Johannine interpretation of baptism, toward the reinterpretation of the ritual in line with Paul's theology (Rom 6) can be summarized in the following pattern:

Main theme in the earliest ritualization process of Syria and Armenia:	Main theme in the baptismal rites in Syro-Palestine[65] from the fourth century onward:
introduction into the faith of the Church and requirement of a wholehearted conversion	excessive development of the cathartic and exorcistic rites as preparation

[65] In substance, this covers also the Latin and Greek baptismal liturgies.

imitation of Jesus' baptism in the Jordan with the Johannine concept of rebirth (Jn 3)	which culminate in a death mysticism,[66] taking up Paul's theology: participation in Christ's death (Rom 6)
emphasis lies on the anointing	central part is baptism proper

The reliable guide in our analysis that led to these conclusions was a close investigation of the terminology for the oil and the anointing. We analyzed the different terms in their context and saw how they were used in the earliest Syriac and Armenian sources, comparing these terms with those of Syro-Palestine of the fourth century. So we can hope to have shed some new light on the evolution of the anointings in the rites of initiation and on the basic theme of baptism. The change in this fundamental aspect of baptism in the fourth century found its clearest expression in the alteration of the original meaning of the anointing before baptism.

[66] It seems that particularly in the late fourth century, the East tended toward a reinterpretation of the liturgy in accordance with what I call here "death mysticism." For instance, in the liturgy of the Eucharist the motif of a burial cortège was introduced by the late fourth century writers of Syro-Palestine. Theodore of Mopsuestia, for example, interprets the procession with the gifts by the deacons as follows: "Christ who is now being led out and going forth to his Passion"; for the placing of bread and wine upon the altar, he says: "Thus we may think of him [Christ] placed on the altar as if henceforth in a sort of sepulchre. . . . That is why the deacons who spread linens on the altar represent by this the figure of the linen cloths of the burial" (Homily 15, 24; quoted in R. F. Taft, *The Great Entrance. A History of the Transfer of Gifts and Other Preanaphoral Rites of the Liturgy of St John Chrysostom*. Orientalia Christiana Analecta 200 [Rome 1975] 35). Narsai (fifth century) took over this interpretation of the procession: "It is the symbol of his death that they [the deacons] carry in their hands, and when they place it on the altar and cover it, they symbolize his burial. . . . All the priests in the sanctuary represent the apostles who gathered at the sepulchre" (Homily 17, also quoted in Taft, *The Great Entrance* 38–39). Very likely it would be worthwhile to investigate more closely this new stream in the thoughts of the growing Church and the eventual ritualization of the reflections. See also my review of Taft's important study on the great entrance in *Oriens Christianus* 62 (1978) 222–225.

Paul F. Bradshaw

5. Baptismal Practice in the Alexandrian Tradition: Eastern or Western?

The liturgical practices of Egypt have not occupied a prominent place in the study of early Christian initiation, at least in part because of the paucity of materials from which to reconstruct just what those practices might have been. The only really extensive investigation was made by Georg Kretschmar in a lengthy German article in 1963,[1] and unfortunately this has not received as much attention as it deserved. In particular such is the insularity of much liturgical scholarship that it has been totally ignored by the authors of subsequent standard English-language works on the history of Christian initiation, including Leonel Mitchell writing on baptismal anointing shortly after Kretschmar,[2] J. D. C. Fisher writing on confirmation in 1978,[3] and E. C. Whitaker in the second edition of his little study of the baptismal liturgy in 1981.[4] All of these have perpetuated the traditional assumption that the early Alexandrian rite was fundamentally Western in character. As our study will show, however, such a simplistic conclusion will not stand up to close scrutiny.

THE BAPTISMAL SEASON

Whereas, at least from the end of the second century onwards, the paschal celebration seems to have constituted the normal occa-

---

[1] "Beiträge zur Geschichte der Liturgie, inbesondere der Taufliturgie, in Ägypten" in *Jahrbuch für Liturgik und Hymologie* 8 (1963) 1–54.

[2] *Baptismal Anointing* (SPCK, London 1966), see esp. 51–58, 73–76.

[3] *Confirmation: Then and Now* (London 1978), see esp. 61–76.

[4] *The Baptismal Liturgy* (SPCK, London, 2nd edn., 1981), see esp. 27–28.

sion for baptism in the West, Coptic tradition claims that in ancient times baptisms were performed at Alexandria on the sixth day of the sixth week of the great fast, i.e. at the end of forty days, and that originally this forty-day fast was situated immediately after Epiphany. Whilst the two principal authorities for this claim are somewhat late (the tenth-century Melchite Eutychius[5] and the fourteenth-century Abu 'l-Barakat[6]), nevertheless support is lent to it by references to a forty-day fast in both Origen[7] and the fourth-century Canons of Hippolytus.[8] The time of year is not specified in those sources, but it is clearly separate from the pre-paschal fast, which at that time lasted only six days.[9] Canon 12 of the Canons of Hippolytus also says that candidates for initiation are to be instructed for forty days prior to their baptism.[10]

To this may perhaps be added the evidence, admittedly of doubtful value, of a Coptic legend which exists in several different recensions. In the version found in the tenth-century history of the patriarchs of Alexandria by Severus of El Asmunein, it refers to a woman who is said to have brought her two children from Antioch to be baptized at Alexandria during the patriachate of Peter (A.D. 300–311), and to have entered the city "in the week of Baptism, which is the sixth week of the Fast, when infants are baptized."[11]

This fast appears to have continued to be separate from the paschal cycle until A.D. 330, when Athanasius attempted to bring Egyptian practice into line with the rest of the world by locating it immediately before Easter, and combining it with the already

---

[5] PG 111.989.

[6] See Louis Villecourt, "Les Observances liturgiques et la discipline de jeûne dans l'Eglise copte" in Le Muséon 38 (1925), 266.

[7] Hom in Lev. 10.2 (PG 12.528B).

[8] Canon 20: see René-Georges Coquin, Les Canons d'Hippolyte (Patrologia Orientalis 31.2, Paris 1966) 118–119; English translation in Paul F. Bradshaw, The Canons of Hippolytus (Alcuin/GROW Jt. Lt. Stud. 2, Grove Books, Nottingham 1987) 25.

[9] Canons of Hippolytus 22: Coquin, 120–121; Bradshaw, 26.

[10] Coquin, 96–97; Bradshaw, 17–18.

[11] B. Evetts (ed.), History of the Patriarchs of the Coptic Church of Alexandria (Patrologia Orientalis 1, Paris 1948), 387. For another version of the legend see below, note 26.

existing pre-paschal fast of six days, so that the total period was of six weeks' duration. Unfortunately, he encountered some resistance to this innovation, and even in A.D. 340, as his letter to his friend Sarapion reveals, his reform was still not being implemented.[12] Eventually, however, it appears to have been successfully accomplished, since we hear of no further problems concerning it.

What then happened to the baptismal season? Thomas Talley presumes that it remained on the traditional day until the patriarchate of Theophilus (A.D. 385–412), when it was transferred to Easter.[13] He bases this on a legend contained in a papyrus of the sixth or seventh century, which tells how "from time immemorial" when the patriarchs had come to administer baptism "on the appropriate day," a beam of light had come and signed the waters of the font, but one year in the patriarchate of Theophilus this miracle failed to happen. While celebrating the eucharist Theophilus heard a voice saying that it would not do so, unless Orsisius, abbot of the Pachomian communities, came. Two deacons were then sent to bring Orsisius to Alexandria, and he arrived just before Easter. Theophilus once more attempted to consecrate the baptismal waters, and this time all went well. In this way, the legend concludes, the feast of the resurrection and baptism were joined together, "and thus it is done until this day."[14]

There is, however, some uncertainty whether this has any historical foundation. Although Albert Ehrhard defended it in an accompanying note when it was first published,[15] both Wilhelm Hengstenburg[16] and Théophile Lefort[17] have been more doubtful

---

[12] See T. J. Talley, *The Origins of the Liturgical Year* (New York 1986), 168–170.

[13] *Ibid.*, 196.

[14] W. E. Crum (ed.), *Der Papyruscodex saec. VI–VII der Phillippsbibliothek in Cheltenham*, (Strasbourg 1915); French translation in L. Th. Lefort, *Les vies coptes de saint Pachôme et de ses premiers successeurs* (Bibliotheque de Muséon 16, Louvain 1943, reprinted 1966), 389–392.

[15] See Crum. *op. cit.* 132ff.

[16] "Pachomiana, mit einem Anhang über die Liturgie von Alexandrien" in A. M. Koeniger (ed.), *Beiträge zur Geschichte des christlichen Alterums und der byzantinischen Literatur* (Bonn 1922, reprinted Rodopi, Amsterdam 1969), 228–252.

[17] *Op. cit.*, LXXXV.

about it, and judged it to have been composed to justify the Alexandrian computation of the date of Easter, and in its present form to reflect Pachomian interests; whilst J. L. Duffes and Claude Geay point out that Orsisius is commonly thought to have died around A.D. 380, five years prior to the patriarchate of Theophilus, and they try to argue that paschal baptism was never practised at Alexandria, but that the story in its present form is a piece of later apologetic seeking to establish Melchite liturgical usages in Egypt. On the other hand, they assert that baptisms continued to be performed on the sixth day of the sixth week of the great fast, apparently failing to realize that at this period the pre-paschal season was only six weeks long in total, and so that day would have fallen on the Friday before Easter — the very day when the story says that Orsisius arrived at Alexandria.[18]

To add further confusion to the picture, we should also note that a briefer version of the legend, which is found in the tenth-century history of the patriarchs of Alexandria by Severus of El Asmunein, merely speaks of it happening "during the week of baptism," and says that it was a deacon, Arsensius, who was sent for, making no reference at all to Easter or to the persistence of paschal baptism.[19] There is yet another version of the legend in which all the bishops go to do homage to Theophilus on his appointment, and they find him in church

"for it was the seventh day after the Sabbath on which the people were baptized. And when they had filled the font with water, the archbishop and the other bishops went in and prayed over the Jordan."

One stayed outside, and when Theophilus went out to him, he was then able to call down fire on the font. Once again no reference at all is made to paschal baptism here.[20]

---

[18] J. L. Duffes and Claude Geay, *Le baptême dans l'église copte* (Cairo 1973), vol. 1, 191a-d. This work, though containing useful information, is not a critical study.

[19] Evetts, 427.

[20] E. A. W. Budge, *Miscellaneous Coptic Texts* (British Museum, London 1915), 469; Translation, 985.

In any case, because of the intimate relationship between the fast and the baptismal day, it seems improbable that the one could have been successfully transferred without the other. It would surely have been difficult to convince the general Christian populace of Alexandria that the forty-day fast itself was to be observed immediately before Easter, so long as baptisms continued to be performed on the traditional day, forty days after Epiphany, and the initial opposition to the relocation of the fast referred to earlier may well have been not unrelated to this. Thus it seems unlikely that it took over fifty years for this step to be taken.

Moreover, there is some evidence to suggest that at least in Pachomian monasticism, if not at Alexandria itself, the transfer of the baptismal season was made at an earlier date than the patriarchate of Theophilus. Among the novices in the various communities there were often those who had not previously been baptized, and a story concerning Pachomius relates that "it was the custom to bring to Phbow during the fast all the catechumens of the monasteries in order to give them baptism."[21] This would have been necessary because of the absence of ordained ministers in the communities. It should be noted, however, that this remark is not part of the story itself but merely a comment by the redactor, and in any case it does not indicate at what point in the year the great fast took place, so it cannot be used as evidence that paschal baptism was practised before the death of Pachomius in A.D. 346. On the other hand, a further story concerning the abbot Theodore says that, when he became sick, the heads of the various monastic houses came to visit him, "especially as the days of the holy Pasch were approaching; indeed, all the brothers gather at Phbow to baptize the catechumens . . ."[22] If this is historically reliable, it seems to suggest that here the baptismal day was transferred prior to the death of Theodore in A.D. 368.

It is important to note, however, that even after the baptisms had been transferred at Alexandria, they were apparently not situated within the paschal vigil itself, as was the case elsewhere, but the legend speaks of Theophilus and Orsisius going to the church

[21] Lefort, 141.
[22] Ibid., 211.

on "the great Friday of the great Pascha; on Saturday morning he [i.e. Theophilus] opens the baptistry and the customary holy ceremonies take place . . ." In other words, the baptism still took place immediately after the conclusion of the forty days. The only other reference to baptism at the paschal season in Egypt concerns the Melchite patriarch Proterios who is said to have been assassinated while baptizing children in A.D. 457, but the descriptions are too imprecise to enable one to judge exactly when in the week the baptism took place.[23]

It is unlikely that this survived as the sole baptismal season for very long. The second series of "Canonical Responses," attributed to Timothy of Alexandria but probably dating from the fifth century, indicate that candidates for baptism are now infants rather than adults, and that — most likely as a result of this — baptisms can be administered by a priest and are apparently not restricted to any one season of the year.[24] A letter of the tenth-century bishop of Memphis, Macarius, maintains that "when the confusion and perturbation had overcome us" (by which he is probably referring to the establishment of the Melchite patriarchate in Alexandria after the Council of Chalcedon, which gave rise to the assassination of Proterios), the initiatory rites were transferred to the monastery of his namesake St. Macarius, but that only the consecration of the chrism continued to be performed then, and not the baptismal rite itself.[25] The disappearance of the baptism was no doubt not unrelated to the fact that there would not have been

[23] Zacharias Rhetor, *Eccl. Hist.* 4.1, speaks of him baptizing children "at the time of the unleavened bread" prior to his death (text in E. W. Brooks, *Historia Ecclesiastica Zachariae Rhetori vulgo adscripta* (Durbecq, Louvain 1953) vol. 1, 171; Latin trans., vol. 3, 119); Evagrius, *Eccl. Hist.* 2.8 (*PG* 86.2526), says only that his death took place during the paschal celebration, but Liberatus, *Breviarium* 15 (*PL* 86.1017), alleges that it was on the day before the Triduum — which seems an unlikely occasion for the baptism itself, but could have been that of the final pre-baptismal scrutiny: see below, 77.

[24] J. B. Pitra, *Iuris Ecclesiatici Graecorum Historica et Monumenta* I (Rome 1864), 638ff; English translation in E. C. Whitaker, *Documents of the Baptismal Liturgy* (SPCK, London, 2nd edn., 1970), 86.

[25] Louis Villecourt, "La lettre de Macaire, êveque de Memphis, sur la liturgie antique du chrême et du baptême à Alexandrie" in *Le Muséon* 36 (1923), 38.

a plentiful supply of children needing initiation in this monastic setting as there had been in the city.

Moreover, another version of the legend of the Antiochene woman, preserved in the fourteenth-century "Book of the Chrism," places the event in the patriarchate of Theophilus, and claims that afterwards he wrote to the other patriarchs and asked them to ordain that baptisms should take place at all times, in every place, and by all priests, except during the great fast, unless it was a case of necessity: "and that has been so until today."[26] The attribution of this change of practice to Theophilus seems unlikely, but it does serve to show that the baptismal season was thought to have disappeared at an early stage.

Sometime between A.D. 577 and A.D. 622 the shape of the Alexandrian Lent underwent a further change, and the forty-day fast was once more detached from the six-day pre-paschal fast, and located immediately before it, so that it now began seven weeks before Easter, and ended on the Friday of the sixth week, with the consecration of the chrism.[27] The following Saturday and Sunday were treated as festal days, and the six-day fast began, as was traditional, on the Monday.[28] This suggests that the memory of the ancient tradition had never really died, and indeed it is quite possible that it had been kept alive in other Egyptian dioceses which had refused to conflate the forty-day fast with the six-day fast and instead compromised by juxtaposing them in this way ever since the fourth century, ultimately persuading the mother

[26] Here there is only one child, and they are said to arrive in Alexandria "on the day of the sixth Friday of the holy fast": see Louis Villecourt, "Le livre du chrême" in *Le Muséon* 42 (1928) 58.

[27] Talley, 200. Abu 'l-Barakat speaks of Palm Sunday as the end of the holy Forty: see *Le Muséon* 38, 314.

[28] During that patriarchate of Benjamin I (A.D. 622–661) the Lenten season was further extended by the pre-fixing of another week of fasting. Known as "the Fast of Heraclius," this is said by Eutychius (*PG* 111.1090) to have been intended as an act of penance for the emperor Heraclius' failure after his conquest of Jerusalem to keep his promise to spare the Jews living there. It seems likely, however, that the real reason for the addition was to bring the total days of actual fasting before Easter up to the biblical total of forty, since Saturdays and Sundays were never kept as fast days. A similar process can be observed in other parts of the ancient Christian world.

church to come into line. It may even have been the traditional custom at the monastery of St. Macarius where the consecration of the chrism had now been performed for more than a century.

Thereafter, therefore, if not before, the consecration of the chrism took place on the Friday nine days before Easter, where it remained, according to the letter of Macarius, until the tenth century when it was again moved, this time to the Thursday of Holy Week in order to fall in line with the custom observed in other parts of the world.[29] Even this, however, is not the end of the story, for by the fourteenth century, according to Abu' l-Barakat, the consecration of the chrism was taking place on the sixth Sunday of Lent,[30] and in current Coptic usage baptisms are actually forbidden between Palm Sunday and Pentecost.

THE CATECHUMENATE

Such Western evidence as there is suggests that originally the catechumenate there was a lengthy process, lasting anything up to three years, but with a very short period of final preparation, probably of only three weeks' duration.

Although there are some indications of the possible existence of a similar three-year catechumenate in early times in Egypt, the evidence is of doubtful value. A passage in the writings of Clement of Alexandria, which compares the catechumenate to the three years of growth required for a tree by Old Testament Law before its fruit is consecrated to the Lord, has been thought by some to be implying that the catechumenate had the same duration,[31] but the comparison may well not be meant so literally. Secondly, the letter of Macarius states that orginally only adults were baptized, after having been taught the Christian religion for three years,[32] but such a statement at this late date could well be dependent on the *Apostolic Tradition* of Hippolytus, which had considerable in-

---

[29] *Le Muséon* 36, 39.

[30] *Le Muséon* 38, 269.

[31] *Strom.* 2.18. See A. Mehat, *Étude sur les 'stromates' de Clément d'Alexandrie* (Paris 1966), 221; M. Dajarier, *A History of the Catechumenate: The First Six Centuries* (New York 1979), 42.

[32] *Le Muséon* 36, 34.

fluence in Egypt. A similar affirmation made in the "Book of the Chrism,"[33] could also derive from the same source, or from the letter of Macarius itself, which is reproduced in that document. Thirdly, Canon 1 of the patriarch Peter, issued in A.D. 305, speaks of penitent apostates, who had done penance for three years, being required to fast forty days, in imitation of the fasting of Jesus, before they could be readmitted to communion.[34] Is this regulation perhaps influenced by an established pre-baptismal catechumenate of similar length?

An important piece of counter-evidence, however, is provided by the *Canons of Hippolytus,* which in Canon 12 entirely omits the reference to three years of pre-baptismal instruction found in its principal source, the *Apostolic Tradition* of Hippolytus, and speaks instead of only forty days of instruction.[35] Although this document apparently comes from some other diocese in northern Egypt rather than Alexandria itself,[36] it does suggest that there at least a longer catechumenate was unknown, or had already become extinct by the early part of the fourth century. Furthermore, it has led René-Georges Coquin to conclude that the post-Nicene expansion of the period of final preparation to forty days elsewhere in the early Church was the result of the influence of the Egyptian tradition, a conclusion shared by Talley.[37] In this regard, therefore, it would appear that it is not so much that the Alexandrian tradition was Western, as that other traditions became Alexandrian.

Equally as significant, however, as any difference in length of the catechumenate between Alexandria and the West is the difference in character. We have no indication of any elaborate ceremonies accompanying admission to this stage of the initiatory process, such as we find in the West, nor reference to a *traditio*

---

[33] *Le Muséon* 41, 57.

[34] Alexander Roberts and James Donaldson (eds.), *Ante-Nicene Fathers* 6 (New York 1926), 269.

[35] Coquin, 96–97; Bradshaw, 17–18.

[36] See H. Brakmann, "Alexandreia und Kanones des Hippolyt" in *Jahrbuch für Antike und Christentum* 22 (1979) 139–149.

[37] R-G. Coquin, "Une Réforme liturgique du concile de Nicée (325)?" in *Comptes Rendus, Académie des Inscriptions et Belles-lettres* (Paris 1967) 178–192; Talley, 214ff.

symboli at any point. Moreover, whereas the *Apostolic Tradition* of Hippolytus apparently expected there to be a daily exorcism of the candidates during the final period of their preparation, and a similar procedure is recorded by Chrysostom for Antioch and by Egeria for Jerusalem[38] (though later Roman practice was to do this only three times during Lent), we have no trace of such a custom in ancient times in Egypt. In place of the daily exorcism recorded in *Apostolic Tradition* 20, Canon 19 of the *Canons of Hippolytus* substitutes a single final scrutiny, apparently without exorcism, which takes place a few days before the baptism.[39] Further information concerning a rite of this nature is given in a baptismal *ordo* interpolated into the Ethiopic version of the *Apostolic Tradition*. This says that the candidates enter the baptistry and give their names; they are then examined to ascertain whether their preparation has taken place, whether they have read the Scriptures and learned the psalms; and someone acts as a guarantor for each one. Prayertexts for those who have given in their names then follow.[40]

The letter of Macarius confirms that this assembly was an ancient Alexandrian practice, held two days before the actual baptism and called *Fishishin*, meaning apparently "scrutiny":

"All the bishops assembled at Alexandria with the people of every country who were present and were admitted to the Jordan on the fourth day of the sixth week . . . They assembled and the book of the patriarch which is called *kathekesis*, that is exhortation, was read to those who were to be baptized . . . On the fourth day of the sixth week of the fast the clergy and people assembled in the church of the Evangelists. They filled the Jordan with water. The lectors read. The archdeacon assembled before him the deacons who had written on a paper roll the names of those to be baptized. They read the prayers of baptism, invocations and supplications. He said to them: fast until the end of the day. Then communicate and depart. And a second day of fasting is also prescribed for them."[41]

[38] See Whitaker, *Documents*, 4, 38, 42.
[39] Coquin, *Les Canons d'Hippolyte*, 108–109; Bradshaw, 21.
[40] English translation in G. Horner, *The Statutes of the Apostles*, (London 1904), 162–164.
[41] *Le Muséon* 36, 35–36, 38.

It seems likely that the practice described in these last two documents represents a conflation of two stages of baptismal preparation which formerly took place on separate occasions, the enrolling of the candidates and the final scrutiny before baptism. The former would seem to belong originally to the beginning of the forty-day period of preparation, as we find it in fourth-century Jerusalem practice and elsewhere,[42] and was very likely joined to the latter when children rather than adults became the normal candidates for baptism and the catechumenate fell into disuse. We can see a similar conflation in the Syrian tradition, where Pseudo-Dionysius seems to speak of scrutiny, enrolment, and baptism as taking place on the same day.[43]

THE PRE-BAPTISMAL ANOINTING

In the ancient Roman rite, if not in the West generally, pre-baptismal anointing was exorcistic. This does not appear to have been the case in the Alexandrian tradition. With one exception, which we shall speak of later, the term "oil of exorcism" is not used by Egyptian sources of the first five centuries. The "Canonical Responses" speak only of "the anointing of oil,"[44] Cyril of Alexandria calls it "the chrism of catechesis";[45] and the prayer over the oil in the *Sacramentary of Sarapion* describes it simply as *aleimma*, "ointment," and suggests that its function was seen as healing and re-creation.[46]

This last document gives no formula for use at the actual moment of anointing, but other sources suggest what it might have been in ancient Alexandrian practice. The fourth-century Didymus the Blind says that "in the name of the Father and of the Son and of the Holy Spirit were we both sealed and baptized."[47] Geoffrey

[42] See, for example, Whitaker, *Documents*, 24, 41.
[43] *De Eccl. Hier.* 2 4–7 (PG 3.396); English Translation in Whitaker, *Documents*, 57.
[44] Pitra, I, 640; Whitaker, *Documents*, 86.
[45] *In Job.* 7 (PG 74.49D).
[46] Text in F. E. Brightman, "The Sacramentary of Sarapion of Thmuis" in *Journal of Theological Studies* 1 (1900), 264; English translation in Whitaker, *Documents*, 85.
[47] *De Trin.* 2.15 (PG 39.720A).

Lampe understood these two verbs to be referring to the same liturgical action, water baptism,[48] but the more natural explanation would appear to be that the sealing here is a pre-baptismal anointing, and that both actions were accompanied by a Trinitarian formula.[49]

Moreover, the legend of the Antiochene woman, to which we have already referred, tells of her baptizing her children while on the voyage to Alexandria, since she feared that they would not survive the journey. She used her own blood to make a sign of the cross on their foreheads and over their hearts in the name of the Father and of the Son and of the Holy Spirit, and then baptized them, saying, "I baptize you in the name of the Father, Son, and Holy Spirit."[50] This confirms not only the nature of the formula but also the great importance apparently attached to the inclusion of this pre-baptismal anointing. A similar formula also seems to have been used in early Syrian practice.[51]

Later, however, changes begin to take place in the understanding of the anointing. In the sixth-century Egyptian baptismal rite interpolated into the Arabic version of the *Testamentum Domini*, the prayer over the oil asks God to

"send on this oil your holy power, and may it be oil which puts to flight all the works of the adversary and destroys every evil and every injustice, so that those anointed with it may receive salvation and life and sanctification and turn to you with faith. . . ."

The minister then signs with oil the candidates' foreheads, eyes, ears, hearts, and hands, saying over each of them,

"Oil putting to flight all the works of the adversary and planting those anointed with it in the holy universal Church."[52]

[48] G. W. H. Lampe, *The Seal of the Spirit* (SPCK, London, 2nd edn., 1967), 241.

[49] See Kretschmar, 44–45.

[50] Evetts, 386–387. In the version in the Book of the Chrism the mother only signs the one child with her blood, and does not baptize him: see *Le Muséon* 41, 58.

[51] See Whitaker, *Documents*, 40, 48.

[52] See A. Baumstark, "Eine ägyptische Mess- und Taufliturgie vermutlich des 6. Jahrhunderts" in *Oriens Christianus* 1 (1901), 35.

A similar formula is also found in the baptismal rite interpolated into the Ethiopic version of the *Apostolic Tradition* of Hippolytus,[53] and a more developed form of this appears not only in the later Coptic rite[54] but also in the Syrian rites.[55] Sebastian Brock has suggested that the formula originally came from Jerusalem to Syria, since its themes feature in Cyril's *Mystagogical Catecheses*.[56] It would seem likely, therefore, that the Coptic tradition in turn inherited it from Syria.

In the later Coptic rite the pre-baptismal oil is called "the *agallielaion* of the oil of exorcism." The term *agallielaion*, "the oil of gladness," is also used of the prebaptismal oil in Syrian circles, where again the anointing did not originally have exorcistic significance.[57] How then did "oil of exorcism" eventually become attached to it in the Coptic rite? The answer to this question seems to lie in the influence wielded in Egypt by the *Apostolic Tradition* of Hippolytus. The *Canons of Hippolytus* adopted the term "oil of exorcism" for the pre-baptismal anointing from the *Apostolic Tradition*, even though it was alien to the indigenous usage,[58] and later this designation starts to appear in texts influenced by either the *Apostolic Tradition* or the *Canons of Hippolytus*. It appears in the baptismal rite of the sixth-century *Canons of Basil*,[59] which makes considerable use of the *Canons of Hippolytus*, and also in both the "Book of the Chrism,"[60] and the Ethiopic translation of the *Apostolic Tradition*.[61] However, the manner of its usage in these last two documents confirms that it was indeed foreign to the indigenous tradition and its significance was not properly appreciated, for it was here

---

[53] See Horner, 170, 174.

[54] See Whitaker, *Documents*, 95.

[55] See Sebastian Brock, "Studies in the Early History of the Syrian Orthodox Baptismal Liturgy" in *Journal of Theological Studies* 23 (1972), 30–32.

[56] *Ibid.*, 38–39.

[57] See, for example, P. W. Harkins, *St. John Chrysostom: Baptismal Instructions* (London 1963), 58.

[58] Coquin, *Les Canons d'Hippolyte*, 110–111; Bradshaw, 22.

[59] See W. Riedel, *Die Kirchenrechtsquellen des Patriarchats Alexandrien* (Leipzig 1900), 279–281.

[60] *Le Muséon* 41, 57.

[61] See Bernard Botte, *La tradition apostolique de saint Hippolyte* (Münster 1963), 47, n. 3.

applied, not to the pre-baptismal anointing at all, but to the post-baptismal unction.

THE CONFESSION OF FAITH

One of the principal reasons why Alexandrian baptismal practice has traditionally been identified as Western has been the apparent presence of a credal interrogation of the candidates similar to that in the *Apostolic Tradition* of Hippolytus and the later Roman rite, rather than a *syntaxis* of the Syrian kind. It is attested by the third-century patriarch Dionysius,[62] and supported by a reference in the works of Origen.[63] This, however, is not of itself sufficient to demonstrate the Western character of the whole rite: it is clear from the evidence presented by other liturgical practices that Egypt was something of a "maverick" in its form of worship, so that the presence of one element found in another tradition does not necessarily mean that all other elements from that tradition must have been there too.

In any case, this interrogatory form of the baptismal confession of faith did not last long in the Alexandrian tradition, but was replaced by a declaratory form with a fivefold shape. Emmanuel Lanne has recently presented evidence for the existence from early times of a fivefold credal affirmation in the Alexandrian tradition,[64] and whilst none of this proves that such a form was used in a baptismal context at an early date, it does suggest that, when the change was made, such a credal form was already an established feature in that ecclesiastical tradition, and it may even have been already in use for some time in baptismal practice in Egyptian dioceses outside Alexandria.

It is possible that the change from the interrogatory to the declaratory form of confession of faith came about when the indicative baptismal formula — "I baptize you in the name of the Father, and of the Son, and of the Holy Spirit" — was adopted.

---

[62] In a letter preserved in Eusebius, *Ecclesiastical History* 7.9.

[63] *In Num.* 5.1. (*PG* 12.603C).

[64] E. Lanne, "La confession de foi baptismale à Alexandrie et à Rome" in A. M. Triacca & A. Pistoia (eds.), *La liturgie expression de la foi* (Bibliotheca "Ephemerides Liturgicae" Subsidia 16, Rome 1979), 213–228.

The first evidence for the use of this formula in Egypt is in Canon 19 of the *Canons of Hippolytus*, where the author apparently has some difficulty in knowing how to combine it with the interrogation, and resorts to the expedient of having it repeated three times, once after each question and answer.[65] Clearly such an arrangement was far from satisfactory, and it is not surprising, therefore, that the later Coptic tradition did what the Western rites would also ultimately do, and placed the confession of faith before the immersion.[66]

THE POST-BAPTISMAL ANOINTING

Among the points which Kretschmar made in his important study was the suggestion that post-baptismal anointing was a later addition to initiatory practice in Egypt and that the rite there originally included only a single pre-baptismal unction, as was also the case in the Syrian tradition.[67] Other scholars, however, have assumed that all references to "chrism" in Alexandrian patristic writers must be a post-baptismal anointing and not to an unction which preceded baptism.[68] This assumption is a dubious one to make, for three reasons. Firstly, at least in some instances the word may be intended in a purely metaphorical sense, as a description of the Holy Spirit, as indeed it seems to be in the New Testament. Secondly, even where it does appear to refer to a literal anointing, it need not necessarily be to a post-baptismal unction, since it was not in early centuries a technical term for this but could be employed in a more general sense.[69]

Thirdly, since none of the early Alexandrian references specify precisely when in the rite this chrism was bestowed, they could well be speaking of a pre-baptismal unction. Thus, for example,

---

[65] See Coquin, *Les Canons d'Hippolyte*, 112–113; Bradshaw, 23.

[66] See Whitaker, *Documents*, 94–95.

[67] 43ff.

[68] Fisher, 72, even included as fourth-century Egyptian evidence extracts from the homilies attributed to Macarius, which are considered by scholars to be the work of Symeon of Mesopotamia.

[69] For example, it is used in reference to the pre-baptismal anointing in *Apostolic Constitutions* 7.22.2, and, as already noted above 92, Cyril of Alexandria, *in Job.* 7 (PG 74.49D), speaks of "the chrism of catechesis."

the allusion to "visible waters and visible chrism" in Origen[70] should be treated with some caution. On the one hand, he could in any case be describing the baptismal practice of Caesarea rather than that of Alexandria here, and on the other, it should be noted that he immediately goes on to speak of baptism "in the Holy Spirit and the water," and elsewhere says that "the unction of chrism and the baptism have continued in you undefiled."[71] The order in these last two passages, spirit/water, unction/baptism, may — or may not — be significant, but it should act as a warning against assuming that "visible chrism" must necessarily be a post-baptismal anointing.

There is furthermore the testimony presented by the legend of the Antiochene woman, where such great stress is laid on the inclusion of the pre-baptismal anointing, but no mention made of a post-baptismal unction.

Finally, there is another piece of evidence not referred to by Kretschmar which, though of a late date, may be of some importance. The "Book of the Chrism" contains two legends concerning the origin of the post-baptismal anointing. The first asserts that its use was traditional at Alexandria, the chrism itself having been obtained from the embalming of Jesus, but that it eventually fell into neglect and the supply of chrism disappeared, so that Athanasius had to write to the bishop of Rome and to the patriarchs of Antioch and Constantinople asking them to compose prayers to read over the baptismal oils, Basil being credited with the composition of those adopted.[72] The second legend, on the other hand, maintains that it was Theophilus who originated the use of chrism. He received from an angel the order to bring balsam trees from Jericho, plant them, extract the balsam and cook the spices, and to do this

"on the Friday of the sixth week in the monastery of St Macarius, if possible, if not at Alexandria, according to the rite which the angel had made known to him. He fixed the *ordo* of the manner which is now well-known. He wrote about it to all the patriarchs.

[70] *In Rom.* 5.8 (*PG* 14.1038C).
[71] *In Lev.* 6.5 (*PG* 12.472D).
[72] *Le Muséon* 41, 57-59.

All were in accord except the Armenians because of their innovation."[73]

I do not, of course, wish to suggest that either of these legends provides us with a reliable account of what actually happened, but I do want to suggest that some historical event must have given rise to them. The admission of the loss of the chrism and of the need to seek help from other churches to restore it in the first version is a somewhat embarrassing tale which does not exactly bring credit to the Alexandrian patriarchate. It is, therefore, difficult to imagine why it should have arisen at all, unless there were behind it some recollection of a genuine innovation during the fourth century. It is interesting that the second version too chooses the fourth century for the introduction of the use of chrism, although it does attempt to give it additional status by means of the angelic command and by the claim that it was from Egypt that other churches derived the custom. Once again, there seems to be no reason for such a late date, unless there is some truth to the story, and post-baptismal anointing was a later addition to the Alexandrian practice.

Thus the *Canons of Hippolytus*, which seems to reveal the existence of an established practice of post-baptismal anointing early in the fourth century,[74] may well indicate only the beginnings of this development, since it is highly likely that innovations in liturgical practice would have been adopted in the smaller dioceses before they were accepted in the more conservative patriarchal church. The same may also be true of the *Sacramentary of Sarapion*, though, on the other hand, it is possible this may have been composed, or at least revised and expanded, later than the middle of the fourth century.[75]

[73] *Le Muséon* 41, 57.
[74] See Coquin, *Les Canons d'Hippolyte*, 112–115; Bradshaw, 23–24.
[75] See Bernard Botte, "L'Eucholge de Serapion est-il authentique?" in *Oriens Christianus* 48 (1964) 50–56; but cf. G. J. Cuming, "Thmuis Revisited: Another look at the Prayers of Bishop Sarapion" in *Theological Studies* 41 (1980) 568–575.

The initiatory process in the West concluded with a celebration of the eucharist, in which the newly-baptized participated for the first time. It is not clear whether or not the same was true at Alexandria. The tradition here with regard to the eucharist, at least up to the end of the fourth century, was for there to be full celebrations only on Sundays, with communion from the pre-sanctified gifts being practised on Wednesdays, Fridays, and Saturdays.[76] Since, as we have seen, baptisms were not performed on a Sunday, there seem to be three possibilities with regard to the communion of the newly-baptized — a special eucharistic celebration on the baptismal day, the reception of communion from the reserved sacrament, or even no reception of communion at all until the next Sunday.

The tenth-century letter of Macarius states that the first of these was the case:

"When they had finished, they consecrated the holy mysteries . . . and gave them to the baptized. And after that they made them drink from a chalice which they had consecrated, in which milk and honey were mixed. . . ."[77]

However, as we have suggested earlier, his account could well have been influenced by knowledge of the procedure described in the *Apostolic Tradition* of Hippolytus. The legend of the Antiochene woman, on the other hand, describes the baptism as taking place "when the patriarch had finished the liturgy" (by which may be meant the liturgy of the pre-sanctified), and after the baptism "he gave to the two children of the holy mysteries."[78] Another version of the legend also speaks of the baptism taking place in the evening after the liturgy,[79] whilst the legend of Theophilus, as we have seen,[80] places it on a Saturday morning, and makes no explicit reference to a eucharistic celebration in conjunction with it.

---

[76] See Socrates, *Eccl. Hist.* 5.22.
[77] *Le Muséon* 36, 35–36.
[78] Evetts, 389.
[79] E. A. W. Budge (ed.), *Coptic Martyrdoms in the Dialect of Upper Egypt* (London 1914), 404.
[80] Above, 74.

Possibly the evening in conjunction with the liturgy of the pre-sanctified represents the earlier tradition, and the morning reflects the later practice when the consecration of the chrism alone was performed.

CONCLUSION

In the light of all this, it does not seem to do justice to the early Alexandrian baptismal rite to classify it as fundamentally Western in character. On the contrary, it should more properly be described as fundamentally Alexandrian in character. This in turn means that we cannot really speak of two principal liturgical traditions in the early Church — Eastern and Western — but should rather acknowledge that there was instead a variety of local practices, since there were also significant differences between the other churches which we designate as forming the rest of the Western liturgical family. These in the course of time increasingly conformed to a more standardized model through a process of mutual borrowing and adaptation, but neither this resultant composite pattern nor any one of its constituent traditions can claim to have been the normative baptismal practice of primitive Christianity, for such a thing appears never to have existed, which would seem to call into question twentieth-century attempts to restore it.

Jean Laporte

6. Models from Philo in Origen's Teaching on Original Sin[1]

My purpose is an investigation of original sin in Origen in the light of Philo of Alexandria. I do not mean by "original sin" the Augustinian definition resulting from the Pelagian controversy, but what the ancients meant by the inheritance of the human sinful condition, and the way Philo and Origen explained it in biblical language.[2]

PHILO OF ALEXANDRIA

I studied this notion in Philo in relation to the theory of the Ages of Life.[3] This theory, which is classical in Greek philosophy, reappears in Philo and acts as a frame for the development of the soul

---

[1] A paper given at the International Congress of Societas Liturgica, 17-22 August 1987, in Brixen, Italy.

[2] A. I. Gaudel, "Péché originel," *DTC* XII/I, 1933, 323-339 on Origen.

H. Rondet, *Le péché originel dans la tradition patristique et théologique*, Paris 1967, ch. 4, 85-90, Origen.

G. Teichtweiert, *Die Suendenlhere des Origenes*, Regensburg 1958, 92-111.

H. Haag, "The Original Sin in Discussion, 1966-1971," *Journal of Ecumenical Studies*, 10, 1973, 259-289.

C. Blanc, "Le Baptême d'après Origène," *Studia Patristica* XI, TU 108, 1972, 113-124.

J. Laporte, "La Chute chez Philon et Origène," *Kyriakon*, Festschrift J. Quasten, 319-335.

H. Rhaner, "Taufe und geistliches Leben bei Origenes," *Zeitschrift f. Aszese und Mystik*, VII, 1932, 205-223.

[3] J. Laporte, "The Ages of Life in Philo of Alexandria," *SBL Seminar Papers* 122, 1986, 278-290 (Abbr. "Ages of Life").

from the first age (complete subjection to the impulse of the irrational) to adulthood and the threshold of contemplative life. The soul progress through several steps, or ages, which include the appearance of reason, that of malice, the victory of reason, and the development of virtue with education and the acquisition of culture.[4]

However, I also found in Philo interesting developments on Adam, although less as the cause of our miseries than as a type of man.[5] Philo distinguishes between the man created according to the image and likeness of God, who enjoys the fullness of the divine spirit; the fashioned man, i.e., the good Adam put in charge of the garden of his own soul and growing the trees of virtue, but exposed also to the trial of the tree of the knowledge of good and evil in his moral conscience; the fallen Adam, who is a type of sinner and of repentance; finally, the "sons of Adam" who are the descendants of Cain, hardened and unrepenting sinners and atheists, which perished in the Deluge.[6]

Since, according to Philo, biblical models stand for our moral constituency, we are a mixture of many biblical types, with the predominance of certain of them.[7] Basically, and sometimes almost perfectly, we are the man created according to the image of God.[8] But, as members of the race of Adam, sin enjoys a priority in our soul in the beginning, and, inclining to sin, we are called to repentance.[9] A "breath of life," or a remnant of the divine spirit

[4] "Ages of Life" 282–286. In Philo, see particularly *Op.* 103–105; *Jos.* 126–130; *Her.* 293–299; *Congr.* 72–88; *Aet.* 58–60; *Sp.Leg.* IV, 68.

[5] "Ages of Life" 286–288.

[6] *Q.G.* I, 8; *Op.* 134 (the man created according to the image of God); *Op.* 134; 149 (the good Adam who was subjected to the trial); *Op.* 151–169; cf. *Leg. Al.* I–II *passim* (the fallen Adam and the allegory of the fight of the logos against the flesh); *Plant.* 60; *Post.* 1–124 (the sons of Adam as a wicked generation).

[7] *Abr.* 53.

[8] *Sobr.* 8–9; *Congr.* 34–38 (Isaac is that perfect man); *Mos.* I *passim*, particularly 1–40; *Virt.* 61–85 (Moses is the perfect man); *Abr.* 53–54 (Abraham is the perfect man).

[9] *Q.G.* I, 90–99; II, 54; *Abr.* 236–243; *Sacr.* 14–17; *praem.* 62–63; *Congr.* 81–88 (10 years in Canaan first).

(*pnoe*, not *pneuma*), warns us about sin, and kindles in us the flame of repentance and virtue.[10]

A third aspect of Philo's notion of original sin is the notion of "defilement."[11] Defilement is communicated to individuals in many ways, particularly through birth. According to Leviticus, a child needs circumcision in order to remove the defilement inherited from the womb, and a sacrifice must be offered for his purification. The mother also is defiled: intercourse makes a purification necessary for the couple; menstruations and delivery bring about an impure blood. Circumcision and purifications are necessary in order to enter the court of the temple, to sacrifice, and even to obtain the remission of sins. This is pure Levitical theology and practice in Judaism. These impurities are cured by circumcision and purifications.[12]

In relation to circumcision and purifications, we must understand that Philo — who requires the material act[13] — extends the requirements and meaning of these rites to the moral life, far more important in his opinion than the material aspect, but in agreement with it. Whereas the prophets seemed to substitute Ethics for Ritual, Philo, through a reflection on the moral implication of rites, established a continuity between Ritual and Ethical life.[14]

Therefore, considered as defilement, original sin in Philo is connected with birth. However, the circumcision on the eighth day does not presuppose the existence of a moral evil, of a sin properly speaking, in the baby at birth. A baby is not circumcised

[10] *Leg. Al.* I, 31–42.

[11] "Ages of Life" 288–289.

[12] *Dec.* 45; *Sp. Leg.* III, 63 (defilement after intercourse); *Q.G.* III, 48, 52 cf. Lev. 15:18 (defilement cured by circumcision); *Sp. Leg.* III, 32, cf. Lev. 18:19 (defilement of a menstruous woman); *Sp. Leg.* I, 113–115 (defilement resulting from intercourse, menstruation, motherhood in the case of priests and high priest); *Deus* 8–9 (undefinite defilement preventing entry to the temple): *Q.E.* I, 10 (priestly purity required of all for passover). I do not see Philo quoting Lev. 12:1-8.

[13] Cf. A. Wolfson, *Philo* I, 127.

[14] Cf. J. Laporte, "Sacrifice and Forgiveness in Philo of Alexandria," a paper presented at the Oxford Patristic Conference, 1983. In Philo, see particulary *Sp. Leg.* III, 88–89; *Det.* 20–21; *Cher.* 95–96; *Sp. Leg.* I 304–306.

for the forgiveness of the Adamic sin. It is a mere question of Levitical defilement. The real moral purification takes place later, and is related with the idea of the priority of the passions, of the flesh, and vice in the soul. Here Philo is in agreement with the Greek theory of the *Ages of Life*. We can also say that he agrees with the biblical notion of the flesh.

According to the theory of the Ages of Life as understood by Philo, a baby is "pure wax" as not having yet lived in good or evil. But, because of the pressure of the passions and of poor early education, he will turn to evil before turning to virtue under the guidance of reason.

Philo also introduces evil as a twin brother of the good, two innate tendencies figured by the conflict of Essau and Jacob in the womb of Rebecca.[15]

Finally, in *Legum Allegoriae*, Philo uses the illustration of the temptation of Adam by Eve to explain the idea that the mind, turning away from direct knowledge from God, yields to sense perception and becomes the slave of the flesh.

Philo recognizes a historical loss of mankind in Adam,[16] not a transmission of the sin of Adam. For Philo, Adam is more the type than the cause of our own failure to master the irrational part. Philo is interested in what happens in our hearts according to the Adamic allegory, not in the past event as such.

ORIGEN

Regarding original sin, there are important similarities between Philo and Origen. There are also important differences owing to the Christian faith of Origen.

Pre-existence and original sin. It seems right to discard old scholarship which ascribed to Origen without distinctions the teachings of Timaeus on the pre-existence of the soul and a fall resulting from a sin in a previous life.[17] Actually, the image of the "cool-

---

[15] *Praem.* 62–63.

[16] *Op.* 151–164; *Her.* 292–293; *Sacr.* 14–16; *Praem.* 62–63.

[17] E. de Faye, *Origène, sa vie, son œuvre, sa pensée*, Paris 1923/28, 3 vol.

H. Koch, *Pronoia und Paideusis*, Studia ueber Origenes und sein Verhaeltnis zum Platonismus, Leipzig 1932.

ing" of the *nous* into a *psuche,* and its restoration as *nous* is one illustration among many others, such as the mirror looking askance, the spoilt painting, etc. which Origen uses to express the idea of fall and restoration.[18]

In his fight against the Gnostics who accused the Creator of injustice, Origen tried to resolve the problem of diversity and inequality by a fall resulting from neglect of participation in the good in the beginning, ultimately by the free-will of the creature.[19]

Origen dealt with the cases of the Prince of Tyre, of Lucifer and of the devils, of heavenly bodies, finally of certain exceptions among men such as the cases of Jacob and Essau, of Eliah, Jeremiah, of John the Baptist, of early possessions by the devil.[20] In the case of Jacob and Essau, Origen, indeed, suggests the

---

H. Rondet, *Le péché originel dans la tradition patristique et théologique,* Paris 1966.

H. Crouzel, *Origène et la philosophie,* Paris 1962, 195–215. Against the thesis of old scholarship affirming that Origen followed Plato's doctrine of reincarnations and of the pre-existence of the soul, the author shows that the so-called quotes of *De principiis* found in Jerome and other later sources, and integrated by Koetschau in his critical edition, are unreliable and contradicted by Origen in the original Greek text elsewhere.

J. Daniélou, *Message évangélique et culture hellénistique,* Paris 1961, 381–390. The author sees Origen in *De principiis* as closer to the Greeks, but as focusing on the radical liberty of men and as rejecting the Gnostic dualism which considered the body as evil by nature.

The dependence of Origen on Plato in *De principiis* was exaggerated by old scholarship which deliberately ignored his exegetical writings, and considered him as a representative of Greek culture. In order to understand Origen's "pre-existence of the soul," we must understand what Philo of Alexandria — who so often inspired him — meant by "existing in the divine Logos."

A. Guillaumont, *Les "Kephalaia Gnostica" d'Evagre le Pontique, et l'histoire de l'origénisme chez les Grecs et chez les Syriens,* Paris 1962, passim. The author situates the "quotes" in the history of Origenism, and shows their dependence on Evagrius and on the Origenists of the time of Justinian.

[18] *Princ.* II, 8, 3 SC 252, 342–348.

[19] *Princ.* II, 8, 4, 9 *passim,* SC 252, 348–372.

[20] *Princ.* I, 5, SC 252, 174–194 (Prince of Tyre, Lucifer, Devils and Satan); I, 7, 206–220 (devils); I, 8, 220–232 (heavenly bodies); II, 9, 7, 366–370 (Jacob-Essau); III, 4–5, Koetschau, 260 (early possessions); *Com. on Mat.* XIII, 1–2 (the spirit of Eliah).

hypothesis of a previous life.[21] If the soul pre-exists the body, he says, the solution of such cases becomes easy,[22] but, because he is aware of the obscurity of the question of its origin, Origen cannot affirm that the soul pre-exists the body (the Platonic thesis of the re-incarnations).[23]

Regarding early possessions, Origen considers the possibility of temptations by evil spirits, and guilt, taking place in the womb in a soul developed in its emotional and sensitive nature, and always in (radical) possession of free-will.[24] On the other hand, in the womb also, some may listen to the Father, and more readily adhere to Christ.[25]

All these speculations are very tentative, and they deal with life in the womb, not with a previous life properly speaking.

Philo also asked questions about the origin of the soul, wondering at the absence of known merit in the cases of certain privileged men such as Melchisedek, Abraham, Isaac, Jacob (Essau), Ephraim (Manasseh), Besalee.[26] His questions may have inspired the questions of Origen. The answers belong to Origen. It is interesting to observe that Philo raises, but does not answer such questions.

Devil and original sin. It seems that the importance of the Devil was so predominant in early Christianity, and particularly in Origen, that the Redemption was conceived as a ransom paid to the devil,[27] and Christian life as a fight against the "Strong one," from beginning to end.[28] Therefore, original sin could only be represented as captivity of the Devil, from which there is no human escape.[29]

[21] *Com. on John* VI, 62, SC 157, 174–194; *On Prayer*, 5, 4, ACW, 28; *Princ.* I 7, 4 SC 252, 214; II, 8, 3, Koetschau, 161; II, 9, 7 SC 252, 368; *Com. on John* VI, 62, SC 157, 174–194; *On Prayer* 5:4, ACW 28.

[22] *Com. on John* II, 182–186, SC 120, 330–332.

[23] *Princ.* "Preface" 5, SC 252, 84; *Com. on Song* II, 5, ACW, 134–136.

[24] *Princ.* III, 3, 4–5, Koetschau, 260.

[25] *Com. on John* XX, 52, SC 290, 182.

[26] *Leg. Al.* III, 79–95.

[27] Cf. G. Aulen, *Christus Victor*, "Christ and the Devil," Tr. A. G. Herbert, Macmillan 1960, 149ff.

[28] *Hom. on Ex.* II, 3, SC 16, 97–98, PG XII, 313–314. *Princ.* III, 2, *passim*.

[29] S. T. Bettencourt, *Doctrina ascetica Origenis, seu quid docuerit de ratione ani-*

Plenty of evidence, indeed, can be found in Origen in support of such a view. However, Origen grants the Devil a rather limited influence. He disagrees with simple Christians who admit the necessity of demonic influence.[30] He maintains the power of free-will to approve and disapprove the suggestions of the Devil.[31] He considers the fight against devils as a fair matching of individuals against individuals, allowed by God for our training and victory. Moreover, the Devil can only foster evil desires existing in our soul; he cannot force our will.[32] Finally, all the temptations do not come from the Devil, but also from ourselves, even sometimes from God.[33]

If we can say that the Devil killed Adam and the whole human race in Adam when he took away from him the true life[34] — which is spiritual —, we must admit, however, that, in our fallen condition, we preserve the sense of good and evil, and the presence of the divine Word in our human reason.[35]

Philo does not offer any parallel to such a theory of the Devil, but he may have provided Origen with the corrective which enables him to escape a psychosis of the Devil, and to make a positive and well balanced analysis of temptation.

Ages of Life, and original sin in Origen. In the same manner as in Philo, the classical theory of the Ages of Life remains in Origen the basic system of the development of the soul and combines with the biblical teachings on flesh and spirit and on the necessity of education as pointed out in biblical wisdom writings and provided in the catechumenate.

In *Commentary on Romans*, Origen writes: "Certain Greeks rightly taught that in our mortal and rational race, when reason reaches

---

mae humanae cum daemonibus, Romae 1945; L. Bouyer, "Le problème du mal dans le Christianisme antique," *Dieu Vivant* 6, 1946, 17–42.

[30] *Princ.* III, 1, Koetschau, 246; *Contra Celsum* VIII, SC 150, 289.

[31] *Princ.* III, 2, 3, 4, Koetschau, 251 (resistance to the devil); *Princ.* III, 6, Koetschau, 263 (watching); *Princ.* III, 3–4, Koetschau, 262 (discernment of spirits).

[32] *Princ.* III, 2, 4–5, Koetschau, 251.

[33] *Princ.* III, 2, 4, Koetschau, 247–252.

[34] *Com. on John* XX, 221, SC 290, 266.

[35] *Contra Celsum* VIII, 52, SC 150, 288.

its full development, vice necessarily appears first, and later on, with time and application, vice is overthrown and virtue arises."[36] *Contra Celsum* distinguishes four steps:

1) there is a time when the individual has not yet received reason;
2) another time when reason is accompanied by malice, and we obtain evil;
3) another time when the individual progresses in virtue;
4) another time when perfection is reached in adulthood.[37]

The Prologue of *Commentary on Song of Songs* describes the progress of the soul toward love according to the schema of the Ages of Life. Infants and children understand nothing of the passion of love. The biblical books of Proverbs, Ecclesiastes, and Song of Songs respectively represent the successive steps in education: Ethics, Physics, Epoptics. But "kisses of his mouth" figure a first communication of the divine Word in elementary instruction (in Scripture). The "maiden souls" are not given all at once the full revelation of the Word, their Bridegroom, but first particles only of the mysteries found in the Law and the Prophets, and "inlays of gold and silver" figuring parables, until complete communion becomes possible.[38]

Therefore, during the first age of life, the soul is under the power of the passions, and bound to vice. "Every soul," Origen says, "before reaching virtue, is covered with the pollution of vice."[39] At the age of reason, we decide for or against vice, for being a son of God or a son of the Devil. The next step is not the ritual of baptism immediately, but the education provided in catechumenate, in which the word of God and the Law exercise their purifying influence.[40]

---

[36] *Com. on Rom.* 3:9-18. Cf. Jean Scherer, *Le Commentaire d'Origène sur Rom. III-5-V-7,* 4, lines 11–14, Le Caire 1957, 136–138.

[37] *Contra Celsum* IV, 64, SC 136, 344.

[38] *Com. on Song.* II, 8, ACW, 148–155.

[39] *Hom. on Luke* XIX, 1, SC 87, 272.

[40] *Hom. on Ex.* IV, 8, PG XII, 323; *Com. on John* I, 273–275, SC 120, 198; XX, 107–109, SC 290, 212; 288–289, SC 290, 298; *Hom. on Jer.* V, 15–16, SC 232, 318–324; 6, 2, id., 330 (the Logos fighting against the passions).

The flesh. All beginners, in the first age of life, and as well in a late conversion, have to fight against, and master, the flesh. This teaching is common to the Greeks, Philo, Paul, Origen. Paul specifies that we must fight, not only the flesh, but also demonic powers. Philo does not know these demonic powers. Origen sees the conflict with demonic powers as the lot of baptized Christians who are advanced in virtue, whereas beginners are still entangled in the flesh.[41]

The couple flesh-spirit belongs to the teachings of the Bible and of Philo. The connection between the flesh and our beginning makes of the flesh an equivalent of "original sin," I mean, of the sinful origin and condition of humanity, in relation, or not, with Adam.

The large number of references to the flesh in Origen, and their diversity, makes it more profitable to turn to the particular aspects of original sin which integrate the flesh, I mean, certain biblical images such as those of Adam, the seed of Abraham, defilement, Egypt and baptism.

Adam. The opening of the eye of Adam to earthly things, and its closing to the contemplation of heavenly things, turns the good Adam, a righteous man and a prophet, into a slave to passions and vices.[42] From the man created according to the image of God, he becomes, as his name indicates, "Adam," the image of the "Earthly," a man living according to the wisdom of the flesh.[43] This teaching is common with Philo.

Origen learnt from Paul that the whole human race is included in Adam and shares in the curse which his sin brought upon the earth.[44] The serpent which beguiled Eve, also poisoned her posterity.[45]

---

[41] *Hom. on Ex.* VIII, 4-5, PG XII, 356-358; *Hom. on Josuah* XV, 4-7, SC 71, 344-356.

[42] *Princ.* 1, 3, 6-7, SC 252, 2156, 158; *Hom. on Luke* XVI, 7, SC 87, 244-248; XVII, 1, 4, id., 252-254.

[43] *Hom. on Num.* XVII, 3, PG XII, 704-705; *Hom. on Jer.* II, 1, SC 232, 240; VIII, 1-2, SC 232, 352-356; *Com. on John* XX, 224-234, SC 290, 268-274.

[44] *Contra Celsum* IV, 40, SC 136, 288; and ref. to notes 42 and 43.

[45] *Com. on Song* III, 12, ACW, 225-226.

Had Adam chosen life, according to Deut. 30:15, things would have turned differently for him and his race.[46] But like Philo, Origen is more interested in the present situation than in the "would-be."

As belonging to the race of Adam, but contrary to Adam, we put on the earthly first, and then must convert to the heavenly.[47] As "sons of the wrath," all sinners must circumcise the foreskin of their heart, master the flesh, mortify their members.[48]

Since the Divine Word is communicated through human reason, the saints of the Old Testament and all of the human race enjoy a way to come to Christ independent of the Incarnation, and therewith a source of purification.[49] The Incarnation adds a new way of salvation, more adjusted to our present condition, and efficient.[50] Christ comes as the counterpart of Adam,[51] and the Bride of Song of Songs and of Ephesians, the right Eve, figures the Church.[52] The reference to Christ is what Origen understands as the "Mystery of Baptism."[53]

Seeds of Abraham (spermatikoi logoi). Philo wrote a book on the *posterity of Cain*. The "sons of Adam" are the posterity of Cain, a series of wicked generations coupled with a series of holy types (Abel, Seth, Enos, Enoch, Noah). The interest of the notion of descendants for the question of original sin is obvious.

Origen considers the theory of Traducianism as a hypothesis which he must maintain as an alternative to the Platonic theory of

[46] *Hom. on Lev.* IX, 11, SC 287, 124.

[47] *Hom. on Jer.* II, 1, SC 232, 240; *Hom. on Luke* XVII, 2–3, SC 87, 252–254.

[48] *Hom. on Jer.* V, 14–15, SC 232, 314–320 (wrath); VIII, 1, *id.*, 252 (mortification); Same theme in *Hom. on Lev.* III, 4, SC 286, 138; *Hom. on Luke* XVI, 7, SC 87, 244–246; *Com. on Rom.*, 124 & 172 on wrath, and 214 on mortification, in Scherer.

[49] *Hom. on Jer.* V, 15–17, SC 232, 318–326; VI, 2, id., 330; *Contra Celsum* I, 48, SC 132, 204; III, 68–69, SC 136, 136; IV, 25, 242; VIII, 72, SC 150, 340.

[50] *Contra Celsum* IV, 15–16, SC 136, 220; *Princ.* II, 6, SC 252, 314–324.

[51] *Com. on John*, XX, 224–233, SC 290, 268–272.

[52] *Com. on Song* IV, 14, AC, 239–240.

[53] *Hom. on Ex.* V, 2 PG XII 328; VI, 7, id., 336; VIII, 5, id., 356–358; *Hom. on Num.* III, 3, PG XII 596; XII, 3, PG XII 665.

the incarnation of a pre-existing soul sent from heaven.[54] Actually, he rejects the two theories in their crude form, i.e., respectively, as transmission of the soul in the seed, and as reincarnation.[55] But he must explain the diversity and inequality of men in their origin without joining the Gnostics who accuse the Creator of injustice.

His answer is that the soul inherits spiritual seeds from ancestors, and adds its personal contribution. Therefore, the seed in its spiritual nature is the fruit of works and merit. Origen proposes a kind of "moral Traducianism," which is of the utmost interest for the question of original sin.[56]

Origen does not grant much importance to the seed of Adam, which is found in Abraham, indeed, but seems to represent mediocrity rather than wickedness, and is superseded by the seeds of Seth, Enos, Enoch, Noah, Shem, finally by the seed resulting from Abraham's own works.[57]

Origen asks how we can be "sons of Abraham." His answer is that we can reach the same spiritual worth by other means, because our particular ancestry — our fathers — is not the ancestry of Abraham. Pharisees and Sadducees rightly claimed their dignity as "seed of Abraham," but they were not "sons of Abraham" because they did not do the works of Abraham. Therefore, what is essential in order to be "sons of Abraham" is to do the works of Abraham.[58]

Similarly there are "sons of the Devil," those who perform the works of the Devil. And all will join their "fathers" after death: either Christ and the Patriarchs, or Cain and his descendants.[59]

Finally, there are those "born of God," who cannot sin (I John 3:8-10).[60]

---

[54] *Princ.* III, 4, 2 Koetschau, 264–267: the "lower soul," according to the Valentinians, comes along with the seed, but Origen doubts Traducianism, and rejects the Gnostic division of the soul. *Com. on Song* II, 5, ACW, 135–136, Origen raises many questions about the soul and its origin.

[55] *Com. on John* VI, 64, SC 157, 176–178; *Com. on John* XX, 2–8, SC 290, 156–158.

[56] *Com. on John* XX, 2–65, SC 290, 156–188.

[57] *Com. on John* XX, 12, 25, SC 290, 162–170.

[58] *Com. on John* XX, 30–43, SC 290, 164–176.

[59] *Com. on John* XX, 77–79, SC 290, 196.

[60] *Com. on John* XX, 106, 110, SC 290, 210–212.

We do not inherit the seed of Cain and of his descendant, because "God destroyed the seed of Cain in the Deluge."[61] It was, indeed, a good way to stop the "Traducianism" of moral evil. Unfortunately, we can always perform the works of the Devil, and repeat the sins of Cain. Moreover, if, according to Origen, nobody is completely deprived of good and salutary seeds,[62] we must admit that we all also inherit seeds of evil in larger or lesser quantity.

Defilement and original sin. I noted in Philo the importance of the ritual of purities in practice and in its moral extensions, particularly the defilement coming from birth and its moral symbolism. Although affirming the Christian freedom from the observance of the levitical laws on purities,[63] Origen inherits the moral interpretations inaugurated by Philo, and even the existence of a real defilement attached to birth.

In *Homilies on Luke* we read that no soul is spotless from the beginning, that a *macula* (stain, defilement) must be removed in order for the soul to be *immaculata*.[64] Even Jesus needed a purification *a sorde* (uncleanness) — not from sin —[65], for he put on the dress sown in corruption, although he was not defiled, like all other men, in his Father and mother. A sacrifice was offered for his purification.

The defilement attached to birth is independent from personal sins, and even from sins committed by forefathers. It is related to birth, to the impure blood accompanying birth, and it has some similarity with the blood of menstruation and with the loss of seed of the male.[66] Origen also sees in intercourse a kind of shame which prevents the presence of the Holy Spirit and prayer.[67]

---

[61] *Com. on John* XX, 25–27, SC 290, 168–170.

[62] *Com. on John* XX, 34, SC 290, 172.

[63] *Com. on Mat.* XI, 12 SC 162, 328–334.

[64] *Hom. on Lev.* VIII, 3, SC 287, 20; *Hom. on Luke* II, 2, SC 87, 112; *Contra Celsum* VII, 50, SC 150, 130–132.

[65] *Hom. on Luke* XIV, 3, SC 87, 218–220.

[66] *Hom. on Lev.* VIII, 3, cf. Lev. 12:2, SC 287, 14–22; XII, 4, SC 287, 178; *Hom. on Luke* XIV, 5, SC 87, 222; XIV 6, 224 *(nativitatis sordes)*.

[67] *Hom. on Num.* XXIII, 3, PG XII, 749; VI, 3, id., 610; *On Prayer* 31:4-5 ACW, 132–134.

Origen brings forth as evidence for a defilement at birth regardless of personal sins, infant baptism which, for him, cannot be given for the remission of sins, but only for the removal of the *macula* attached to birth.[68]

Regarding original sin, Origen can repeat the statement of Psalm 51 ascribed to David, "My mother conceived me in sin." It seems that, from a mere question of impure blood, he passes to the consideration of the defilement of our sinful condition and of our past sins, just as the Psalmist probably himself did.[69]

Baptism. Origen does not theologically relate baptism to the fall of Adam, but to the typology of Exodus.

The image of the crossing of the Red Sea, and of leaving Egypt for the desert where the people of Israel is trained by Moses and taught in the Law, becomes in Origen, as it was in Philo, a symbol of purification from the passions, and of the catechumenate.[70] Philo developed the same symbolism.[71]

In this context of thought, Egypt represents a beginning in evil, and the Exodus a moral and religious conversion. Egypt also figures the body which enslaves the soul, and Pharaoh, who, not allowing the service of the true God to take place, becomes the champion of an earthly and atheistic philosophy.

Origen reinforces this outline. Egypt is attachment to carnal vices, dependance on demons, enslavement in the life of the body, in the image of the earthly man.[72] We all begin in Egypt, in the moral laxity and doctrinal error of youth, before reaching virtue through reason and education.[73] We must all "descend to Egypt," fight the temptation of Egypt, remove the "shame of Egypt" from ourselves.[74]

---

[68] *Hom. on Lev.* VIII, 3 SC 287, 20; *Hom. on Luke* XIV 5, SC 87, 222; *On Prayer* 5, 4, ACW, 28.

[69] *Contra Celsum* VII, 50, SC 150, 130; *Hom. on Luke* XIV, 6, SC 87, 224.

[70] *Contra Celsum* II, 4, SC 132, 288; *Hom. on Lev.* VI, 2, SC 286, 274; *Hom. on Num.* XXVI 3, XXVII, PG XII, 774–801.

[71] *Sp. Leg.* I, II, 147 (*Diabateria*); *Leg. Al* II, 71–108 (the serpent of Eve is pleasure, and the brazen serpent of Moses is self-mastery).

[72] *Hom. on Gen.* XVI, 2, PG XII 247.

[73] *Hom. on Ex.* IV, 8, PG XII 323–325.

[74] *Hom. on Gen.* XV, 6, PG XII 245.

The Apostle Paul sees in the Exodus from Egypt a figure of the purification of baptism. Origen accepts this Pauline tradition,[75] and sees in the crossing of the Red Sea the mystery of our burial and resurrection in Christ through baptism.[76]

However, Origen prefers to spread the interpretation of baptism over two crossings instead of one. The first is the crossing of the Red Sea, and the second is the crossing of the Jordan. The first is closer to the renunciation of catechumens to idolatry, and leads them to instruction in the Law and its purifying influence. It is baptism, indeed, but in some regard superficial, fragile, still in need of the guidance of Moses.[77]

The second crossing is that of the Jordan, the "river which rejoices the City of God," a symbol of Christ.[78] Baptism now becomes deep and serious, and focuses on the mystery of Christ. It consists of sharing in Christ's burial and resurrection. We mortify our members, and we are renewed, regenerated, by the Spirit of God.[79] Origen likes to relate this baptism in the Jordan to the "second circumcision" accomplished by Josuah after the crossing.[80] This "second circumcision," or "circumcision of the heart," removes the impurities which prevent the edification of the "new man" with his "internal senses" and his ability to see God. With the baptism in the Jordan we are already living in the heavenly Kingdom in its eschatological reality.[81]

---

[75] Rom. 6:1-11; I Cor. 10:1-5.

[76] Hom. on Ex. V, 1 PG XII 326; Hom. on Num. XXII, 4, id., 745; Hom. on Josuah V, 1, SC 71, 146-156; XV, 5 id., 346-354; Com. on John VI, 166 SC 157, 254.

[77] Hom. on John VI, 2, 248-251, SC 157, 316-318; Hom. on Josuah V, 6, SC 71, 174-176; V, 2-3, 166-172; Hom. on Ex. V, 1-5, PG XII 325-331.

[78] Hom. on Luke XXI, 4, SC 87, 294; Hom. on Josuah IV 2, SC 71, 150; V, 1, id., 160-162; Com. on John VI 227-251, SC 157, 302-318; Hom. on Num. XVI, 4, PG XII 776-777.

[79] Hom. on Josuah IV, 1-2 SC 71, 146-154; Com. on Song IV, 14, ACW, 240-246; Hom. on Luke XIV, 1, SC 87, 216; XXVI, SC 87, 338-342; XXVII, 5, id., 348; XXIX, 1, id., 360.

[80] Hom. on Josuah V, 1, SC 71, 160-162; Com. on John VI, 217-237 SC 157, 294-308.

[81] Hom. on Josuah I, 7 SC 71, 114; V, 5-6, SC 71, 164-172; Hom. on Jer. V, 14, SC 232, 316-320; Hom. on John VI, 168-169, SC 157, 256; Dialogue with Heraclides 16-22, SC 67, 88-98; Com. on Mat. XI 20; cf. K. Rahner, "Les débuts

Josuah removed from the sons of Israel the "shame of Egypt," and "he was exalted." Our Josuah — Jesus —, in the mystery of baptism, in the exaltation of the cross, removes from our hearts the "shame of Egypt," i.e., the servitude of the flesh, which is far more difficult to uproot, because internal, than idolatry.[82]

Origen warns the catechumens against returning to the "shame of Egypt" after baptism, that is, against maintaining the routine of sin and going back to the old habits and vices of the flesh.[83]

In addition, a return to the "shame of Egypt" implies the prostitution of a member of Christ, and the profanation of a temple of the Holy Spirit.[84] A Christian returning to sin can be purified only through a baptism of fire, i.e., through penitence,[85] unless he or she has repented and become an accuser of self while "on the way," before being accused by the Adversary on the Day of Judgment.[86]

Therefore, Origen would have defined the original sin as our evil beginning in Egypt, an image belonging to the biblical language of baptism, instead of emphasizing the inheritance of Adam's sin. Adam was not a prominent figure like Abraham or Moses in the gallery of the Fathers. Paul "dramatized" the case of Adam, in whom we have all sinned, only, it seems, in order to show salvation in Christ, the New Adam.

CONCLUSION

Origen does not rely on infant baptism as a model for his theology of original sin and baptism. He interprets the sin of Adam

---

d'une doctrine des cinq sens spirituels chez Origène" RAM 13 (1932) 113-145; Hugo Rhaner, "Taufe und geistliche Leben bei Origenes" ZAM 7 (1932) 205-223.

[82] Hom. on Josuah, I, 7, SC 71, 112-114; V, 6, id., 170-172; Hom. on Num. XXVII, 2, PG XII 783.

[83] Hom. on Ex. V, 4, PG XII, 329-330; Hom. on Josuah V, 6, SC 71, 172-176; XXVI, 2, id., 492.

[84] Hom. on Josuah V, 6, SC 71, 172-174.

[85] Hom. on Lev. VIII, 10, SC 287, 50-52; XI, 2, id., 156-158; Hom. on Jer. XVI, 5-8. SC 238, 144-150; Hom. on Luke XXIV, 1, SC 87, 324-326; XXVI, 3, id., 340; Com. on John VI, 125, SC 157, 226.

[86] Hom. on Ps. 37 II, 6, PG XII, 1396; Hom. on Lev. III, 4, SC 286, 140.

as a loss for mankind, indeed, but counterbalanced by the presence of the Word from the beginning, the gift of the Law, the mission of the prophets and of Christ. The seed of Adam is unimportant. Baptism is the remission of our sins and our integration to Christ's Mystery. In the case of children, who have not sinned, baptism only purifies the defilement of birth. We must also remember that there is a priority of evil which results from the predominance of the flesh before the development of reason. Origen agrees with biblical statements affirming that we are sinners from the beginning.[87]

As in Philo, in Origen Adam is still a type: the type of the "earthly" man, and the type of the sinner who repented. We cannot ascribe to him the classical notion of original sin developed by Augustine. Paul's sentence, "In Adam we all sinned" does not have the same meaning in Origen and in Augustine. In Origen it means the universality of sin. In Augustine it means the inheritance of sin.[88]

[87] *Hom. on Num.* XXV, 6, PG XXII 767 (Nobody is pure when leaving this life); *Hom. on Lev.* II, 3, SC 296, 100–102. 106 (sin is contagious); *Hom. on Jer.* V, 15, SC 232, 318; VIII, 1–2, *id.*, 120; *Com. on John* I, 121, SC 120, 124; XX, 224–244, SC 290, 268–278; *On Prayer* V, 4, ACW, 28; *Hom. on Luke* XXIV, 2, SC 87, 324–326; *Com. on Mat.* XV, 22.

[88] The use of Origen's *Commentary on Romans* (PG XIV) raises problems because of changes made by the Latin translator Rufinus, but it is still Origenian thought. Concerning original sin and baptism, all the other themes reappear (especially the "ages of life" (PG XIV 931, 938–939, 1013–1018, 1031–1033, 1079–1083, 1162–1163, 875), the Devil and the Redemption interpreted as a sacrifice for sin (especially 1017–1018, 950–951, 1095, 1203), the flesh, etc.). However, because Origen is interpreting Paul, the emphasis here is on the image of *baptism as death and resurrection with Christ*: death to sin, circumcision of the heart, putting off the "body of sin" and the "old man," being renewed into a new life by the Holy Spirit. Concerning Adam, Origen here inclines to see in the sin of Adam a sin of concupiscence and in the Adamic inheritance the transmission of concupiscence (1094–1095): *pollutionem peccati quae ex concupiscentiae motu conceptis tradetur.* In spite of A.I. Gaudel ("Peché originel," DTC XII/1, 1933, 232–239), Philo does not see a sexual sin in the sin of Adam or in its inheritance as will Augustinian theology later on. This interpretation by Origen is, I would say, occasional, depending on the place in Paul, but does not become the chief consideration which absorbs all others (as the snake of Moses swallowed the Egyptian snakes), because the various images of original

But, besides Augustine's so-called "historical" interpretation of the original sin, which seems to discard, or absorb, all other explanations, it is not pointless to notice — with a bit of humour — that Augustine himself witnesses to another view of original sin, unrelated to Adam, well known in Greek literature, in Philo of Alexandria, in Origen and other Fathers, the theory of the Ages of Life. The terrible report of the sins of babies which he gives in the beginning of his *Confessions* is the best illustration of the "first age" in which the child is totally subjected to the influence of his passions and of his environment.

One word seems to contain the essential teaching of Origen on baptism: the Mystery of Christ. In relation to it, everything else is but image or preparation. One does not build a theology on the basis of the original sin, but on the Mystery of Christ. In baptism rightly understood, we get rid of the "old man," and die to sin; then, being raised again together with Christ, we are regenerated and live to God.

Origen's notion of original sin might, by the variety of its aspects, help today's believers and theologians to look into the early Christian tradition for more than one way to conceive of our sinful origin, and to accept one answer without rejecting the others. It would also free us from the now impossible Augustinian system of original sin abusively built on the corner-stone of Adam. Certainly, sin is as old as mankind, and its beginnings in ourselves is beyond remembrance. The story of Adam and Eve remains a powerful symbol of this mysterious reality.

---

sin and baptism survive and coexist. And this Origenian interpretation is well explained by his ascetical tendency as a "servant of God" living in contemplation and celibacy, who could not admit that the Holy Spirit would not be horrified by the conjugal bed room. For opposing views on this see the *Didascalia Apostolorum* and Augustine.

Maxwell E. Johnson

7. From Three Weeks to Forty Days: Baptismal Preparation and the Origins of Lent

In the context of his radical reconstruction of the origins of Lent (as stemming from the pre-Nicene post-Epiphany forty-day fast in the Alexandrian Christian tradition) Thomas Talley makes reference to the much disputed statement of the fifth-century Byzantine historian, Socrates, concerning Lenten practice at Rome.[1] Socrates writes that "the fasts before Easter will be found to be differently observed among different people. Those at Rome fast three successive weeks before Easter, excepting Saturdays and Sundays."[2] This reference, inaccurate for its own fifth-century context, when combined with the Roman traditions of the *missae pro scrutiniis* on the third, fourth, and fifth Sundays in Lent in the *Gelasianum*, the course reading of the Gospel of John from the third Sunday in Lent to Good Friday,[3] and the titles *Hebdomada in Mediana* and *Dominica in Mediana* provided by various *ordines Romani* and lectionaries for the fourth week and fifth Sunday in Lent respectively, leads Talley to the following conclusion:

"If it is possible that Socrates' inaccurate description of the Roman Lent throws some light on the length of the final period of candidacy for baptism in the third century, it is no more than possible. In the end, we must be satisfied with later data. Nonetheless, in

[1] Thomas J. Talley, *The Origins of the Liturgical Year* (New York 1986) 165-7.
[2] Socrates, *Historia ecclesiastica* V. 22.
[3] The fact of the matter is that the "course reading" from the Gospel of John in the Roman books begins on the *Friday* of the third week in Lent, not on the third Sunday.

the third century, Pascha is appearing as the preferred time for baptism in many parts of the Church, and the final preparation of candidates is a concern of the period just preceding the great festival. That preparation for baptism is antecedent at Rome to any extended period of ascetical preparation for the festival itself. That being the case, we can say that the masses *pro scrutiniis* on the third, fourth, and fifth Sundays in the Gelasian Sacramentary point to the older core of preparation for paschal baptism. Around that grew the more extended Lent of 'forty days or more' of which Siricius spoke in 385."[4]

However, on the basis of supporting evidence from other liturgical traditions his conclusion can be made even stronger. In other words, Socrates' "inaccurate description" of a three-week "Lent," as shall be demonstrated in what follows, is indeed *quite* possible, and it is quite possible not only for third-century Rome but also for other liturgical centres prior to the post-Nicene shift to a Lent of forty days.

A THREE-WEEK LENT IN EARLY ROME?

It is Antoine Chavasse who has argued most strongly for the existence of an earlier three-week Lenten pattern in Rome. In a series of related essays,[5] Chavasse interpreted Socrates' statement quite literally as a description of early Roman practice and pointed to a number of factors in support of this. To the "evidence," supplied by the title *mediana*, the John cycle of readings, and the three scrutiny masses of the *Gelasianum*, Chavasse added: (1) that the Roman tradition of ordination on the Saturday before the *Dominica in mediana* can best be understood if it once came in the context of an original three-week period;[6] (2) that the *Depositio Martyrum* of

---

[4] Talley, 167.

[5] See "La préparation de la Pâque, à Rome, avant le Ve siècle. Jeûne et organisation liturgique" in *Memorial J. Chaine* (Bibl. de la Fac. Cath. de Theol. de Lyon, vol. 5), Lyon 1950, 61–80; "La structure du Carême et les lectures des messes quadragesimales dans la liturgie romaine" in *La Maison-Dieu* 31 (1952) 76–120; and "Temps de préparation à la Pâque, d'après quelques livres liturgiques romains" in *Rech. de Sc. relig.* 37 (1950) 125–145.

[6] Chavasse argued that since the Saturdays of the first three weeks of a six-week Lent remained without a proper synaxis until the sixth century and the

354 is an indirect witness to an earlier Lenten period of three weeks, in that the calendar is vacant from March 7th to May 19th, i.e., exactly enough time for a three-week Lent and the fifty days of Easter;[7] and (3) that the Roman year, reckoned as beginning on March 1st, offers only a three-week period before Easter in those years that Easter falls on March 22nd, its earliest possible date. On the basis of all this, therefore, Chavasse concluded that there was an original three-week Lent at Rome which disappeared sometime between 354, the date of the *Depositio Martyrum*, and 384, the date of Jerome's letter to Marcellus in which is the first datable reference to a Roman Lent of six weeks.[8]

Saturday of the fifth week remained vacant until the eighth, the presence of ordination on the fourth Saturday may well indicate the remains of an older Lenten structure (See "La préparation de la Pâque," 75). Similarly, he noted a parallel between ordination on this fourth Saturday and the tradition of ordination of the *first* Saturday in Lent which he considered to be a later development (See "La structure du Carême," 83). While he did not go into detail on this question, it is certainly reasonable to assume that the celebration of ordination on the fourth Saturday in Lent *is* an earlier tradition than ordination on the first. That is, it is easy to understand how a celebration on the Saturday of the first week of an original "three-week Lent" might be later duplicated and ultimately replaced by one on the first Satuday of a six-week Lent. A development in the other direction is much more difficult to comprehend. If ordinations were celebrated on the first Saturday in Lent prior to their appearance on the fourth Saturday, then why would it have been necessary to add this second celebration after an interval of only three weeks?

[7] In this context Chavasse also notes that the *sanctorale* of the Gelasian Sacramentary ceases between March 7th and May 1st and that the Gregorian liturgical documents show that the formulas for Ascension and Pentecost have been inserted into the *sanctorale* after May 12. See "Temps de préparation à la Pâque," 127.

[8] See "La préparation de la Pâque," 69 and "La structure du Carême," 83-4. Cf. also P. Jounel, "The Year" in A. G. Martimort, et.al. (eds.), *The Church at Prayer*, IV (Collegeville 1986) 67; Patrick Regan, "The Three Days and the Forty Days" in *Worship* 54 (1980) 5; and Cyrille Vogel, *Medieval Liturgy: An Introduction to the Sources*, translated and revised by William Storey and Niels Rasmussen (Washington, D.C. 1986) 309-10. Vogel even supports Chavasse's attempt to relate a three-week Lent to the secular Roman calendar. He writes (p. 310); "We can deduce the reason for the three-week preparatory fast. Since the Roman year began on March 1, there were exactly three weeks available before March 22, the earliest possible date of Easter. In such a case

Chavasse's speculations on the date of a six-week Lent at Rome, the *Depositio Martyrum*, and the supposed relationship between "Lent" and a (fourth-century?) March 1st Roman New Year can be criticized.[9] His greatest contribution to the question of early Roman Lent, however, is his analysis of the apparent relationship between the Johannine cycle of Lenten readings and the *missae pro scrutiniis* of the *Gelasianum*. Beginning with the oldest surviving Roman lectionary, the *Würzburg Capitulary* (*c.* 700),[10] Chavasse[11] noted that Gospel readings on the Sundays, Wednesdays, and Fridays of the last three weeks of Lent (which parallel the readings in the Tridentine *Missale Romanum*) produce a rather confusing sequence. The first Johannine reading occurs on the Friday of the current third week in Lent and sets the following course of readings in motion:[12]

LENT III

Sunday:	Luke 11:14-28
Wednesday:	Matt 15:1-20
Friday:	*John 4:5-42* (The woman at the well of Samaria)

---

one would have a beginning of the year fast the would coincide with a fast before Easter. . . . In any case, the three week period could not begin before New Year's (March 1) since Easter could not fall earlier than March 22."

[9] Talley, for example, has argued (166, 170) on the basis of the Festal Letters of Athanasius that Rome was already observing the fast of forty days in 340. While this may certainly call into question the dates Chavasse assigned to the beginning of the forty-day Lenten observance at Rome, it does not necessarily mean that the *Depositio Martyrum* does not reflect an earlier and authentic Roman liturgical practice. In the supposed relationship of Lent to the Roman New Year, however, there is simply no evidence to support the notion that the Roman church consciously related its pre-paschal fast to the secular calendar. Therefore, while Chavasse *may* be correct in this, his conclusion is simply too speculative to be accepted uncritically.

[10] For the list of the Lenten Gospel readings from this lectionary see G. Morin, "Liturgie et basiliques de Rome au milieu du VII siècle d'après les listes d'évangiles de Würzburg" in *Revue Bénédictine* 28 (1911) 302-4; W. H. Frere, *Studies in Early Roman Liturgy II: The Roman Gospel Lectionary* (London 1934) 8-10.

[11] For the description and discussion which follows see especially "La structure de Carême," 82-4, 89-90, 94-7, and 113-4.

[12] Ibid., 78.

LENT IV

Sunday: *John 6:1-15*
Wednesday: *John 9:1-38* (The man born blind)
Friday: *John 11:1-45* (The raising of Lazarus)

LENT V

Sunday: *John 8:46-59*
Wednesday: *John 10:22-38*
Friday: *John 11:47-54*

HOLY WEEK

Sunday: Matt 26-27
Monday: *John 12:1-36*
Tuesday: *John 13:1-32*
Wednesday: Luke 22-23
Friday: *John 18-19*

In analyzing this non-sequential series of readings Chavasse argued that they represented a shift from a pattern that would have placed the John 4, 9, and 11:1-45 readings on the Sundays to which the Gelasianum assigns its three scrutiny masses. Noting that the sermons of Pope Leo the Great indicate that the first two Sundays in Lent already had, respectively, the Matthean pericopes of the temptation and transfiguration of Jesus[13] and that the Matthean Passion was read on Palm/Passion Sunday, Chavasse reconstructed what he considered to be the Roman Lenten series in the time of Leo:[14]

LENT III

Sunday: *John 4:5-32*
Wednesday: Matt 15:1-20
Friday: Luke 11:14-18

[13] It should be noted, however, that the *Würzburg Capitulary* lists the second Sunday in Lent as *Die Dominico vacat*. See Morin, 302.
[14] Chavasse, "La structure du Carême," 78.

LENT IV

Sunday:	John 9:1-38
Wednesday:	John 6:1-14
Friday:	John 8:46-59

LENT V

Sunday:	John 11:1-45
Wednesday:	John 10:22-38
Friday:	John 11:47-54

HOLY WEEK (as above)

Such a series of readings, at least for the Sundays, Chavasse found parallelled also in the Milanese and Beneventan liturgical traditions, with the exception that John 4:5-32 was read on the second Sunday in Lent rather than on the third.[15] Similarly, in the Gelasian Sacramentary itself reference is explicitly made to both

[15] Ibid., 113–14. For a list of the Lenten Gospel pericopes in the Milanese liturgical tradition see A. Paredi, "L'evangeliario di Busto Arsizio" in Miscellanea liturgica in onore di sua Em. il card. G. Lercaro 2 (Rome 1967) 218; and E. C. Whitaker, Documents of the Baptismal Liturgy (London 1970) 133. In his study of the communion antiphons related to these three Sundays in the Beneventan liturgical tradition (Qui biberit, Lutum fecit, and Videns Dominus) R. J. Hesbert has argued that the original Roman pattern inherited by other Western traditions (e.g., Spain, Gaul, and North Italy) placed John 4:5-32 on the Second Sunday in Lent prior to its eventual and final placement on the third Friday. See R. J. Hesbert (ed.), Graduel bénéventain: Le Codex 10673 de la Bibliothèque Vaticane, fonds latin. XI siècle (Paléographie Musicale 14), Tournai 1931–1936, 219–22, 225–34. Chavasse, however, claimed that the reason for this pericope being on the Second Sunday in Lent in these non-Roman Western rites was that these other churches ignored the Roman tradition of the Ember Days. See Chavasse, "La structure du Carême," 114, and idem., "Le Carême romain et les scrutins prébatismaux avant le IXe siècle" in Rech. de Sc. relig. 35 (1948) 348–51, 364–5. Hesbert, of course, may be correct in his conclusion. Yet, it would be extremely difficult to explain the shift of this pericope from the Second Sunday all the way to the third Friday if it did not originally belong to that series of Johannine readings which continue to be present exclusively in the last three weeks of Lent. The best explanation, perhaps, is that these other non-Roman Western traditions merely adapted the Roman cycle to their own situations. I am grateful to Dr. Peter Jeffery for referring me to the work of R. J. Hesbert.

the John 9 and 11:1-45 pericopes in the context of the exorcism
"over females."[16] Chavasse concluded, therefore, that this
particular cycle of readings on the third, fourth, and fifth Sundays
was certainly the cycle designed to parallel the three scrutiny
masses themselves.

Nevertheless, even this cycle is still not in sequence; it represented, according to him, a yet earlier shift from a three-week
preparation period which must have included a sequential reading
from John. He, therefore, reconstructed this "original" series in
the following manner:[17]

LENT I (IV)

Sunday:	*John 4:5-32*
Wednesday:	John 6:1-14
Friday:	John 8:46-59

LENT II (V)

Sunday:	*John 9:1-38*
Wednesday:	*John 10:22-38*
Friday:	*John 11:[1-45] 47-54*

LENT III (HOLY WEEK) (as above)

Since Holy Week with its Passion readings from Matthew (Sunday), Luke (Wednesday), and John (Friday) had, in his opinion,
developed prior to this three-week period, it was necessary to skip
over "Passion" Sunday and Wednesday when the Lenten Johannine cycle was formed.[18] This "skip" he found confirmed by the
fact that the John 11:1-54 reading is also paralleled on the Friday
before Holy Week in the ancient Neapolitan evangeliary, which
"has generally conserved the structure of the ancient Roman evan-

---

[16] "I exorcise thee, unclean spirit, through the Father and the Son and the
Holy Spirit, that thou mayest go away and depart from these servants of
God. For he himself commands thee, accursed one, damned one, *who opened
the eyes of the man born blind, and on the fourth day raised Lazarus from the tomb*"
(Whitaker, 172) [emphasis added].

[17] "La structure du Carême," 78.

[18] Ibid., 96, 81-2.

geliary."[19] On the basis of all this, Chavasse maintained that, in terms of the later development of Lent, two further steps were made. First, when Rome adopted a six-week Lent (sometime between 354 and 384 according to his calculations) the "scrutiny" gospel readings (John 4:5-32; 9:1-38; and 11:1-45) were each transferred back one week to the Sundays indicated by the scrutiny masses in the *Gelasianum* (i.e., the third, fourth, and fifth Sundays in Lent). Second, the later shift of the catechetical scrutinies themselves to ferial days caused an "exchange" to take place between the Sunday and ferial gospel readings. This exchange thus resulted in the rather confusing sequence of Johannine readings in both the *Würzburg Capitulary* and the Tridentine *Missale Romanum*.

Did Rome, then, have a three-week paschal and baptismal preparation period before the post-Nicene development of a six-week Lent? Chavasse's conjectural but reasonable argument, based primarily on the Johannine cycle of readings, may certainly lead one in that direction. In fact, even in the later sources these Johannine pericopes, despite their sequence, are all contained (with the addition of the Friday of the third week) within the time-frame of the final three weeks of Lent. This, combined with the tradition of *mediana*, the scrutiny masses, and the other possible evidence indicated by him, makes his argument a strong one indeed. In any event, it certainly supports Talley's hypothesis that the scrutiny masses of the *Gelasianum* "point to the older core of preparation for paschal baptism,"[20] and that Socrates, while inaccurate for the fifth century, may certainly be pointing to what was a well-ingrained and early Roman tradition.

A THREE-WEEK LENT IN EARLY JERUSALEM?

Basing his work on the methodology and conclusions of Chavasse, Mario F. Lages argues that a three-week period of Lenten preparation for catechumens existed also in Jerusalem before the end of

---

[19] Ibid., 96. For the reference to this Gospel reading in the Neapolitan Evangeliary see G. Morin, "La liturgie de Naples au temps de saint Grégoire d'après deux evangeliaires du septième siècle" in *Revue Bénédictine* 8 (1891) 492. Interestingly enough this lectionary refers to this day as *Post. V. dominicas de XLgesima feria. VI. de lazarum.*

[20] Talley, 167.

the third century, a period which is discernible from an analysis of the contents of the Armenian Lectionary.[21] According to Lages, the canon of Lenten readings for the Wednesday and Friday afternoon synaxes at Zion, the canon of readings for Holy Week, and the nineteen biblical readings assigned to Lenten catechesis (which parallel the baptismal catecheses of Cyril of Jerusalem) all constituted independent *libelli* before being incorporated into this important fifth-century liturgical document.[22] Most pertinent to the question of a three-week Jerusalem Lent, however, are his analyses of the psalm series which concluded each of the Wednesday and Friday synaxes and of the nineteen catechetical readings themselves.

Lages claims that the psalm series accompanying the canon of readings at Zion on the Wednesday and Friday stations of the Armenian Lectionary's six-week Lent (excluding Holy Week) fall into two three-week groups as follows:[23]

	LENT I	LENT IV
Wednesday:	Ps.50	Ps.76
Friday:	Ps.40	Ps.82
	LENT II	LENT V
Wednesday:	Ps.56	Ps.83
Friday:	Ps.60	Ps.84
	LENT III	LENT VI
Wednesday:	Ps.64	Ps.85
Friday:	Ps.74	Ps.87

[21] M. F. Lages, "'Étapes de l'evolution de carême à Jérusalem avant le Ve sièle. Essai d'analyse structurale" in *Revue des Études Armeniénnes* 6 (1969) 67–102. See also Maxwell E. Johnson, "Reconciling Cyril and Egeria on the Catechetical Process in Fourth-Century Jerusalem" in Paul F. Bradshaw (ed.), *Essays in Early Eastern Initiation*, Alcuin/GROW Liturgical Study 8, Bramcote (Notts.) 1988, 24–6. For the Armenian Lectionary see A. Renoux, *Le Codex armenien Jérusalem 121*, II (Turnhout 1971).

[22] Lages, 72–81.

[23] Ibid., 81–2. See also Renoux, 239–55.

Noting, however, that weeks four, five, and six appear to indicate the debris of a once continuous psalmody from Pss. 82–87 and the Georgian Lectionary places Ps.56 on the Friday of the first week while retaining Ps.87 on the Friday of the sixth,[24] Lages seeks to reconstruct the "original" series in the following manner:[25]

	LENT I	LENT IV
Wednesday:	Ps.50	Ps.82
Friday:	Ps.56	Ps.83
	LENT II	LENT V
Wednesday:	Ps.64	Ps.84
Friday:	Ps.70	Ps.85
	LENT III	LENT VI
Wednesday:	Ps.74	Ps.86
Friday:	Ps.76	Ps.87

Furthermore, the fact that the Georgian Lectionary also assigns Ps.87 to Good Friday (where the Armenian Lectionary assigns Ps.22) suggests to him that this "original" series once belonged to an earlier three-week period of preparation before the further development of Holy Week itself.[26] Lages concludes, therefore, that the psalm series in the first three weeks of Lent developed only when the canon of Wednesday and Friday Lenten readings was established, but the psalm series in the last three weeks, given its structural continuity, represents a much earlier development and dates to an original three-week Lenten period.

Further evidence for this conclusion, he claims, is offered by the Armenian Lectionary's nineteen catechetical readings. According to him, these readings served as the basis for Cyril of Jerusalem's pre-baptismal catecheses and belong to the last three weeks of Lent. Yet, prior to the development of Holy Week they would

[24] See Michael Tarschnischvili, *Le grand lectionnaire de l'Église de Jérusalem*, I (Louvain 1959) 68–79.
[25] Lages, 82–3.
[26] Ibid., 98–9.

have concluded on Good Friday itself.[27] Lages bases this assumption on two pieces of evidence, namely, the introductory rubric in the Canon of Baptism of the ninth- or tenth-century Armenian liturgy and a reference to catechetical instruction in the Georgian Lectionary. The introductory Armenian baptismal rubric reads in part:

"The Canon of Baptism when they make a Christian. Before which it is not right to admit him into church. But he shall have hands laid on beforehand, *three weeks or more* before the baptism, in time sufficient for him to learn from the Wardapet [Instructor] both the faith and the baptism of the church."[28]

Because of the similarity in content (i.e., the Creed) between this rubric, the nineteen readings, and Cyril's catecheses, as well as the specification of a "three-week" instruction period, Lages asserts that this rubric is "primitive" and that pre-baptismal catechesis would have been originally given at Jerusalem during the three weeks before Easter baptism.[29] This three-week instruction period may also be indicated by a reference to catechetical training in the Georgian Lectionary. Unlike the Armenian Lectionary, which does not indicate the day on which the nineteen readings are to begin or conclude, a rubric in this lectionary indicates that on the Monday of the fifth week in Lent, that is, exactly *nineteen* days before Holy Saturday baptism, the instruction of catechumens is to begin (*Tertia hora incipiunt legere lectiones instruentes catechumenos ad portas ecclesiae*).[30]

---

[27] Ibid., 99–100.

[28] Whitaker, 60 [emphasis added].

[29] Lages, 100.

[30] Ibid., 98–100 and Tarschnischvili, 68. John Baldovin, in *The Urban Character of Christian Worship: The Origins, Development, and Meaning of Stational Liturgy*, Orientalia Christiana Analecta 228 (Rome 1987) 90–3, and in *Liturgy in Ancient Jerusalem*, Alcuin/GROW Liturgical Study 9 (Bramcote (Notts.) 1989), 13–14, has argued that the catechetical lectures indicated by the nineteen readings in the Armenian Lectionary were delivered *only* on non-stational days in Jerusalem. Hence, according to him, Egeria's description of daily catechetical instruction in both the Bible and the Creed during Lent is either incorrect or must be interpreted rather loosely as referring both to the special catechetical gatherings and to the stational liturgies themselves. Against Baldovin, I have

North Africa. On the basis of the sermons of Augustine and Quod-vultdeus of Carthage, I have suggested elsewhere that a three-week final preparation of catechumens prior to Easter baptism might be discernible in fourth-century North Africa as well.[31] In a sermon given on the occasion of the delivery of the Lord's Prayer,

---

argued elsewhere that Lages' hypothesis is extremely helpful in reconciling the apparent discrepancies between Cyril of Jerusalem's eighteen pre-baptismal lectures and Egeria's description of Lent. These eighteen lectures, parallelled by the designated readings in the Armenian Lectionary, can easily be assigned to every day (except Sundays) in the final three weeks of Lent prior to the beginning of Holy Week. Furthermore, if this is the case, then Egeria's statement about the Creed being delivered to the catechumens "after five weeks teaching" is easily squared with Cyril's delivery of the Creed in his fifth catechetical lecture. For, the third week prior to Holy Week in Egeria's eight-week Lenten schema is the fifth week of Lent (see Johnson, 24-9). A particular problem, however, is that in his fourteenth lecture Cyril refers to the narrative of the ascension which had been read and upon which he had commented during the previous Sunday liturgy. Since the Armenian Lectionary does not list the Lenten Sunday readings it becomes rather difficult to determine the particular Sunday to which he refers. In a recent essay ("A Lenten Sunday Lectionary in Fourth-Century Jerusalem?" in J. Neil Alexander [ed.], *Time and Community* [Washington D.C. 1990] 115-22). Baldovin suggests that Jerusalem may have adopted the Lenten lectionary of Constantinople, in which case the pericopes from Hebrews 4:14–5:6, 6:13-20, and 9:11-14, read respectively on the third, fourth, and fifth Sundays in Lent, may have provided for Cyril the necessary reference or allusion to the ascension. Though Baldovin admits that "it is easier to see a reference to the ascension in the reading from Hebrews assigned to the Fifth Sunday of Lent," he argues that the Sunday in question was the Fourth because: "if the four-teenth lecture followed the Fifth Sunday of Lent there would be too few days left before the beginning of Great Week. A lecture would have to be given every day of that week to conclude before Lazarus Saturday." His argument, thus, continues to stand or fall on his proposed schema of the catechetical lec-tures themselves. But, if, in fact, it *is* easier to see a reference to the ascension in the Hebrews reading assigned to the fifth Sunday, then my schema re-mains equally plausible. For, the Fifth Lenten Sunday in Constantinople and the Armenian Lectionary is the *sixth* Sunday in Egeria (i.e., the day before the seventh week of Lent) and it is to *this* Sunday where my schema assumes that the ascension reference was made and it is precisely for "daily cateche-sis" that I have argued.

[31] Johnson, 27, note 1.

Augustine refers to the return of the Creed which had just taken place. Therein he says not only that the Lord's Prayer would have to be returned in a week's time but that those who had not made a "good return of the Creed" still had time to learn it prior to its recitation at baptism itself.[32] Similarly, in a sermon on the Creed, Quodvultdeus of Carthage refers to what seems to have been an enrolment of catechumens on the previous night.[33] By joining these two together one might reasonably conjecture a three-week pattern of final baptism preparation: the *traditio symboli* in week one, its return and the delivery of the Lord's Prayer in week two, the return of the Lord's Prayer in week three, and the final profession of faith in the celebration of baptism.[34] Despite the fact that the scrutinies were on Saturdays in this tradition and that Rome delivered the Creed on a different day, one cannot but be struck by the fact that these three scrutinies offer a curious parallel to the scrutiny masses in the *Gelasianum*. Consequently, it appears quite possible that, whatever may have taken place in the first three weeks of Lent, it was the three weeks prior to Holy Week in North Africa that were singled out as a special time for catechumenal preparation.

Spain. The sources of the Mozarabic Liturgy also seem to point in a similar direction. In both the *Liber commicus*[35] and the *Liber Mozarabicus sacramentorum*[36] a distinction is made between the first three and last three weeks of Lent. While during the first three weeks of Lent week-day mass is celebrated only on Mondays,

---

[32] Sermon 58, in Whitaker, 103.

[33] "I am to explain to you the sacraments of the past night and of the present holy Creed . . . For you are not yet re-born in holy baptism, but by the sign of the cross you have been conceived in the womb of holy mother Church" (Whitaker, 107).

[34] In his hypothetical reconstruction of the North African lectionary in the time of Augustine, G. G. Willis comes to a similar conclusion. Yet, he omits any reference to Quodvultdeus of Carthage in this context. See G. G. Willis, *St. Augustine's Lectionary*, Alcuin Club Collection XLIV (London 1962) 63.

[35] F. J. Perez de Urbel and A. Gonzales y Ruiz-Zorilla, *Liber commicus, Edición crítica*, I, Monumenta Hispaniae sacra, Series liturgica, II (Madrid 1950).

[36] M. Ferotin (ed.), *Liber Mozarabicus sacramentorum*, Monumenta Ecclesiae liturgica 6 (Paris 1912).

Wednesdays, and Fridays, it is celebrated on every day except Thursdays in the final three weeks. Thus, the last three weeks have a different liturgical character and emphasis altogether, with readings and mass formulas assigned to each day. The reason for this shift and change of emphasis is undoubtedly due to the fact that it was on the Fourth Sunday in Lent (called either in vicessima[37] or in mediante die festo[38]) that the catechumens were enrolled for Easter baptism. "En este dia entre los españoles," note F. J. Perez de Urbel and A. Gonzales y Ruiz-Zorilla, "'los catecumenos daban sus nombres al sacerdote.'"[39] This they support by referring to the first canon of the Second Council of Braga (572) which directs that diocesan bishops:

". . . shall teach that catechumens (as the ancient canons command) shall come for the cleaning of exorcism twenty days before baptism, in which twenty days they shall especially be taught the Creed, which is: I believe in God the Father Almighty. . . ."[40]

The evidence for Spain, therefore, would seem strongly to indicate that the final three weeks of Lent, *including* Holy Week in these sources, have a tradition and history which may, in fact, antedate the formation of a later six-week Lenten period itself.

Naples. It was to the Neapolitan liturgical tradition that Chavasse appealed for evidence to confirm his argument that John 11:1-54 was originally read on the Friday before Holy Week. Not surprisingly, three weeks of final preparation for Easter baptism seem to be part of this tradition as well. In the Neapolitan evangeliaries studied by Morin it is to be noted that, while the first two Sundays are entitled simply, *Dominica I or II XLgisima paschae,* the three Sundays prior to Holy Week all receive special names obviously related to catechumenal preparation, namely: *Dominica tertia quando psalmi (salem) accipiunt, Dominica IIII quando orationem accipiant,* and *Dominica V quando symbulum accipiunt.*[41] Again, the close

---

[37] *Liber commicus,* 274.
[38] *Liber Mozarabicus sacramentorum,* 190.
[39] *Liber commicus,* 274, note 1. See also A. W. S. Porter, "Studies in the Mozarabic Office" in *Journal of Theological Studies* 35 (1934) 280–2.
[40] Whitaker, 227. See also *Liber commicus,* 274, note 1.
[41] Morin, "La liturgie de Naples," 530.

parallel to the scrutiny masses in the *Gelasianum* is striking. Morin himself, in fact, was so convinced that this referred to a three-week baptismal preparation period that, as early as 1891, he concluded that: "à Tolede, à Naples et à Rome il n'y avait que trois semaines entre l'inscription des competents et l'administration du baptême."[42]

Constantinople. It is again Talley who has drawn attention to the fact that in the *typica* of the ninth- and tenth-century Byzantine tradition there is a complete liturgy of initiation on Lazarus Saturday (the day before Palm Sunday) presided over by the patriarch in the little baptistery of Hagia Sophia. He has further noted that a vestige of this liturgy remains on Lazarus Saturday in the current Byzantine rite where the baptismal troparion (based on Galatians 3:27) is sung in place of the entrance chant.[43] What Talley does not note, however, is that the *first* reference to Lenten catechesis and baptismal preparation in the tenth-century typicon edited by Juan Mateos comes on the third Sunday in Lent. On that day an announcement was to be made stating that, because of the necessity of catechesis and examination before baptism, no one would be permitted to enter the catechumenate after this week.[44] Such an announcement certainly looks as though it means that in the Byzantine tradition final preparation for Easter baptism took place during the last three weeks of Lent before Holy Week. M. Arranz, in fact, has argued that, including Holy Week, there was only a four-week period possible for such instruction.[45] Yet, if one maintains the possibility of a baptismal liturgy on Lazarus Saturday, which Talley wants to argue is ancient, then the presence of this rubric on the Sunday which concludes the third week of Lent would leave precisely *three* rather than four weeks for final baptismal preparation.

[42] Ibid., 535. Actually, by adding Holy Week to this period, there would be four and not three weeks before Easter baptism.

[43] Talley, 188.

[44] Juan Mateos, *Le Typicon de la Grande Église*, II, *Le cycle des fêtes mobiles*, Orientalia Christiana Analecta 166 (Rome 1963) 38–9.

[45] M. Arranz, "Évolution des rites d'incorporation et de réadmission dans l'Église selon l'Euchologe byzantin," in *Gestes et paroles dans les diverses familles*

During the final weeks of Lent in the various liturgical sources of
Rome, Jerusalem, Armenia, North Africa, Spain, Naples, and Constantinople it appears that an earlier three-week period of final
preparation for baptism has left certain traces or debris. The fact
that some of these sources include "Holy Week" within that
three-week period, while others conclude this period before the
beginning of that week, might also serve to indicate that the tradition itself is older than the various adaptations made of it in these
liturgical traditions.

Talley has suggested that the three scrutiny masses of the
Gelasianum may reflect the final period of baptismal preparation in
the third century, a time when Easter was becoming the preferred
baptismal day in many places. However, granted that the indications of this three-week period in the various sources do occur
during the final portion of Lent, this period devoted to baptismal
preparation need *not* be understood only in relationship to Easter.
As Talley himself has shown on the basis of the Alexandrian tradition, there is not a necessary correlation between baptism and the
celebration of Easter. Baptism could and did occur at other times
of the year. In fact, while paschal baptism is referred to for the
West (at least for North Africa) as early as Tertullian in *De baptismo*
19, we simply do not know when it became the preferred day in
the East. And, on the basis of the early Armenian and Syrian traditions, Gabriele Winkler has argued that the dominant pre-Nicene
interpretation of baptism in the Christian East was that it was a
pneumatic ritual of rebirth related to Jesus' own baptism in the
Jordan and John 3 rather than a ritual of death and resurrection in
Christ along the lines of Romans 6. The latter interpretation makes
its full appearance in the East only in the fourth century with the
result that the baptismal rite itself becomes transformed.[46]

---

liturgigues (Rome 1978) 39. I am grateful to the Rev. Peter Galadza for directing
me to this reference.

[46] Gabriele Winkler, *Das Armenische Initationsrituale*, Orientalia Christiana
Analecta 217 (Rome 1982) passim., and idem., "The Original Meaning of the
Prebaptismal Anointing and its Implications" in *Worship* 52 (1978) 24-25.

Nevertheless, whenever baptism was celebrated and however it was interpreted, it is reasonable to assume that it was preceded by some kind of preparation period for the *competentes* or *photizomenoi*. Consequently, it is quite possible that the three-week period reflected in the Lenten materials of later liturgical sources was a very early "free-floating" baptismal preparation period without any *necessary* relationship to the liturgical year at all. Whenever baptism was administered it would have been preceded, as the rubric in the Armenian baptismal liturgy directs, by "three weeks or more" of instruction. And, at least at Jerusalem and Rome, specific biblical readings related to catechesis (e.g., the nineteen catechetical readings of the Armenian Lectionary and the course reading from John) may have been assigned to this period.

In his reconstruction of the Johannine lectionary cycle for Rome, Chavasse argued that the reason for the occurrence of John 11:1-54 on the second (fifth) Friday was because Holy Week (with its Passion readings on Sunday, Wednesday, and Friday) had developed prior to the formation of this three-week cycle. Such an assumption is certainly plausible in that, given the structure of the ancient Christian week and its focus on Sundays, Wednesdays, and Fridays, one might surely expect that this week above all would be organized and receive specific readings rather early in its development. Yet, the first reference to Holy Week at Rome is in the fifth century and we simply do not know what may have characterized the week before Easter prior to then.[47] Because of this, it is just as plausible to assume that the Johannine cycle existed either prior to or independent of the development of Holy Week itself as a series of baptismal preparation readings organized around John 4, 9, and 11. And, if this is the case, there need be no reason to assume that the Lazarus reading from John 11 originally fell on a Friday but, rather, it could have occurred on the third Sunday of this period. Such would certainly better explain the supposed shift of the Sunday readings back one week at that later period presumably indicated by the scrutiny masses in the *Gelasianum*. Furthermore, reference to Lazarus in the context of "Palm Sunday" is not unknown in other liturgical traditions. In the propers assigned to the *traditio*

[47] See Vogel, 309.

symboli mass on Palm Sunday in the Gallican sacramentaries, for example, the raising of Lazarus and the entry into Jerusalem are *both* the object of attention.[48] And, the fact that the early Alexandrian tradition, according to Talley, could conclude its post-Epiphany baptismal preparation period with reference to both a Lazarus-like narrative *and* Jesus' "Palm Sunday" entrance into Jerusalem underscores the fact that neither the raising of Lazarus nor Jesus' entry must necessarily be related to a "pre-paschal" period.[49]

I should like to suggest, therefore, that the three-week period of baptismal preparation indicated in the Lenten portions of various liturgical sources refers originally not to a pre-paschal Lent at all, but to an early and perhaps independent period of final baptismal preparation by itself. Such a hypothesis is admittedly conjectural and speculative but, if correct, would go a long way towards explaining how Lent itself may have developed. When Easter finally became the preferred time for baptism, this independent "free-floating" three-week period would have naturally become attached to it as the final period of catechetical instruction and preparation now in a pre-paschal context. Then, after Nicea, and under the influence of the Alexandrian forty-day post-Epiphany fast, Lent itself came to be created in various ways on the basis of this "core" resulting in the differing lengths calculated in the various traditions. For the East, however, it may be that the post-Nicene adoption of the forty-day Lent also coincided with the adoption of Easter itself as the preferred baptismal day. Yet, even if this is the case, a previously independent three-week period of final baptismal preparation could certainly have been integrated into this new pre-paschal period.

The development of Holy Week also seems to have played a significant role in this process, at least in two places. Contrary to Chavasse, either the further development of Holy Week itself with its Passion pericopes or the merging of this independent three-week cycle with an already established Holy Week could have eas-

---

[48] Cf. L. C. Mohlberg (ed.), *Missale gothicum* (Rome 1961) 53; idem., *Missale gallicanum vetus*, (Rome 1958) 25; and E. A. Lowe (ed.), *The Bobbio Missal,* Henry Bradshaw Society 58 (London 1920), 59.

[49] Talley, 194–214.

ily caused the backwards "shift" of the three Sunday readings while, nonetheless, maintaining a Johannine cycle on other days during the final three weeks at Rome. A similar shift may also be conjectured for Jerusalem. It is interesting to note that it is only in the second week of the Armenian Lectionary's seven-week Lenten period (including Holy Week) that readings and psalms are also provided for Monday, Tuesday, and Thursday stations at the Anastasis. According to Lages, such a peculiarity may indicate that this week was originally the first week of a six-week Lent.[50] When Holy Week developed as a separate week altogether in Jerusalem, the beginning of Lent was thereby shifted back one week in order to retain a six-week period of preparation.

CONCLUSION

Scholars have often concluded that Socrates was mistaken in his claim that the Roman church fasted for three weeks in preparation for Easter at any time in its history.[51] Yet, given the indications of a three-week period in various and unrelated liturgical sources, it may well be that Socrates points us to what was the earliest "core" of Lenten development not only at Rome but, with the notable exception of Egypt, in other traditions as well, a core originally based not on Easter but on final baptismal preparation. Around this baptismal core Lent developed only when Easter became the preferred baptismal day. And, if this is correct, then the forty days of Lent represent a synthesis of two traditions, both of which are baptismal in their origins and orientation: the forty-day Alexandrian post-Epiphany fast, and a three-week baptismal preparation period elsewhere. In its origins, therefore, "Lent" has nothing to do with Easter at all but everything to do with the final training of candidates for baptism.

---

[50] Lages, "Étapes," 102.
[51] Cf. G. G. Willis, "What is Mediana Week?" in Essays in Early Roman Liturgy, Alcuin Club Collections XLVI (London 1964) 101–4; C. Callewaert, "La semaine 'mediana' dans l'ancien Carême romain et les Quatre-Temps" in Sacris Erudiri: Fragmenta Liturgica (Steenbruge 1940) 561–89. Neither Willis nor Callewaert, however, deals with the baptismal scrutinies or the Johannine lectionary readings.

Paul F. Bradshaw

8. "Diem baptismo sollemniorem": Initiation and Easter in Christian Antiquity

Liturgical scholars have been unanimous in affirming that a preference for baptizing at Easter rather than at other times of the year was widespread — some would say universal — in the third-century Church.[1] But does the evidence really support such a conclusion? And did paschal baptism ever really become the normative feature of ancient Christianity that contemporary enthusiasts for liturgical reform would like it to have been?

PASCHAL BAPTISM BEFORE THE FOURTH CENTURY
It has frequently been assumed that the *Apostolic Tradition* attributed to Hippolytus offers evidence for paschal baptism at Rome in the early third century. Not only, however, is the authenticity of this document under question, and hence its reliability as a witness to early Roman liturgical customs,[2] but it is strangely reticent about a baptismal season. Apart from the statement that "catechumens shall hear the word for three years," no indication is given as to when the various stages of the catechumenate are to take place, and scarcely any more information is provided for the occa-

[1] See for example Robert Taft, "Historicism Revisited," *Studia Liturgica* 14 (1982) 101 = idem, *Beyond East and West* (Washington DC: Pastoral Press, 1984) 20; Thomas J. Talley, *The Origins of the Liturgical Year* (New York 1986) 36–37, 167; Geoffrey Wainwright, "The Baptismal Eucharist before Nicea," *Studia Liturgica* 4 (1965) 10.

[2] The most recent case against Hippolytean authorship is presented by Marcel Metzger, "Nouvelles perspectives pour la prétendue *Tradition Apostolique*," *Ecclesia Orans* 5 (1988) 241–259.

sion of the baptism itself: candidates are to bathe "on Thursday," fast "on Friday," and assemble "on Saturday" for a final exorcism by the bishop, before spending the whole night in vigil and being baptized at cockcrow.[3]

Such a description is of course consistent with baptism at Easter, but it does not require it. Moreover, since the paschal season is mentioned elsewhere in the document (ch. 33), there would seem no reason why it would not have been specified here as the occasion for baptism if that indeed was what was meant. It appears more likely, therefore, that Raniero Cantalamessa is correct in seeing it as referring to a vigil which was not peculiar to Easter but would have taken place whenever baptism was administered.[4]

One of the undisputed works attributed to Hippolytus, however, does refer to the practice of baptism at Easter. Commenting on Daniel 13.15 (= Daniel and Susanna 15: "And while they were watching for an opportune day, she went into the garden as usual with only her two maids; it was very hot, and she wished to bathe there"), Hippolytus says:

"What is 'an opportune day' but that of the Pasch? On that day the bath is prepared in the Garden for those who are burning and the Church, washed like Susanna, is presented to God as a pure bride; and faith and charity, like her two companions, prepare the oil and the unguents for those being washed. What are the unguents but the commandments of the Word? What is the oil but the power of the Holy Spirit, with which, like perfume, believers are anointed after the bath?"[5]

A similar preference for baptism at Easter also occurs in the writings of Tertullian:

"The Passover offers the day of most solemnity for baptism, when our Lord's passion, into which we are baptized, was completed. . . . After that, Pentecost is a most joyful time for conferring baptisms, when also the resurrection of the Lord was

[3] *Apostolic Tradition* 17, 20–21.
[4] *Ostern in der alten Kirche* (Bern 1981) 79, no. 48, n. 1.
[5] Gustave Bardy and Maurice Lefévre, *Hippolyte: Commentaire sur Daniel*, Sources chrétiennes 14 (Paris 1947) 100.

frequently made known to the disciples and the grace of the Holy Spirit first given and the hope of the coming of the Lord was indirectly revealed. . . . However, every day is the Lord's day: any hour, any season, is suitable for baptism. If there is a difference in solemnity, there is no difference in the grace."[6]

Scholars have been divided over whether "Pentecost" here means the whole fifty-day period or just the fiftieth day itself.[7] Whatever conclusion is reached on that question, however, it would seem most unlikely that Tertullian viewed it as an entirely separate occasion for initiation. For he goes on to say that baptism is preceded by a period of prayer, fasting, and vigils.[8] Such activities would have been inconsistent with the joyous character of the whole fifty-day post-Easter period, which Tertullian elsewhere states involved the complete cessation of fasting and kneeling.[9] Those who were baptized at "Pentecost," therefore, can surely only have been candidates who had made their preparation before Easter but who had been unable, for one reason or another, to receive baptism at the preferred season and so had to defer the completion of their initiation until this later date.

The most we can say, then, is that in Rome and North Africa a preference for baptism at Easter appears to have existed by the beginning of the third century, but that it was only a preference and baptisms could still be performed at other times of the year. But did this situation extend to the rest of the early Church, or was it merely a characteristic of these two regions which in liturgical matters seem in general to have been closely related?

One place where a preference for paschal baptism certainly appears to have been unknown before the middle of the fourth century is in the patriarchate of Alexandria. René-Georges Coquin and Thomas Talley have presented impressive evidence for believing that there existed in Egypt from early times a forty-day fast in commemoration of Jesus' fasting in the wilderness which did not take place immediately before Easter, but began on the day after

[6] De Baptismo 19.
[7] See Robert Cabié, La Pentecôte (Tournai 1965) 40–41.
[8] De Baptismo 20.1.
[9] De Corona 3.4; De Oratione 23.2.

January 6, observed by the Alexandrian church as the celebration of the baptism of Jesus, and thus was situated in the correct chronological sequence of the gospel accounts. Furthermore, this also seems to have functioned as the final period of preparation for baptism, with the rite itself being celebrated at the very end of the forty days, whenever that happened to fall.[10]

There are even signs that a similar practice may once have existed in northern Italy. In the fourth century Ambrose refers to the enrolment of catechumens for paschal baptism at Milan as taking place at Epiphany,[11] and the same day seems to have been chosen at nearby Turin: Maximus addresses two sermons preached on the days immediately after Epiphany to catechumens apparently preparing for baptism at Easter.[12] Since elsewhere at this time candidates were enrolled at the beginning of Lent, is the north Italian custom the vestigial remains of an older tradition of baptizing forty days after Epiphany?[13]

For the rest of the ancient world, there is no trace at all of Easter as the preferred baptismal season before the fourth century. Of course, arguments from silence are notoriously unreliable, but there is more here than just an argument from silence. As both E. C. Ratcliff and Gabriele Winkler have demonstrated, early Syrian Christianity understood baptism as being a *mimesis* of the baptism of Christ in the Jordan and made no reference to the idea contained in Romans 6:3-5, of Christians being baptized into the death and resurrection of Christ.[14] Winkler has also suggested that

[10] René-Georges Coquin, "Les origines de l'Épiphanie en Égypte," in Bernard Botte et al., *Noël, Épiphanie: retour du Christ,* Lex Orandi 40 (Paris 1967) 139-170; Talley, "The Origin of Lent at Alexandria," *Studia Patristica* 18 (1982), 594-612 = idem, *Worship: Reforming Tradition* (Washington D.C. 1990) 87-112; idem, *The Origins of the Liturgical Year* (New York 1986) 189-214. See also Paul F. Bradshaw, "Baptismal Practice in the Alexandrian Tradition: Eastern or Western?" in idem (ed.), *Essays in Early Eastern Initiation,* Alcuin/GROW Liturgical Study 8 (Nottingham 1988) 5-10.

[11] Ambrose, *In Expos. Ev. Luc.* 4.76.

[12] *Serm.* 13; 65.

[13] See Talley, *The Origins of the Liturgical Year,* 217.

[14] E. C. Ratcliff, "The Old Syrian Baptismal Tradition and its Resettlement under the Influence of Jerusalem in the Fourth Century," *Studies in Church History* 2 (1965) 28 = A. H. Couratin and David Tripp, eds., *E. C. Ratcliff.*

a similar interpretation of baptism may belong to the most ancient stratum of the Gallican rites.[15] Indeed, André Benoit long ago pointed out that nowhere in the patristic literature of the second century is there the slightest echo of the Pauline baptismal imagery.[16] Moreover, in the third century it only makes an appearance in literature from North Africa and Alexandria.[17] In such a theological climate, therefore, there simply would have been no reason to see baptism at Easter as particularly appropriate.

In an article entitled "Paschal Baptism" published in 1973,[18] Stuart Hall tried to present the most favourable case possible for an early date for the adoption of the paschal season for baptism, but even he was forced to admit how indefinite were the alleged allusions to paschal baptism in early sources, and some years later in his edition of the *Peri Pascha* of Melito of Sardis he concluded that the case for paschal baptism in the second century was an unproven supposition.[19] Raniero Cantalamessa, too, has expressed serious reservations about the suggestion that paschal baptism was practised among the Quartodecimans in the second century: the allusions to baptism in Quartodeciman sources dealing with the Pascha do not refer explicitly to the actual administration of baptism at that season, and so that practice should not automatically be assumed to underlie them.[20]

Liturgical Studies (London 1976), 142; Gabriele Winkler, "The Original Meaning of the Prebaptismal Anointing and its Implications," *Worship* 52 (1978) 36.

[15] Gabriele Winkler, "Confirmation or Chrismation? A Study in Comparative Liturgy," *Worship* 58 (1984) 2–16.

[16] *Le baptême chrétien au second siècle* (Paris 1953) 227.

[17] Tertullian expounds Romans 6 in his *De Resurrectione Carnis* 47 and may be alluding to it in the phrase "symbolum mortis" in *De Penitentia* 6. Clement of Alexandria, *Excerpta* 77, refers to death in connection with baptism, but not explicitly to Paul's imagery; Origen, however, makes frequent use of it: see for example *Contra Celsum* 2.69; *Com. in Ev. Joan.* 1.27; *Hom. in Jer.* 1.16; 19.14; *In Jesu Nave* 4.2.

[18] In E. A. Livingstone, ed., *Studia Evangelica* VI (Texte und Untersuchungen 112, Berlin 1973) 239–251.

[19] S. G. Hall (ed.), *Melito of Sardis: On Pascha and Fragments* (Oxford 1979) xxviii.

[20] *L'Omelia "In S. Pascha" dello pseudo-Ippolito di Roma* (Milan 1967) 285–287.

Testimony to a seemingly universal tradition of regarding Easter as the preferred occasion for baptism, therefore, emerges quite suddenly in the second half of the fourth century, much in the same way as does the evidence for the season of Lent a little earlier in the same century. Of the latter, Talley has commented: "Prior to Nicea, no record exists of such a forty-day fast before Easter. Only a few years after the council, however, we encounter it in most of the Church as either a well-established custom or one that has become so nearly universal as to impinge on those churches that have not yet adopted it."[21] He inclines towards the conclusion that "the establishment of the principal fast prior to Pascha is a reflection of the ever-growing custom of conferring baptism at that principal festival."[22]

Talley appears to be right in suggesting that there is some link between the emergence of these two liturgical phenomena — paschal baptism and the season of Lent — but is the relationship in fact somewhat different than he surmises? Could it be that both alike are results of post-Nicene attempts to bring the divergent customs of different churches into some conformity? Alexandria (and perhaps other places) already knew of a pre-baptismal fast of forty days, but not connected to Easter; in Rome and North Africa there was a tradition which regarded Easter as the preferred occasion for baptism, but preceded only by a shorter fast, of perhaps three weeks' duration; and other churches were familiar with the same three-week preparation[23] but did not associate baptism with any particular period of the year. The arrangement which then became universal in the fourth century, of a preference for baptism at Easter preceded by forty-day season of fasting and preparation, would thus have been a post-Nicene amalgamation of these variant practices.

Nevertheless, even after the emergence of paschal baptism in the fourth century, we need to note some significant differences in

[21] *Origins of the Liturgical Year*, 168.
[22] Ibid., 217.
[23] For the length of the baptismal preparation, see Maxwell Johnson, "From Three Weeks to Forty Days: Baptismal Preparation and the Origins of Lent," *Studia Liturgica* 20 (1990) 185–200.

its status in different parts of the ancient world. In northern Italy, for example, it was apparently intended to be the one and only occasion in the year for the conferral of the sacrament. Ambrose, bishop of Milan, reminded his hearers that in the Old Testament the high priest entered the inner sanctuary of the Temple only once a year. "What is the purpose of this? To enable you to understand what this inner sanctuary is, into which the high priest led you, where the custom is for him to enter *once a year*: it is the baptistery. . . ."[24]

Some confirmation of the exclusive character of paschal baptism in this region is provided by Maximus at Turin in the early fifth century. In a sermon preached on the feast of Pentecost he drew attention to the similarities between that feast and Easter, noting that both occasions were preceded by a Saturday fast and a vigil of prayer through the night,[25] but made no mention of the celebration of baptism as being common to both; and in another Pentecostal sermon he took up the same theme and remarked that "at Easter all the pagans are usually baptized, while at Pentecost the apostles were baptized [with the Holy Spirit]."[26] It seems impossible to imagine, therefore, that Maximus can have been familiar with the practice of baptism at Pentecost and failed to refer to it here. Similarly, for both Ambrose and Maximus, a major theme of the feast of the Epiphany was the baptism of Christ, and yet neither ever alludes to a custom of baptizing converts at this season.[27]

At Rome, on the other hand, according to a letter of Pope Siricius to Himerius of Tarragon written in 385, both Easter and Pentecost were the regular seasons for baptism. Siricius acknowl-

[24] *De Sacramentis* 4.1-2 (emphasis added).

[25] *Serm.* 40.1.

[26] *Serm.* 44.4. In this sermon, however, he seems to contradict what he says in *Serm.* 40 about fasting on the Saturday before the feast of Pentecost by affirming that there was an unbroken period of fifty days during which no fasting took place. See Cabié, *La Pentecôte*, 141–142.

[27] See Hieronymus Frank, "Die Vorrangstellung der Taufe Jesu in der alt-mailändischen Epiphanieliturgie und der Frage nach dem Dichter des Epiphaniehymnus Illuminans Altissimus," *Archiv für Liturgiewissenschaft* 13 (1971) 115–132.

edged that his fellow-bishops elsewhere (probably in northern Spain where the letter is directed) permitted the administration of baptism at Christmas, Epiphany, and on the feasts of apostles and martyrs. But "with us and with all the churches"(!) these two feasts were the only days in the year for the regular celebration of the sacrament.[28] Pope Leo in 447 similarly wrote to the bishops of Sicily expressing astonishment that baptism could be celebrated at Epiphany, contrary to the tradition of the Apostles: because of its connection with the resurrection, baptism belonged to Easter and also to the feast of Pentecost, which commemorated the coming of the Holy Spirit and was linked to the paschal festival. Moreover, did not St Peter baptize 3000 people on the day of Pentecost? And because, according to the apostolic rule, baptism should be preceded by exorcism, fasting, and frequent instruction, only these two occasions should be kept.[29] Leo's sermons, however, make it clear that regular fasting was not resumed at Rome until the feast of Pentecost was over,[30] which suggests that the preparation of candidates for baptism at Pentecost must have taken place during Lent together with that of the candidates for paschal baptism. In other words, Pentecost was still really only an "overflow" from Easter and not a baptismal season in its own right.

Nevertheless, we need to treat the Roman evidence for the normative character of baptism at Easter and Pentecost with some caution. The letters of Siricius and Leo both reveal that in other parts of the West Epiphany and other festivals were regarded as regular occasions for the conferral of the sacrament; and in a further letter written in 459 Leo also referred to certain bishops from central Italy who celebrated baptism on the feasts of the martyrs.[31] Augustine knew Easter and Pentecost as regular baptismal seasons, but also acknowledged the existence of baptismal celebrations at other times in the year.[32] Thus, the alleged "apostolic

---

[28] *Ep. ad Himerium* (PL 13.1154-1155). Cabié, *La Pentecôte*, 120, argues that Pentecost is to be understood here as referring to the fiftieth day alone and not to the whole Easter season.

[29] *Ep.* 16 (PL 54.699-702).

[30] See *De Pentecoste* II.9 (PL 54.411); *Serm.* LXXVIII-LXXXI (PL 54.415-422).

[31] *Ep.* 168 (PL 54.1209-1211).

[32] *Serm.* 210.2. For baptism at Pentecost see *Serm.* 266, 272 (PL 38.1225-1229,

tradition" did not apparently extend beyond Rome and northern Italy, and even at Rome itself it was certainly not absolute. For in the very same letter to Himerius, Siricius admits that infants and those in danger of dying are not to wait until one of the two occasions but should be baptized with all haste; and Innocent I at the end of the fourth century claimed that not a day passed at Rome on which "the divine sacrifice or the office of baptism" did not take place.[33] Even after making allowance for some degree of exaggeration in this remark, it would seem that, whatever the theory, in actual reality the celebration of baptism must have been a fairly frequent occurrence in that city and by no means merely a single annual event.

We can also document similar traditions in the East to those in the West condemned by Siricius and his successors. Gregory of Nazianzus in a sermon preached in 381 rejects excuses made by catechumens that they want to wait for Epiphany, Easter, or Pentecost to be baptized because it is better to be baptized close to the baptism of Christ, to receive the new life on the day of the resurrection of Christ, or to honour the manifestation of the Spirit. Gregory himself recommends them not to delay their baptism, and thereby avoid the risk of dying unbaptized.[34] This passage reveals that not only was Epiphany an established occasion for baptism in Cappadocia along with Easter and Pentecost, but that there was here no limitation on baptism at any time in the year. On the other hand, we must note that John Chrysostom twenty years later (c. 400/401) was opposed to Pentecost being a baptismal season at Constantinople.[35] Because he is forced to argue the case, however, this may mean that this restriction is a relatively recent innovation, as Robert Cabié has suggested,[36] or at least an attempt to stop a widespread custom from being adopted in that city.

Finally, we should note that baptism at the paschal season did not everywhere mean baptism within the Easter vigil itself. In-

---

1246); Cabié, *La Pentecôte*, 206. Ambrosiaster (*In Eph.* 4: PL 17.888) also refers to baptism at other times of the year.

[33] *Ep. ad Victricium* 9 (PL 20.476).

[34] *Oratio XL, In Sanctum Baptisma* 24 (PG 36.392).

[35] *In Acta Apostolorum Hom.* 1.6 (PG 60.22).

[36] *La Pentecôte*, 202–203.

deed, Cantalamessa has warned against assuming that Tertullian was necessarily referring to the vigil when he spoke of baptism at the Passover.[37] Moreover, when sometime in the middle of the fourth century Alexandria finally transferred its older post-Epiphany forty-day fast culminating in the celebration of baptism to a location immediately before Easter, it apparently did not incorporate the baptismal rite within the paschal vigil. Although witnesses to the Alexandrian tradition are rather limited and not entirely reliable, it seems that the baptisms may have taken place at first on the Saturday morning before Easter, and later, when a further week was prefixed to the Lenten season, were moved back to the end of the previous week, so that they still came at the conclusion of forty days.[38]

Something similar may once have been the case at Constantinople. The typika of the ninth and tenth centuries there include provision for a full baptismal liturgy both on the morning of Lazarus Saturday (one week before Easter and at the end of the forty-day Lenten season) and also at the paschal vigil itself. Furthermore, one tenth-century typikon, *Hagios Stavros 40,* adds a rubric directing the patriarch to perform the baptisms after the morning office on Holy Saturday. Juan Mateos suggested that the two Saturday morning celebrations were introduced in order to reduce the numbers to be baptized at the vigil itself. Such an expedient was never found necessary in any other major city in Christian antiquity, however, and Talley thought it more probable that the Holy Saturday morning celebration had been added as a more convenient occasion for the baptism of infants, with the other two older celebrations being thereafter retained in the liturgical books but rarely, if at all, being found in practice.[39]

Even if Talley is correct, that still leaves the question as to which of the other two occasions — Lazarus Saturday morning and the paschal vigil — was the older of the two, since it seems improb-

---

[37] *L'Omelia "In S. Pascha"* dello pseudo-Ippolito di Roma, 283–284; see also Talley, *Origins of the Liturgical Year,* 35.

[38] See Bradshaw, "Baptismal Practice in the Alexandrian Tradition: Eastern or Western?" 8–9.

[39] *Origins of the Liturgical Year,* 188–189.

able that both can claim equal antiquity at Constantinople. It is difficult to imagine that if the custom of baptizing at the vigil already become firmly established there, it would then have been possible to introduce a second baptismal occasion one week earlier. But the reverse possibility does seem more plausible: that the custom of baptizing on Lazarus Saturday morning at the conclusion of the forty-day Lent was introduced first, in imitation of Alexandrian practice, but that later it was necessary to add the celebration of baptism at the Easter vigil in order to bring the Constantinopolitan church into line with liturgical practice elsewhere. It is interesting to note that the last day on which candidates for baptism at the paschal season were permitted to enroll in the catechumenate at Constantinople was exactly three weeks before Lazarus Saturday — precisely the length of time which Maxwell Johnson has argued was the original length of the final preparation for baptism in many parts of the primitive Church.[40]

CONCLUSION

Prior to the middle of the fourth century preference for paschal baptism seems to have been merely a local custom of the Roman and North African churches, and long before the fourth century drew to a close there is clear evidence that in many parts of the ancient world other festivals in the liturgical year were challenging the exclusive claims of the paschal season — and indeed may always have done so — to say nothing of signs of the continuing acceptance of the legitimacy of baptisms at any time of the year. Whatever the *theory* may have been in some places, therefore, it looks as though baptism at Easter was never the normative *practice* in Christian antiquity that many have assumed. The most that can be said is that it was an experiment that survived for less than fifty years. Like the seed sown on rocky ground, it endured for a while but eventually withered away.

---

[40] See Johnson, "From Three Weeks to Forty Days," esp. 193.

Aidan Kavanagh

9. Confirmation:
A Suggestion from Structure

The tenor of modern work on confirmation has been to regard this rite as a part of baptism and to restore it to the baptismal synaxis. Confirmation as a synaxis in its own right, apart from baptism preceding it and eucharist coming after it, has been characterized as a degeneration in the unitary ensemble of the sacraments of Christian initiation in the Roman rite. It is as though confirmation represents a long-term misunderstanding of baptism, reduplicating baptismal chrismation and denigrating baptism itself by implying that confirmation adds to, completes, or otherwise develops realities begun but not finished in baptism itself.

It should be noted that these arguments and attitudes arise almost entirely from the area of interpretation. But what if confirmation, which is unique to the initiation procedure of the Church of Rome and its derivatives, is in fact a synaxis in its own right with its own archaic structural integrity distinct if not wholly separable from baptism and eucharist? And what if confirmation's undeniable relationship to baptism is *primarily structural* and only secondarily theological at base?

It cannot be ruled out that failing to attend carefully to the structure of confirmation as it is found *in situ* following straightaway on baptism-chrismation, and to the structural precedents of such an act, may be confusing the way in which confirmation is perceived and interpreted. For example, placing high emphasis on confirmation's anointing may be making some Eastern data on a single postbaptismal chrismation seem the universal norm, and the second Roman postbaptismal anointing in confirmation seem hypertrophaic and unnecessary. Similarly, placing high emphasis on confirmation's invocation of the Holy Spirit upon the newly baptized may be making baptism itself seem pneumatically incomplete, and may give rise to the notion that confirmation either "completes" baptism's unfinished business or supplies (*ad robur*) other means for the baptized to live their Christian lives on other levels at a later time. This latter emphasis is what seems to serve as one reason for denying the eucharist to the newly baptized who are infants: like the Samaritans (Acts 8:1-17), they have not yet received the Holy Spirit. The implications of this interpretation for the integrity of baptism cannot go unnoticed.

The suggestion made here is that such interpretations signal a weakness in our grasp of what confirmation's synaxis structure really is. We submit that the structural evidence points to what we today call confirmation being in fact the dismissal or *missa* terminating the baptismal synaxis itself.[1] This means that Roman consignation or confirmation is nothing more nor less than a surviving, and probably quite archaic, *missa* of baptism, and that baptism is complete with the washing in water and a chrismation which is *christic* in nature and intent. I am not aware of any historic Christian baptismal rite other than that of Italy and North Africa which had or has such a baptismal *missa*. One must look therefore to rites other than those of initiation for illustrative examples.

The Missa of the Jerusalem Office. At the end of the fourth century, Egeria notes that all regular assemblies for prayer in Jerusalem ended with formal dismissals. So elaborate did these become that they took on the character of a synaxis in their own right, even to the point that Egeria uses the term *missa* to refer to the whole prayer service — a terminological usage which will later be extended in the West to refer also to the eucharist.[2] More notably the *missa* is a *leitourgia* proper to the bishop. Even when he is not actually present for the psalms and antiphons of the office, he

[1] This possibility was suggested to me by my student, Mr David Hall. Its accuracy is his, its possible defects mine.

[2] See John Wilkinson, *Egeria's Travels* (London 1971; rev. ed. Jerusalem, Ariel and Warminster 1981) 57-58.

is sent for in order to preside at the *missa*.[3] This is done more elaborately at evening prayer than at morning and midday, but in all three instances the basic structure is the same:

1 A call to pray with bowed head: done by a deacon.

2 A petitionary prayer, called a "blessing," for those dismissed: done by the bishop.

3 All then "come to his hand."[4]

The same procedure is employed to dismiss both catechumens and faithful from prayer services.

The Eucharistic Missa of Apostolic Constitutions. Book 8 of the late fourth century *Apostolic Constitutions,* from around Antioch in West Syria, contains no less elaborate dismissals for four categories of Christians at the end of the eucharistic word service. Catechumens, those possessed of "unclean spirits," the elect, and penitents are dismissed in order according to the following procedure:

1 A call to prayer with bowed head or prostration, a litany, and a call to arise and receive a "blessing": done by a deacon as his "ministry for them."

2 A petitionary prayer, called a "blessing," for the group being dismissed: done by the bishop.

3 In some mss, later titles call this "blessing" of the bishop a "laying on of hands."

That these dismissals end, as in Egeria, with some sort of coming to the bishop's hand is further suggested by Canon 19 of the contemporary Council of Laodicea: "After the homily of the bishop, the prayer of the catechumens should be made, *and when these have had hands laid on them,* and have gone out, there should be three prayers of the faithful. . . ."[5]

The Catechumenal Missa of Apostolic Tradition. In addition to office and eucharist dismissals, Hippolytus' *Apostolic Tradition* in the

[3] This is definite practice at midday and evening prayer. It may be implied also for morning prayer. See Egeria, 24:2-7 in Wilkinson, 123–124.

[4] "Presumably to kiss it," says Wilkinson, 57. That the bishop may also have laid his hand upon them and signed their foreheads with his thumb cannot be ruled out, as one sees even today in parts of Germany.

[5] See *A Select Library of Nicene and Post-Nicene Fathers,* ed. P. Schaff and H. Wace (1899; rpt Grand Rapids n.d.), vol. 15, 136.

early third century says that each time the catechist finishes an instruction "the catechumens pray by themselves apart from the faithful" (18:1). Then, "after the prayer let the teacher lay hands on them and pray and dismiss them. Whether the teacher be an ecclesiastic or a layman let him do the same" (19:1).[6] The previous *missa* pattern is reproduced here in its earliest manifestation:

1 Prayer by the group.

2 Prayer, certainly of a petitionary type, done by the catechist who has presided at the instruction.

3 Handlaying during or after the catechist's prayer.[7]

Leaving aside oblique references in other sorts of literature to *missa* components, these examples from early liturgical texts themselves may allow us to appreciate something of the form and function of a liturgical structure which has receded in importance and declined in use in subsequent centuries. They may also help us understand why in the West the eucharist came to be called *missa* — not in view of its final blessing and diaconal dismissal, but because of the extensive dismissals of catechumens, penitents, and perhaps others which took place at the end of the word service and required a significant amount of time.[8]

With these things in mind, one turns now to Hippolytus' *Apostolic Tradition* 22:1-4, where what would become Roman consignation, and later confirmation, can be seen for the first time.[9] After the candidates have been first anointed with the oil of exorcism, baptized in water, anointed with the oil of thanksgiving by a presbyter with the words "I anoint thee with holy oil in the

---

[6] Gregory Dix, *The Treatise on the Apostolic Tradition of St Hippolytus of Rome*, 2nd ed., rev. Henry Chadwick (London 1968) 29-30.

[7] The development of this catechumenal practice of prayer with handlaying (although not as dismissals) may be seen in the baptismal *Ordo Romanus XI* (8th-9th century, representing older practice). In the election rite of the first scrutiny on the third Sunday of Lent alone, there are no less than *eight* handlayings with prayers proper to each, only two of which are done by a presbyter, the others by "acolytes." See M. Andrieu, *Les Ordines Romani du Haut Moyen Age*, Spicilegium Sacrum Lovaniense (Louvain 1948), vol. 2, 417-425.

[8] A vestige of these may be seen in *Ordo Romanus XI*; see Andrieu, 425.

[9] See Dix, 38-39.

Name of Jesus Christ," and dressed, Hippolytus says ". . . let them be together in the *ecclesia*." The Latin suggests, by *in ecclesia ingrediantur*, that the newly baptized are now prepared to stand as equals in the assembly of the baptized. But *before* they do so, or perhaps *as* they do so, the bishop, who until now seems to have done nothing more in the baptismal liturgy than bless the oils at the beginning of the service, performs his special *leitourgia* for the baptized. This episcopal *leitourgia* takes the form of a *missa* such as we have seen in the Jerusalem office, in the eucharist of *Apostolic Constitutions*, and in the catechumenate of this same document where it was done by the catechist. The *missa* in this instance is *from* baptism *into* full fellowship in the baptized assembly, a fellowship shortly to be consummated in the celebration of the *oblatio*, as Hippolytus calls the eucharist. The form this unique solemn *missa* takes is as follows:

1 Prayer of petition for the Holy Spirit along with handlaying: done by the bishop.

2 All come to his hand and are anointed in the name of the Trinity, signed on the forehead, exchange for the first time the kiss forbidden to catechumens (18:3), and are greeted as Christians with "The Lord be with you."

With this, the *missa* of baptism ends. The eucharistic synaxis then begins with the neophytes and the already baptized joining together in the prayers of the faithful concluding with the kiss of peace (22:5-6).

It will be noted that the *missa* sustains its own structural integrity despite the proximity to it of baptism-chrismation before and the eucharist after: it anoints again after baptism-chrismation and it exchanges the kiss between bishop and neophyte despite the kiss of peace ending the prayers of the faithful which follow.[10] This suggests that the *missa* recounted in *Apostolic Tradition* is being governed in its structure by principles which are proper to it rather than to the two initiatory mysteries which bracket it. These principles seem to be those which are later enunciated for dismis-

[10] The *missa* kiss, perhaps significantly, is not called "the kiss of peace" in all mss, nor is the oil used in the *missa* anointing called "the oil of thanksgiving" in all mss. See Dix, 39.

sals by Laodicea and exemplified in the dismissal structure of the Jerusalem office, the eucharist of *Apostolic Constitutions,* and indeed in the catechumenal dismissal mentioned in *Apostolic Tradition* itself. If our suggestion is correct, then several results seem to follow. First, as a *missa,* Roman consignation-confirmation has a claim to being a synaxis with its own internal logic and integrity, structurally distinct from baptism while remaining related to it and to the eucharist as well. Its structural distinctness from eucharist is signaled by the kiss between bishop and neophyte being *repeated* after the "prayers" in *Apostolic Tradition* 22:6: "And after the prayers let them give the kiss of peace." Similarly, confirmation's structural distinctness from baptism is signaled by the presbyteral anointing with chrism being *repeated,* this time by the bishop, as the neophytes "come to his hand" at the end of the baptismal *missa.* Both kiss and anointing make liturgical sense only if consignation-confirmation is aboriginally a synaxis having its own distinct structure and internal logic.

Second, the structural distinctness of consignation-confirmation as a *missa* synaxis might help to account for the tenacity with which it retains its character as a service distinguishable from baptism-chrismation and associated fundamentally with the bishop's *leitourgia* in the Roman rite. In *Ordo Romanus XI* consignation is done not at the font but in another place, namely, at the bishop's chair placed elsewhere in the *ecclesia fontis* or in another hall. Here the neophytes are vested, prayed over, come to the bishop's hand and are anointed with chrism a second time. From here they enter the church (*ingrediuntur ad missas*) to a litany followed by the Gloria of the Easter eucharist.[11] It is this tenacious structural distinctiveness and association with the bishop which contributed to the perception of medieval interpreters that confirmation could and should be explained beyond baptism and apart from it. While we today are justified in thinking that these interpreters went *theologically* too far in separating confirmation from baptism, it should perhaps be said that their *liturgical* perception of Roman consignation-confirmation may not have been far off the mark. They at least realized that consignation-confirmation, whatever

[11] See Andrieu, 446

else it might be, was not merely the postbaptismal chrismation solemnized out of all proportion by bishops so as to be repeated yet again to the confusion of baptism.

Third, the structural distinctness of consignation-confirmation as a *missa* synaxis may help to clarify the priorities one should assign to its various parts. The *missa* is an episcopal *leitourgia*, whether the baptismal synaxis was or not, just as the office *missa* was in Egeria and as the eucharistic *missa* was in *Apostolic Constitutions*.[12] The liturgical structure of consignation-confirmation from *Apostolic Tradition* to the present is a *missa* like others:

1 A petitionary prayer "blessing" said by the bishop.
2 A "coming to his hand" by those he has blessed.

In consignation-confirmation the "blessing" of petitionary prayer is an epiclesis for the Holy Spirit upon the baptized. This ends baptism rather as a similar form of prayer over the water began baptism. The "coming to his hand" is accomplished in this very solemn instance more solemnly than was usual in other *missae:* a handlaying together with anointing with baptismal chrism being traced on the forehead, perhaps with the thumb of the hand as it lies on the head, and ending with a kiss and greeting. The *missa* of baptism being thus accomplished, the eucharist begins directly with the prayers of the faithful as in *Apostolic Tradition,* or with the Gloria of Easter as in *Ordo Romanus XI* (by which time the prayers of the faithful had disappeared and the kiss of peace had moved to after the Our Father).

This suggests that the anointing with chrism in consignation-confirmation is an element in the *missa* synaxis which should not be regarded as more than secondary in the structure. It may well be that this anointing is included here, when all come to the

---

[12] The statement of J.D.C. Fisher in *Confirmation Then and Now* (London 1978) 126, that confirmational rites were associated with the bishop precisely because those rites had to do with bestowing Holy Spirit, is typical of interpretative-theological attempts to explain things without recourse to structure and its precedents. In our view confirmation is associated with bishops due to the special association of the *missa* with episcopal *leitourgia*. This continued in the Roman and other liturgies of the eucharist when the bishop gave the *missa* blessing even when he did not preside.

bishop's hand, for reasons similar to those which prompt the addition of a cup of milk and honey and a cup of water to the first communion of the neophytes in *Apostolic Tradition* 23:2-3.[13] The cup of milk and honey is said to be "in fulfillment of the promise," the cup of water "a sign of the washing." In view of this it seems possible that consignation-confirmation's anointing with baptismal chrism may have been a similar "fulfillment" or "sign" of the chrismation in baptism, which was messianic and christic: "I anoint thee with holy oil in the name of Jesus Christ" (i.e., the Anointed One). The *missa* anointing would have functioned as a reminder of this in context of petitioning for the Holy Spirit whom the Father sends so that the neophytes may serve him according to his divine will as did Jesus the Anointed One.[14]

In this view the recent Roman reform, which omits the baptismal chrismation when confirmation follows immediately,[15] has the effect of removing precisely that which the anointing in confirmation looks back to as fulfillment and sign. Such a thing would be analogous to Hippolytus attempting to simplify and enhance the significance of the cup of milk mixed with honey and the cup of water at the neophytes' first communion by suppressing baptism. Anomalously, the attempt of the Roman reform to restore confirmation to baptism according to the serious theological reasons mentioned in the Rite of Christian Initiation of Adults, 34[16] knocks out the postbaptismal chrismation with its christic-messianic symbolism and transmutes it into pneumatic symbolism, thus obscuring rather than enhancing "the close relationship (= *necessitudo*) between the mission of the Son and the pouring out of the Holy

[13] Dix, 40-41. Significantly, in contemporary North Africa Tertullian knows the baptismal *missa without* an anointing: "Dehinc manus imponitur per benedictionem advocans et invitans Spiritum" (*De Baptismo* 8). In *De Corona* 3 Tertullian mentions a cup of milk and honey.

[14] As I have noted in *The Shape of Baptism* (New York 1978) 66, this epiclesis prayer in *Apostolic Tradition* is the basis of that larger prayer in the *Gelasian Sacramentary*, which continues in Roman use today. See the Rite of Confirmation, 25, in *The Rites of the Catholic Church*, vol. 1, 2nd ed. (New York 1983) 329.

[15] See the Rite of Christian Initiation of Adults, 35, in *The Rites of the Catholic Church*, 30.

[16] Ibid.

Spirit."[17] Furthermore, while most other historic Christian baptismal rites have a postbaptismal chrismation which appears to have been originally christic-messianic (as the Roman chrismation, when it is used, continues to be),[18] the reformed Roman rite appears to be putting in its place something peculiar to itself, confirmation. The current situation is thus filled with paradox.

CONCLUSIONS

If there is a lesson to be learned in all this it may be that the felt need to "do something" about confirmation invariably complicates the problem further when doing something is undertaken without first establishing *what* it is that is being dealt with.

Our suggestion is that consignation-confirmation, something unique and peculiar to the Roman out of all other rites, seems to be, in terms of structural analysis, the distinct yet inseparable *missa* synaxis which consummates baptism-chrismation on the one hand and sends the neophytes directly into eucharist on the other. As the *missa* of baptism-chrismation, confirmation may be said to "complete" baptism in the same sense that the *missa* of the eucharist may be said to "complete" the eucharist. Neither *missa*, however, adds anything to either liturgy that each does not already possess except its apolysis or ending. To say, therefore, that confirmation "completes" baptism is to say something structural rather than theological. This means that later attempts to explain confirmation as adding something to baptism which baptism itself does not accomplish, whatever else may be said about such attempts, have no basis in the original structure of confirmation itself or in the history of the rite's development. We suggest that all

---

[17] Ibid.

[18] See the Rite of Christian Initiation of Adults, 224, in *The Rites*, 101; the Rite of Baptism for Children, 62, in *The Rites*, 208–209. For a historical example from third century North Africa see Tertullian's *De Baptismo* 3; from fourth century Jerusalem see Cyril's *Mystagogical Catechesis* 3:1-5, where the postbaptismal chrismation is called "the emblem of that wherewith Christ was anointed; and this is the Holy Spirit." This motif reaches its clearest expression in the Barberini ms of Byzantine usage, where the postbaptismal chrismation, which is *not* confirmation, is said to be "the seal of the gift of the Holy Spirit."

confirmation ever was or really has been is episcopal prayer over neophytes and their coming to the bishop's hand, where they are reminded solemnly of their chrismation by a second anointing and dismissed into their first eucharist.

If this be true, then it counsels that making too much out of confirmation either theologically or educationally may well be what continues to fuel our current anomalies, paradoxes, and dilemmas over this rather modest rite. As in other matters, questions and answers as to *why* and *how* become inextricably tangled and begin to swell when they are not constantly related to *what* the matter at hand really consists in. If *what* confirmation is, in its own integrity, is the solemn episcopal *missa* of baptism-chrismation, then *when* it is administered is revealed to be not a catechetical or educational issue but a baptismal one;[19] *how* it prepares for Christian life is a baptismal question which has only a eucharistic answer;[20] *why* it exists at all is a baptismal matter whose explanation seems to lie, at least in part, in baptismal chrismation and its christic implications for pneumatic prayer not only in confirmation but in the eucharist as well. As the eucharistic prayer of Hippolytus says after its anamnesis and oblation: "And we pray Thee that Thou wouldest send Thy Holy Spirit upon the oblation of Thy Holy Church (and that) Thou wouldest grant to all who partake to be united that they may be fulfilled with the Holy Spirit for the confirmation of faith in truth."[21]

Finally, if our suggestion is correct it has the advantage of helping to pinpoint the spot at which both structural and interpretative anomalies concerning confirmation begin to occur. This neuralgic

---

[19] Being the *missa* of baptism, if our suggestion is correct, confirmation should never be separated from baptism any more than the eucharistic *missa* should be separated from Mass, even if this means that confirmation must be done by a baptizing presbyter in the bishop's absence — a stance already taken for adults and children of catechetical age by the Rite of Christian Initiation of Adults, 46, in *The Rites,* 34.

[20] The *missa* of confirmation dismisses neophytes of whatever age *from* baptism *into* eucharist. When confirmation is separated from these two mysteries its character and function *as missa* is destroyed and anomalies in practice and interpretation then adversely affect the whole of sacramental initiation.

[21] *Apostolic Tradition* 4:12 (Dix, 9).

point seems to be twofold: the separation of the *missa* from baptism and, then, the separation of eucharist from the same *missa*. When the first happens, confirmation's epiclesis makes baptism seem pneumatically incomplete at the same time that it makes confirmation's anointing seem reduplicative or baptism's chrismation unnecessary. When the eucharist is separated from the *missa*, the latter's immediate purpose, which is to dismiss neophytes into the assembly's *oblatio* as certified Christians whose *baptism* has been publicly "confirmed," is frustrated. Confirmation is left as a floating *missa* from nothing, into nothing — its historic structure, integrity, and purpose no longer detectable even by trained eyes and minds.

Joseph L. Levesque

10. The Theology of the Postbaptismal Rites in the Seventh and Eighth Century Gallican Church

Many people today say that they have a problem with the Sacrament of Confirmation. They will ask questions such as: what does it mean, how do you celebrate it, at what age should it be received, and they ask these questions not necessarily in that, but a reverse order of importance.

In reading the historical development of the Sacrament of Confirmation one finds something similar to the contemporary problem. In a book such as J. D. C. Fisher's *Baptism in the Medieval West*,[1] one discovers many unsolved questions in the historical development of Christian Initiation in the West, just one of those being the nature of the Gallican postbaptismal rites during the seventh and eighth centuries.

Some recent research led me to examine at length the extant Gallican liturgical sources which bear witness to the Order of Christian Initiation. After the study of this material I came to appreciate that the analysis of liturgical texts does not tell you everything (which one can well imagine), but it does let you see the liturgical practice of a particular church, and more importantly, it

[1] J. D. C. Fisher, *Christian Initiation: Baptism in the Medieval West: A Study in the Disintegration of the Primitive Rite of Initiation* (Alcuin Club, 47), (London 1965).

also allows you to discover the inner, theological meaning of a particular liturgical rite.

If one can join to the valuable insights drawn from the study of liturgical texts, the evidence provided by patristic/ecclesiastical writers, and conciliar teaching, or studies within a particular historical context, then one is contributing not to archaism (as is often the criticism) but hopefully to a better and developing theological understanding of liturgical rites and their celebration.

In this article I will explore the baptismal and postbaptismal ceremonies of one of the most important Gallican sacramentaries of the seventh and eighth centuries, the *Missale Gothicum*.[2] Then I will offer some supporting evidence (other sacramentary witness, the use of Sacred Scripture, patristic and conciliar teachings) to help present the theological nature of the Gallican postbaptismal rites.

The time period covered in this study is the era of the seventh and eighth centuries, a period in which the Gallican church was suffering because of barbarian invasions into Europe, as well as a time of decadence in the social and religious life of the people. The Gallican liturgy of this period was also influenced by Eastern, Spanish, North Italian and Roman churches and this combined influence brought about a very interesting theological result evident in the liturgical texts. And this was the period of history that preceded the great Carolingian reform; yet, during this time the various liturgies of individual countries retained much of their own liturgical forms.

Michael Andrieu once wrote a very interesting summary of the historical details of the seventh and eighth century Gallican

---

[2] *Missale Gothicum, Vat. Reg. Lat. 317*, ed. L. C. Mohlberg, Rerum Ecclesiasticarum Documenta. Series Major, Fontes, 5, (Rome 1961).

There are two other major sacramentaries that will be referred to frequently in this text: (1) *Bobbio Missal: A Gallican Mass Book, Paris, B.N. Ms. Lat. 13246*, II: Text 58, ed. E. A. Lowe (London 1920); III: Notes and Studies 61, ed. A. Wilmart, E. A. Lowe and H. A. Wilson (London 1924), Henry Bradshaw Society; (2) *Missale Gallicanum Vetus, Cod. Vat. Palat. Lat. 493*, ed. L. C. Mohlberg Rerum Ecclesiasticarum Documenta. Series Major, Fontes 3, (Rome 1958). A schema of the postbaptismal ceremonies will be provided and placed immediately before an analysis of the *Missale Gothicum* to help the reader more easily identify the most important (postbaptismal) texts.

church. Some of the important elements of that account are offered here for the reader:

"La première moitié du VIIIe siècle fut pour l'Eglise franque une période de désorganisation et de désarroi. La décadence commencée au siècle précédent s'accéléra, sous l'action de multiples causes.

"Dans le Midi et dans le Centre, les invasions arabes ruinent églises et abbayes. De la chute de Narbonne, en 725, jusqu'à sa délivrance, par Pépin le Bref, le Musulmans, maîtres de la Septimanie, ne cessent durant cette trentaine d'années d'envoyer vers l'est et vers le nord des armées ou des bandes de pillards, qui s'en prennent surtout aux villes et aux monastères opulents . . .

"Même lorsqu'elles ne font que passer, les hordes sarrasines anéantissent les quelques foyers d'étude, où subsistait encore un peu de vie intellectuelle. Ceux qui avaient le plus glorieux passé ne sont pas épargnés. A Lérins (vers 736) comme à Luxeuil (732), les moines sont massacrés et les bâtiments incendiés. Dans la métropole monastique de l'Est, la *laus divina* s'interrompit durant quinze ans. Les abbayes saccagées forment le cadre habituel des récits hagiographiques se rapportant à cette époque. Partout les sanctuaires sont pillés et souvent réduits en cendres . . .

". . . on ne pouvait espérer d'amélioration foncière, si l'on ne ravivait la ferveur des clercs et des moines, et par eux celle du peuple chrétien. Tout tentative de réforme supposait un réveil liturgique. Tant que les clercs des deux ordres, dans les cathédrales, les églises monastiques et les sanctuaires paroissiaux, n'auraient pas réappris à célébrer correctement la messe, à administrer les sacrements, à s'acquitter de l'office canonique, les maux que l'on voulait guérir persisteraient.

"Malheureusement les traditions étaient perdues. Il eût été chimérique de vouloir les ranimer par simple résurrection de la vieille liturgie indigène. Celle-ci, qui n'avait jamais été uniforme, s'était trop profondément dégradée et ne pouvait plus être revivifiée. Les livres d'église transcrits au VIIIe siècle, par des copistes de plus en plus ignorants, avaient en grande partie disparu dans les troubles des guerres et des sécularisations. Ceux qui subsistaient encore offraient une déconcertante variété de rites et de prières. D'un diocèse, d'une paroisse à l'autre, on rencontrait les usages les plus différents, dont nul ne savait l'origine et où les coutumes anciennes n'apparaissaient plus que défigurées."[3]

SCHEMA OF POSTBAPTISMAL CEREMONIES

The following schema contains the most important sections of the three major Gallican sarcamentaries. The schema is placed here so that the reader can make quick reference to important texts, as well as to provide a summary and comparative presentation of these texts.

This schema is based on the format offered by M. C. Vanhengel in his article, "Le Rite et la Formule de la Chrismation postbaptismale en Gaule et en Haute Italie du IVe au VIIIe siècle d'après les Sacramentaires Gallicans aux origines du Rituel primitif," *Sacris Erudiri* 21 (1972–73) 165–66.

---

[3] This text is found in Les *"Ordines Romani" du Haut Moyen Age,* ed. Michel Andrieu, Spicilegium Sacrum Lovaniense. Etudes et Documents, 23, II: *Les Textes* (Louvain 1960) XVII–XX. The following works have also been consulted and provide a good bibliography for the historical material of seventh and eighth century Gaul: C. de Clercq, *La Législation Religieuse Franque de Clovis à Charlemagne (507–814),* (Louvain 1936); Jean Daniélou and Henri Marrou, *The Christian Centuries,* Vol. I: *The First Six Hundred Years,* trans. Vincent Cronin (New York 1964); David Knowles and Dimitri Obolensky, *The Christian Centuries,* Vol. II: *The Middle Ages* (New York 1968); Charles W. Previté-Orton, *The Shorter Cambridge Medieval History,* Vol. I: *The Later Roman Empire to the Twelfth Century* (Cambridge 1971); Elie Griffe, "Les Paroisses Rurales de la Gaule," *La Maison-Dieu* 36 (1953) 33–62; Elie Griffe, *La Gaule Chrétienne à l'Epoque Romaine,* Vol. II: *l'Eglise des Gaules au Ve Siècle. Première Partie: l'Eglise et Les Barbares; l'Organisation Ecclésiastique et la Hiérarchie* (Paris 1957); Elie Griffe, *La Gaule Chrétienne à l'Epoque Romaine,* Vol. III, *L'Eglise des Gaules au Ve Siècle. Deuxième Partie: La Cité Chrétienne* (Paris 1965); Elie Griffe, "L'Episcopat Gaulois et Les Royautés Barbares de 482 à 507," *Bulletin de Littérature Ecclésiastique* 76 (1975) 261–84; Elie Griffe, "A Travers Les Paroisses Rurales de la Gaule au VIe Siècle," *Bulletin de Littérature Ecclésiastique* 76 (1975) 3–26.

GOTHICUM (Mohlberg, §§ 260–65)	BOBBIO (Lowe, §§ 248–54)	VETUS (Mohlberg, §§ 173–77)
260. Dum baptizas interrogas ei et dicis: Baptizo te illum in nomine patris et filii et spiritus sancti in remissionem peccatorum ut habeas vitam aeternam Amen.	248. Baptisas eum et dicis: Baptizo te in nomine patris et filii et spiritus sancti unam abentem substancia ut abias vitam aeternam parte cum sanctis.	173. Dicis: Baptizo te? Responsio: Baptiza. 174. Baptizo te credentem in nomine patris et filii et spiritus sancti ut habeas vitam aeternam in saecula saeculorum.
261. Dum crismas eum tangis, dicis: Perungo te crisma sanctitatis, tonicam immortalitatis qua(m) dominus noster iesus christus traditam a patre primus accepit ut eam integram et inlibatam perferas ante tribunal christi et vivas in saecula saeculorum.	249. Suffundis crisma in fronte eius dicens: Deus Pater domini nostri iesu christi qui te regeneravit per aqua et spiritu sancto quicquid tibi dedit remissione peccatorum per lavacrum regeneracionis et sanguine + ipse te liniat crismate suo sancto in vitam aeternam.	175. Infusio crismae. Deus pater domini nostri iesu christi qui te regeneravit ex aqua et spiritu sancto quique tibi dedit remissionem peccatorum ipsi te lenet cri(s)mate suo sancto ut habeas vitam aeternam in saecula saeculorum.
	250. Superindues eum veste dicens: Accipe vestem candidam, quam immacolatam perferas ante tribunal christi.	

The Theology of the Postbaptismal Rites 163

GOTHICUM (Mohlberg, §§ 260-65)	BOBBIO (Lowe, §§ 248-54)	VETUS (Mohlberg, §§ 173-77)
262. Dum pedis cius lavas, dicis: Ego tibi lavo pedis sicut dominus noster iesus christus fecit discipulis suis, tu facias hospitibus et peregrinis ut habeas vitam aeternam	251. Collectio ad pedis lavando Ego tibi labo pedis sicut dominus noster iesus christus fecit discipolis suis: ita tu facias hospitibus et peregrinis.	176. Ad pedes lavando
	252. Dominus noster iesus chri-stus de lenteo quo erat precinctus tersit pedis dis-cipolorum suorum et ego facio tibi tu facias peregri-nis, hospitibus et pauperibus	Dominus et salvator noster iesus christus apostolis suis pedes lavit: ego tibi pedes labo ut et tu facias hospitibus et peregrinis qui ad te venerint. Hoc si feceris, habibes vitam aeternam in saecula saeculorum. [Amen.

Dum vestimentum ei
inponis, dicis

263. Accipe vestem candi-
         [dam,
quam immaculatam perfe-
         [ras ante
tribunal domini nostri iesu
christi. Amen.

Coleccio 264. Oremus, fratres ka-rissimi, dominum et deum nostrum pro (neo)-	253. Post baptismum. Laudis et gracias domi-no referemus, fratres	Post baptismum. 177. Deus ad quem scu-bias veteris homines in-

GOTHICUM (Mohlberg, §§ 260–65)	BOBBIO (Lowe, §§ 248–54)	VETUS (Mohlberg, §§ 173–77)
fetis suis, quo modo baptizati sunt, ut cum in maiestate sua salvator advenerit, cuius regeneravit ex aqua et spiritu sancto, faciat eos ex aeternitate vestire salutem: per domnum.	dilectissimi quod augere dignatus est aeclesie suae congregacione per carus nostros qui modo baptizati sunt petamus ergo de domini misericordia ut baptismum sanctum quod acciperunt inlibatum inviolatum et immaculatum perferant ante tribunal christi.	fundit et depositas novella subolis propago discendit, dum in novam aeternamque substanciam salutaribus aquis exuemur et nascimur: conserva in nos tui(s) laticis purum liquorem, ut nequas superinduere maculae non valeat inimicus, nec auferatur pater a filiis, nec patri subtrahatur heredi- [tas.
265. Item alia Baptizatis et in christo coronatis, quos dominus noster a crisma petentibus regeneracione donare dignatus est, praecamur, omnipotens deus, ut baptismum, quod acceperunt, inmaculatum ipsum perferant usque in finem: per dominum.	254. Item alia Domine deus omnipotens famolus tuos quos iussisti renasci ex aqua et spiritu sancto, conserva in eis baptismum sanctum quod acceperunt et in nomenis tui sanctificacionem perficere dignare: ut proficiat in illus gracia tua semper et quod de donante susciperunt vite suae integritate custodiant.	

EXAMINATION OF THE MISSALE GOTHICUM

Before the texts of the sacramentary are examined some background information about the manuscript is offered:

Manuscript. Rome: *Codex Vaticanus Reginensis* lat. 317. This manuscript was formerly in the Petau Library; it is frequently called the *Sacramentary of Autun.*[4]

[4] K. Gamber, *Codices Liturgici Latini Antiquiores*, 2nd ed., Spicilegii Friburgensis Subsidia I (Freiburg 1968), n. 210, 161–62. See J. Quasten, "Gallican Rites," *New Catholic Encyclopedia* (NCE), (New York 1967), 259.

Edition. Missale Gothicum, ed. L. C. Mohlberg, Rerum Ecclesiasticarum Documenta, Series Major, Fontes, 5, Rome: Casa Editrice Herder, 1961. Also very helpful, because of its notes is the *Missale Gothicum: A Gallican Sacramentary, Ms. Vatican. Regin. lat. 317*, ed. H. M. Bannister, I: *Text and Introduction*, Henry Bradshaw Society, 52, London: Harrison & Sons, 1917; II: *Notes and Indices*, Henry Bradshaw Society, 54, London: Harrison & Sons, 1919.

Date of the Manuscript. Mohlberg himself dates this manuscript at some time between 690–710. He sets the *terminus post quem* as 679, when Leodegar, Bishop of Autun, died as a martyr, since the missal contains a Mass of St Leodegarius (lxiii). He sets the *terminus ante quem* close to 835. While there is a great deal of speculation as to the precise year of the origin of the manuscript, most scholars are agreed that the manuscript originated around the end of the seventh or beginning of the eighth century.[5]

Origin of the Manuscript. For Bannister, this manuscript "is a copy of a Gallican sacramentary made in Burgundy, probably at Luxeuil or some daughter house, or even further east in Switzerland, for general use in Gaul from an archetype which also served for part of the Missale Gall. Vetus . . ." Gamber cites Eastern France as the place of origin, probably from Autun. Lowe says that its origin is Burgundy and that "the manuscript was written, it seems, for Autun, at an important centre where the script of Luxeuil was practiced." Delisle also feels that the manuscript was copied for the Church of Autun. Dom Morin has rendered this theory: "Pour ma part je ne vois, présentement du moins, en pays franc vers l'an 700, aucun milieu auquel les traits caractéris-

---

[5] L. C. Mohlberg, ed., *Missale Gothicum* (1961), xxii–xxiii; H. M. Bannister, ed., *Missale Gothicum: A Gallican Sacramentary, MS Vatican. Regin. lat. 317.* I: *Text and Introduction* (1917), xlvii; C. Vogel, "Les échanges liturgiques entre Rome et les pays Francs jusqu'à l'époque de Charlemagne," in *Le Chiese nei regni dell'Europa Occidentale e i loro rapporti con Roma sino all'800*, Settimana di Studio del Centro Italiano di Studi Sull'Alto Medioevo, VII, i, (Spoleto 1960), 185–295; E. Bourque, *Etude sur les Sacramentaires Romains.* II: *Les textes remaniés*, 1. *Le Gélasien du VIIIᵉ siècle*, (Québec 1952), 390, which also offers Lowe and Wilmart's dating for the same period.

tiques du *Missale Gothicum* puissent s'appliquer aussi bien qu'au monastère alsacien de Gregorienmünster."[6]

Missa in Symbuli Traditione. This Palm Sunday Mass has traditional baptismal themes throughout its text. The *Praefatio* (§ 196) has no counterpart in any Roman sacramentary, yet it does have parallels in the *Bobbio* (§ 189) and the *Gallicanum Vetus* (§ 81), both of which mention the resurrected Lazarus, and the crowds of Bethany going out to meet Jesus with palm branches in their hands.

The most important text in the entire Mass is the *Collectio Post Nomina.* The first part of the prayer alludes to the biblical notion of the seed having to die in order to bring new growth (John 12:24), describing Jesus as Redeemer because of his saving death. The latter part of the prayer describes those soon to come to the baptismal font:[7]

"Sed et si qui inter hos adstantes ⟨qui⟩ ad baptismi salutaris sacramenta praeparentur, quaesomus, domine deus noster, ut inbutos in fide, instructos in sensu, confirmatos in gratia, ad percipiendam plenitudinem gratiae tuae spiritus tui munere iobeas praeparare, ut sancti lavacri fonte desiderato merea ⟨n⟩ tur renasci. Quod . . ." (§ 198).

The candidates are by now well prepared and they are ready to receive the "fullness of grace" (plenitudinem gratiae); this fullness of grace (by which they are reborn) is given as gift by the Holy Spirit. In most of these texts the Spirit functions in cooperation with Jesus Christ, but at times only the Spirit is explicitly mentioned, as is done here. It is interesting to note the use of the plural form, *sacramenta (ad baptismi salutaris)* and the developing

---

[6] Bannister, *Gothicum*, I lxviii; Gamber, *Codices*, § 210, 162; E. A. Lowe, *Codices Latini Antiquiores*, Part I: *The Vatican City* (Oxford 1934), p. 32; L. V. Delisle, "Mémoire sur d'anciens Sacramentaires," *Mémoires de l'Institut National de France. Académie des Inscriptions et Belles-Lettres*, Vol. 39 (Paris 1886), p. 69; G. Morin, "Sur la provenance du Missale Gothicum," *Revue d'Histoire Ecclésiastique* (RDH), 37 (1941) 30; Mohlberg, *Gothicum*, xx–xxvi, who offers some theories given by others.

[7] The symbols used in cited texts are standard: ⟨ ⟩ = that which is incorrectly omitted by the scribe; [] = that which is incorrectly included by the scribe; and /// = erasure in the text.

sequence of verbforms: *inbutos, instructos, confirmatos, ad percipien-dam*. One could say that there is reference to "sacraments of initiation," culminating in the reception of the fullness of God's grace.

The *Immolatio Missae* (§ 200) has its parallel in the Bobbio (§ 193), which describes the events usually proper to the day, that is, the New Testament description of the procession of palms during Jesus' entry into Jerusalem.

Orationes In Biduana.[8] The *Praefatio in Vespera Paschae* begins:

"Domini gracia ⟨ m ⟩ per aquam et spiritum renati . . . agni immaculati sanguine corporum nostrorum postibus aspersis . . ." (§ 221).

This phrase "begotten of water and the Spirit" is at the very heart of the baptismal liturgy: "respondit Iesus amen amen dico tibi nisi quis renatus fuerit ex aqua et Spiritu non potest introire in regnum Dei . . ." (John 3:5).[9] God's sanctifying power is conveyed by means of the baptismal water and the Holy Spirit. Water is that necessary element which the Spirit of God uses to symbolize the cleansing, sanctification and dedication that is effected within the person.

When the pericope 1 John 5:8 is considered, one sees that there are three elements, the Spirit, the water, and the blood that testify to the central salvific event of Christ: "6. hic est qui venit per aquam et sanguinem Iesus Christus non in aqua solum sed in aqua et sanguine et Spiritus est qui testificatur quoniam Christus est veritas. 7. quia tres sunt qui testimonium dant 8. Spiritus et

---

[8] *DACL*, 1914, ed., s.v. "Biduana," by W. Henry. "C'est le terme qui est donné dans certains livres liturgiques au vendredi et au samedi-saint. On dit quelquefois *Triduana* en y comprenant le jeudi-saint: le mot est composé d'après *Biduum*, ou *Triduum*." However, during the time when the Gallican Sacramentaries were used the *Triduum* was understood to be Good Friday, Holy Saturday and Easter Sunday: See C. Callewaert, *Sacris Erudiri* (Steenbrugge 1940), 529–41; B. Fischer, "Vom einen Pascha-Triduum zum Doppel-Triduum der Heutigen Rubriken," *Paschatis Sollemnia*, ed. B. Fischer and J. Wagner (Freiburg, 1959), 146–56.

[9] All Scripture quotes used in this text will be in Latin; this is done to make it easier for the reader to identify similarities between the phraseology of the Scripture passage and the liturgical text. The biblical text used was *Biblica Sacra Iuxta Vulgatam Versionem*, 1975 (the edition has no punctuation).

aqua et sanguis et hi tres unum sunt . . ." (1 John 5:6-8). If this same passage were part of a baptismal context (which is the concern here), one finds that just as water, blood, and the Spirit testified that Jesus once came into the world for the sake of mankind, so now these same three elements testify to His coming to a particular person. Through water, and empowered by the Spirit, the person receives the new life of Christ, won for him through His blood poured out on the cross.

Both of the above Johannine passages are frequently found within the Gallican baptismal liturgy, and especially in the *Missale Gothicum*. Reference to John 3:5 is found in § 221, above, and again within the Easter baptismal context in the following:

§ 256 ". . . ut quibus perfusi famuli tui accipiant remissionem peccatorum ac renati ex aqua et spiritu sancto . . ."

§ 264 ". . . quo modo baptizati sunt, ut cum in majestate sua salvator advenerit . . . cuius regeneravit ex aqua et spiritu sancto . . ."

§ 290 ". . . ut omnes in Christo renati ex aqua et spiritu sancto . . ."

§ 307 ". . . Conserva, domine, familiam tuam, quos ex aqua et spiritu sancto propicius redimisti . . ."

One can find allusion to the 1 John 5:8 passage in:

§ 267 ". . . Redimisti nos, domine, deus, per lavacrum regeneracionis et sanguinem crucis . . ."

§ 309 ". . . quo labacrum abluti, quo spiritu regenerati, quo sanguine sunt redempti . . ."

Oraciones Paschalis Duodecim Cum Totidem Colleccionibus. These prayers correspond to the *Orationes Solemnes* of Good Friday in the Roman Rite. There really are only two prayers out of this group-

---

[10] Bannister, *Gothicum*, II §§ 228-51 (especially 228 and 229), 55-56; §§ 228-251: "Similar prayers are found in a corresponding place in G. V.; in Bo. they come before the Exultet; they correspond to the *Orationes sollemnes* on Good Friday in the Roman rite. In each of these 12 suffrages the *Praefatio* or Bidding prayer, precedes and invites the *Oratio* which follows. The *Orationes* in Bo. are different; the 12 classes of persons prayed for are the same, though at times

ing that seem worthwhile to comment upon. The first one speaks of the three stages of the baptismal ceremony:[10]

"Sancte domine, omnipotens pater, exaudi, tuere ac sanctificare plebem tuam / praemonitam signo crucis, baptismate purificatam, crismate delibutam, quos ad celebrandam praesentis sollemnitatis beatitudinem congregasti, universisque noticiam tui participacionem sancti spiritus propicius infunde: per (§ 229)."

The paragraph, *Pro Caticuminis*, specifically prays for those soon to experience baptism (§ 250). The second important baptismal prayer, however, is:

"Creator omnium, domine, et fons aquae vivae, per lavacrum baptismi peccata corum dele, quibus iam donasti resurreccionis fidem, ut mortem huius saeculi non timeant, reple eos spiritu sancto, ut formari in illis Christum ac vivere glorientur: per (§ 251)."

The two major themes of the initiation ceremony are: (1) through the font of baptism, sins are forgiven and (2) filled with the Holy Spirit, Christ is formed in the candidates. Although there is reference to the Holy Spirit *(reple eos spiritu sancto)*, there is no explicit mention of chrismation or any postbaptismal rite related to His coming. The best conclusion regarding this final prayer (§ 251) is that through the ceremony of Christian Initiation described here one receives forgiveness of sin, and through the power of the Holy Spirit, Christ is formed in one's life.[11]

---

under different denominations." §§ 228, 229. "It will be noticed that these are the only *Praefatio* and *Oratio* which are not for a class of persons; they are really a thanksgiving *(gratiarum actio)* (cfr. Bo. 843, L. 214), *ex gratiarum actione sumat exordium, pro neobaptizatis; praemunitam signo crucis, baptismate purificatum, chrismate delibutam* represents the three stages of the baptismal ceremony, cf. §§ 259–261."

[11] One can find in Isidore of Seville, references to baptism effecting forgiveness of sin, and chrismation effecting sanctification; see A. Chavasse, "La Bénédiction du Chrême en Gaule avant l'adoption intégrale de la Liturgie Romaine." *Revue du Moyen Age Latin* 1 (1945), 112; some of the texts cited are: (a) *Etymologiarum*, VI, ch. 19, n. 51: "Nam sicut in baptismo peccatorum remissio datur, ita per unctionem santificatio spiritus adhibetur, et hoc de pristina disciplina, qua ungi in sacerdotium et in regnum solebant, ex quo et Aaron a Moyse unctus est" (PL 82:256c); (b) *De Fide Catholica Contra Judaeos*, Liber II, ch. 24, 1: "Quod per baptismum erat purgatio peccatorum futura . . ." (PL

Ad Christianum Faciendum. The prefatory prayer (§ 252) found here is quite difficult to untangle and analyze. The two prayers which follow the preface actually make it easier to understand. The first of these two collects (§ 253) indicates the giving of the sign of the cross to the candidate with the formula: *Accipe signaculum Christi.* This is a slight change from the usual form: *Accipe signum crucis.*[12] The second prayer reads:

"Signo te in nomine patris et filii et spiritus sancti, ut sis christianus; oculos, ut videas claritatem dei, aures ut audias vocem domini, nares, ut odoris suavitatem Christi, ⟨linguam⟩ conversus ut confitearis patrem et filium et spiritum sanctum, cor, ut credas trinitatem inseparabilem. / Pax tecum: per Iesum Christum dominum nostrum, qui cum patre [et filio] et spiritu sancto vivit" (§ 254).

The forehead is probably signed first, and then the eyes, ears, nostrils, tongue, and heart, in turn. While the use of oil is not indicated, it is accepted that during the sixth century this ritual of signing the various parts of the body actually did use oil and that this prayer and rite were considered an old baptismal anointing.[13] The frequent and clear references to the Trinity, mentioned explicitly four times within this one prayer (§ 254), reminds one of the Gallican anti-Arian tendency evident in its prayers; even the formula for the signing of the heart illustrates this:

"Signo . . . cor, ut credas trinitatem inseparabilem."[14]

Collectio Ad Fontes Benedicendos. It is difficult to discern the proper reading of the beginning of the *Praefacio* (§ 255), but the second half is clear enough:

"Locus quidem parvus, sed gracia plenus. Bene gubernatus est spiritus sanctus. Oremus ergo dominum et deum nostrum, ut santificet hunc fontem, ut omnes qui discenderint in hanc fontem,

---

83:530c); (c) *De Fide Catholica Contra Judaeos,* Liber II, ch. 25, 2: "ut sacri chrismatis unctione delibuti omnes sanctificentur, atque sanctificati in Dei gloriam praeparentur" (PL 83:534a).

[12] Bannister, *Gothicum* II, § 253, 59.

[13] L. L. Mitchell, *Baptismal Anointing,* Alcuin Club 48 (London 1966), 113.

[14] See J. Jungmann, *The Place of Christ in Liturgical Prayer* (Staten Island 1965), 92, 213–38.

faciat eis lavacrum beatissimi regeneracionis in remissione omnium peccatorum: per dominum.''

A fullness of grace *(gracia plenus)* is received in baptism through the work of the Holy Spirit. The blessed baptismal font will be the context for the candidate's regeneration by the forgiveness of all his sins *(remissione omnium peccatorum)*.

The *Contestacio* indicates that these waters are to be filled with the power of the Holy Spirit:

"Benedic, domine, deus noster, hanc creaturam aquae et discendat super eam virtus tua, desuper infunde spiritum sanctum paraclytum, angelum veritatis'' (§ 257).

From the rest of the prayer one sees that because of the special blessing, the baptismal bath will mediate the forgiveness of sins *(peccatorum veniam)* and the infusion of the Holy Spirit *(sancti spiritus infusionem)*.[15]

---

[15] Mohlberg, *Gothicum,* § 257, pp. 66–67: "Contestacio. Dignum et justum est, domine, sancte pater, omnipotens aeterne deus, iniciatur sanctorum, crismatum pater et novi per unicum filium tuum dominum et deum nostrum indetur sacramenti, qui portantibus aquis spiritum tuum sanctum ante diviciae mundi largires, qui Bethsaida aquas angelum medicante procuras, qui Iordanis alueum / Christo filio tuo dignante sanctificas. Respice, domine, super has aquas, qui praeparatae sunt ad delenda hominum peccata, angelum pietatis tuae his sacris fontibus adesse dignare, vitae prioris abluat et parvum habitaculum sanctificet tui procurans, ut regenerandorum viscera aeterna floriscat, et vere baptismatis novitas reparetur. Benedic, domine, deus noster, hanc creaturam aquae et discendat super eam virtus tua, desuper infunde spiritum tuum sanctum paraclytum, angelum veritatis. Sanctifica, domine, huius latecis undas, sicut sanctificasti fluenta Iordanis, ut qui in hanc / fontem discenderit in nomine patris et filii et spiritus sancti, et peccatorum veniam et sancti spiritus infusionem consequi mereantur: per dominum.''
There is a constant reference to an Angel who makes the water holy. It is difficult to identify the Angel with the Holy Spirit since there is not enough evidence. There is an interesting tradition to this which stems from Tertullian. See R. F. Refoulé, ed., *Tertullien. Traité du Baptême,* 2, Sources Chrétiennes, 35, (Paris 1952), ch. IV 71; and E. C. Whitaker, *Documents of the Baptismal Liturgy* Alcuin Club 42, (London 1960), 7: "Thus when the waters have in some sense acquired healing power by an angel's intervention, the spirit is in those waters corporally washed, while the flesh is in those same waters spiritually cleansed.''

The exorcism which follows is almost identical to the *Praefacio* (§ 255) in its reference to regeneration by the forgiveness of all one's sins:

". . . qui discenderint in hanc fontem fiat eis lavacrum baptismi regeneracionis in remissione omnium peccatorum . . ." (§ 258).

A rubric next directs the celebrant to blow three times upon the water, and to put chrism into the water in the form of the cross, saying:

"Infusio crismae salutaris domini nostri Jesu Christi, ut fiat fons aquae salientis cunctis discendentibus in ea in vitam aeternam. Amen" (§ 259).

After the actual baptism, administered with the Trinitarian formula, the celebrant performs the chrismation (§ 261). He touches the newly-baptized person with the chrism, and says:

"Perungo te crisma sanctitatis, ⟨indua te⟩ tonicam immortalitatis, qua ⟨m⟩ dominus noster Iesus Christus traditam a patre primus accepit, ut eam integram et inlibatam perferas ante tribunal Christi et vivas in saecula saeculorum" (§ 261).

This prayer has an interesting and controversial reference to the "Chrism of sanctification" which seems to be identified with the "tunic of immortality." The ceremony of putting on the white vestment is apparently misplaced here in the Gothicum because this ceremonial action usually comes immediately after the post-baptismal chrismation, and before the washing of the feet. Is the reference to the "tunic of immortality" at this point actually a

---

E. G. C. F. Atchley, *On the Epiclesis of the Eucharistic Liturgy and In the Consecration of the Font*, Alcuin Club 31 (London 1935), 164: "There is mentioned *angelus benediccionis tuae* (John 5:4); *angelus pietatis tuae* who (so operates), *vitae prioris (maculas, peccata) abluat;* and finally, *Spiritus tuus sanctus paraclytus angelus veritatis.* This last reference is undoubtedly to the third person of the Holy Trinity; but who are the Angels of blessing and piety? Who is the angel who can wash away the stains of sin?"

B. Botte has an interesting reference to Christ as the "Angel of Counsel," found in the Roman Liturgy, "L'ange du Sacrifice et l'Épiclèse de la Messe Romaine au Moyen Age," *Recherches de Théologie Ancienne et Médiévale,* 1 (1929) 285–308, especially 308.

mistake, or is it simply a duplication of the investiture with the white garment (§ 263)? Does this reference have a special, and perhaps even theological, meaning attached to it?

In his critical edition of the Gothicum Mohlberg inserts *indua te* as that phrase which the scribe incorrectly omitted, and he gives no further explanation of that usage. In a footnote, the only comment Mohlberg writes is "tonicam *vorher* induo te *oder* induere." Bannister comments on this important line in the text and indicates that Mabillon and Neales-Forbe suggest inserting *induo te* or *induere* before the word *tonicam*.[16]

In his book, *Baptismal Anointing*, Mitchell argues that Mohlberg (who offers the critical edition cited above) is wrong to insert the word *indua te* into the chrismation text before the phrase *tonicam immortalitatis*. Mitchell cites the chrismal preface in the Mass for Maundy Thursday in the *Ancient Gelasian Missal* where chrism is referred to as a *vestimentum incorrupti muneris*. And Coptic and Byzantine rites refer to the chrism as an "incorruptible robe." Mitchell concludes that the *tonica immortalitatis* is actually the chrism itself, and not a garment. Duchesne, writing many years before Mitchell, had come to the same conclusion regarding this identity of the chrism.[17]

In his study of the chrismation in the *Missale Gothicum*, Chavasse notes that some scholars have thought that the text was inaccurate due to the mistake of a copyist who may have placed next to one another the beginning of a chrismation formula and the end of a formula which should have accompanied the investiture of the white garment on the neophyte.[18]

But the Gothicum is not the only witness to this imagery of chrismation as a garment. The famous homily on grace by Faustus

---

[16] Mohlberg, *Gothicum*, 67; Bannister, *Gothicum*, II, 61.

[17] Mitchell, *Baptismal Anointing*, 121; L. Duchesne, *Origines du Culte Chrétien* (Paris 1925), 313–14. Bannister, *Gothicum* II, § 261, 61: "I had felt that, as the rubric and the form for the white garment came later in § 263 it might be possible to take the 'chrisma' as the Christian's first and immortal dress; I have unfortunately lost the reference to a passage in a (? Mozarabic) sacramentary to that effect."

[18] Chavasse, "Bénédiction du Chrême," 109–11; the resumé of opinions can be found in Bannister, *Gothicum*, II, 61–62, § 261.

of Riez also uses this imagery. And the Holy Thursday chrismal preface of the Gelasian Sacramentary (*Vaticanus reginensis* 316) uses the phrase *vestimento incorrupti muneris induantur* which refers to the chrism which is being blessed.[19]

Chavasse says that both the Gelasianum and the Gothicum can explain their juxtaposition and comparison of the chrismation to the *tunica immortalitatis* by two biblical texts: Isaiah 61:1: which invites the comparison between a garment and an unction which confers "the Spirit of the Lord"; and Luke 24:49: which speaks of "putting on the Holy Spirit" on the day of Pentecost.

There are some famous Pauline texts which also make reference to these concepts of personal renewal as if one were putting on special clothing: e.g., putting on the new man and taking off the old man, and putting on immortality at the time of the Resurrection:[20] 22. "deponere vos secundum pristinam conversationem veterem hominem qui corrumpitur secundum desideria erroris 23. renovamini autem spiritu mentis vestrae 24. et induite novum hominem qui secundum Deum creatus est in iustitia et sanctitate veritatis" (Ephesians 4:22-24); "opertet enim corruptible hoc induere incorruptelam et mortale hoc induere inmortalitatem" (1 Corinthians 15:53).

Many of these passages can be found especially in the analysis of the *Missale Gallicanum Vetus*. Any observant reader of the New Testament soon becomes aware that one is being urged, especially in the Pauline writings, to "put on Christ." The imagery of clothing is easy to read into the texts, but even more so when the con-

---

[19] Faustus, *De Gratia*, I, 14; *Fausti Reiensis et Ruricii Opera*, ed. A. G. Engelbrecht, CSEL, 21, (Vienna 1891), 47; Gelasian reference, *Liber Sacramentorum Romanae Aeclesiae Ordinis Anni Circuli* (Cod. Vat. Reg. lat 316) ed. L. C. Mohlberg et. al., Rerum Ecclesiasticarum Documenta, Series Major, Fontes 4, (Rome 1960), § 378, 60.

The full text of the *Gelasian* Preface is: "V. D. Clementiam tuam suppliciter obsecrare, ut spiritalis lavacri baptismum renovandis creaturam chrismatis in sacramentum perfectae salutis vitaeque confirmes, ut sanctificatione unctionis infusa, corruptionis primae nativitatis absorpta, sanctum uniuscuiusque templum acceptabilis vitae innocens odor redolescat: ut secundum constitutionis tuae sacramentum regio et sacerdotali propheticoque honore perfusi, vestimento incorrupti muneris induantur. Per quem maiestatem tuam. . . ."

[20] Chavasse, "Bénédiction du Chrême," 112.

text is one of initiation into the Christian Mystery. (The practice of using a white baptismal robe or garment was common in the baptismal liturgy, at least in Medieval Gaul and Germany.)[21]

Along with many references to the baptismal garment found in the Gallican sacramentaries there can also be found strong theological interpretation attached to these references. Usually the garment is spoken of as Christ Himself, or that which symbolizes the power of God coming to man. All of this clothing imagery simply yet profoundly speaks of man's relationship to God in and through Christ. There are studies available which offer important insights into the theological understanding of the baptismal garment.[22]

A recent doctoral study by John Farrell, "The Garment of Immortality," provides a fine synthesis of much of the writing in this area. Some of his conclusions are valuable to this paper, particularly his conclusions 7 and 9:

(7) "Baptism symbolizes man's burial and resurrection with Christ, the Second Adam. Through Baptism man is incorporated into Christ. Christ possesses this right relationship to God for he as man is the eternal Son. Christ offers man participation in his own likeness to God. Thus, of water and the dynamism of the Holy Spirit, primordial nudity, the Garment of Immortality, is rewoven."

(9) "The symbol par-excellence of man's restored condition is the white baptismal robe woven of linen. The baptized, thus clad, have entered the community of those who through Jesus Christ in the Spirit call God "Abba" and look for his appearance."[23]

---

[21] Cf. *Vetus*, § 168; Fischer, *Baptism in Medieval West*, 48.

[22] Some of the studies which have been quite helpful: Johannes Quasten, "Theodore of Mopsuestia on the Exorcism of the Cilicium," *Harvard Theological Review* 35 (1942) 209–19; Erik Peterson, *Pour une théologie du Vêtement* (Lyons 1943); Salvatore Famoso, "Accipe Vestem Candidam," *Rivista Liturgica* 42 (1955) 26–44; Jean Daniélou, *The Bible and the Liturgy* (Notre Dame 1956) 51ff.; Edgar Haulotte, *Symbolique du Vêtement selon la Bible*, Théologie 65, (Paris 1966); Jonathan Z. Smith, "The Garments of Shame," *History of Religions* 5 (1966) 217–38; Johannes Quasten, "The Garment of Immortality: A Study of the 'Accipe Vestem Candidam,' " *Miscellanea Liturgica in onore di Sua Eminenza il Cardinale Giacomo Lercaro* (Rome 1966) 391–401.

[23] John E. Farrell, "The Garment of Immortality: A Concept and Symbol in

Now, let us look more carefully at the texts which Chavasse offers in his thesis regarding the comparison of chrismation to the *tunica immortalitatis:*

1. "spiritus Domini super me eo quod unxerit Dominus me ad adnuntiandum mansuetis misit me ut mederer contritis corde et praedicarem captivis indulgentiam et clausis apertionem. 10 gaudens gaudebo in Domino et exultabit anima mea in Deo meo quia induit me vestimentis salutis et indumento iustitiae circumdedit me . . ." (Isaiah 61:1, 10). The Isaiah text was the passage that Jesus applied to Himself as He began His ministry in Galilee (Luke 4:17-18). Just previous to this Lucan passage one finds the description of Jesus' own baptism when the Spirit visibly came upon Him, to anoint Him at the beginning of His ministry:

21. "Factum est autem cum baptizaretur omnis populus et Iesu baptizato et orante apertum est caelum 22. et descendit Spiritus Sanctus corporali specie sicut columba in ipsum et vox de caelo facta est tu es Filius meus dilectus in te conplacuit mihi" (Luke 3:21-22).

Later, in Luke 24:49, the Risen Lord appears to the eleven and says: ". . . et ego mitto promissum Patris mei in vos; vos autem sedete in civitate quoadusque induamini virtutem ex alto" (Luke 24:49). The same "Spirit of God" of Isaiah 61:1, Luke 3:21-22 and 4:17-18, will be sent down upon these Apostles (Luke 24:49). And they and their disciples will continue to do the same thing in the life of the church: to call down the Spirit of God upon men, and He will come in a special way through the Christian community's liturgical celebration of Christian Initiation.

The conclusion of Chavasse's article is so fine an explanation and summary, it is quoted at length: "C'est dans un tel contexte d'idées qu'ont pris naissance les expressions que nous étudions, grâce à un rapprochement qui devenait comme fatal, entre l'idée que la chrismation apporte la vie nouvelle au baptisé et l'idée qu'elle 'revêt' le baptisé de l'homme nouveau, étant elle-mème symboliquement, ce vêtement d'incorruptibilité, d'immortalité,

Christian Baptism," (Ph.D. dissertation, The Catholic University of America 1974) 310–12.

dont parlait saint Paul. La *préface chrismale* conservée dans le *sacramentaire gélasien* nous en est garantie, puisque la chrismation y apparaît comme assurant, à ceux que doit 'rénover' l'ablution baptismale, 'le salut et la vie parfaite,' la 'corruption de la première naissance' étant abolie dans l'ablution, ceux-ci sont 'revêtus du vêtement du don de l'incorruptibilité dans et par le sacrement de la vie parfaite qu'est le chrême.' [17] - *Footnote* [17]: "Plusieurs des expressions utilisées dans cette préface, et à peu près toutes les idées exprimées, sont inspirées par les textes de Paul cités ci-dessus notes 13 et 14." (The references there are to Ephesians 4:22-24; Colossians 3:9-10 and 1 Corinthians 15:53).[24]

The chrismation brings new life to the baptized person, and it allows one to "put on the new man"; it is symbolically the "garment of immortality." Almost immediately, those who have received baptism and chrismation will receive the white baptismal robe which is customary for the newly baptized. What has been "put on" in baptism and the chrismation (a new and more perfect life leading to eternal life through water and the Holy Spirit) is now symbolized by a special white linen garment "worn" by the initiated as the garment of incorruptibility and immortality.

Chavasse makes a strong statement here: "ceux-ci sont 'revêtus du vêtement du don de l'incorruptibilité' *dans* et *par* le sacrement de la vie parfaite qu'est le chrême."[25] [Emphasis by this author.] If Chavasse acknowledges this chrismation as the means by which man puts on new life, salvation, perfection, incorruptibility, and immortality, then he judges this postbaptismal chrismation to be a very special ceremony for the Christian community. Chavasse does not explicitly say so, but he appears to give the postbaptismal ceremony a distinction all its own, although not separated from the baptism.

In his study of the Gallican postbaptismal rituals, Vanhengel indicates that the key to the problem of the Gothicum chrismation formula lies in a study of the origin of the postbaptismal formula, *Accipe Vestem:*

---

[24] Chavasse, "Bénédiction du Chrême," 113.
[25] *Ibid.*

"Dum vestimentum ei inponis, dicis: Accipe vestem candidam, quam inmaculatam perferas / ante tribunal domini nostri Iesu Christi. Amen" (Gothicum, § 263).

Vanhengel admits that the origin of the formula (§ S 263) is very complex, and that this particular version of the formula (also found in Bobbio § 250) is known only in the Gallican liturgy. Vanhengel's hypothesis regarding this formula is that it only serves as practical information because the formula really only tries to accentuate what the robe symbolizes for the newly baptized. If Vanhengel is correct, then § 263 is not part of a rite at all; it is only there to emphasize what took place the chrismation.[26]

Even though Vanhengel admits that the origin of the formula is complex, he offers some clear indications of its historical development. His study concludes that what seems to be a literary doubling in § 261 (the chrismation formula) and therefore appears as superfluous, indicates that the formula *Accipe Vestem* is an addition to the postbaptismal rite which is later than the *Perungo te* formula. In light of this, it can be mentioned here that some authors say that the Gothicum chrismation formula, *Perungo te,* consists in a combination of two prayers.[27]

Vanhengel indicated that comparing the chrism to a vestment seems to be an established custom within the Gallican liturgy. He cites the example of Faustus of Riez († 480) who writes about the validly baptized heretic being reconciled to the church: ". . . sed ita operante gratia ablutus iudicetur ut tantum benedictione chrismatis induatur . . ."[28]

For Vanhengel, the expression *tonicam immortalitatis* and the beginning *Perungo te crisma sanctitatis,* have no parellel in any other liturgical text precisely that way. Vanhengel develops his thought

---

[26] M. C. Vanhengel, "Le Rite et la Formule de la Chrismation postbaptismale en Gaule et en Haute Italie du IVᵉ au VIIIᵉ siècle d'après les Sacramentaires Gallicans aux origines du Rituel primitif," *Sacris Erudiri* 21 (1972–73) 161–222, 190.

[27] *Ibid.,* 191–93; H. M. Bannister, *Missale Gothicum,* II: *Notes and Indices* 61 § 261; Mohlberg, *Gothicum,* 67.

[28] Vanhengel, "Le Rite et la Formule de la Chrismation," 196; *Fausti Reiensis et Ruricii Opera,* ed., A. G. Engelbrecht (CSEL, 21), 1891, Liber I, xiii, *De Gratia,* 47, lines 13–15.

by indicating that the indicative form of the verb, and the symbolism of the charismation-vestment enable one to assert that the Gothicum's *Perungo te* formula is very definitely an ancient Gallican prayer of chrismation.[29]

Therefore one concludes from Vanhengel that the chrismation formula is a genuine ancient Gallican prayer and that the *Accipe Vestem* is a later addition. There is no mistaken duplication in the chrismation formula. The phrase *tonica immortalitatis* in the chrismation formula is genuine, probably coming from the Gallican custom to describe and identify chrismation that way.

Returning to the regular order of the postbaptismal ceremonies, one finds that the washing of the feet (§ 262) follows immediately after the chrismation; and after the ceremonies of the foot-washing and bestowal of the white robes (§ 263) there are two concluding prayers. The first prayer develops:

''. . . pro aufetis suis, quo modo baptizati sunt, ut cum in maiestate sua salvator advenerit, cuius regeneravit ex aqua et spiritu sancto, faciat eos ex aeternitate vestire salutem: per dominum'' (§ 264).

Presumably the prayer is for neophytes (it seems that the word found here, *aufetis*, is a corrupted form of that word). The previous *Accipe Vestem* (§ 263) was eschatological in tone; this prayer (§ 264) refers to the vesting *(vestire salutem)*, but it also has an eschatological emphasis.

The final prayer speaks of the baptismal crown:

''Baptizatis et in Christo coronatis, quos dominus noster a crisma

---

[29] Vanhengel, ''Le Rite et la Formule de la Chrismation,'' 197, 199; Vanhengel cites where there is a very similar reference with the same meaning in the Mozarabic liturgy. It is the manuscript Paris, Bibl. Nat. nouv. acq. lat. 2199 (9-10th century), and cited in an Appendix by M. Férotin, *Liber Mozarabicus Sacramentorum*, 1912, 891. The reference is an antiphon for the ceremony *ad oleandum altare:* ''Induit te Dominus tunica iucunditatis et inposuit tibi coronam et ornavit ornamentum sanctis.'' (The interesting image of *crown* is also raised here.) The Gothicum text shares its peculiarity of having the chrismation formula in the indicative mood with the *Stowe Missal* and the *Apostolic Tradition* of Hippolytus; see: Vanhengel, ''Le rite et la Formule de la Chrismation.'' 198-99.

petentibus regeneracione donare dignatus est, praecamur, omnipotens deus, ut baptismum, quod acceperunt, inmaculatum ipsum perferent usque in finem: per dominum'' (§ 265)[30]

Reference to a crown in the Eastern churches pertains to the sacrament of confirmation. Perhaps its use here in the Gothicum formula, and its relationship to the phraseology found in § 265 which is just a little unusual: a *crisma petentibus* would indicate that one has a special postbaptismal ritual here. Could the Gallican church also have considered the postbaptismal chrismation (accompanied by their other ceremonies and formulas) equivalent to the sacrament of confirmation? The evidence here urges that at least the question be raised.

Missa In Vigiliis Sanctae Paschae. This Mass has many references to the events of the baptismal liturgy, but only the first prayer will be studied:

''Redimisti nos, domine, deus, per lavacrum regeneracionis et sanguinem crucis, ut illa caro, quae prius in Adam mortalis fuerat effecta, per passionem maiestatis tuae rursum revocaretur in coelum, salvator'' (§ S 267).

The emphasis of the prayer is on man's redemption. This redemption through the blood of Christ is received by the baptizand now through the baptismal font of regeneration. The latter

[30] Bannister, *Gothicum,* II, § 265, 63; see: footnote 43 on the same page: '' 'coronatis.' It is possible that there is here reminiscence of the Eastern (Armenian and Syrian Jacobite) rite of attaching to the neck a small red and white cord with a wax cross (cf. Denzinger, *Ritus Orientalium,* 1863, I, 389, 397), with the rubric *Mox induit eum et coronat,* and the prayer ''Corona domine hunc servum tuum decore et gloria,'' etc. (*DACL* I, c. 3127).

There are references to this custom at Alexandria in the seventh century: ''tum induunt qui baptizati sunt vestem albam et coronam super capita sua de myrtho et palma.'' (*Bibl. maxima patrum,* Paris 1654, VI, 25). Durandus (*Rationale,* VI, c. 82) refers to a Narbonne use in his time of the white garment having sewn on to it a red band like a 'corona.'

Should the reference here be to some such custom, we should have to read, 'Pro baptizatis, crisma petenibus et in Christo coronatis, quibus dominus noster regenerationem donare dignatus est praecamur,' etc. (There is an erasure in the manuscripts after 'coronatis.')''

part of the prayer reminds one of several Pauline themes, i.e., 1 Corinthians 15:22. Romans 8:6, and Galatians 6:8. It is the baptismal liturgy celebrated on this solemn Easter Vigil which permits one to live a new life in the Spirit, and thus someday to share in eternal glory.

Missa Prima Die Sanctum Paschae. The first prayer of the day, *Collectio Post Prophetia*, summarizes those gifts received by the newly baptized on the evening before, at the Easter Vigil Ceremony:

"Summe omnipotens deus, qui cornuum salutis nostrae in crucis tuae mysterium extulisti, ut nos in domo David pueri tui regali fastigio sublimaris, in quo etiam trifario titulo trinitatis nobis unitas manifestata clariscens ostenditur, salvator nempe in hominem, sacerdos quippe in chrismate, rex scilicet secundum carnem ex genere, praeces nostras tuae supplices prosternimus maiestati, ut quos in tuo nomine per lavacrum regeneraciones consecrare dignatus es, prestis etiam / in sanctitate et iustitia tibi domino servientes unanimitatem fidei per infusionem spiritus tui sancti inviolabiliter custodire ac per viam pacis liberis gressibus properantes caelestia regna conscendere: per resurgentem" (§ 273).

It is through the mystery of the cross that all men are saved and are thus able to come to the *lavacrum regeneraciones*. There is mention of the Trinity in whose name the baptism takes place *in remissionem peccatorum* (§ 260). Then there is a developed sketch of Christ's roles as Savior, priest and king. Not only is man incorporated into Christ's life, but he shares specific powers or roles, namely, the priestly and royal functions of His life. The principal purpose of the prayer is to seek help for these newly baptized people. Considering the awesome dignity in which they now share, one prays that they may live and serve the Lord well. The Holy Spirit Himself will one day bring them into heavenly glory, just as He conducts and guides them through this life on earth.

Missa Matutinalis Per Totam Pascha Pro Parvolis Qui Renati Sunt. Secunda Feria: On this Monday of Easter Week the prayers are significantly influenced by the baptismal ceremonies of the Easter Vigil. As compared to the Mass texts of the other days of the week, three of the prayers for this Mass refer clearly and directly to the effects received by those who shared in the baptismal font. These three prayers (§§ 282, 283, 286) stress rebirth, regeneration, and the destruction of death effected by Jesus' Resurrection. These prayers support the emphasis that has already been discovered in the Gothicum Missal.[31]

On the other two days during Easter Week, Mass prayers can be found which will repeat common baptismal themes. Some of the more pertinent texts are written here to show precisely how the themes are nuanced:

Tercia Feria.

§ 287: "Deus, qui omnes in Christo renatos genus regium et sacerdotale esse fecisti, da nobis velle et posse quod praecipis, ut populo ad aeternitatem vocato una sit fides mencium et pietas accionum."

§ 288: "Omnipotens sempiterne deus, per quem nobis redempcio praestatur et adopcio, respice in opera pietatis tuae, et quae dignatus es conferre, conserva, ut in Christo renatus aeterna tribuatur / hereditas et vera libertas."

§ 290: ". . . ut omnes in Christo renatis ex aqua et spiritu sancto regnum caelorum ingredi mereantur."

Missa Die Sabbato Octava Paschae.

§ 307: "Conserva, domine, familiam tuam, quos ex aqua et spiritu sancto propicius redimisti, ut veterem hominem cum suis actibus expoliantes in ipsius conversacione vivamus. . . ."

§ 309: "Deus misericordiae sempiterne, qui in ipso paschalis festae recursum fidem sacratae tibi plebis accendis, auge graciam quam dedisti, ut digna omnes intellegencia conpraehendant, quo

---

[31] Mohlberg, *Gothicum*, §§ 282, 283, 286, 73: § 282: "Deus qui credentes in te populus graciae tuae largitate multiplicas, respice propicius ad electionem tuam, ut qui sacro baptismatae sunt renati, regni caelestis mereantur introitum."

§ 283: "(Collectio). / Famuli tui, domine, qui ad tuam sunt graciam vocati, tuo indesinenter protegantur auxilio, ut qui divino sunt baptismo regenerati, numquam a tui regni potencia possint evelli."

§ 286: "Immolacio. Vere dignum et iustum est, quia verus ille agnus qui pro nobis est immolatus, / qui mortem nostram resurgendo reparavit Jesus Christus dominus noster. Cui merito omnes angeli."

labacrum abluti, quo spiritu regenerati, quo sanguine sunt redempti.''

This last prayer (§ 309) has some very interesting qualities. The opening phrase: *Deus misericordiae sempiterne,* is the only one of its kind in the entire *Ordo.*[32] In the *Expositio* there is reference to the fact that the Greek word ἔλαιον used for the Latin word *oleum,* is translated at times as *misericordia.*[33] The prayer goes on to ask for an increase of grace (or mercy) which has already been given. May those baptized understand precisely what has happened to them: they are cleansed by water, given new life through the Spirit, and redeemed by Christ's blood. The principal event of salvation history, Redemption, was accomplished through Christ's blood, by His death on the cross. Everyone can share in this salvation event today, baptized by water and the Spirit. The water cleanses (or forgives sin), and the Spirit regenerates man (empowers him to lead a new life, configured to Christ). Once again there is evidence of the close cooperation between Christ and the Holy Spirit found in the Gothicum texts.

The last two prayers (§§ 307 and 309) provide summaries of the baptismal liturgy of the Easter Vigil, and quite appropriately since they are prayed in the Christian community on this last (summarizing) day of Easter Week.

Missa In Die Sancto Pentecosten. The Mass texts for Pentecost Sunday allude to the presence of the Holy Spirit and His operation in man's life. These texts have been analyzed to find if there are any special references or phrases regarding the Holy Spirit operating in a way similar to that spoken of within the baptismal ordo.

The first prayer of Pentecost Sunday alludes to adoption by the Spirit:

"Da populis tuis capire intellectu, quod dicere miraculo, ut adopcio, quam in eos spiritus sanctus advocavit, nihil in dileccione tepidum, nihil habeat in confessione diversum: per (§ 358).''

[32] Cf. also in other Gallican texts, Georg Manz, *Ausdrucksformen der Lateinischen Liturgiesprache bis in Elfte Jahrhundert. Texte und Arbeiten,* I, (Berlin 1941).

[33] E. C. Ratcliff, *Expositio Antiquae Liturgiae Gallicanae* (Henry Bradshaw Society 98, 1971) 19, § 5b.

The Spirit will help the Christian keep his love alive, and prevent him from error in the profession of his faith. There is reference to the "adoption" which the Holy Spirit offered man on the occasion of his baptism, having taken place either at the Easter Vigil, or some other previous time, or even immediately preceding this Pentecost Mass. The "Spirit of Adoption" is a common phrase in the prayer texts of baptismal ceremonies, and it is interesting to have some reference to it cited here on Pentecost, which was not most probably a day for celebrating the ritual of Christian Initiation.

The prayer *Ad Pacem* pleads for a preservation *(conserva)* of the grace of sanctification within the new offspring of God's family:

"Domine, sancte pater, omnipotens aeterne deus, cuius spiritu totum corpus eclesiae multiplicatur et regitur, conserva in novam familiae tuae progeniem sanctificacionis graciam, quam dedisti, ut corpore et mente renovati puram tibi animam cum securitate ⟨m⟩ pacis et purum pectus semper exhibeant: per (§ 361)."

This prayer seems to refer to the newly baptized, for the phrase, "Conserva in novam familiae tuae progeniem sanctificacionis graciam," is frequently used in a baptismal context. Again, it is not clear whether the baptism referred to here was that of the Easter Vigil or one that might have taken place earlier in the day (Pentecost Day). The concept of "preservation" *(conserva)*, frequently used in reference to the baptismal graces, is stressed here as it is in other baptismal prayer texts. Both of the concepts which are highlighted, namely, adoption and preservation, could refer to the special working of the Holy Spirit as may be found in the chrismation ceremony. Pentecost Sunday is an appropriate time for such important events to be celebrated.

Missa In Vigiliis Ephiphaniae. Because of the tradition in the church to celebrate baptism on the feast of the Epiphany, the texts for this Mass have been consulted. There is no significant evidence for this day in the Bobbio, and the Gallicanum Vetus does not even have a text for the day. There are some noteworthy references in the Gothicum texts however.[34]

[34] Cf. Mitchell, *Baptismal Anointing*, 163.

There is no indication that this Vigil Mass followed any baptismal ceremony. Most of the Mass texts do not focus their concern on baptism, and even though the *Praefatio* (§ 76) refers to Our Lord's baptism in the Jordan and the miracle at Cana, these are traditional examples of the special manifestation of God in the world, which the Epiphany feast would probably emphasize. The first collect of the Mass (§ 77) refers to the sanctification given to man through the waters of regeneration, and the Holy Spirit coming to man in the form of a spiritual dove.[35]

Missa In Diem Sanctum Ephyphaniae. The *Praefatio* of the Mass directly refers to the infusion of the Spirit:

"Et qui aliis saturitatem meri potatione concessit nos potationis suae libamine et paraclyti spiritus infusione sanctificet" (§ 82).

The context of this passage is one of "drinking." If God could satisfy people's thirst by a mere drink (of wine), those who share of His drink, that is, those who share in His life, and receive the infusion of the Spirit of God, will be sanctified. The reference then is to a sharing in God's life, and receiving an infusion of the Spirit.

In the context of speaking of God's wonderful works, the first collect of the Mass (§ 83) describes the regeneration of man through the sacrament of baptism, effected by the Holy Spirit. Another reference is made in the same prayer to man's dying (to the world) and rising (to Christ).[36]

It is not until the *Contestatio* that one finds a somewhat sustained reference to baptism, and in particular, the baptismal font.

---

[35] Mohlberg, *Gothicum*, § 77, 23: "Collectio Sequitur. Deus, qui per unigenitum Iesum Christum filium tuum dominum nostrum sanctificationem salutis aeternae aquas regenerantibus praestisti et veniente super caput illius spiritali columba per spiritum sanctum ipse venisti . . ." Cf. *DACL*, 1914 ed., s.v. "Colombe," by J. P. Kirsch, c. 2198–2231.

[36] Mohlberg, *Gothicum*, § 83, 24. "Collectio Sequitur . . . Qui in / corpore nostro mirabilis baptismi sacramento regeneratos ex spiritu nos abluens renascendo et ineffabilis potentiae dono hodie aquas in vina mutando discipulis tuis tuam manifestasti divinitatem: Exaudi nos supplices tuos ob diem sacratissimae sollempnitatis et praesta, ut gloria tua inluminati saeculo moriamur, tibi / regi Christo vivamus, salvator mundi."

The function of the baptismal font is described in terms of the effects of baptism, i.e., remission of sin and a regeneration of man:

". . . fontem purificasti et tuum unicum per columbam sancti spiritus demonstrasti. Susceperunt fontes hodie benedictionem tuam / et tulerunt maledictionem nostram, ita ut credentibus purificationem omnium delictorum exhibeant et deo filios regenerando faciant ad vitam aeternam, quos ad temporalem vitam carnalis nativitas fuerat . . ." (§ 86).

The word *hodie* in the text is interesting. One could translate the sentence as "The fonts have *today* received . . ." followed by the descriptive narrative. The baptismal font is usually blessed within the baptismal ceremony, and so from the textual evidence it might be said that baptism was celebrated on the feast of the Epiphany. In other words, the prayers and prefaces of the Vigil and the Epiphany feasts make clear that the Ordo of Christian Initiation was celebrated on these days.

A Brief Summary of the Gothicum. The Missale Gothicum stresses the role of the Trinity which provides a context for the missal's theology of initiation.

The role of Christ in the Redemption, and the role of the Holy Spirit imparting the "fullness of grace" predominate the baptismal and postbaptismal texts. The prayers constantly refer to man's new life born of "water and the Spirit and blood." The *lavacrum* contains the water through which God bestows: (1) forgiveness and healing of sin; (2) "adoption" by which man is made co-heir with Christ; (3) priestly and kingly powers; and (4) the power to form Christ within man's life.

The chrismation formula in this missal is very important. When the formula speaks of the chrismation given to the baptizands, it refers to the bestowal of a garment. The putting on of the chrism is the putting on of the Holy Spirit. That fact described in concrete terms determines the use of the analogy of "putting on a garment." The chrismation bestows the Spirit who gives the special gifts of new life: salvation; perfection; incorruptibility; and immortality (an eschatological theme runs throughout the missal's text).

The references to the Holy Spirit in the Gothicum chrismation formula leads one to hypothesize that this chrismation was a special Gallican postbaptismal ceremony. The exclusive references to the Spirit and His special coming upon man in the fullness or perfection of grace suggest the importance of this rite. The texts stress the roles in man's life shared by Christ and the Spirit.

The Gothicum texts reveal that water baptism effects in man the forgiveness of sin and a new adoption by Christ who begins to be formed in men especially through man's reception of priestly and kingly powers. It is the postbaptismal chrismation which seems to allow man to put on the robe of incorruptibility and immortality, that is, the fullness of grace which guarantees that he can now live out his "new life" and walk on toward eternal life "sealed" by the Holy Spirit.

BRIEF WITNESS OF THE TWO OTHER
MAJOR GALLICAN SACRAMENTARIES

The Bobbio Missal. The prebaptismal prayers of this missal stress the concepts of rebirth (1 Corinthians 5:7b) and strength (making firm, preserving), which are celebrated through the power of the Holy Spirit.

The postbaptismal chrismation clearly refers to the work of the Holy Spirit. The prayers speak of regeneration, the life of the "New Man" (§§ 249, 261) and the forgiveness of sins (§§ 237, 249, 310).

The Mass prayers refer to the gifts of the Holy Spirit under the titles of "Spirit of Adoption" (§§ 235, 310), and "Spirit of Sanctification" (§ 257).

The principal thrust of this sacramentary, then, is the work of Christ to change a person's life: to remove the "Old Man" from his life, to grant him "regeneration" through water and the Holy Spirit, and forgiveness of sins.

Even though reference to the Holy Spirit has been made rather clearly, the Spirit in these texts effects in man's life what Jesus Christ has won for man in His Redemption. Christology, then, seems to be emphasized here rather than Pneumatology.

There is no intention to draw any opposition between the Gothicum and the Bobbio and their different emphases. It is interesting to see that although one sacramentary may have one principal theological emphasis, all the sacramentaries have references to both Jesus Christ and the Holy Spirit, and their "cooperation" in the work of man's salvation.

The Missale Gallicanum Vetus. The predominant thought pattern in this missal is Pauline: the frequent reference to the "Old Man vs. New Man" theme (§§ 124, 168, 169, 177), the person dying and rising with Christ (§§ 124, 166, 168), and living according to truth and justice (§ 60). There are frequent references to Johannine theology, especially baptism ex *aqua et spiritu* (§§ 126, 175), and reference to the "Spirit of Adoption" (§§ 164).

One of the most interesting theological insights gained in this sacramentary was from a study of the Chrismal Preface (§ 82) which borrowed part of its theme from 1 Peter 2:9: through the chrismation, one shares in Christ's kingly, priestly and prophetic roles in the world, empowered by the Holy Spirit.

The role of the Holy Spirit is adequately emphasized in the Chrismal Preface for Maundy Thursday (§§ 82 ff.), and in the prayers over the blessing of the Font (§ 166). The Holy Spirit thus is the life-principle of the new Christian, directly strengthened by the Spirit so as to configure his life more and more to Christ's: dying ("Old Man") and rising ("New Man") with Him.

USE OF SACRED SCRIPTURE IN THE INITIATION RITES

It can be seen from the close scrutiny given to the *Missale Gothicum* (and the brief account of the other two major sacramentaries) that it is above all the use of Scripture that truly characterizes a particular liturgical rite.

One of the most interesting and valuable Gallican liturgical sources is the *Luxeuil Lectionary,* which has the distinction of being that manuscript in the Gallican corpus which is the least influenced by Roman practice.[37]

In the readings found in the *Luxeuil* for the days *In Symboli Traditione, In Vigiliis Pasche,* and *In Pasche* one can find references to themes such as new life in Christ, baptismal forgiveness of sin,

---

[37] *Le Lectionnaire de Luxeuil, Paris, B. N. ms. lat. 9427,* ed. P. Salmon, I: *Edition et Etude comparative,* Collectanea Biblica Latina, 7, (Vatican 1944): II: *Etude paléographique et liturgique,* Collectanea Biblica Latina, 9, (Vatican 1935): see especially I, p. lxxviii.

and life in the Holy Spirit. These particular emphases are found in Masses where the Scriptural readings emphasize the Resurrection event as well.

There are two days in the Luxeuil whose development of readings would be interesting to look at more closely:

Clausum Paschae. *Clausum Paschae* was important in the Gallican church because it was the day when the newly baptized took off their white baptismal garments received on Easter morning.[38]

The *Luxeuil Lectionary* has three readings for this day, with the recitation or singing of the Canticle from Daniel (Daniel 3:52-59) to be used between the second and third readings. The first reading is from Isaiah 61:1-7, about which much was said when the Gothicum's postbaptismal chrismation formula was treated. The verses refer to a "putting on of the Spirit," the image of someone putting on a garment: ". . . spiritus Domini super me eo quod unxerit Dominus me ad adnuntiandum mansuetis misit me ut mederer contritis corde et praedicarem captivis indulgentiam et clausis apertionem" (Isaiah 61:1). On this day when the newly baptized would take off their white baptismal garments, this passage could have been chosen because it very appropriately reminded people of the more important garment which they put on at their baptism, that is, the Holy Spirit. The baptismal robe which they removed was a symbolic reference to the important baptismal event of a week earlier.

The second reading is from 1 Corinthians 15:12-28, a passage which primarily speaks of the Resurrection of Christ and the importance of one's faith in the Resurrection. But there is a reference also to the power of Christ's Resurrection in a person's life: ". . . quoniam enim per hominem mors et per hominem resurrectio mortuorum et sicut in Adam omnes moriuntur ita et in Christo omnes vivificabuntur" (1 Corinthians 15:21-22).

The Christian actually shares in Jesus Christ's life, death and Resurrection by the fact of his baptism.

The third reading is from John 20:19-25, the post-Resurrection account of Jesus appearing to the disciples where He wished them peace and "showed them his hands and his side." The entire pas-

[38] Salmon, *Luxeuil* 1, xcii–cxiii.

sage has significance for this important day at the end of Easter week; it recalls the Resurrection event of Jesus Christ, emphasizing the giving of the Spirit: ". . . hoc cum dixisset insuflavit et dicit eis accipite Spiritum Sanctum. Quorum remiseritis peccata remittuntur eis quorum retinueritis detenta sunt" (John 20:22-23) and serves as a reminder of the special coming of the Holy Spirit at baptism just one week earlier. One can say further that if this lectionary's author or redactor were aware of the type of initiation ceremonies described by Alcuin (735–804), i.e., having the episcopal chrismation (or what today we term confirmation) on this day *(Clausum Paschae)*, this passage of John 20:19-25, as well as the first two, would be most fitting and even descriptive of such an important liturgical event (especially Isaiah 61:1-7 and John 20:19-25). These readings are theologically rich, filled with significant references to the Holy Spirit and His work with man; and they certainly belong to a day (or a week) that must have been considered quite important to the Gallican church of this era.[39]

In Sancto Pentecosten. The Luxeuil Lectionary has three readings for this festive day, the first of which is Joel 2:21–3:5, the promise of God to grant material blessings to Judah as well as the spiritual outpouring of the spirit on Judah. The famous passage of Joel is: ". . . et erit post haec effundam spiritum meum super omnem

---

[39] This *Luxeuil* lectionary was in the late seventh or early eighth century, perhaps a little too early to have any similarity with Alcuin's practice. However, in the rite of Alcuin and Rabanus Maurus the bishop laid his hand upon the baptized not immediately after the Mass of the Paschal Vigil, but a week later, i.e., on the *Clausum Paschae; Monumenta Germaniae Historica* IV, Epp. Merov. et Karol. Aevi II, Ep 143, 226 *(MGH):*

"Et tunc maxime, dum alba tolluntur a baptizatis vestimenta (eos) per manus impositionem a pontifice Spiritum sanctum accipere conveniens est, qui in baptismo omnium receperunt remissionem peccatorum et per septem dies in angelico castitatis habitu et luminibus coelestis claritatis sanctis adsistere sacrificiis solent."

Fisher translates: "and then especially, when their white robes are taken away from the baptized, it is convenient through the imposition of hand by the bishop for them to receive the Holy Spirit, who in baptism received remission of all their sins and for seven days in the angelic attire of purity and with the lights of heavenly brightness are wont to assist at the eucharist." J. D. C. Fisher, *Christian Initiation: Baptism in the Medieval West,* 65.

carnem et prophetabunt filii vestri et filiae vestrae senes vestri
somnia somniabunt et iuvenes vestri visiones videbunt . . ."
(Joel 2:28).

The second lesson is Acts 2:1-21, a description of the Pentecost
event, as well as the beginning of Peter's discourse to the Jews
witnessing the event, in which he quotes the Joel passage. Peter
says that this promise in Joel is fulfilled in the event of that first
Pentecost day.

The third and last lesson in the Luxeuil document is John 14:15-
29; Jesus promises that He will not leave His disciples abandoned
but will send the Spirit, the Paraclete. In this particular passage,
John refers to the "Spirit of Truth," one who reveals all truth and
helps man to understand God and to act accordingly; this is the
Spirit that Jesus sends, who will teach people all things, and bring
to their remembrance all that He (Christ) has said to them. An important excerpt of this passage is the reference to the "Spirit of
Truth": 16. ". . . et ergo rogabo Patrem et alium paracletum dabit
vobis ut maneat vobiscum in aeternum. 17. Spiritum veritatis quem
mundus non potest accipere quia non videt eum nec scit eum vos
autem cognoscitis eum quia apud vos manebit et in vobis erit"
(John 14:16-17).

The last Supper discourse in John's Gospel has further references to the "Spirit of Truth" coming as Jesus' gift; and the Spirit
helps people to understand all that Jesus taught while He was
with them: 26. "cum autem venerit paracletus quem ego mittam
vobis a Patre Spiritum veritatis qui a Patre procedit ille testimonium perhibebit de me. 27. et vos testimonium perhibetis quia ab
initio mecum estis" (John 15:26-27); ". . . cum autem venerit ille
Spiritus veritatis docebit vos omnem veritatem non enim loquetur
in semet ipso sed quaecumque audiet loquetur et quae ventura
sunt adnuntiabit vobis" (John 16:13).

The three Luxeuil lessons fit together as a perfect development
of thought: the promise of God's spirit as a blessing (Joel 2:21-3:5);
the Pentecost events (Acts 2:1-21) as fulfillment of the promise
made to mankind; and the life of a person in the world today,
empowered by the Spirit (John 14:15-29) as He continues to reveal
what Jesus Christ had wished for all to know and would only in
time be able to understand.

That which gives one the ability to know the truth which the Spirit reveals is his baptism *ex aqua et spiritu*. Because of this baptism one is an heir to all that God promised, particularly in Jesus. The prayer-texts of the sacramentaries sometimes refer to the "Spirit of Adoption," that Spirit which enables or empowers one to function as a Christian (e.g., Bobbio, §§ 235, 310; Gothicum §§ 288, 358; Vetus § 164). Once a person is born of water and the Spirit, he has received the "Spirit of Adoption," and he can also be said to have received the "Spirit of Sanctification" (e.g., Bobbio § 257, Vetus § 178), and the "Spirit of Truth" (e.g., Gothicum § 257, Vetus § 60). It is this latter title which the Luxeuil readings emphasize on this Pentecostal day.

The Luxeuil manuscript, the most complete and clear of the lectionaries available from the Gallican Church, stresses many Scriptural themes which have direct or parallel references within the Gothicum baptismal liturgy.

These principal Scriptural themes found in the Luxeuil (and related lectionaries), as has been mentioned above, would be forgiveness of sins, the "Old Man vs. New Man" theme, and the role of the Holy Spirit in the Christian's life.

The following *schema* of themes indicates: (1) a few of the major themes, (2) where they are most clearly found throughout the manuscript, and (3) a suggested Scriptural background which most probably provided the basis for the theology of the Gallican baptismal and postbaptismal texts.

Forgiveness of sins. The "forgiveness of sins" theme is one of the important baptismal emphases contained in all three of the principal sacramentaries:

Gothicum § 251 (*Oraciones Paschalis Duodecim - Pro Caticuminis*)
Gothicum § 255 (*Collectio Ad Fontes Benedicendos - Praefacio*)
Gothicum § 258 (*Collectio Ad Fontes Benedicendos - Exorcism*)
Bobbio   § 237 (*Easter Vigil - Benedictio Fontis*)
Bobbio   § 249 (*Easter Vigil - Infusio Crismae*)
Bobbio   § 310 (*Missa in Quinquagesima - Collectio Ad Pacem*)
Vetus   § 167 (*Opus Ad Baptizandum - Benedictio Fontis*)
Vetus   § 175 (*Opus Ad Baptizandum - Infusio Crismae*)

Old Man versus New Man. This is certainly one of the most popular themes found in a variety of expressions throughout the sacramentaries. Only some of the most explicit references are offered here:

Bobbio	§ 237 *(Easter Vigil - Benedictio Fontis)*
Bobbio	§ 249 *(Easter Vigil - Infusio Crismae)*
Vetus	§ 261 *(Missa In Vigiliis Pasche - Contestacio)*
Vetus	§ 124 *(Oratio Post Lectiones Sabbati - Oratio in Sabbati Hora Nona)*
Vetus	§ 166 *(Opus Ad Baptizandum - Praefacio ad Benedicendum Fontis)*
Vetus	§ 167 *(Opus Ad Baptizandum - Benedictio Fontis)*
Vetus	§ 168 *(Opus Ad Baptizandum - Contestatio Fontis)*
Vetus	§ 177 *(Opus Ad Baptizandum - Post Baptismum).*

Both of the above themes can find their origins in a variety of Scripture passages, but some of the following pericopes seem to be the clear inspiration for the sacramentary texts:

22. ''. . . deponere vos secundum pristinam conversationem veterem hominem qui corrumpitur secundum desideria erroris. 23. renovamini autem spiritu mentis vestrae. 24. et induite novum hominem qui secundum Deum creatus est in justitia et sanctitate veritatis'' (Ephesians 4:22-24).

9. ''nolite mentiri invicem expoliantes vos veterem hominem cum actibus eius. 10. et induentes novum eum qui renovatur in agnitionem secundum imaginem eius qui creavit eum'' (Colossians 3:9-10).

''. . . oportet enim corruptibile hoc induere incorruptelam et mortale hoc induere immortalitatem'' (1 Corinthians 15:53).[40]

''. . . et sicut in Adam omnes moriuntur ita et in Christo omnes vivificabuntur'' (1 Corinthians 15:22).[41]

---

[40] *Jerome Biblical Commentary,* s.v. ''The Letter to the Ephesians,'' by Joseph A. Grassi, 347–48; G. R. Beasley-Murray, *Baptism in the New Testament* (Grand Rapids 1962), 147–48, 149, 286; *Jerome Biblical Commentary,* s.v. ''The Letter to the Colossians,'' by Joseph Grassi, 339.

[41] Rudolph Schnackenburg, *Baptism in the Thought of St Paul,* trans. by G. R. Beasley-Murray, (New York 1964), 113–15.

21. "in hoc enim vocati estis quia et Christus passus est pro nobis, vobis relinquens exemplum ut sequamini vestigia eius. 22. qui peccatum non fecit nec inventus est dolus in ore ipsius. 23. qui cum malediceretur non maledicebat cum pateretur non comminabatur tradebat autem iudicanti se iniuste. 24. qui peccata nostra ipse pertulit in corpore suo super lignum ut peccatis mortui iustitiae viveremus cuius livore sanati estis. 25. eratis enim sicut oves errantes sed conversi estis nunc ad pastorem et episcopum animarum vestrarum" (1 Peter 2:21-25).[42]

4. "conseputil enim sumus cum illo . . . 5. si enim conplantati facti simus similitudini mortis eius . . . 6. hoc scientes quia vetus homo noster simul crucifixus est . . . 8. si autem mortui sumus cum Christo . . . credimus quia simul etiam vivemus cum Christo" (Romans 6:4-8).[43]

Ex Aqua Et Spiritu. Along with the other themes, the liturgical texts are filled with references to the theme of the person's rebirth *ex aqua et spiritu.* The following sacramentary texts make such clear references:

Gothicum § 221 (*Orationes in Biduana - Praefatio in Vespera Paschae*)
Gothicum § 256 (*Collectio Ad Fontes Benedicendos*)
Gothicum § 264 (*Collectio Ad Fontes Benedicendos*)
Gothicum § 290 (*Missa Matutinalis Per Totam Pascha Pro Parvolis Qui Renati Sunt. Tercia Feria*)
Gothicum § 307 (*Missa Matutinalis Per Totam Pascha Pro Parvolis Qui Renati Sunt. Missa Die Sabbato Octava Paschae*)
Vetus   § 166 (*Opus Ad Baptizandum - Praefacio Ad Benedicendum Fontis*).

Themes that are closely related to this one refer to regeneration and renewal, as well as to "adoption" received through the power of the Holy Spirit. This "adoption" theme is found in several texts:

---

[42] Beasley-Murray, *Baptism in the New Testament*, 251–58.
[43] Burkhard Neunheuser, *Baptism and Confirmation*, trans. J. J. Hughes, The Herder History of Dogma, (New York 1964), 24; Beasley-Murray, *Baptism in the New Testament*, 132.

Gothicum § 288 (*Missa Matutinalis Per Totam Pascha Pro Parvolis Qui Renati Sunt - Tercia Feria*)

Gothicum § 358 (*Missa In Die Sancto Pentecosten*)

Bobbio § 235 (*Ordo Baptismi*)

Bobbio § 258 (*Missa In Vigiliis Pasche - Collectio*)

Bobbio § 310 (*Missa In Quinquagesima - Collectio Ad Pacem*)

Vetus § 164 (*Opus Ad Baptizandum - Collectio sequitur*).

The themes of rebirth *ex aqua et spiritu*; regeneration and renewal of man, and "adoption" through the Holy Spirit are closely interrelated, and most probably depend on some of the following pericopes:

3. "respondit Iesus et dixit ei: amen amen dico tibi nisi quis natus fuerit denuo non potest videre regnum Dei 4. dicit ad eum Nicodemus: quomodo potest homo nasci cum senex sit numquid potest in ventrem matris suae iterato introire et nasci 5. respondit Iesus: amen amen dico tibi nisi quis renatus fuerit ex aqua et Spiritu non potest introire in regnum Dei" (John 3:3-5).

6. "hic est qui venit per aquam et sanguinem Iesus Christus; non in aqua solum sed in aqua et sanguine et Spiritus est qui testificatur quoniam Christus est veritas. 7. quia tres sunt qui testimonium dant: 8. Spiritus et aqua et sanguis: et hi tres unum sunt" (1 John 5:6-8).

5. "non ex operibus iustitiae quae fecimus nos sed secundum suam misericordiam salvos nos fecit per lavacrum regenerationis et renovationis Spiritus Sancti. 6. quem effudit in nos abunde per Iesum Christum salvatorem nostrum. 7. ut iustificati gratia ipsius heredes simus secundum spem vitae aeternae" (Titus 3:5-7).[44]

In addition to the above themes the reader should note that there are frequent references, expressed in a variety of forms, which stress the abundance or fullness of grace which is given to the candidate in the initiation ceremonies. There is also reference to the important sevenfold gift of the Spirit, preparing one totally to live out the newly-received life in Christ.

[44] Raymond E. Brown, *The Gospel According to John*, The Anchor Bible, (London 1971), 144; Beasley-Murray, *Baptism in the New Testament*, 231-32, 239-42.

These themes found in the Gallican sacramentaries are closely intertwined and they pervade the entire initiation ceremony. The very same themes could be found in a Palm Sunday *collectio*, or in a Preface for the blessing of the baptismal font, or even within the postbaptismal ceremonies. In other words, the themes are not logically separated from one another, enabling one to see a methodical progression of themes. Rather, the themes overlap one another and one can find a mention of two or three of the themes within the one same prayer which could be found anywhere within the initiation ceremony. This use of repeated themes in all parts of the baptismal liturgical texts renders the impression that one is discovering here in the initiation ritual a "unified" theological statement.

One might also assert that this unity which derives from the consistent overlapping and repetition of all the major Western theological (baptismal) themes, also indicates that the Gallican church must have perceived their initiation rites as equivalent to a complete ceremony.[45]

WITNESS OF THE FATHERS AND ECCLESIASTICAL WRITERS

Many of the Fathers and Ecclesiastical writers[46] spoke of the priestly postbaptismal anointing in which they described a per-

[45] For an interesting development of the difference between the Eastern and Western approaches to the baptismal ceremony, see G. Kretschmar, "Die Geschichte des Taufgottesdienstes in der alten Kirche," in *Leiturgia, Handbuch des Evangelischen Gottesdienstes*, eds. K. Müller, W. Blankenburg, Vol. V. *Der Tauf-Gottesdienst* (Kassel 1970); Kretschmar describes how the Greeks saw baptism as an unfolding from around the central event of the baptismal bath; the Eastern approach is a circular or elliptical one, as contrasted to the Western mode of thought which is linear, that is, one ceremony following the other in a definite progression (236). This reference is also cited and developed in Hugh M. Riley, *Christian Initiation* . . . Studies in Christian Antiquity, 17, (Washington, D.C. 1974), 399, n. 144.

[46] The writers that have been studied will be indicated here with no further attempt to identify their particular contribution: St Hilary of Poitiers (c. 315–367); Salvian of Marseilles (c. 400–480); Faustus of Riez (c. 408–490); Gennadius of Marseilles († 492–505); St Avitus of Vienne († c. 519); St Caesarius of Arles (c. 470–542); St Gregory of Tours (c. 540–594); St Bede the Venerable (c. 673–735); Alcuin (735–804); Leidrad of Lyons († 813); Magnus of Sens († 818); Jesse of

son's relationship to the Holy Spirit, as well as the strength to live one's new Christian life. These authors explained the postbaptismal rites celebrated by the priest in such a way that they seemed to perceive the rites as theologically complete ceremonies. However, they almost all referred to the episcopal postbaptismal chrismation also, to which they ascribed some important theological notions such as a share in Christ's kingly and priestly powers, and the reception of the fullness of the Holy Spirit. It must be remembered, however, that most of the writers that have been cited here wrote, for the most part, either before or after the time of the principal Gallican sacramentaries. They may be speaking of an era and rites other than that which produced the Gallican sacramentaries under consideration here, but their witness would nevertheless be related to these same sacramentaries and provide some further insight.

Despite the semi-Pelagian tendencies evident in fifth century Southeastern Gaul, which could have affected the doctrine of the Gallican texts and/or the writers' teachings, the theological position of almost all of these writers (as is certainly true of the Gallican sacramentary texts) was almost totally unaffected by it. Some of the writers developed a special theological explanation for the postbaptismal rites (Faustus, Alcuin, Rabanus)[47] and their empha-

---

Amiens († 836); Maxentius of Aquileia († 826); Odilbert of Milan (Archbishop from 803–814); Amalar of Trier (775–850); Theodulf of Orleans (c. 750–821); Jonas of Orleans († 843); and Rabanus Maurus (776 or 784–856).

[47] Faustus' position was that the episcopal postbaptismal anointing completed or perfected the process of Christian Initiation: these postbaptismal rites gave strength to a person at a moral level, so that he could live out his baptismal commitment: for Faustus, this anointing was a second birth "from above"; see L. A. Van Buchem, L'Homélie pseudo-eusébienne de Pentecôte: l'origine de la Confirmation en Gaule Méridionale et l'interprétation de ce rite par Fauste de Riez (Nijmegen 1967), especially 40–41, 52–53, 154–60, 164–67.

Alcuin wrote that through the postbaptismal ceremonies one receives the sevenfold gift of the Spirit, whereby he can preach to others in words and examples; see MGH, Epistolae IV, Epistola 110, pp. 157–59; Epistola 137, 210; Epistola 134, 202–03; Epistola 143, 226.

Rabanus Maurus distinguishes between the two postbaptismal anointings and attributes the candidate's role of habitatio or dwelling-place of God to the priestly anointing while describing the conferral of the sevenfold gift of the

sis on the effect of these latter rite as "strengthening" the newly baptized appears to have some strains of semi-Pelagianism (especially Faustus).

The Fathers and Ecclesiastical writers made no new contribution to the theology of the Gallican postbaptismal rites, with the exception of Faustus of Riez. But the witness these writers did offer corroborated the theological significance of the Gallican postbaptismal rites discovered in the sacramentary texts.

WITNESS OF THE COUNCILS

The Gallican councils[48] indicated that, more than anything else, much reform was needed in the Gallican church of the sixth-eighth centuries. The conciliar witness emphasized the role of the bishop not only in the postbaptismal ceremony but in all the ecclesial activities of the diocese. The conciliar statements indicated that on the one hand the bishop and clergy were mandated to assume their functions, and that on the other hand no one else should dare usurp their power and authority.

These councils do point out that the bishops of the Gallican dioceses at this time were not doing all that they should. This is important information when one asks why no episcopal functions were indicated in the Gallican sacramentaries (e.g., the episcopal anointing or imposition of hand); the sacramentaries contained only a simple postbaptismal anointing.

Spirit as that which is received through the episcopal anointing; see *De Clericorum Institutione*, PL 107: 312–14.

[48] The Councils that were studied for statements regarding the baptismal and postbaptismal practice of the Gallican Church were: Council of Riez (Nov. 18, 439); First Council of Orange (Nov. 8, 441); Third Council of Arles (c. 449–461); Frankish Council of 798 (Concilium Rispacense); Council of Aix-la-Chapelle (802); Council of Paris (829); Council of Aix-la-Chapelle (836); Council of Meaux (845); and Council of Tribur (May 5, 895). For the earlier councils the following texts were used: C. Munier, ed., *Concilia Galliae A. 314-A. 506*, Corpus Christianorum. Series Latina, 148 (Turnhout 1963); C. De Clercq, ed., *Concilia Galliae A. 511-A. 695*, Corpus Christianorum. Series Latina, 148A (Turnhout 1963); for the later councils various sources were used: *Monumenta Germaniae Historica (MGH)*; Mansi, and Hefelé-Leclercq's, *Histoire des Conciles* (1907).

CONCLUSIONS

The title and introduction to this article have indicated that its concern has been with the theological understanding of the Gallican postbaptismal rites of the seventh and eighth centuries. Each section of this study has brought forward some witness regarding such a theology. The sole motivation for investigating the Gothicum as well as the other Gallican liturgical texts has been to let the texts reveal their theological content.

It must be clearly understood that, especially from a short study such as this, it is only the *cumulative* force of all the expositions and insights indicated here which will provide the most appropriate understanding for the theology of the liturgical texts of the Gallican postbaptismal liturgy.

Despite the fact that an individual sacramentary or liturgical book might have stressed one particular theological position, the Pauline and Johannine themes emphasizing the Christological and Pneumatic theologies in the baptismal liturgy were found in almost all the Gallican texts. The roles performed by Christ and the Holy Spirit and their cooperation in one's salvation pervaded the prayer-texts whether in the prebaptismal, baptismal, or postbaptismal ceremonies. The Scriptural passages in the liturgical texts provided the thematic integration of the ritual celebrations.

The Gallican sacramentaries clearly indicated how Sacred Scripture influenced them: recall the Johannine pericopies which referred to rebirth *ex aqua et spiritu* (John 3:5; 1 John 5:8), and the Pauline passages which referred to one's incorporation into Christ's life by the power of His death and resurrection (Romans 6:1-11; Titus 3:5-7). These texts formed the core-theology of the sacramentaries, and they clearly emphasized cooperation between Jesus Christ and the Holy Spirit in effecting man's salvation.

The texts also revealed how the candidate received the fullness of God's grace through the initiation ceremonies. The postbaptismal chrismation is symbolically spoken of as a garment which had theological overtones based on the Pauline imagery (Romans 6) of man putting on new life in Christ, and the Isaian (61:1) passage whereby man is described as receiving the fullness of grace. The postbaptismal chrismation conferred a fullness of grace because through this rite man shared in the kingly, priestly, and prophetic roles of Christ.

The Gallican sacramentary texts revealed a theological completeness; one did not have to look elsewhere for the texts indicated
that theologically the complete initiation of man into the body of
Christ had taken place. Jesus Christ and the Spirit have accomplished all that is necessary for one to live his "new life," and the
ceremonies spoke of this *fact* in detail. The fullness of grace was
given in this rite and nothing more was needed; the picture that is
formed from the superimposition of the various themes in the
sacramentary texts is a complete one.

The study of the Gallican postbaptismal rites of the seventh and
eighth centuries, especially as found in the Gothicum, asks this
author to recommend for consideration that these rites were
equivalent to the effects of the sacrament of episcopal confirmation.
That is, *theologically*, these rites present themselves as complete
and integral, not even demanding the episcopal consignation. This
conclusion is drawn from all of the evidence that has been studied
in another place, and admittedly could only be partially revealed
in this limited space.

Whether one terms these Gallican postbaptismal ceremonies a
rite of confirmation or not is not very important. The principal
concern of this article was to discern the theological content of
these rites as found in the well-known Gallican sacramentaries
and to discover if there was support for this in other Gallican witnesses. This concern has been satisfied. The primary sacramentary
texts, especially the Gothicum, have repeated references to Scriptural themes such as the forgiveness of sins, rebirth *ex aqua et
spiritu*, regeneration, the "Old Man vs. New Man," and the
"Spirit of Adoption." Along with references indicating the fullness of grace and the sevenfold gift of the Spirit these themes
blend and pervade all the baptismal and postbaptismal texts and
convince one that the ceremony is a complete unit. This author
believes that "theologically" the rites celebrated were adequate
and complete as a celebration of full Christian Initiation.

Gabriele Winkler

11. Confirmation or Chrismation?
A Study in Comparative Liturgy

The Apostolic Constitution of Paul VI *Divinae consortium naturae*
(1971) specifies that confirmation is conferred through an anointing
with chrism on the forehead and that the effect of the sacrament
is a sealing with the gift of the Spirit.[1] This decree, representing
as it does a virtually unprecedented receptivity on the part of the
Roman See to the tradition of the Eastern churches, seems to require a radical reevaluation of the Western doctrine and practice of
confirmation. Since the term "confirmation," ultimately the basis
for so much Western theological speculation concerning the nature
of the sacrament, is first encountered in Gallican documents, it
seems useful to reexamine carefully the pertinent documents and,
more generally, the Gallican tradition with regard to postbaptismal rites.

In studying the Gallican tradition concerning postbaptismal rites
it is necessary to take careful account of the provenance of the
relevant documents and also, more important, to distinguish
clearly between the language of liturgical formularies, that is, the
text of prayers, and the juridical formulations of decrees of synods
of south Gaul. With these necessary distinctions it is at once apparent that the terms *confirmare* and *confirmatio* never occur in the

---

[1] *Constitutio Apostolica de Sacramento Confirmationis: Divinae consortium naturae*
in *Acta Apostolicae Sedis* 63 (1971) 657–664; for an English version see *Documents
on the Liturgy 1963–1979. Conciliar, Papal, and Curial Texts* (Collegeville 1982)
766–770 (nos. 2499–2598). I am preparing a detailed commentary on this extremely important decree for publication in a future issue of *Worship*.

earliest liturgical formularies, all of which derive from northern or eastern areas of Gaul. Furthermore, it becomes clear that these terms, which are never used in a technical sense in the earliest patristic sources, are employed by local synods of south Gaul in dealing with disputes about juridical aspects of the postbaptismal rites and that the terms, even here, are not applied to the essence of rites associated with the conferral of the Spirit, such as post-baptismal anointing.

THE WITNESS OF THE GALLICAN MISSALS

The extant Gallican liturgical books relevant to our present study are the so-called *Missale Gallicanum Vetus*,[2] the *Missale Gothicum*,[3] and the *Bobbio Missal*,[4] all of them documents of the early eighth century. Although they are commonly classified with the vague *Sammelbegriff* "Gallican missals," I consider it important to indicate for each of them the place of origin, or if this is disputed, at least the general region of origin. In the opinion of B. Bischoff, cited by Mohlberg in his edition of the manuscript,[5] the *Missale Gallicanum Vetus* (second half of Cod. Vat. Palat. 493) was apparently written in northeastern France. The *Missale Gothicum* (Cod. Vat. Reg. Lat. 317) stems either from the region of Autun or from Alsace,[6] and the *Bobbio Missal* (Cod. Paris. Bibl. Nat. 13246) was probably written in the northwestern region of the Alps, although its provenance is still very much disputed.[7] Thus two of these documents derive from the northern or northeastern part of Gaul and the other probably from the region of the Alps. None of them derives from south Gaul.

[2] See L. C. Mohlberg, *Missale Gallicanum Vetus (Cod. Vat. Palat. lat. 493)*, Rerum Ecclesiasticarum Documenta. Series major: Fontes III (Rome 1958).

[3] See L. C. Mohlberg, *Missale Gothicum (Vat. Reg. lat. 317)*, Rerum Ecclesiasticarum Documenta. Series major: Fontes V (Rome 1961).

[4] See E. A. Lowe, *The Bobbio Missal: A Gallican Mass-Book (Ms. Paris lat. 13246)*, Henry Bradshaw Society 58 (London 1919).

[5] See Mohlberg, *Missale Gallicanum Vetus*, xxii–xxiii.

[6] See Mohlberg, *Missale Gothicum*, xxiv–xxvi.

[7] Scholars such as A. Wilmart (and Mabillon) suggested Burgundy (more precisely, Luxeuil), while others proposed Irish centers in northern Italy; see A. Wilmart, E. A. Lowe, H. A. Wilson, *The Bobbio Missal (Ms. Paris. lat. 13246): Notes and Studies*, Henry Bradshaw Society 61 (London 1924) 36–39.

Missale Gallicanum Vetus. The *opus ad baptizando* of this document is of considerable interest, since it contains no reference to a separate episcopal rite after baptism. It assumes that the presbyter, after baptizing, recites the formula for the *infusio crismae:*

"Deus pater domini nostri Iesu Christi,
qui te regeneravit ex acqua et spiritu sancto [cf. John 3:5],
quique tibi dedit remissionem peccatorum,
ipsi te lenet cri[s]mate suo sancto,
ut habeas vitam aeternam in secula seculorum. Amen.'[8]

This ceremony is followed by the footwashing, as in Ambrose, probably an indication of Syrian influence.[9] The prayer *post baptismum*, which follows the footwashing, does not refer to the bestowal of the Spirit, but serves simply as a concluding prayer of the rite of initiation.[10] Thus there is only one anointing, performed by the presbyter, with no reference to a laying on of the hand. And there is no indication of a separate episcopal postbaptismal rite.

Missale Gothicum. This document provides for a postbaptismal rite similar to that of the *Gallicanum Vetus*. The baptismal formula is followed by a short rubric and a formula for postbaptismal anointing:

"Dum crisma eum tangis, dicis:
Perungo te crisma sanctitatis,
[indua te] tonicam immortalitatis,
qua[m] dominus noster Iesus Christus traditam a patre
*   primus accepit . . .'*[11]

---

[8] Mohlberg, *Missale Gallicanum Vetus*, 42 (175). For the corresponding Gelasian formula see Mohlberg, *Liber Sacramentorum Romanae Aeclesiae Ordinis Anni Circuli*, Rerum Ecclesiasticarum Documenta, Series major: Fontes IV (Rome 1960) 74 (450). (The reader should be aware of the variety in the orthography of Latin in this period.)

[9] For the best survey see E. J. Duncan, *Baptism in the Demonstrations of Aphraates the Persian Sage*, Catholic University Studies in Christian Antiquity 8 (Washington 1945) 67–78

[10] Mohlberg, *Missale Gallicanum Vetus*, 42 (176–177).

[11] Mohlberg, *Missale Gothicum*, 67 (261). English translation in E. C. Whitaker, *Documents of the Baptismal Liturgy* (London: S.P.C.K. 1970) 162: "I

According to Finnegan "'this prayer belonged with the bestowal of the white garment.'"[12] This, in my opinion, is incorrect. In the Syrian tradition, as is well known among specialists of the Christian East, the anointing or the ascent from the water is often referred to as "putting on" that garment which Adam had lost in paradise.[13] Since there is good reason for admitting Syrian influence on these "Gallican" documents, this reference to being robed with immortality at the anointing can be considered a case of such influence.[14]

The formula for the anointing is followed by formulas for the footwashing and the bestowal of the white garment and then by a concluding prayer which, like that of the *Gallicanum Vetus*, contains no reference to the gift of the Spirit.[15]

Bobbio Missal. This codex has at the rubric *suffundis crisma in fronte* a formula similar to that of the *Gallicanum Vetus*.[16] In contrast to the *Missale Gothicum* the vesting follows immediately after the anointing,[17] and then follows the washing of the feet.[18] The subsequent prayer is again only a concluding prayer.[19]

It is of great interest that the rite *ad christianum faciendum* of the *Bobbio Missal* features, after the prebaptismal signing, the rubric and formula: *insufflabis in os eius ter et dices: Accipe spiritum sanctum*

---

anoint thee with the chrism of holiness, [put on] the garment of immortality, which our Lord Jesus Christ first received from the Father . . .'"

[12] E. M. Finnegan, *The Origins of Confirmation in the Western Church. A Liturgical-Dogmatic Study of the Development of the Separate Sacrament of Confirmation Prior to the Fourteenth Century* (Dissertation, Trier 1970) I, 256.

[13] See now the superb article of S. Brock, "Clothing Metaphors as a Means of Theological Expression in Syriac Tradition," in Margot Schmidt, C. F. Geyer (eds), *Typus, Symbol, Allegorie bei den östlichen Vätern und ihren Parallelen im Mittelalter*, Eichstätter Beiträge 4 (Regensburg 1982) 11–40.

[14] See note 10.

[15] See Mohlberg, *Missale Gothicum*, 67–68 (262–265).

[16] See Lowe, *The Bobbio Missal*, 75 (249); see also the parallels pointed out by Lowe in Wilmart, *Notes and Studies*, 131 (249).

[17] See Lowe, *The Bobbio Missal*, 75 (250); Wilmart, *Notes and Studies*, 131 (250).

[18] See Lowe, *The Bobbio Missal*, 75 (251–252); Wilmart, *Notes and Studies*, 131 (251–252)

[19] See Lowe, *The Bobbio Missal*, 75–76 (253–254).

in cor retenias.[20] This, of course, invokes the Genesis story of the breathing of life into Adam (Gen 2:7). It is also remarkably reminiscent of the bestowal of the Spirit *before* baptism in the Syrian tradition.[21]

The prebaptismal anointing in the *Bobbio Missal,* with its imagery of the anointing of David, also recalls the Eastern tradition. The text for this prebaptismal anointing reads as follows:

"Unges eum de oleo sanctificato dicens:
Ungo te de oleo sanctificato
sicut unxit samuhel david in rege et propheta.''[22]

In my studies devoted to the history of initiation in the East I have demonstrated that the anointing of the head is intimately associated with the pouring of oil over David's head when he was anointed, and that this anointing is related to the outpouring of the Spirit.[23] While there is no explicit reference to the bestowal of the Spirit in this prebaptismal anointing in the *Bobbio Missal,* the reference to the anointing of David suffices to invest this anointing with pneumatic implications.[24]

The *Bobbio Missal* is characterized by a generally strong pneumatic emphasis. We find it not only in the postbaptismal anoint-

---

[20] *Ibid.,* 72 (233); English translation in Whitaker, *Documents,* 209: "After this you shall breathe into his mouth three times and say: N., receive the Holy Spirit, mayest thou guard him in thy heart."

[21] See Winkler, *Das armenische Initiationsrituale. Entwicklungsgeschichtliche und liturgievergleichende Untersuchung der Quellen des 3. bis 10. Jahrhunderts,* Orientalia Christiana Analecta 217 (Rome 1982), 77, 161, 405, 407–413, 420, 442.

[22] Lowe, *The Bobbio Missal,* 74 (242); English translation in Whitaker, *Documents,* 211: "You anoint him with sanctified oil and say: I anoint thee with sanctified oil, as Samuel anointed David to be king and prophet."

[23] See Winkler, *Das armenische Initiationsrituale,* 138, 409–412, 458–459; idem, "The Original Meaning and Implications of the Prebaptismal Anointing," *Worship* 52 (1978) 36.

[24] It is of interest that in the Syrian (and some Armenian) sources the emphasis lies on the imagery of the anointing of the *Messiah-King* (see previous note), whereas in Latin documents the imagery of *priesthood* is stressed: see, for example, Tertullian's *De baptismo,* vii (ed. R. F. Refoulé in Sources Chrétiennes 35 [Paris 1952] 76) where the postbaptismal anointing is associated with the priesthood of Aaron.

ing, but also in the rite of insufflation and anointing before baptism and in the formula for the blessing of the font (see in particular the *oracio* [sic], *collectio*, and *sursum corda*). Thus it can be compared with the Eastern sources where the coming of the Spirit is likewise not exclusively associated with the anointing, which is perceived only as the highpoint of initiation.

The blessing of the font with the reference to being born of water and the Spirit (John 3:5), as well as the allusion to Jesus' baptism in the river Jordan[25] in all three of these Gallican documents, mirrors the earliest Syrian tradition.[26] It is also important to note in this context that neither the *Missale Gothicum* nor the *Bobbio Missal* ever cite Romans 6. In other words, Paul's baptismal theology, with its christocentric "death-mysticism," is quite absent here,[27] as it is in the earliest Syrian (and Armenian) tradition.[28] The key New Testament text here is John 3:5, with the result that being born again of water and the Spirit provides the fundamental *leitmotiv* for initiation. The *Gallicanum Vetus* represents a special case, since it does twice allude to Romans 6:4. Nevertheless, the position of this citation at the end of two prayers,[29] as well as the way in which it is inserted into the text and juxtaposed to John 3:5, makes one suspect that it represents a subsequent interpolation. It could well be that Paul's baptismal theology was also originally absent from the text to which the *Gallicanum Vetus* is witness. The absence of any allusion to Romans 6 in the *Missale Gothicum* and the *Bobbio Missal* tend to support such a hypothesis.

When one takes account of the fact that the rite of footwashing as well as the pneumatic character of the anointings point to

[25] See Mohlberg, *Missale Gallicanum Vetus*, 40; idem, *Missale Gothicum*, 66–67; Lowe, *The Bobbio Missal*, 72–73.

[26] See Winkler, *Das armenische Initiationsrituale*, 77, 143, 153, 155, 162, 170–171, 209, 211, 424–425, 427–432, 434–448, 461–462.

[27] It is significant that in many early Western sources (particularly in non-Roman witnesses) the Johannine baptismal theology (and not the Pauline) is underlying baptism. For the *Missale Gothicum* see Mohlberg, 65–68, for the *Bobbio Missal*, Lowe, 71–76.

[28] See Winkler, *Das armenische Initiationsrituale*, 77, 162, 211, 424–425, 427–430, 434, 443–446, 448, 462 (= Johannine baptismal theology); 77, 163, 416, 429–430, 432, 434–438, 440–441, 444–446, 452, 454, 462 (= Pauline baptismal theology).

[29] See Mohlberg, *Missale Gallicanum Vetus*, 40 (163, 166).

Syrian influence, one must seriously doubt whether the initiation rites represented by these documents ever included any postbaptismal rite other than the one anointing, performed either by a bishop or a presbyter. There probably never was a separate laying on of the hand combined with a second anointing reserved to the bishop. Finnegan believes that the "Gallican" documents portray a later shape of initiation rites where an episcopal action was no longer customary.[30] However, I believe that these liturgical formularies reflect an archaic shape of initiation rites where either the bishop or the presbyter could confer baptism, including the postbaptismal anointing.

Evidence from Spain dating from the fourth to the seventh century tends to corroborate this hypothesis. The first council of Toledo (c. 397?) determined that while deacons should not perform the anointing, presbyters could, in the absence of the bishop, and that only the blessing of the oil used in this anointing was reserved to the bishop.[31] The second council of Barcelona, at the end of the sixth century, still allowed a presbyter to anoint the baptized in the absence of a bishop.[32] Not until the beginning of the seventh century, with the second council of Seville, does one find presbyters forbidden to anoint the forehead of the baptized — evidence, surely, of increasing Roman influence.[33] Yet even then the prohibition does not seem to have been taken very seriously, since the bishop Braulio of Saragossa (631–651) allowed his presbyters to perform the anointing as long as the oil was blessed by the bishop.[34]

Our Gallican sources, which derive from the northern part of Gaul and possibly from the northwestern region of the Alps, seem to indicate that there were communities outside of Rome which practiced only one postbaptismal anointing. This anointing was done apparently by either the bishop, if he was present, or by a presbyter. The same was, of course, true in the Christian East,

[30] See Finnegan, *The Origins of Confirmation* 1, 260–261.
[31] See J. Vives, *Concilios Visigoticos* . . . (Barcelona/Madrid 1963) 24–25; English translation in Whitaker, *Documents*, 223–224.
[32] See Vives, *Concilios Visigoticos*, 159.
[33] *Ibid.*, 167–168
[34] See his letter to the bishop of Toledo; PL 87, cols 406–407.

where it became normal for a presbyter to preside over the entire rite of initiation, and only the blessing of the oil was reserved to the bishop or, according to the present custom of the Syrian and Armenian communities, to the highest ranks of the hierarchy.[35]

Let us summarize the evidence provided by the Gallican missals. The rites of initiation to which they witness included only one postbaptismal anointing. The structural simplicity of the rites as a whole support this assumption. Furthermore, early Spanish documents, such as the treatise on baptism of Ildefonse of Toledo[36] and the *Liber Ordinum*,[37] attest only one postbaptismal anointing.

These "Gallican" sources reflect manifold Syrian influence: the conferral of the Spirit before baptism, Johannine baptismal theology (and an absence of the Pauline christocentric "death-mysticism"), an allusion to the Jordan event in the blessing of the font, and the ceremony of the footwashing. What the communities who employed these rites obviously did was to introduce the postbaptismal anointing customary throughout Greco-Latin regions while retaining, to a marked extent, other Eastern traits.[38] However, there is no evidence for the use of the terms *confirmare* and *confirmatio*, in a technical sense, with regard to the postbaptismal rites. For this one must look to local synods of south Gaul.

THE EVIDENCE OF GALLICAN SYNODS

For the technical use of *confirmare* and *confirmatio* the evidence of the Gallican local councils of Riez, Orange and Arles is crucial. Canons 3 and 4 of the council of Riez (18 November 439) dealt with juridical questions concerning the illegal consecration of a bishop, and it determined that the illegal consecration of a bishop did not

---

[35] See my contribution in *Oriens Christianus* 66 (1982) 240.

[36] See English translation in Whitaker, *Documents*, 115.

[37] See M. Ferotin, *Le Liber Ordinum en usage dans l'Église visigothique et mozarabe d'Espagne du Ve au XIe siècle*, Monumenta Eccles. Liturg. V (Paris 1904) 32–34; English translation in Whitaker, *Documents*, 121. The bestowal of the Spirit is, however, connected with the laying on of the hand after the anointing. The same is true for Isidore of Seville; see English translation in Whitaker, *Documents*, 111.

[38] For further Eastern borrowings see the interesting article of J. Quasten, "Oriental Influence in the Gallican Liturgy," *Traditio* 1 (1943) 55–78.

interfere with his power to "confirm neophytes" (*confirmare neophytos*).[39] Armentarius, who had been illegally consecrated a bishop and subsequently deposed, could, nevertheless, "confirm neophytes." The wording suggests something special, apart from the ordinary rite of initiation.

A decade or two later, sometime between 449 and 461, the third council of Arles addressed the issue of episcopal power, as distinct from that of an abbot.[40] It was the task of the bishop to "confirm the neophytes (*neophyti si fuerint ab ipso confirmentur*)."[41] Again it appears that the bishop administered something apart from the customary baptism. The data seem to indicate that the postbaptismal anointing, previously a part of the baptismal rite, had either been separated from baptism or that it had been duplicated: the presbyters either omitted the anointing in anticipation of the bishop's visit or they anointed the baptized and then presented them to the bishop on the occasion of his visit. This twofold possibility may very well conform to the practice in rural areas where the bishop could not always be present to preside over the rites of initiation.

Somewhat earlier than the third council of Arles, the council of Orange (8 November 441) dealt with the question of postbaptismal rites in its second canon:

> I a *Nullum ministrorum, qui baptizandi recipit officium,*
> b *sine chrismate usquam debere progredi*
> c *quia inter nos placuit semel chrismari.*
> II a *De eo autem qui in baptismate, quamcumque necessitate faciente, non chrismatus fuerit,*
> b *in confirmatione sacerdos commonebitur.*
> III a *Nam inter quoslibet chrismatis ipsius nonnisi una benedictio est, non ut praeiudicans quidquam,*
> b *sed ut non necessaria habeatur repetita chrismatio.*[42]

---

[39] See ed. of C. Munier, *Concilia Galliae: A. 314–A. 506*, Corpus Christianorum Series Latina 148 (Tournhoult 1963) 67–68.

[40] *Ibid.*, 131–134.

[41] *Ibid.*, 133.

[42] See Munier, *Concilia*, 78. The first part of canon 2 (Ia-c) is also found in the *Collectio Canonica* of the second council of Arles: see Munier, 120 (27/26). I

There is considerable ambiguity in this text, and much ink has been spilled over it.[43] The *crux interpretationis* lies in several passages:

1 Who is meant by "ministers" [Ia]? Chavasse is of the opinion that the term refers to deacons, who sometimes baptized in rural areas.[44] It seems, however, that this term could have been chosen in order to include presbyters as well as deacons.

2 There can be little doubt that only one (postbaptismal) anointing was customary [Ic, IIIa], which ought not to be repeated [IIIb]. The allusion in IIIb seems to imply that the baptized had sometimes been anointed twice (despite the fact that this was not originally the ordinary practice in Gaul): anointed first right after baptism by the presbyter, and perhaps occasionally by the deacon, when the bishop was not present, and then anointed a second time when the bishop visited. This presupposes, of course, that this abuse happened in rural areas where the bishop could not regularly preside over baptism.

---

have provided the numeration for the successive clauses of the canon. Let me propose the following English translation of the canon: (Ia) None of the ministers who has received the office of baptizing (Ib) shall ever proceed without chrism, (Ic) for we have agreed that the anointing should be done once; (IIa) however, in the case where someone, for whatever reason, has not been anointed at baptism, (IIb) let the bishop be reminded of this in confirmation; (IIIa) as for the chrism itself, there is in every case but one blessing, not to prejudice anything, (IIIb) but so that a repeated chrismation not be considered necessary.

[43] See for example A. Chavasse, "Le deuxième canon d'Orange de 441. Essai d'exégèse," in *Mélanges E. Podechard* (Lyons 1945) 103-120; J. D. Fisher, *Christian Initiation in the Medieval West* (London 1965) 143; P. De Puniet, "La liturgie baptismale en Gaule avant Charlemagne," *Revue des Questions Historiques* 72 (1902) 382-423; *idem*, "Onction et confirmation," *Revue d'Histoire Ecclésiastique* 13 (1912) 450-466; *idem*, "Confirmation," *Dictionnaire d'archéologie chrétienne et de liturgie* 3 (1914) cols 2515-2544; D. Van den Eynde, "Le deuxième canon du concile d'Orange de 441 sur la chrismation," *Recherches de Théologie Ancienne et Médiévale* 11 (1939) 97-109; *idem*, "Les rites liturgiques latins de la confirmation," *La Maison Dieu* 54 (1958) 53-78; Finnegan, *The Origins of Confirmation* I, 159-160, 247-251; and the most important study: L. A. Van Buchem, *L'homélie Pseudo-Eusébienne de Pentecôte. L'origine de la confirmatio en Gaul Méridionale et l'interprétation de ce rite par Fauste de Riez* (Nijmegen 1967) 95-110.

[44] Chavasse, "Deuxième canon," 104-105.

3 Moreover, Ia ("none of the ministers . . . shall anywhere proceed without chrism") and IIa ("if . . . someone for whatever reason was not anointed at baptism") seem to imply that the presbyters in rural areas might sometimes have failed to procure the required chrism from the bishop. Just one year after the council of Orange another synod, held in Vaison, had prescribed that the presbyters or ministers (*presbyteri uel ministri*) were to obtain chrism from the bishop before Easter.[45] This same regulation is found in the *Statuta Ecclesiae Antiqua*.[46] Thus it may very well be that the second canon of the council of Orange refers to the negligence of presbyters in procuring chrism, and that some presbyters in rural areas performed baptism without the baptismal anointing, for which chrism was needed, and that they waited for the occasion of the bishop's visit. This would explain the prescription of the canon that none of the ministers should baptize without the required chrism, as well as its provision that the bishop should be informed, *in confirmatione*, in case some of the baptized had not been anointed.

4 What, precisely, is meant by *in confirmatione* [IIb]? Contrary to Fisher,[47] I assume hypothetically that the term *confirmatio* is used here in a technical sense. However, does this term signify the postbaptismal anointing, or the laying on the hand, or both, or does it simply signify the visit of the bishop, who on that occasion confirmed, or ratified, what had been done previously by the presbyter (or deacon)? One must be careful not to read the evidence of Gaul with Roman presuppositions. In Rome not only had a double anointing become customary, but there was also a distinct laying on of the hand. Van Buchem remarks, a propos of this canon: "Cela signifie donc que l'intervention personelle de l'évêque est limité au minimum de l'imposition de main. . . ."[48] However, I am not as convinced as Van Buchem, and other scholars as well,[49] that in this canon the term *confirmatio* assumes an imposi-

[45] See canon 3 of the council of Vaison; Munier, *Concilia*, 97.

[46] See Munier, *Concilia*, 180 (87).

[47] J. D. C. Fisher, *Christian Initiation: Baptism in the Medieval West*, Alcuin Club 47 (London 1965) 143.

[48] Van Buchem, *L'homélie Pseudo-Eusébienne*, 108.

[49] See, for example, Van den Eynde, "Le deuxième canon du concile d'Orange," 105.

tion of the hand. Perhaps the expression in *confirmatione* does not allude to the laying on of the hand, but to the postbaptismal anointing. Quite possibly the situation envisioned by the canon was the following: on the occasion of his visitation of rural areas the bishop confirmed, or ratified, the ministry of the local presbyter (or deacon). In the process he anointed those who had not been anointed when they were baptized. Perhaps, on the occasion of his visitation he presided at the celebration of the rites of initiation. In that case he anointed those previously baptized and not anointed along with those whom he was presently baptizing.

5 While the council of Orange was concerned with the omission of anointing, it was also evidently concerned with its unnecessary repetition. This seems to be the import of the third sentence of the canon, with its expression *ipsius chrismatis . . . una benedictio.* The sentence is ambiguous. How, exactly, does *una benedictio* relate to *ipsius chrismatis?* Does *benedictio* refer to the blessing of the chrism by the bishop? Since the presbyters received the chrism from the bishop and passed it on to the baptized with the postbaptismal anointing, one could speak of one single blessing, imparted through the ministry, or agency, of various ministers — the bishop and the presbyter (or deacon). However, the reference to one single *benedictio* could also be intended to counter the opinion of rural ministers who tended to consider two anointings better than one. In this case, the reminder that there is only one single "blessing" served to challenge the practice of presbyters who did anoint after baptism and then presented the neophytes to the bishop during his visit *in confirmatione* for an additional anointing by him.

Let us summarize the data we have from the synods of south Gaul. In general this evidence from the mid-fifth century seems to indicate that *confirmatio* developed in the context of juridical issues concerning the postbaptismal rite and the office of bishop. When Armentarius was deposed by the council of Riez because he had been illegally consecrated, he was not divested of his right to "confirm" the baptized in the "parish" to which he was assigned. The council of Arles distinguished the prerogatives, or power, of bishops from those of abbots, assigning to bishops their traditional function of presiding over the rites of initiation; this episcopal function was characterized, however, as one of "confirmation": *neophyti si fuerint ab ipso confirmentur*. The terminology *confirmare neophytos* seems to suggest that in rural areas where the bishop could not regularly be present, the postbaptismal anointing had been omitted in some parishes, while in other parishes it was being duplicated, that is, presbyters anointed after baptism and then subsequently presented the neophytes to the bishop for a second anointing. If I understand it correctly, this is the situation with which the second canon of the council of Orange was concerned.

Thus I find no compelling reason why the expressions *in confirmatione* and *una benedictio* should be interpreted as referring to the laying on of hands and why the possibility of an allusion to the anointing after baptism should be *a priori* excluded from consideration. It may well be that postbaptismal anointing is meant, and not laying on of the hand. This anointing may or may not have included a laying on of the hand, but I do not believe that the rites included a laying on of the hand *distinct* from the anointing. The laying on of the hand as a separate rite was customary in Africa (e.g., Tertullian, *De baptismo*, viii) and in Rome (e.g., Hippolytus, *Traditio Apostolica*, xxii), but there is no really clear evidence for the existence of the laying on of the hand as a separate rite in Gaul, except for the reconciliation of heretics.[50] The only document that can be cited in support of the existence of the laying on of hands as a separate Gallican rite of initiation is an anonymous homily on Pentecost.

A HOMILY ON PENTECOST AND "CONFIRMATION"

This homily on Pentecost, fated to greatly influence Western understanding of "confirmation," used to be attributed to Eusebius of Emesa. More recently it has been ascribed by Van Buchem to Faustus of Riez (a fifth century Gallican bishop).[51] While I am persuaded that the homily is probably Gallican in provenance, I have reservations about accepting Faustus as its author. Compared with

[50] See, for example, the *Collectio Canonica* of the second council of Arles; Munier, *Concilia*, 117 (17).

[51] See Van Buchem, *L'homélie Pseudo-Eusébienne*, 23–82.

the authentic works of Faustus, the homily seems to reflect significant development in theological reflection about initiation. The author could have used the works of Faustus as a source. Perhaps he was personally acquainted with him. This would account for some of the similarities in vocabulary. Thus, although I grant the Gallican provenance of the homily, I do not think it can be dated as early as the middle of the fifth century.

This rather mediocre homily, which does indeed refer to a separate laying on of the hand and repeatedly employs the term *confirmare*,[52] was destined to a quite unmerited notoriety. In the ninth century it was metamorphosed into a letter of Pope Melchiades, and thus invested with papal authority, was incorporated into the so-called False Decretals, a canonical collection attributed to Isidore of Seville, but in reality the work of a Frankish cleric. The False Decretals, in turn, were incorporated into the authoritative Decretum of Gratian. Ultimately our homily on Pentecost, duly canonized, found a place in the Sentences of Peter Lombard, a basic source for scholastic theologians! Thus it acquired great influence on the Western understanding of "confirmation." Let us note the nature of this influence.

The homily has two parts: the first part formulates a distinction between confirmation and baptism, and the second compares the Holy Spirit (associated with confirmation) with Christ. Thus confirmation, with its pneumatic associations, is understood as distinct from baptism, with its christological reference. The artificial distinction between baptism and confirmation can be clearly seen in the following passage:

"In baptism we are born anew for life,
after baptism we are confirmed for battle (*confirmamur ad pugnam*);
in baptism we are washed,
after baptism we are strengthened (*post baptismum roboramur*)."[53]

In this text we note two fateful shifts in meaning: the concept of baptism is no longer anchored in the original pneumatic imagery

---

[52] *Ibid.*, 40–41, Finnegan, *The Origins of Confirmation* IV, 463 (1568).

[53] See Van Buchem, 411. For a good survey in English on Faustus of Riez, see Finnegan, *The Origins of Confirmation* III, 501–513.

of John 3:5; and the pneumatic character of the postbaptismal rite is limited to the notion of being "strengthened for battle."

Such an explanation of the role of the Spirit is far removed from the imagery employed in the Pentecost story of Acts 2, with its reference to an overwhelming theophanic event which held the disciples in its grip for their entire lives: the mighty wind and the tongues of fire, which announced an outpouring of the Spirit in such profusion that those present, quite transformed, were able to proclaim the mighty works of God with hitherto unheard of eloquence (Acts 2:1-11).

No doubt the disciples were "strengthened," but this was the *consequence* of much deeper currents, of an infinitely more forceful event! At the core of this event stood the transformation of the disciples into apostles — a transformation expressed with the imagery of divine fire with its power, on the one hand, to burn to ashes that which cannot withstand the divine presence, and, on the other hand, to effect total illumination. The disciples are now apostles sent as their master was sent. Just as the descent of the Spirit upon Jesus at the Jordan marked the beginning of the "public" life of Jesus as the Christ, so did the outpouring of the Spirit on the disciples effect a profound change in their lives. With the force of the Spirit they now went forth to proclaim the mighty works of God. . . .

COMPARATIVE LITURGY AND LITURGICAL RENEWAL
Such is the Pentecost event we celebrate in baptism, with its complementary rite of "confirmation." To substitute the image of soldier for that of apostle, as the homily on Pentecost does, tends to trivialize the Pentecost event. Images of battle have their place in the rites of initiation. However, as the study of comparative liturgy clearly shows, such "defensive" and prophylactic connotations — the imagery of military battle, of being armed for combat — belonged originally to the *prebaptismal* context! There we find the same imagery, but it is not associated with the coming of God's Spirit, but with the pursuit and expulsion of the evil spirit. In my study of the origins and historical development of the baptismal anointings I have shown that from the second half of the fourth century onwards the prebaptismal anointing is related, with

its imagery, to preparation for battle with evil.[54] The occurrence of military imagery, with its "defensive" connotations, in the postbaptismal rite, tends to reduce the gift of the Spirit to the effect of strengthening. But strengthening is the outcome, not the essence, of a much deeper and infinitely more consequential event — the bestowal of those mysterious currents of life which have their source in the inner divine stream of life.

Thus there is great significance in the fact that the decree of Paul VI regarding the reform of confirmation forcefully reasserts the relation of this rite to the Pentecost event by explaining the nature of chrismation on the basis of Jesus' baptism, so strongly pneumatic in character, and the outpouring of the Spirit on the disciples. Indeed, the reference to the descent of the Spirit at Jesus' *baptism* reflects a new and extraordinary vision of the pneumatic quality of baptism itself, and thus of the intrinsic unity of the baptismal event: baptism and the outpouring of the Spirit are *one* mystery and sacrament.

Let us recall, in this regard, that the liturgical formularies of north Gaul did not restrict the gift of the Spirit to, or identify it with, the postbaptismal rite as (Pseudo?-) Faustus of Riez did in his Pentecost homily. Thus the prayers and other formulas before baptism, during baptism, and after baptism in the *Bobbio Missal* all exhibit a considerable pneumatic character, and the vocabulary and concepts of being "strengthened" or "confirmed" are absent from the liturgical formularies of all three Gallican missals.

It is with the Gallican councils of Riez, Orange and Arles that we observe the onset of a problematic evolution focused on the ministers of initiation. At the origins of this unfortunate development we find the perception that the validity of the rites of initiation depends on the personal intervention of the bishop, who had to "confirm" or "ratify" the baptismal rite of the presbyters on the occasion of his visitation of rural parishes. Nowhere do we find the slightest clue which would allow us to conclude that the term *confirmare* had any reference to the gift of the Spirit as such.

---

[54] See Winkler, *Das armenische Initiationsrituale,* 415–423; *idem,* "Zur frühchristlichen Tauftradition," 296–298; *idem,* "The Original Meaning and Implications of the Prebaptismal Anointing," *Worship* 52 (1978) 39–43.

Considerations about the outpouring of the Spirit contributed in no way to the growing usage of such terminology. It was adopted for reasons strictly juridical in nature, not as a result of theological reflection on the essence of the rite.[55]

The study of comparative liturgy helps us to see historical developments in perspective. It can, for example, help us to clarify the question of who should preside at the celebration of the rites of initiation. The inherent unity of these rites cannot be fully evident unless one and the same minister performs both baptism and the postbaptismal rite with, preferably, one anointing. Just as practical considerations led to an artificial separation of chrismation and baptism proper, so practical considerations, combined with a sensitive appraisal of historical development and sound theological reflection, can lead to a desired change with regard to the minister of postbaptismal chrismation. The Christian East was also confronted with the question of who should preside at the celebration of initiation. Originally the bishop presided at all the rites of initiation. When, just as in the West, this was no longer feasible, it became the practice for presbyters to preside over all the rites, and thus the integral unity of baptism was preserved.

Since a strongly juridical conception of the postbaptismal rite of confirmation, developed in south Gaul, has in the course of history exerted such singular influence over the entire West, it seems important at this time of liturgical reform and renewal to highlight the tradition of north Gaul by calling to attention the extant liturgical formularies. Not only do these exhibit a structural unity between baptism proper and the postbaptismal conferral of the Spirit (ritualized in *one* anointing), but they represent a coherent ritual sequence marked throughout with a pervasive pneumatic character. These formularies, which were undoubtedly inspired by the heritage of the Christian East, can serve as a bridge between the Eastern and Western understanding of the rites of Christian initiation. As such they represent a source of inspiration for contemporary reform. Convinced of this, I consider it important to bring the results of current scholarly research in comparative liturgy, as it relates to confirmation, to the attention of a wider audience.

[55] See Van Buchem, 192.

Frank C. Quinn

12. Confirmation Reconsidered: Rite and Meaning

One of the most vexing issues in contemporary theology, liturgical reform, and pastoral practice is confirmation. Again and again the same questions are asked: what are the origins of confirmation; what does the rite of confirmation mean; what is the relation of confirmation to baptism; when should it be celebrated? It is not surprising, then, that new articles and books continue to appear on the subject. Among the authors who have written extensively on confirmation and/or Christian initiation in the recent past, Aidan Kavanagh and Thomas Marsh have again brought confirmation to our attention.[1] Although these two authors are in agreement in certain areas (e.g., the origin and general meaning of the second postbaptismal anointing), they are in strong disagreement over such questions as the origin of handlaying and the reasons for it.

Aidan Kavanagh suggests that confirmation's relation to baptism may be more structural than theological. He theorizes that the ritual complex later called confirmation was originally an episcopal conclusion to baptism and had the character of a liturgical *missa*, i.e., an archaic and independent rite. Although as dismissal rite it would conclude baptism, this rite would add nothing to it; in other words, "baptism is complete with the washing in water and chrismation which is *christic* in nature and intent."[2] Kavanagh fur-

[1] Aidan Kavanagh, "Confirmation: A Suggestion from Structure," *Worship* 58 (1984) 386–395; Thomas Marsh, *Gift of Community:* Baptism and Confirmation (Wilmington 1984).

[2] Kavanagh, 387.

ther suggests that the second postbaptismal anointing (a consignation of the forehead, peculiar to Rome among all the western rites)
is "fulfillment and sign" of that baptismal chrismation which is
performed immediately after the baptism itself (the so-called presbyteral chrismation on the crown of the head). Furthermore, any
emphasis on the invocation of the Holy Spirit would seem to indicate that baptism is "pneumatically incomplete," giving rise to the
notion that confirmation actually adds something to baptism.[3]

An immediate response to this interesting theory is that "confirmation" did conclude baptism and prepare for eucharist. Early
terms for the postbaptismal, episcopal rites assert this: *perficere* and
consummare, as well as the later *confirmare*, all had the meaning "to
complete" or "to perfect."[4] And certainly the episcopal rites in
the *Apostolic Tradition* of Hippolytus,[5] which the author cites as his
major source, have the appearance of a formal conclusion to the
liturgy of baptism, particularly since they are so spatially and tem-
porally separated from the actual baptisms themselves. But can
one conclude from this that the origin of the rite of confirmation is
to be found in the *Apostolic Tradition,* and that "all confirmation
ever was or really has been is episcopal prayer over neophytes
and their coming to the bishop's hand, where they are reminded
solemnly of their chrismation by a second anointing and dismissed
into their first eucharist"?[6]

For his part, Thomas Marsh argues that baptism primitively consisted of two rites, water bath and handlaying. He finds his
"proof" for this in the Acts of the Apostles and in the Lukan theology of the Holy Spirit. This ritual structure — water and hand-

[3] Ibid., 386–87, 390, 392

[4] E.g., see Cyprian, *Ep.* 73:9, for *consummare*; cf. Ambrose, *De Sacramentis*
3:8, for *perficere*, in *Des Sacrements; des Mystéres*, ed. Bernard Botte, Sources
chrétiennes 25 bis (Paris 1961) 96.

[5] Bernard Botte, *La Tradition apostolique de saint Hippolyte*, LQF 39 (Münster:
Aschendorff 1963) 52–55.

[6] Kavanagh, 394; in a study group on January 3, 1985, during the annual
meeting the North American Academy of Liturgy, Kavanagh discussed his
article. At that time he spoke of the prayers of the episcopal postbaptismal
rites in *Apostolic Tradition* as the *Urtext* for confirmation and the rites as the
"genesis point" of confirmation.

laying — is found in the major western rites: Rome, Spain, North Africa, and Gaul. The only other important addition to the post-baptismal complex, appearing sometime in the second century, is a unique anointing occurring immediately after baptism. The second postbaptismal anointing testified to in *Apostolic Tradition* and in later Roman documents is an anomaly which Marsh explains, as does Kavanagh, as actually referring back to the first postbaptismal anointing: "The important conclusion which emerges from this discussion of the origin of this anointing in the Roman rite is that originally it was a feature of the post-baptismal anointing and formed no part of the rite of imposition of hand, but at some stage in Rome, for practical reasons, it was incorporated into this latter to become there, with the kiss of peace, the concluding act of the initiation ritual."[7] Not surprisingly Marsh comes to a different conclusion than does Kavanagh, arguing that handlaying is an essential element of baptism, has a pneumatic note and completes baptism from the point of view of both ritual and meaning.

These authors, then, raise a number of questions. What was the meaning of the primitive Roman second postbaptismal anointing? Was not handlaying with its prayer both more traditional and more important than this anointing? Was handlaying not the original episcopal rite, the ritual action covered by the term "confirmation"? Will not evidence of practice in Gaul, as well as North Africa, help us to view handlaying as a more important rite than some scholars consider it to be?[8] As for the meaning of the episcopal rites, are they simply a structural conclusion to initiation, or do they add anything to baptism? Does the rite of handlaying

[7] Marsh, 126.

[8] Evidence from North Africa is contemporaneous with *Apostolic Tradition;* that from Gaul and Spain is, admittedly, somewhat later. But all of these rites witness to the same episcopal postbaptismal rite of handlaying without the peculiar Roman second postbaptismal anointing. Perhaps North African practice is not totally derived from that of Rome, as Kavanagh suggests (387). Also, despite Gabriele Winkler's assertion that evidence for handlaying in Gaul is attested to only by "an anonymous homily on Pentecost," one wonders if her statement is not based on a misinterpretation of a number of other sources which testify to the existence of handlaying *without* subsequent anointing; cf. her "Confirmation or Chrismation?: A Study in Comparative Liturgy," *Worship* 58 (1984) 13.

have special reference to the Holy Spirit? And, if so, does this mean that the Spirit has no connection with baptism?

To attempt some answer to these questions it will be of help to explore the following issues: the overall structure of the postbaptismal episcopal rites; episcopal handlaying and prayer; the origin and meaning of the term confirmation; and the involvement of the Holy Spirit in the confirmation rite.

THE EPISCOPAL RITES: THEIR STRUCTURE

Toward the end of the second century we find the first relatively full descriptions of baptism. In them we discover that the actual baptismal complex has two foci: (1) water baptism with those rites directly associated with it, especially the consecration of the water and the postbaptismal anointing, which prepare for or unfold the meaning of baptism and have a christic focus; and (2) other postbaptismal rites which are associated with the bishop in a way that the rest of the baptismal rites are not. As indicated above, Kavanagh regards these rites as a liturgical conclusion to baptism, and Marsh thinks they not only conclude baptism but add something new to it. In particular he notes that one of these rites, handlaying with epicletic prayer, has a clear pneumatic focus.[9]

An outline of the rites may help to make the picture clear. Since Roman practice adds an element not found in the rest of the West (the second postbaptismal chrismation), evidence from two Latin-speaking regions will be utilized: North Africa, represented by Tertullian and Cyprian,[10] and Rome, represented by the *Apostolic Tradition*.[11] These witnesses are roughly contemporary.

[9] See page 197f. In the modern Roman rite of initiation we also find a number of postbaptismal rites which are baptismal in character; they are called "Explanatory Rites." The other postbaptismal rites, the "confirmation" rites, are quite clearly separated from baptism, much more so than in the primitive rites, because of the new structuring of this section of the postbaptismal ritual. Both handlaying with prayer and anointing now have a pneumatic focus. Cf. RCIA 223-231.

[10] The outline of North African rites is based upon the writings of Tertullian and Cyprian; the order follows that of Tertullian as in his *De carnis resurrectione* 8 (CSEL 47:36), except for the position of the sealing with the cross. Both authors' writings may conveniently be found in E.C. Whitaker, *Documents of the Baptismal Liturgy*, 2nd ed. (London 1970) 7-12.

[11] Botte, 44-55.

NORTH AFRICA	ROME
1. Blessing of water	1. Blessing of water.
2. Renunciation of Satan	2. Stripping off of garments and renunciation of Satan
3. Water baptism: threefold dipping in answer to credal questions	3. Water baptism: threefold dipping in answer to credal questions.
4. Anointing of body with oil unto royal priesthood	4. Anointing of body with oil of thanksgiving in name of Jesus
	[Clothing and procession to place where assembly and bishop are gathered]
5. *Manus impositio*, pneumatic in character [presumably with prayer for the Holy Spirit]	5. *Manus impositio* [over all the neophytes], with epicletic prayer
	6. Anointing of head with oil of thanksgiving, using a trinitarian formula, by individual hand-laying [and?]
6. Signing of forehead with the cross [perfected with the Lord's seal][12]	7. Signing of forehead with the cross
[7. Kiss of peace?]	8. Kiss of peace

It is quite clear that the rites are the same except for the one peculiarity of the second postbaptismal anointing found in the *Apostolic Tradition*, an anointing of the head which is accomplished by an (additional) imposition of hand. This second anointing will continue to be found in later Roman practice; it will be combined, however, with the signing of the forehead (no. 7 above).[13] The

---

[12] Cyprian, Letter 73, to Januarius (Whitaker 11).

[13] Both Marsh and Kavanagh assume that the anointing of the head is already combined with the sealing with the cross in the *Apostolic Tradition*. Although this could possibly be true and at least the specification of episcopal

consignation with chrism will eventually provide the whole complex of the Roman episcopal rites with its title. A witness to these changes is *Reginensis 316* (*Gelasianum vetus*) where we find the following order of the baptismal ritual.[14]

1. Procession to the font, with litany
2. Blessing of water
3. Water baptism: threefold immersion in response to credal questions
4. Presbyteral consignation on crown of head with chrism, employing chrismation prayer [not an administration formula as in *Apostolic Tradition*]
5. Handlaying with epicletic prayer for the sevenfold Spirit (*Deinde ab episcopo datur eis spiritus septiformis. Ad consignandum imponit eis manum in his verbis.*)
6. Consignation of forehead with chrism and christological formula
7. Peace exchanged between bishop and candidate

Which of these latter rites is the rite of "confirmation"? The signing with the cross, as in other liturgical rites, seals and completes the whole baptismal ceremony; the greeting and pax introduce the candidate into the eucharistic assembly. Handlaying with epicletic prayer for the Holy Spirit seems to be the most important element; this is particularly clear in the non-Roman western rites, where no episcopal consignation with chrism occurs. Why do we find this second anointing only in Rome during the first eight centuries? As found originally in the *Apostolic Tradition* it seems to be a continuation and completion of the presbyteral anointing of the body. The congregation had seen none of the

---

anointing as a signing of the forehead with chrism is indicated by the time of the letter of Innocent I to Decentius of Gubbio (19 March 416; Henry Denzinger and Adolf Schönmetzer, *Enchiridion symbolorum*, 32nd ed. [Barcelona 1963] 215), we have indicated a separation of rites in *Apostolic Tradition* both because the document can be read in this fashion and because such a division clearly indicates the addition of a new element to the Roman postbaptismal rites.

[14] *Liber Sacramentorum romanae Aeclesiae ordinis Anni circuli*, ed. Leo Cunibert Mohlberg (Rome 1968) 444–452, pp. 72–74

earlier ceremonies so there is a recapitulation of these within the assembly by the head of the assembly, the bishop. The final post-baptismal rites of imposition of hand with prayer followed by sealing with cross are interrupted by a visible remembrance of the effects of baptism which demonstrates the bishop's role in all of baptismal initiation, even if he has not been immediately present at the rites. Certainly, the formulas used for each anointing do not lead us to any other conclusion. The first mentions Jesus Christ, the second the Trinity of persons into whom the candidates have been baptized.[15]

In this context Aidan Kavanagh's remarks about the episcopal anointing being sign and fulfillment of the presbyteral postbaptismal anointing would seem to be given strong support.[16]

THE ORIGIN AND MEANING OF THE TERM CONFIRMATION

When the word baptism is mentioned most think of a rite including water and trinitarian formula, a ritual act having something to do with the forgiveness of sin. But when one speaks of confirmation it is not always clear what rite is being referred to or what meaning is being assigned to the term. Some will think of the postbaptismal, episcopal rites which conclude baptism; they will emphasize either handlaying or anointing. Others will immediately understand confirmation to refer to the medieval sacrament, with its emphasis on anointing and moral strengthening, or to the rite of the churches of the Reformation which completed one's religious education and admitted the confirmand to the communion

---

[15] Cf. Joseph Coppens, *L'Imposition des mains et les rites connexes dans le N.T. et dans l'Eglise ancienne* (Wetteran 1925) 350; Thomas Marsh, "A Study of Confirmation," *Irish Theological Quarterly* 39 (1972) 322; also see Marsh's earlier article, "The History and Significance of the Postbaptismal Rites," *Irish Theological Quarterly* 29 (1962) 184.

[16] Kavanagh, 394. As already indicated, Thomas Marsh also feels that the unique Roman practice of repeating an anointing after the laying on of hand arose because the bishop was not personally involved in the baptism and anointing of the numerous candidates initiated at Rome: "it would be felt desirable to maintain the act and role of the bishop here. An obvious solution to this practical, and in no way doctrinal, problem would be to combine this signing of the forehead with oil with the individual imposition of hand after the prayer for the Spirit" (*Gift of Community,* 126).

table. Twentieth century catechists have bolstered the medieval and Reformation views by comparing confirmation to a coming of age or puberty rite. It is important, then, to speak of the meaning or meanings of the word confirmation in order to avoid confusion.

As indicated above,[17] terms such as *perfectio* or *consummatio* were used of those final rites of baptism which were associated with the bishop. The terms do not so much refer to specific rites as to the perfecting or completing of baptismal initiation by the bishop. A study of liturgical and canonical texts referring to the bishop's role in baptism, whether or not he was present at the actual baptism, or to an analogous situation, the readmission of heretics to the church, informs us of the rites which these terms cover. We may conclude the following: (1) certain baptismal rites are not bound as closely to the baptismal ritual as are others; (2) such rites are directly associated with the bishop; (3) of the rites mentioned, handlaying with prayer for the Holy Spirit is *the* rite intended to perfect baptism or admit heretics to the church. The Council of Elvira (300–305) demands, in canon 38, that in cases of clinical baptism the candidate "be brought to the bishop so that he may be *perfected* with the handlaying" (*ad episcopum perducat, ut per manus impositionem* perfici *possit*; emphasis mine), and, in canon 77, "the bishop shall *perfect* them with the blessing" (*episcopus eos per benedictionem* perficere *debebit*; emphasis mine).[18] The Council of Arles (314), speaking of the readmission of heretics to the church prescribes that "such a one should receive the handlaying only, for the reception of the Spirit" (*manus ei tantum imponatur, ut accipiat Spiritum*).[19] Other rites which the bishop performs, such as the final sealing with the cross, simply conclude a series of ritual actions.

As a technical term *confirmatio* first appears in the fifth century, in documents reporting practice in southeast Gaul.[20] As with *per-*

---

[17] See above, 197.

[18] Council of Elvira cc. 38, 77 (Denzinger 120–121).

[19] Council of Arles c. 9 (8); *Concilia Galliae A.314-A.506*, ed. T. Munier, CCSL 148. (Turnhot: Brépols 1963) 10–11. Innocent I also speaks of this same practice: cf. J. MacDonald, "Imposition of Hands in the Letters of Innocent I," *Studia Patristica* 2 (Berlin 1957) 49–53

[20] See, among others, Bernard Botte, "Le vocabulaire ancien de la confirma-

fectio and *consummatio, confirmatio* did not refer directly to a particular rite or to the bestowal of the Holy Spirit. Instead it referred to the personal intervention of the bishop in baptismal initiation, especially when the bishop had not been present at the baptism itself. This happened regularly in the initiation of those living in rural areas of southeast Gaul since during this period there was an increase in the number of persons to be initiated. In such situations, according to the Council of Riez (18 November 439) the bishop (in this case a *chorepiscopus*) was to *neophytos confirmare*,[21] to complete baptismal initiation by personal involvement with the newly baptized when he encountered such members of his flock.

Quite clearly, the rite involved is the imposition of hands with prayer for the Holy Spirit. This is indirectly indicated in the famous canon 2 of the Council of Orange (8 November 411), which seems to be arguing against the introduction of the Roman practice of a double postbaptismal chrismation. The canon insists on only one postbaptismal anointing (the presbyteral anointing which ordinarily must take place immediately after baptism); if the latter had been omitted when deacons or presbyters baptized in their rural parishes — presumably because they did not have chrism with them at the time they baptized — the bishop is to supply it when he "confirms."[22] In his famous Pentecost homily, Faustus of

---

tion," *La Maison-Dieu* 54 (1958) 15–18; Thomas Marsh, "St. Patrick's Terminology for Confirmation," *Irish Ecclesiastical Review* 93 (1960) 145–54; and especially L.A. van Buchem, *L'Homélie pseudo-Eusébienne de Pentécôte.* "L'Origine de la "Confirmatio" en Gaule méridionale et l'interprétation de ce rite par Fauste de Riez (Nijmegen 1967).

[21] *Concilia Galliae*, c. 3, p. 67–68.

[22] Ibid., 78; cf. Van Buchem, 95–98, who follows the interpretation of Anton Chavasse, "Le deuxieme canon de Concile d'Orange de 441, Esquisse d'exégèse," *Melanges E. Podéchard* (Lyon 1945) 103–20. This author argues that the canon insists on the Gallican practice of one baptismal anointing (against the incursion of the Roman custom?) because there is only one *benedictio* of the chrism. Other authors have asserted that "blessing" refers to the imposition of hand, which is therefore always connected to chrismation. Gabriele Winkler has recently written that *in confirmation* most likely simply refers to chrismation, that, in other words, handlaying does not exist; see "Confirmation or Chrismation?", 10–11. It seems to me that a careful reading of this controversial canon supports Chavasse's interpretation that bishops are not to repeat a

Riez clearly indicates that such a confirmation is provided by episcopal handlaying.[23] As is also well known, in the course of his delivery Faustus provided a theological explanation of confirmation quite different from the notion of a completion of baptismal initiation through the personal involvement of a bishop with the neophyte. The preacher equates *confirmare* with *roborare*. Because of the accidents of history this new meaning for confirmation will have a profound effect upon future theology.

Outside of southeast Gaul the word *confirmation* is not used of the postbaptismal rites but of eucharistic communion. The chalice "completes" the eating of the consecrated bread,[24] or, as with Alcuin, the bread and cup "confirms" the participants: *Sic corpore et sanguine dominico confirmatur.*[25] But whether confirmation is used of an episcopal, postbaptismal involvement with the baptized or of eucharistic communion, its technical meaning, the same as that of *perfici* and *consummare*, is simply one of completing, validating, or ratifying something.

Neither Alcuin nor his disciple Rabanus Maurus uses the word *confirmation* to describe the episcopal conclusion to initiation; for it is quite clear that the ritual itself consists of *manus impositio* for the conferral of the sevenfold Spirit. Rabanus also mentions, for the first time in Gallican literature, the Roman practice of the second postbaptismal chrismation. He adds an explanation of this rite to his explanation of baptism (which is essentially an expansion of

---

chrismation, since there is only one blessing of the chrism, when they "confirm," that is, when they impose their hand upon those who have already been baptized.

[23] Van Buchem, 40–44. Although Winkler quite correctly states the fact that confirmation is "juridical in nature," i.e., it has to do with a bishop's connection with the neophyte, this does not necessarily mean, as she asserts, that it has no connection with the Holy Spirit; insofar as confirmation assumes the rite of handlaying with prayer for the Spirit it has something to do with the Spirit. See Winkler, 16.

[24] This usage is found in the following *Ordines Romani:* I, IV, XXIV, XXVII, XXVIII, XXIX; see Michel Andrieu, *Les Ordines Romani du haut moyen Âge,* 5 vols, Spicilegium Sacrum Lovaniense 11, 23, 24, 28, 29 (Louvain 1931–1961).

[25] *Epistola* 134: *Alcuino Oduino presbytero baptismi caeremonias exponit;* in Ernest Duemmler, *Epistolae Karolini Aevie* 2, Monumenta Germaniae Historica, Epistolarum 4 (Berlin 1895) 203.

Alcuin's own statements).[26] This may reflect actual practice or simply be a commentary upon a Roman *ordo*. In either case it signals the end of the western non-Roman practice of completing baptism with one anointing and sometime later following this with handlaying by the bishop. It also signals the problems theologians will have in explaining just what constitutes the rite of confirmation.

Outside of southeast Gaul the use of the word *confirmation* to refer to the postbaptismal episcopal rites is first found in *Ordo Romanus XI*, a Roman church order brought across the Alps around the year 750. The term is used in association with the bishop's handlaying and prayer for the Spirit.[27] Since such usage is Gallican, perhaps we are justified in suggesting that the word was added to the text in Gaul itself. As already noted above,[28] *consigno* was the term Roman texts used for the episcopal postbaptismal actions, including under this term not only the consignation with chrism but also handlaying with prayer for the Holy Spirit. This suggestion might also explain why *confirmans eos* is directly related to the prayer for the Holy Spirit rather than to the chrismation.[29] Whatever the truth of the matter, through *Ordo Romanus XI* confirmation terminology enters into rubrical texts that are, or will become, part of the Roman rite.

The word enters the actual rite in *Ordo Romanus L*, where it is part of the chrismation formula.[30] This order of service, the great grandfather of the Roman pontificals, was redacted not in Rome but by a monk in Germany.

Scholastic theologians titled the second sacrament "confirmation," probably due in part to the reappearance of Faustus of Riez' Pentecost homily. This time, however, his words were be-

---

[26] Rabanus Maurus, *De Clericorum institutione* 30, PL 107:314.

[27] *Dat orationem . . . super eos, confirmans eos cum invocatione septiformis gratiae spiritus sancti* (emphasis mine): OR XI 96–104; Andrieu, 2:445-47.

[28] See above, 224.

[29] I explore this in more detail in Frank Quinn, "Contemporary Liturgical Revision: The Revised Rites of Confirmation in the Roman Catholic Church and in the American Episcopal Church" (Ph.D. diss., University of Notre Dame 1978) 112–14.

[30] *Confirmo (et consigno) te in nomine patris et filii et spiritus sancti*; OR L 29:74; Andrieu, 5:290.

lieved to be those of two popes.[31] Confirmation is not used as the title of the Roman rite until the Castellani Pontifical of 1520, and then it shares honors with consignation as *De Confirmandis seu Chrismandis.* In the *editio typica* of the Roman Pontifical of Clement VIII (1596), confirmation finally becomes the exclusive title for the episcopal rites: *De Confirmandis.*[32]

Conclusions: 1. Confirmation is a word of Gallican provenance. Originally it referred to the bishop's role in initiation, particularly with reference to his personal involvement with those neophytes whom he had not baptized. Used in this manner, "confirmation" does not indicate any addition to baptism.

2. The specific rite used by the bishop "in confirming," however, was the imposition of hand along with prayer for the Holy Spirit.

3. Confirmation continues to refer to episcopal handlaying in the Roman *ordines* and pontificals; but it is also identified with chrismation, even entering into the formula of administration. When western rites outside of Rome accept the peculiar second postbaptismal anointing into their baptismal structure, confirmation terminology with reference to consignation becomes general in western Europe. Most likely, chrismation seemed more important, or at least more concrete, than did handlaying and prayer.[33]

How should we understand the term today? Although some authors such as Thomas Marsh emphasize handlaying with reference to confirmation[34] it is clear from the context of their discus-

---

[31] This fictitious attribution of the homily of Faustus is due to the False Decretals: *Decretales Pseudo-Isidorianae et Capitula Angilramni,* ed. Paul Hinschius (Leipzig: Tauchnitz 1893) 146, 245–46.

[32] *Pontificale Romanum Clementis VIII jussu restitutum atque editum* (Rome 1596) 1.

[33] Similar ritual shifts occurred in the ordination rites when, in the Middle Ages, the *traditio instrumentorum* was emphasized over the more ancient handlaying with prayer for the Spirit. This change was finally corrected by Pius XII in 1947 when he restored *manuum [sic] impositionem* and the words in the accompanying prayer emphasizing the particular order being received and the special grace of the Holy Spirit as the essential "matter" and "form" of the sacrament; *Sacramentum Ordinis* (30 November 1947) *AAS* 40 (1948) 5–7.

[34] See, e.g., his "A Study of Confirmation," *Irish Theological Quarterly* 39 (1972) 149–63; 319–36; 40 (1973) 125–47 as well as his latest publication, *Gift of*

sions that most Roman Catholic and Anglican writers intend chrismation when they use the term confirmation. Aidan Kavanagh speaks this way in *The Shape of Baptism*.[35] In his 1984 article, he contrasts consignation-confirmation with baptism-chrismation.[36] This comparison is not immediately clear. Does Kavanagh mean to contrast baptism-in-water — chrismation with consignation-with-chrismation — confirmation/handlaying? Hardly, since the latter is not the order found in the confirmation rites. One is, therefore, left with questions about this peculiar designation. For myself, and since this is how the rites exist today, it would seem clearer, and more attuned to tradition, to contrast baptism-in-water — chrismation with confirmation/handlaying — consignation with chrism. And although originally it would seem that this latter chrismation simply completed the baptismal chrismation and was a sign of it, as Kavanagh notes,[37] today that same identification may be questioned.

THE HOLY SPIRIT IN CONFIRMATION

Thomas Marsh asks whether we cannot find a primitive pattern of water and handlaying in the book of Acts, a pattern which is the basis for western practice. This pattern is already adumbrated in the baptism of Christ in the Jordan, an event paradigmatic for Christian baptism.

But why two rites in Acts? For Luke the Spirit is a prophetic force, a mighty wind, not, as in Paul and John, a personal and internal principle of life. In the new age, according to Luke, the Spirit which had inspired the great prophets but had been quenched for centuries returns to the new Israel, first to Jesus himself — at his baptism in the Jordan — and then to the new community founded by Jesus — at Pentecost and at subsequent

---

Community. I am particularly indebted to this author for his insights into the origin of both the rite and theology of confirmation.

[35] Aidan Kavanagh, *The Shape of Baptism: The Rite of Christian Initiation,* Studies in the Reformed Rites of the Catholic Church 1 (New York 1978) 17–27 and *passim;* see also J.D.C. Fisher, *Confirmation Then and Now,* Alcuin Club Collections 60 (London 1978) 52–60 and *passim.*

[36] "Confirmation: A Suggestion from Structure," 391.

[37] Ibid., 386, 390, 392.

celebrations of baptism. Such an ecstatic Spirit is poured out upon the baptized through the imposition of hands, a rite which ordinarily follows baptism. The outpouring of such a Spirit ordinarily occurs *after* baptism since the former is not the agent of the forgiveness of sins. Finally, the delivery of the ecstatic Spirit is through the hands of the apostles or their delegates.[38]

Although Luke's view of the Spirit was that common to the Judaism of his time, other, more advanced, theologies of the Spirit exist in the New Testament, particularly in the writings of Paul and of John. In both authors the Spirit is more than a prophetic force; it is also an internal principle of life, a personal and, in John, abiding presence. John speaks of our being born of water *and* Spirit (Jn 3:5), Paul of our dying with Christ in baptism (Rom 6). It is quite evident, then, that with these authors the Spirit is involved in baptism itself. As the agent of new life it is through this Spirit that sins are forgiven.[39]

Marsh is of the opinion that the Lukan rite of baptism in the name of Christ for the forgiveness of sins and handlaying for the prophetic Spirit is the key to the development of the baptismal liturgy, especially in the West. Later on the more advanced theologies of the Spirit of Paul and John would become dominant in the interpretation of Christian initiation. This is especially evident in the writings of the fourth century mystagogues, for whom Paul is so important,[40] as well as in that same century's debate over the personhood of the Holy Spirit. The more developed theology of the Spirit resulting from such emphases would insist on the Spirit's involvement in all aspects of baptism: in the journey to conversion, in incorporation into Christ through baptism and chrismation, and in the pneumatic rite of handlaying with prayer.

Thus, a baptismal rite evolved, patterned on the primitive, Lukan understanding of the Spirit and its role in the life of the

[38] See, e.g., Marsh, *Gift of Community*, 27–67.

[39] Ibid., 68–101; see also Marsh's "The Holy Spirit in Early Christian Teaching," *Irish Theological Quarterly* 45 (1978) 101–16.

[40] On this see Hugh M. Riley, *Christian Initiation: A Comparative Study of the Baptismal Liturgy in the Mystagogical Writings of Cyril of Jerusalem, John Chrysostom, Theodore of Mopsuestia and Ambrose of Milan*, Studies in Christian Antiquity 17, ed. Johannes Quasten (Washington, D.C. 1974) 213–23.

church. But several centuries after the birth of Christianity a much more profound theology of the Holy Spirit, also found in the New Testament, though not part of the ordinary theology of the early church, began to affect the understanding and interpretation of baptismal initiation.

Problems which would later arise with confirmation had their origin, according to Marsh, not in the fourth century but in Paul's view of the Spirit: "His [Paul's] concept of the life-giving Spirit and his application of this concept logically obliges him, in his references to christian initiation, to associate this gift with the union with Christ established by baptism. What is nowadays called the problem of confirmation has its source here in this theologically correct intuition of Paul. Writers who seek this source in later developments, when the problem explicitly manifests itself, are therefore following a wrong trail."[41]

Because of these developments problems have continuously arisen with regard to the meaning of confirmation and the role of the Holy Spirit. Numerous solutions have been proposed, many quite without foundation in fact. Augustine explicitly claimed that there were two gifts of the Spirit in initiation, one the Easter gift in John 20:22-23, the other the Pentecost gift of Acts 2.[42] The preacher Faustus of Riez, who had to convince the newly baptized to be confirmed, told his hearers that although through the Holy Spirit they received the fullness of Christian life in the water of baptism, still they needed the other rite so that through the action of the Holy Spirit they might be [morally] strengthened to fight the good fight and to live through the terrors of their world.[43] Alcuin wrote that we receive the Spirit of sevenfold grace "that one endowed with the grace of eternal life in baptism may be strengthened by the Holy Spirit for preaching to others."[44]

[41] *Gift of Community*, 86–87.

[42] Ibid., 162; Augustine in *Sermo* 265:7 says: *Bis glorificatus, resurgendo et ascendendo, bis dedit Spiritum.*

[43] *L'Homélie pseudo-Eusébienne* 41, lines 20–25.

[44] *Epistola* 134: *ut roboretur per Spiritum sanctum ad praedicandum aliis, qui fuit in baptismo per gratiam vitae donatus aeternae,* Marsh claims that Alcuin's use of the word *roboretur* indicates the survival of Faustus' homily on confirmation (in which confirmation is equivalent to *robur*); however, even if this is so he

Scholastic theologians had at their disposal statements about confirmation which had been handed on by the canonical collections. From these they began to develop a systematic theology of confirmation. This was brought to completion by Thomas Aquinas.[45] His theology of confirmation has been in use with little change since the thirteenth century, and remains at the heart of Paul VI's Apostolic Constitution. Thomas quotes all the authorities that medieval theologians relied upon. He speaks of the reception of the Spirit as enabling public witness to the faith, following in the footsteps of Alcuin, as interpreted by Rabanus Maurus.[46] But since almost every article of question 72 is filled with the imagery of growth and strengthening, all based upon Ps.-Melchiades (i.e., Faustus of Riez), it is very difficult to conclude anything but Thomas' radical indebtedness to a minor, fifth century, semi-Pelagian bishop. This imagery, along with a lack of sophistication on the part of those reading Thomas, would lead to a deemphasis of the role of the Holy Spirit in confirmation. Furthermore, confirmation's relationship to baptism or eucharist, as well as its social dimensions, would be lost. Instead, confirmation would become a support for the moral virtue of fortitude; one became a soldier of Christ in order to fight the battle of life. Thus one was "confirmed," i.e., strengthened, in the name of the Blessed Trinity. So it has remained into the twentieth century.

CONFIRMATION'S STRUCTURE AND THEOLOGY

We began this article by questioning whether Aidan Kavanagh's very interesting theory of confirmation's origin as a primitive liturgical *missa* was the only explanation for the appearance of this rite. It seems to me that although in the *Apostolic Tradition* of Hippolytus the bishop's rite has the appearance of a *missa*, the post-

---

notes the rejection of Faustus' moralistic interpretation of such strengthening since, in Alcuin's interpretation, we are dealing with *robur* as consecration to a life of "preaching" or service (*Gift of Community*, 166).

[45] ST 3:72.

[46] Ibid. Whether such statements truly indicate that "Aquinas places himself solidly in the tradition which sees confirmation as characterized by a gift of the prophetic Spirit," as Marsh thinks (*Gift of Community*, 174), is certainly arguable.

baptismal episcopal rites may be more than that. If Marsh's views have any merit, the genesis for the western rites of confirmation is to be found in the practice of water and hand described in the Acts of the Apostles and based upon the ordinary view of the Spirit held by the Jews of the first century C.E. Even when Paul's more developed theology of the Spirit was later used to interpret baptism, the two-part baptismal rite, with handlaying having reference to the prophetic Spirit, remained as part of the western church's praxis.

Sometime in the second century a chrismation was added to water baptism. Thoroughly christic, the now explicit anointing symbolized the newly baptized's participation in the *Christos*, the anointed one, who is both king and priest. The baptized became a member of the priestly people, sharing in Christ's priesthood and kingship (1 Pt 2:9). With the introduction of this anointing a third element was added to the two earlier ones. The sequence thus became: first, baptism with confession of the Trinity and washing in water for the forgiveness of sins,[47] followed by chrismation of the newly baptized as anointed ones in their own right, sharing in Christ's royal priesthood, and, finally, the imposition of hand with prayer for the sevenfold prophetic Spirit, so that those baptized into the death of the Lord might now preach to others what they themselves have received.

Unfortunately, a second postbaptismal anointing came into existence in Rome. Here I think Kavanagh and Marsh are quite correct in their assumption that this was a completion or sign of the postbaptismal anointing. But once such a chrismation became a standard feature of the western rites it acquired a meaning of its own and began to change the focus and practice of the postbaptismal episcopal rites.

Today it seems that an emphasis upon the classic rite of handlaying with prayer for the Spirit would be quite healthy. Not only

[47] Important as it is, I do not consider the profession of faith to be a separate element since, originally, it was part of the baptismal rite itself; I feel the same about the consecration of the font since it is a rite associated with the use of water, although admittedly its prayer, which explores the total meaning of baptism in the history of salvation, tells us more about baptism than the actual washing.

does the prayer offer much food for thought to the preacher; it is absolutely necessary for understanding the rite. As Louis Ligier has noted, the new formula of administration which was borrowed from the Byzantine rite was taken out of context. In the East such a formula simply ratified or sealed for each individual candidate that which had been asked for in the preceding prayer; in fact the chrismation formula is simply a phrase from that prayer, and is not even a complete sentence since it lacks a verb.[48] Individual chrismation in western confirmation, then, is an illustration for each candidate of that which the church prays for with imposition of hand and prayer.[49]

One does not have to agree with Marsh's pastoral solution to the confirmation problem, that is, that since in origin the handlaying was so loosely connected to baptism, a separate confirmation is no real problem, properly understood and explained.[50] Such practice, in point of fact, gives undue prominence to confirmation and separates it from its very raison d'être, baptism. It should be remembered that one becomes a full member of the church, the body of Christ, through baptism, confirmation and eucharist. Confirmation is not like marriage or orders; it does not confer some particular office or role upon an individual.

On the other side one does not have to fully agree with Aidan Kavanagh's assertion of confirmation's origin as a primitive liturgical *missa* in order to agree with him that it would be best perma-

---

[48] Ligier, *La Confirmation*, 50–94; although not immediately pertinent to this article, it should be noted that one of Ligier's purposes in writing his book was to treat the question of baptismal handlaying in the eastern baptismal rites.

[49] Cf. Adrian Nocent, "Vicissitudes du rituel de la confirmation," *Nouvelle revue théologique* 94 (1972) 718: "On comprend mieu la formule *signaculum doni spiritus sancti* comme l'illustration des dons qui viennent d'étre conférés par l'imposition des mains."

[50] *Gift of Community*, 186–93; Marsh justifies the prior reception of the eucharist when he notes on p. 195: "If confirmation . . . meant the first conferring of the Spirit on the baptized, that prior to this their Christian life was not life in the Spirit, then indeed the argument that full participation in the eucharist should follow confirmation would be absolutely cogent." It seems to me that he is simply theologizing a pastoral practice sanctioned by long usage.

nently to join confirmation with baptism in order to get on to other issues.

One thing that many agree upon is the anomaly, in the Rite of Christian Initiation of Adults, of omitting the postbaptismal chrismation in favor of the confirmation consignation.[51] Since the prayer accompanying the postbaptismal chrismation rite speaks so strongly of incorporation into the church, a principal focus of baptism, it is odd indeed that this rite can be omitted. Even odder is the addition of the image of prophet to the kingship and priesthood with which this rite has been associated for centuries.[52] Ironically, such an assertion removes confirmation's right to be, if what has been said above has any validity at all.

[51] Kavanagh, "Confirmation," 393; Nocent, *La Confirmation*, 216–17.

[52] *Ut, ejus aggregati populo, Christi sacerdotes, prophetae et regis membra permaneatis, in vitam aeternam*, RCIA 224. The combination of the three functions of Christ is not ancient; rather kingship and priesthood are found together (as in 1 Pt 2:9) and prophecy is spoken of separately. On this cf. Joseph Leo Levesque, "The Theology of the Postbaptismal Rites in the Gallican Liturgical Sources of the Seventh and Eighth Centuries" (Ph.D. diss., The Catholic University of America 1977) 100 and *passim*.

Paul Turner

13. The Origins of Confirmation:
An Analysis of Kavanagh's Hypothesis

INTRODUCTION

Confirmation: Origins and Reform by Aidan Kavanagh[1] may be the most important book on its topic in the last four hundred years. One would have to return to Martin Luther's *De captivitate Babylonica*[2] to find another work with such far-reaching consequences.

Scholars have long regarded the *Apostolic Tradition* (AT) of Hippolytus[3] as the oldest liturgical document describing the ritual we have come to call "confirmation." Kavanagh proposes that the initiation rites of AT do not include "confirmation" at all, but rather a baptismal dismissal rite performed by the bishop. AT says the neophytes come to the presbyter who baptized them to receive an anointing, and then they proceed to the bishop who prays for them while imposing a hand. Kavanagh believes we are seeing a presbyteral anointing with a christic, not a pneumatological, meaning, and an episcopal handlaying in the style of a dismissal, not of conferring the Holy Spirit.[4]

If Kavanagh is right, he has dethroned confirmation from its traditional pneumatic interpretation to one almost rubrical in ori-

---

[1] (New York 1988). Kavanagh's thesis first appeared in *Worship* 58 (1984) in his article, "Confirmation: A Suggestion from Structure," 386–395.

[2] "De captivitate Babylonica ecclesiae praeludium," *D. Martin Luthers Werke, Kritische Gesammtausgabe* (Weimar 1883), vol. 6, 497–573.

[3] *Sources Chrétiennes*, intro. and trans. Bernard Botte, OSB (Paris 1968), vol. 11 bis.

[4] Kavanagh, 69–72.

gin. When displaced from its intercalary position between baptism and eucharist, it carries more weight than it was ever intended to bear, and its meaning becomes problematic, especially in its distinction from baptism.

To build this theory, he gathers rites of dismissing groups from the liturgy, and examines the similarity between them and AT's postbaptismal handlaying. The strength of this argument is that similarities exist; the weakness is that the patterns are incomplete.

This article intends to analyze the sources upon which Kavanagh builds his argument and to test their impact upon his conclusion. The sources are grouped into catechumenal *missa* texts, *missae* of the West, the *missae* of the order of penitents, *missae* in the monastic offices, and prayers of inclination. After these groups have been analyzed, the critical passage from AT 22 will be examined. Each section gives 1) the context of the cited source, 2) its application to Kavanagh's argument, and 3) a critique.

CATECHUMENAL *MISSA* TEXTS

Hippolytus: Apostolic Tradition 18-19. Hippolytus describes the conclusion of a catechumenal session "Let the catechumens pray by themselves, separated from the faithful. . . . After the prayer, when the teacher has laid a hand upon the catechumens, let him pray and dismiss them."[5]

Structurally speaking, Kavanagh's assertion is that prayer and handlaying are elements belonging to the ritual genre of *missae*. Since Hippolytus is familiar with the structure, it is possible he will apply it to other circumstances — e.g., the rites following baptism.[6]

Although prayer and handlaying are evident in this and other *missae*, they are elements of other liturgical rites as well. Observing these two elements together, one may be looking at a dismissal, an ordination, a reconciliation, or an exorcism. In addition, it will be noteworthy that the presider who imposes hands on, prays for, and dismisses the group at the conclusion of this catechumenal session may be a member of the laity.

---

[5] *"Catechumeni orent seorsum, separati a fidelibus. . . . Cum doctor post precem imposuit manum super catechumenos, oret et dimittat eos."* SC 11 bis, 76.

[6] Kavanagh, 5-8.

Hippolytus: Apostolic Tradition 20. Those to be baptized gather on Saturday before the vigil. "They shall all be told to pray and kneel. And laying his hand upon them, (the bishop) exorcizes all alien spirits, that they may flee from them and never return to them. . . . And when he has signed their forehead, ears, and nose, he shall raise them up. And they shall spend the whole night in vigil."[7]

Kavanagh believes this is another example of a *missa* since prayer and handlaying are elements of this rite over which the bishop presides. There is no formal dismissal since those to be baptized will spend the night in prayer.[8]

Although the rite contains what Kavanagh calls "dismissal elements" (prayer, handlaying, and episcopal presidency), what it obviously lacks is a dismissal: those to be baptized remain in place. It's clear this is an exorcism; it's less clear it's a dismissal.

The Canons of Laodicea, 19. Composed perhaps after 365, this canon describes the conclusion of the eucharistic Word service. "First, after the sermons of the bishops, the prayer of the catechumens is to be made apart; and after the catechumens have gone out, those who do their penance offer a prayer; and after these have approached the hand and departed, the prayers of the faithful should thus be offered three times."[9]

This text illustrates two dismissals. Kavanagh believes their structure is similar to the dismissals from the catechumenal session in AT 19 and the pre-vigil exorcism in AT 20.[10]

The structure is similar, but the occasions are different: The dismissal at AT 19 concludes a catechetical session, presumably after

---

[7] "*Iubeatur illis omnibus ut orent et flectent genua. Et imponens manum suam super eos, exorcizet omnes spiritus alienos ut fugiant ex eis et non revertantur iam in eos. . . . Cum signaverit frontem, aures et nares eorum, suscitabit eos. Et agent totam noctem vigilantes.*" SC 11 bis, 78–80.

[8] Kavanagh, 6.

[9] "*Oportere seorsum primum, post episcoporum sermones, catechumenorum orationem peragi; & postquam exierint catechumeni, eorum qui poenitentiam agunt, fieri orationem; & cum ii sub manum accesserint, & secesserint, fidelium preces sic ter fieri.*" *Sacrorum conciliorum nova et amplissima collectio*, ed. Joannes Dominicus Mansi (Graz: Akademische Druck-U. Verlagsanstalt, 1960) vol. 2, col. 567–568.

[10] Kavanagh, 8–10.

the catechumens have already been dismissed from the assembly (a dismissal which Laodicea now describes). AT 20's dismissal is in the non-eucharistic context of a pre-vigil exorcism. Similarities are evident: prayer, handlaying, and dismissals while the assembly continues its prayer (except in AT 20). However, the text is silent on key points: It is unclear if the "hand" belongs to a bishop, and if catechumens in addition to penitents "approach" it. If the text argues that handlaying is part of the *missa* structure for penitents, it does so less clearly in the case of catechumens.

The Apostolic Constitutions 8, 6. This Antiochean church order compiled c. 370–380 outlines the rubrics for the eucharist of a newly ordained bishop. Several groups are dismissed from the liturgy: catechumens, energumens, illuminated, penitents, and finally the faithful. In the case of catechumens, the deacon invites them to pray. "And all the faithful pray attentively for them, saying, 'Kyrie eleison.' "[11] The deacon invites all to pray, then commands, "Arise, catechumens, ask the peace of God through his Christ."[12] After the petitions, "while the catechumens bow their heads, let the ordained bishop bless them."[13] Following his prayer, the deacon announces, "Leave, catechumens, in peace."[14]

Kavanagh calls attention to this structure's similarity to Laodicea. He accordingly reconstructs the Apostolic Constitutions (AC) and suggests that groups were dismissed by group prayer, episcopal prayer, and handlaying by the bishop.[15]

The similarity to Laodicea is that prayer precedes the dismissal. But handlaying in AC cannot be established. While it is true that AC dismisses various groups from the liturgy in a repeatable pattern and with a variable prayer, the unit concludes when the groups bow heads for the blessing, not with the bishop imposing hands. Granted, if individual handlaying had been customary in

---

[11] "*Et omnes fideles pro illis cum attentione orent dicentes: Kyrie eleison.*" *Didascalia et constitutiones apostolorum,* ed. Francis Xavier Funk (Turin 1979) vol. I, 479.

[12] "*Surgite, catechumeni: pacem Dei per Christum eius petite.*" *Didascalia* I, 481.

[13] "*Catechumenis autem capita inclinantibus episcopus ordinatus benedicat eis.*" *Didascalia* I, 481.

[14] "*Exite, catechumeni, in pace.*" *Didascalia* I, 481.

[15] Kavanagh, 10–12.

dismissals, it is possible that it had further evolved into a group blessing by this time. But AC does not specify handlaying for any of the five groups dismissed from the liturgy.

Egeria's Travels, 24.2 et al. Egeria the pilgrim visited Jerusalem for Lent and Easter of 383 and recorded her impressions. Excerpts from her diary reveal frequent usage of the term *missa*. The bishop prays over and "blesses" the pilgrims (e.g., 16.7, 19.16-17, and 21.1), and at Lauds the following occurs: "But at the time when it begins to dawn, then they begin to sing the morning hymns. And then the bishop appears with the clergy, and he immediately enters within the cave, and from within the enclosure he first says the prayer for all; he also remembers the names of those he wishes, and thus blesses the catechumens. Similarly he says a prayer and blesses the faithful. And after this, when the bishop goes out from within the enclosure, all approach him to his hand, and while going out he blesses them one by one, and thus the dismissal happens presently at dawn."[16] Other offices conclude in similar fashion.

Kavanagh sees here a pattern of episcopal prayer and handlaying which concludes a liturgical service, sometimes immediately before another service begins. This practice of dismissing from one liturgy into another will compare favorably with his thesis that the post-baptismal handlaying in AT concludes with a dismissal into another liturgical rite; viz., the eucharist. Kavanagh believes the structural evidence is similar to that found in Laodicea, AC, and AT.[17]

Egeria's *missae* conclude different events. Called a "blessing" (24.11), the rite accompanies the departure of pilgrims from certain sites and the conclusion of certain liturgical services. The hand of the bishop is clearly and consistently in evidence. In describing

---

[16] "*Iam autem ubi ceperit lucescere, tunc incipiunt matutinos ymnos dicere. Ecce et superuenit episcopus cum clero et statim ingreditur intro spelunca et de intro cancellos primum dicet orationem pro omnibus; commemorat etiam ipse nomina, quorum uult, sic benedicet catechumenos. Item dicet orationem et benedicet fideles. Et post hoc exeunte episcopo de intro cancellos omnes ad manum ei accedunt, et ille eos uno et uno benedicet exiens iam, ac sic fit missa iam luce.*" "Itinerarium Egeriae," *Corpus Christianorum*, ed. Aet. Franceschini and R. Weber, Series latina (Turnhout 1965), vol. 75, 67.

[17] Kavanagh, 12-14.

the liturgy of baptism, Egeria is silent about a post-baptismal *missa* and even about an anointing. Compared with other sources, Egeria describes diverse occasions with the term *missa*, but she does describe handlaying in the ministry of the bishop more clearly than do Laodicea, AC, and AT.

WESTERN *MISSAE*

Western evidence of dismissals is rare and maddeningly terse. Kavanagh gives several examples.

Augustine, Sermon 49.8 In speaking about the virtue of forgiveness, Augustine reminds the faithful that after the catechumens are dismissed, they will ask God for forgiveness: "Then, after the sermon comes the dismissal for the catechumens. The faithful will remain. . . . What will we have said to God first? 'Forgive us our sins.' "[18]

Kavanagh simply cites this passage as evidence of dismissals in the West.[19]

Sadly, Augustine gives too few details to argue about the rite's structure.

Cassian, Institutes 11.16. Cassian relates the anecdote of an elder who visited a brother. Approaching the cell, the elder heard sounds from inside. Eavesdropping, he discovered the brother imagined he was delivering a sermon of exhortations for the people. "While standing outside the elder heard him finish the treatise and enact as a deacon the dismissal for catechumens after the office had been changed again: then finally he knocked on the door."[20]

Kavanagh's illustration is another reference to the practice of liturgical dismissals in the West.[21]

---

[18] "*Ecce post sermonem fit missa catechuminis. Manebunt fideles. . . . Quid prius deo dicturi sumus? Dimitte nobis debita nostra.*" CChr.SL 41, ed. Cyril Lambot (1961) 620.

[19] Kavanagh, 15.

[20] "*Cumque subsistens senex audisset eum finisse tractatum et mutato rursus officio celebrare uelut diaconum catechumenis missam, tum demum pulsauit ostium.*" SC 109 (1965) 442.

[21] Kavanagh, 15.

As far as it goes, the reference is sound. Once again, there is no clue to the elements of the dismissal.

THE *MISSAE* OF PENITENTS

Kavanagh includes a selection of texts describing the dismissal of penitents from the liturgy. Although they form a separate category from catechumenal dismissals, they still reveal the structure Kavanagh is pursuing.

Augustine, Letter 149, 16. At the turn of the fifth century Augustine writes about the blessing of penitents in the liturgy: "Intercessions . . . happen when the assembly is blessed, for then the bishops, as advocates, offer their constituency to the most merciful Power through the laying on of hands. When these things have been completed and so great a sacrament has been shared, thanksgiving concludes everything."[22]

Kavanagh says Augustine complains about the long lines coming to him for the dismissal, inferring that it was customary for penitents to come individually under his hand.[23]

Augustine refers neither to the length of the line nor the number of penitents. Nor does he specifically state that "offering" the constituency means dismissing them with the blessing. Still, he does imply that episcopal handlaying is part of the blessing of individual penitents.

Augustine, Sermon 232, 8. Augustine complains about the line of penitents coming to him for the imposition of hands: "Penitents abound here: When the hand is laid on them the service becomes exceedingly long."[24]

Again, Kavanagh sees this as evidence that individual handlaying was a part of the episcopal *missa.*[25]

---

[22] "*Interpellationes . . . fiunt, cum populus benedicitur; tunc enim antistites uelut aduocati susceptos suos per manus inpositionem misericordissimae offerunt potestati, quibus peractis et participato tanto sacramento gratiarum actio cuncta concludit.*" *Epistvlae, Corpvs scriptorvm ecclesiasticorvm latinorvm,* ed. Al. Goldbacher (Vienna 1904) vol. 44, 363.

[23] Kavanagh, 15.

[24] "*Abundant hic poenitentes : quando illis imponitur manus, fit ordo longissimus.*" *Patrologiae cursus completus,* ed. Jacques-Paul Migne, Series latina (Paris 1845), vol. 38, col. 1111.

[25] Kavanagh, 15.

This passage implies that individual handlaying upon penitents was part of the bishop's responsibilities.

Sozomen, Historia Ecclesiastica 7, 16. Sozomen describes the prayer for penitents in Rome around 450: "Then the bishop himself, turning away with tears, likewise prostrates to the ground: and the entire multitude of the church, confessing similarly, pours forth with tears. But afterwards the bishop arises first and raises up those prostrate: and these things having been done, as it is fitting, he dismisses them with a prayer on behalf of those sinners doing penance."[26]

Kavanagh maintains the same structural elements here support the *missa* structure.[27]

Although Sozomen reports the role of a praying bishop in the dismissal, he gives no indication here of handlaying.

Damasus, Epistle 5. Writing in the late fourth century, Pope Damasus forbids presbyters to reconcile penitents, a responsibility reserved for bishops: "None may publicly reconcile any penitent *in missa.*"[28]

Kavanagh sees in this text evidence that the *missa* structure — here used in reconciling penitents — was reserved for bishops.[29]

The line does not occur in Migne's edition of Letter 5.[30]

Second Council of Carthage, 3. Convened in 390, the Second Council of Carthage reserved certain rites for bishops: "Let the making of chrism and the consecration of young women not be done by presbyters: and it pleases all not to permit a presbyter to reconcile anyone with a public dismissal."[31]

---

[26] "*Tum episcopus cum lacrymis ex adverso occurrens, pariter ipse humi provolvitur: et universa Ecclesiae multitudo simul confitens, lacrymis perfunditur. Posthaec vero primus exsurgit episcopus, ac prostratos erigit : factaque, ut decet, precatione pro peccatoribus poenitentiam agentibus, eos dimittit.*" PG 67 (1864) col. 1462.

[27] Kavanagh, 15.

[28] Cited in Ibid., 15.

[29] Ibid., 15.

[30] PL 13 (1845) col. 365–369.

[31] "*Chrismatis confectio, & puellarum consecratio, a presbyteris non fiant : vel reconciliare quemquam publica missa presbytero non licere, hoc omnibus placet.*" Mansi 3 (1960) col. 693.

The text demonstrates the prerogative of the bishop in the penitential *missa*.[32]

Although the reservation to the bishop is clear, the text is not conclusive about the presence of other *missa* elements. One may also surmise that the legislation appeared because presbyters had been performing these rites.

Third Council of Arles, 24. This Council (538) describes the blessing given to penitents: "Let no one presume to entrust the blessing of penance to young persons: certainly let no one dare give it to spouses, except by consent of the parties, and if their age is already mature."[33]

Kavanagh believes that "blessing of penance" is dismissal under another title.[34]

Granting this, the text shows how plentiful references to penitential dismissals may be.

Vita S. Hilarii 13, 16. The *Vita* describes the prayers for penitents in general, and then relates this anecdote: "For a certain blind woman, while she was blessed by the laying on of Hilary's hand, proclaimed that she had received sight."[35]

The text implies that the structural element of handlaying was part of the prayer for penitents.[36]

It seems clear that episcopal handlaying was part of Hilary's ritual for penitents.

Caesarius of Arles, Sermon 74. At the turn of the sixth century, Caesarius complains that people are leaving church too early. "For the one who understands what is being done in church when the divine mysteries are celebrated realizes how much evil they do

---

[32] Thus, Kavanagh, 15–16.

[33] *"Ut ne quis benedictionem poenitentiae juvenibus personis credere praesumat : certe conjugatis, nisi ex consensu partium, & aetate jam plena, eam dare non audeat."* Mansi 9 (1960) col. 18.

[34] Kavanagh, 16, n. 31.

[35] *"Nam mulier quaedam caeca, dum manus ejus impositione benedicitur, visum se recepisse proclamat."* PL 50 (1865) col. 1233-1234.

[36] Kavanagh, 16, n. 31.

who without any great necessity leave from the church when Mass is not finished."[37]

Kavanagh surmises that the complaint arose because too many people were leaving after the readings and the sermon, at the time catechumens and penitents were dismissed. This could have contributed toward the ultimate suppression of dismissals.[38]

Caesarius never mentions the formal dismissals of catechumens or penitents in this sermon. Rather, he admits various occupations prevent people from staying: "for a sickness of the body holds some, public necessity holds others, a whim tempts others and binds them like captives."[39] But he mentions neither catechumens nor penitents, nor that the premature departure of the faithful occurred at a regular point in the service, whether after the sermon or before communion. It is unclear whether or not his assembly was familiar with dismissals at all.

Still, the evidence from these sources is strong that episcopal handlaying was in many places part of the ritual for dismissing penitents.

MISSAE IN THE MONASTIC OFFICE

There are several references to the conclusion of monastic offices with a formal dismissal.

Cassian: Institutes 3.7.1. Cassian mentions the occurrence of a *missa* in the monastic office when he covers the case of a monk arriving late for prayer: "But he who at tierce, sext, or none, will not have run to prayer before the first psalm is finished, does not dare to enter the oratory later, nor to admit himself to the singing of psalms, but standing outside the entrance he awaits the dismissal of the congregation."[40]

---

[37] "*Qui enim intellegit quid in ecclesia agatur, quando divina mysteria celebrantur, agnoscit quantum male faciunt illi, qui de ecclesia non expletis missis sine aliqua grandi necessitate discedunt.*" Opera omnia, Sermones seu admonitiones, ed. D. Germanus Morin (Maredsous 1937) vol. 1, 297.

[38] Kavanagh, 19.

[39] "*Alios enim tenet corporis infirmitas, alios publica necessitas, alios ligat et quasi captivos trahit cupiditas.*" Sermones, vol. 1, 298.

[40] "*Is uero, qui in tertia, sexta uel nona, priusquam coeptus finiatur psalmus, ad orationem non occurrerit, ulterius oratorium introire non audet nec semet ipsum ad-*

This describes the custom of concluding a monastic office with a formal dismissal.

Cassiodorus: Expositio in Psalmis, 25. Cassiodorus uses *missa* as a term for the eucharist: *"Sanctus, sanctus, sanctus Dominus Deus Sabaoth (Isa. vi, 3).* After the psalmist has heard these things and recognized them with the greatest devotion, he tells the people all the marvels which even today the Church sings in the blessed celebration of the holy *missae* (eucharist)."[41]

As time progressed, the term *missa* came to describe the entire ritual which it concluded — in this case, the eucharist.[42]

The Rule of the Master 33-49. This sixth-century document details the life of a monastic community. It describes compline (37) as follows: "Three Compline psalms, a responsory, a reading of the apostle, a reading of the gospels — which the abbot always says when he is present — the prayer of God, and the concluding verse ought to be said."[43]

Since this section of the rule patterns that of Benedict (see below), Kavanagh sees in its liturgical rubrics an argument for the presence of monastic *missae.*[44]

Although its services end in prayer, the Rule of the Master never uses the term *missa* or describes the dismissal rite.

The Rule of Benedict 8-20. Another sixth-century monastic treasure, this Rule describes the conclusion of offices in more detail. Litanies conclude six offices, and after compline a "blessing" follows. But in each case, offices end with a *missa*; e.g., at compline,

---

miscere psallentibus, sed congregationis missam stans pro foribus praestolatur." SC 109, 108.

[41] *"Sanctus, sanctus, sanctus Dominus Deus Sabaoth (Isa. vi, 3). Quae cum audiret, et devotione maxima cognovisset, narraret populis universa mirabilia quae hodieque in sanctarum celebratione missarum beata canit Ecclesia."* PL 70 (1865) col. 185.

[42] Kavanagh, 20.

[43] *"Psalmi conpletorii tres dici debent, responsorium, lectionem apostoli, lectionem euangeliorum, quam semper praesens abbas dicat, rogus Dei et uersum clusoriae."* SC 106 (1964) 194.

[44] Kavanagh, 20ff.

"after the psalms come the hymn of the same hour, a single reading, a verset, the *kyrie eleison*, and the dismissals with a blessing."[45]

Kavanagh hypothesizes that these *missae* combined a formal ritual of prayer and a coming of the monks individually to the abbot's hand. He admits the reconstruction cannot be absolutely certain.[46]

What is missing here is a clear explanation from the Rule of Benedict about just what these *missae* are. The text itself gives no indication that the blessing, which one might expect to be given generally over the assembly, was given individually to the monks.

In short, the evidence of monastic *missae* never mentions hand-laying.

PRAYERS OF INCLINATION

Another ritual category with similarities to *missae* is the Eastern prayer of inclination.

Byzantine Liturgy of St. John Chrysostom. The Prayer of Inclination from the liturgy of Chrysostom seems to be a misplaced liturgical unit. Coming immediately before the distribution of communion, it asks protection for the people instead of preparing one for eucharist. "Look down from heaven above, O master, on those who have bowed their heads to you. . . . Smooth out for all of us, for (our own) good, according to each one's need, whatever lies before us."[47]

Kavanagh follows Robert Taft's hypothesis that this prayer originally accompanied a dismissal of those faithful who were not receiving communion that day. This would lend order to a point in the service that had become increasingly chaotic. The prayer and blessing might then be a fourth or fifth century innovation based on a liturgical structure (the *missa*) to which the people were already accustomed.[48]

---

[45] "*Post quos (psalmos) hymnum eiusdem horae, lectionem unam, versu, Kyrie eleison, et benedictione missae fiant (17:10).*" *The Rule of St Benedict*, ed. Timothy Fry (Collegeville 1981), 212.

[46] Kavanagh, 26–27.

[47] Robert Taft, "The Inclination Prayer before Communion in the Byzantine Liturgy of St John Chrysostom: A Study in Comparative Liturgy," *Ecclesia orans* 3, 1 (1986) 31–32.

[48] Kavanagh, 29–30.

If Taft's thesis is acceptable, there is additional evidence that the bishop's blessing and dismissal of individual groups was a recognized liturgical form adapted to different circumstances.

The Council of Agde, 47. This council in 506 forbade anyone to leave before the blessing of the bishop. "We advise that all dismissals from the Lord's Supper by the laity be held by a special regulation: so that the people may not presume to leave before the blessing of the priest. If they do, they may be publicly admonished by the bishop."[49]

Kavanagh interprets this blessing not as a final dismissal, but as a Western prayer of inclination, further evidence of the practice of episcopal dismissals. In a footnote he indicates that the Councils of Orange and Orange III promulgated similar canons.[50]

The evidence does support the practice of episcopal dismissals, but textually this blessing may as well refer to the final dismissal. Orange and Orange III are pseudonymous conciliar texts dating from the Middle Ages.

The Council of Milevis, 12. This early fifth century council of northern Africa resolved, "that prayers or orations, or dismissals which have been approved in council, whether prefaces or commendations or handlayings, shall be used by all."[51]

Kavanagh proposes that these dismissals may also have been for non-communicants — similar to prayers of inclination.[52]

It is difficult to know who is dismissing whom, and what is the occasion of the dismissals, but Kavanagh's interpretation is one possibility.

Gregory the Great, Dialogues 2, 23. Gregory, writing at the turn of the 7th century, indicates a similar dismissal by the deacon for

---

[49] *"Missas de dominico a saecularibus totas teneri speciali ordinatione praecipimus: ita ut ante benedictionem sacerdotis egredi populus non praesumat. Qui si fecerint, ab episcopo publice confundantur."* Mansi 8 (1960) col. 332.

[50] Kavanagh, 30, n. 66.

[51] *". . . ut preces vel orationes seu missae quae probatae fuerint in concilio, sive praefationes, sive commendationes, seu manus impositiones, ab omnibus celebrentur."* Mansi 4 (1960) col. 330.

[52] Kavanagh, 30–31.

those not receiving communion. He tells the story of two "sanctimonious women" who privately led a not-so-pious life, but were buried nonetheless in the local church. "And when in the same church were celebrated the solemnities of the Mass, and the deacon proclaimed according to the custom: 'If anyone is not receiving communion, let him or her leave,' their nurse, who used to bring an offering to the Lord for them, saw them arise from their tombs and leave the church."[53]

Kavanagh surmises that the deacon's instruction indicated another Western prayer of inclination.[54]

His argument is plausible, although the text is silent about the elements of the rite.

AT'S POSTBAPTISMAL HANDLAYING

We may now analyze Hippolytus' postbaptismal handlaying to see if it fits the pattern of liturgical dismissals.

Hippolytus, Apostolic Tradition 21-22. At the conclusion of baptism at the Easter celebration, each neophyte

"is anointed from the oil which was consecrated (by the thanksgiving prayer of the bishop) by the presbyter saying: I anoint you with holy oil in the name of Jesus Christ. And thus, drying themselves, the individuals are vested, and afterwards are brought in the church.

"But the Bishop laying his hand on them prays, saying: 'Lord God, who made them worthy to merit the forgiveness of sins by the washing of rebirth of the Holy Spirit, send your grace onto them, that they may serve you according to your will; for to you is the glory, to the Father and to the Son with the Holy Spirit in the holy Church, both now and for ever. Amen.'

"Afterwards, pouring the consecrated oil from his hand and laying it on the (neophyte's) head, let him say: 'I anoint you with

---

[53] "*Cumque in eadem ecclesia missarum sollemnia celebrarentur, atque ex more diaconus clamaret: 'Si quis non communicat, det locum,' nutrix earum, quae pro eis oblationem Domino deferre consueuerat, eas de sepulcris suis progredi et exire ecclesiam uidebat.*" SC 260 (1979) 206–208.

[54] Kavanagh, 31.

holy oil in the Lord, the Father Almighty and Christ Jesus and the Holy Spirit.'

"And sealing (the neophyte) on the forehead, let him offer the kiss and say: 'The Lord be with you.' And let him who has been sealed say: 'And with your spirit.' Let him do thus to the individuals."[55]

This is commonly regarded as the ritual predecessor to confirmation. However, Kavanagh challenges this assumption by analyzing the earliest manuscript edition of AT, the eighth century Verona *Urtext*. This edition does not include the prayer for the Holy Spirit commonly associated with confirmation. Verona's text simply prays for God's grace, that the neophyte may serve according to God's will. Kavanagh believes the anointing has a christic, not a pneumatological meaning.[56] He builds a convincing argument that later generations added the epicletic formula during an age which developed the theology of the Holy Spirit.[57]

If the Verona manuscript, the earliest, is the most correct, and if the epicletic formula is a later accretion, one is left with a disturbing question: If AT 22 is not confirmation, what is it? Kavanagh's response is that it is a baptismal *missa*. He believes the bishop's action is the public conclusion of a rite begun privately. The rite of baptism, Kavanagh says, would conclude with the assembly's prayer in preparation for the Eucharist. The steps of prayer, hand-

---

[55] ". . . ungueatur a praesbytero de illo oleo quod sanctificatum est dicente : Ungueo te oleo sancto in nomine Ie(s)u Chr(ist)i. Et ita singuli detergentes se induantur et postea in ecclesia ingrediantur.

"Episcopus uero manu(m) illis inponens inuocet dicens : D(omi)ne D(eu)s, qui dignos fecisti eos remissionem mereri peccatorum per lauacrum regenerationis sp(irit)u(s) s(an)c(t)i, inmitte in eos tuam gratiam, ut tibi seruiant secundum uoluntatem tuam; quoniam tibi est gloria, patri et filio cum sp(irit)u s(an)c(t)o, in sancta ecclesia, et nunc et in saecula saeculorum. Amen.

"Postea oleum sanctificatum infunde(n)s de manu et inponens in capite dicat : Ungueo te s(an)c(t)o oleo in d(omi)no patre omnipotente et Chr(ist)o Ie(s)u et sp(irit)u s(an)c(t)o.

"Et consignans in frontem offerat osculum et dicat : D(omi)n(u)s tecum. Et ille qui signatus est dicat : Et cum sp(irit)u tuo. Ita singulis faciat." SC 11 bis, 86–90.

[56] Kavanagh, 39–52.

[57] Kavanagh, 52–72.

laying, signing the forehead, and offering the kiss of peace, he maintains, are steps later sources call a *missa*.[58]

Does the evidence cited above prove this hypothesis? Not really. That's why it remains a hypothesis. Patterns of episcopal *missae* are evident, but tantalizingly incomplete. Since the genre takes various forms it is tempting to apply it to the baptismal liturgy. But the thesis remains unprovable in the end, despite Kavanagh's forceful rhetoric.

There are other problems. A postbaptismal dismissal would be logistically awkward in AT 22: The neophytes have already left the place of baptism and entered the place of communion when the bishop imposes hands on them. Entrance is an unusual moment for a dismissal. And if there had been a dismissal from baptism, surely that would have occurred at the font, before coming to the bishop. One also wonders why baptism would be a separate liturgical unit requiring a dismissal. Other *missae* have marked the completion of an office, the end of the liturgy of the Word, or the blessing of pilgrims. When Egeria's pilgrims were dismissed into another service, they went from one complete liturgy to another; when catechumens, energumens, illuminated, penitents, non-communicants, and the faithful are dismissed from the liturgy, they leave the place of assembly completely. The baptismal rites of AT seem integral to the liturgy. This would be the sole instance of a dismissal *within* a liturgical unit. In addition, the appearance of oil, which has been absent in other *missae*, remains unexplained.

Another difficulty concerns the content of the episcopal prayer. Among the three examples from AT which Kavanagh proposes may be *missae*, only this one presents the actual content of the prayer spoken on the occasion. By taking pains to include the prayer, Hippolytus may be indicating he has a special meaning for this ritual. In fact, among all the dismissal texts cited above, the presentation of the prayer's content is exceptionally rare.

Apart from these texts, the difficulty of chronology remains. AT is the earliest text under consideration. Other examples of *missae* postdate it sometimes by centuries. Contemporaneous evidence is scant. In Tertullian (155–220) the theological treatise on baptism

---

[58] Kavanagh, 67.

recounts its ritual contrary to the way Kavanagh interprets the Verona *Urtext* of Hippolytus: After baptism and anointing, "the hand is imposed for a blessing, calling and inviting the Holy Spirit."[59] Although Kavanagh dismisses this as "allusive evidence,"[60] it gives witness to an epicletic handlaying as part of the baptismal ritual. The possibility of this rite being a dismissal remains open, but Tertullian has given it a pneumatological meaning.[61]

One also has the very difficult passages from Acts of the Apostles to reckon with. Kavanagh is right that the application of the events in Acts to the postbaptismal handlaying comes fairly late, around the fifth century.[62] But surely the coming of the Spirit in Acts, both at Pentecost and through the apostolic handlaying, remains in the background in early Christian initiation proceedings. The gift of the Spirit is what baptism is all about. It should not be surprising to find a pneumatic handlaying in early Christian initiation rites since it was part of apostolic testimony.

Thus the original problem returns: If the episcopal handlaying of AT 22 is not confirmation, what is it?

It seems there are two possibilities, depending on the reliability of the Verona *Urtext*. One is that Verona is incorrect, and that there really was an epiclesis in Hippolytus' prayer. The witness of Tertullian makes this possible. In this case, calling the rite "confirmation" is anachronistic, but it would remain a forerunner to what developed as confirmation later in the Church: a postbaptismal, episcopal, epicletic handlaying. It would be part of the "symbolic overflow" of baptism, to use Pamela Jackson's expression.[63]

[59] ". . . *manus inponitur per benedictionem aduocans et inuitans spiritum sanctum.*" De baptismo 8, 1, CSEL, vol. 1, 282–283.

[60] Kavanagh, 53.

[61] A similar case may be made for Cyprian (200–258) in his *Epistula ad Jubajanum*, 9: "*Quod nunc quoque apud nos geritur, ut qui in Ecclesia baptizantur, praepositis Ecclesiae offerantur, et per nostram orationem ac manus impositionem, Spiritum sanctum consequantur et signaculo Dominico consummentur.*" PL 3 (1865) col. 1160.

[62] Kavanagh credits Innocent I with this innovation, p. 59. Actually, Jerome made the connection a few years earlier in *Contra Luciferianos* 6–9. See PL 23 (1865) col. 169–173.

[63] "The Meaning of 'Spiritale Signaculum' in the Mystagogy of Ambrose of Milan," *Ecclesia orans* 7, 1 (1990) 90.

The meaning of baptism is so rich that additional rites explore its wealth.

Another possibility is that Verona is correct, and there is no support to the epicletic nature of Hippolytus' postbaptismal prayer. In this instance, instead of asking why do the neophytes come back to the bishop, it may be as helpful to ask why did they first go away? The neophytes were baptized in private and then led back into the assembly where the bishop laid hands on them. Since baptism in the nude was a private matter, the handlaying may have been the first public gesture of ratification for the bishop and the faithful who did not witness the pouring of water. It could have been a neophytic version of the catechumenal exorcism: Instead of praying for protection from evil, the bishop now prays for the bestowal of grace.

AFTERWORD

As with any historical study of confirmation, one can only be amazed here at the journey confirmation has taken to arrive at its present status. What began as a fairly simple ritual embedded in grander initiation rites has mushroomed into a sacramental declaration of independence for teenagers. Whatever the origins of confirmation, it was never intended to overshadow baptism and eucharist. To pretend it is the completion of initiation[64] is to cast doubt on one's faith in the communal dimension of the eucharist. If unconfirmed children receiving eucharist have not completed their initiation into the Church, just what is the nature of the common faith we express in the eucharistic banquet?

[64] In the Diocese of Kansas City-St. Joseph, for example, teenagers requesting the sacrament of confirmation send a letter to the ordinary which is to include this sentence: "At this time, I am formally requesting to become a full member of the Catholic faith by asking to receive the Sacrament of Confirmation." "Confirmation Letter to the Bishop," (undated).

One teen expanded on the notion: "Confirmation means to me that I'm sort of one of God's many deciples (sic) now, ofically (sic)." Another expressed a contrary theological opinion, that the sacrament has more to do with accomplishment than initiation: "I wish to be confirmed because I had worked my ass off trying to get my service projects (done and) getting to retreats." Various letters to the bishop, St John Francis Regis Parish, 1990.

Kavanagh's book is important because it scrutinizes the meaning of confirmation from the point of view of a ritual scholar. By analyzing ritual texts, he proposes a ritual solution to what confirmation means. Martin Luther, by contrast, scrutinized the meaning of confirmation from the point of view of a biblical scholar. By analyzing biblical texts, he proposed a biblical solution to what confirmation means.[65] There are those today who scrutinize confirmation as catechetical scholars. By analyzing the process of catechesis, they propose a catechetical solution to what confirmation means. To sacramental theologians who vainly strive to reclaim the modest beginnings of an overgrown rite, Kavanagh offers hope.

Response by Aidan Kavanagh

I thank Paul Turner for his analysis of my *Confirmation: Origins and Reform* and for the complimentary things he says about it. The following are some comments in gratitude.

First, the postbaptismal anointing by a presbyter in AT is certainly not pneumatic but christic: "I anoint you with holy oil in the name of Jesus Christ." This early third-century witness enunciates a tradition still in the Roman Rite to this day (RCIA no. 228).

Second, I am not trying to "dethrone" confirmation. I am merely seeking its genesis as a sacramental, and thus liturgical, act by examining closely its liturgical structure compared across the various families of rites. If it is anything, confirmation is a liturgical act with a liturgical grammar before it is a theological problem, a biblical allusion, or a catechetical opportunity. The *origins* of confirmation cannot dependably be determined by theological reflection, biblical exegesis (even of Acts 8), or catechetics. Its origins can only be discerned through structural and comparative analysis of the rite itself, after which these other approaches may or may not be helpful. As in any other research procedure, there come

[65] Paul Turner, *The Meaning and Practice of Confirmation: Perspectives from a Sixteenth Century Controversy*, American University Studies Series VII, Theology and Religion, vol. 31 (New York 1987) 7–13.

times when the evidence runs out and one must risk well-informed hypotheses that plausibly bridge the gaps. This I have tried to do.

Third, Fr Turner says "The gift of the Spirit is what baptism is all about." I agree entirely, and so does the bishop's "confirmation" prayer in AT 21: "Lord God, you have made them worthy to receive remission of sins through the washing of regeneration of the Holy Spirit. . . ." In this case, however, as I point out, the neophytes engage the Holy Spirit *in their baptism* into that Anointed One whose first gift is Spirit, not in a subsequent epicletic prayer of the bishop, which is absent here and witnessed only some two centuries later in Roman procedure by Innocent I. On this basis I claim that "confirmation" is not in AT, but that the liturgical elements peculiarly associated with bishops — namely, prayer and handlaying of a *missa* — are there and will later be pneumaticized for good and sufficient reasons, even though the split continues to give us trouble today. That "confirmation" is not in AT should not surprise: Gallican churches appear never to have had it originally, and the Eastern churches do not have it to this day (although some have pneumaticized the postbaptismal anointing by a presbyter, none yet have a second anointing with prayer and handlaying by a bishop, the very structure which distinguishes both a *missa* and confirmation from a postbaptismal anointing by a presbyter).

Fourth, I remain convinced that the formal *missa* structure of prayer and handlaying during the first five or six centuries is definite no matter whether it was called *missa* or *impositio manuum* or inclination prayer or the blessing of penance; so definite indeed that mere allusion to it was enough for contemporaries to know what was meant (thus the incompleteness of evidence we today would prefer not to have). So large a part did *missae* play in early liturgical structure and growth that they came to give their name to even larger structures such as offices in Spain and the entire eucharist in the West, *missarum solemnia*, the Mass. Given this, I would not be surprised that there remains a sort of informal "*missa* instinct" among even some modern Christian groups. In the early 1960s while a doctoral student in Trier, Germany, I was struck by how fervently the people pressed around the bishop after a pontifical service to have him lay his hand on their children's heads and mark the sign of the cross on their foreheads with his thumb. One also sees something similar among Greek Orthodox. This liturgical protocol in antiquity, formal or informal, has been well described by Robert Taft.[1]

Finally, whether my *missa* suggestion for the origins of confirmation stands scrutiny or not (hypothesis is a risky business) is not the point. The point is that the law of prayer founds and establishes the law of belief, not vice versa. What I have tried to do is let the *lex supplicandi,* so far as I can evoke it, speak for itself on a matter of origins where the *lex credendi* has had all the lines. I hope my small work might prod further studies by those of such competence as Fr Turner exhibits.

---

[1] "The Inclination Prayer before Communion in the Byzantine Liturgy of St John Chrysostom: A Study in Comparative Liturgy," *Ecclesia Orans* 3/1 (1986) 29–60, especially 57–58.

Aidan Kavanagh

14. Unfinished and Unbegun Revisited: The Rite of Christian Initiation of Adults

I am asked to do another of my unfinished-and-unbegun jobs, this time on the Rite of Christian Initiation of Adults. Like a previous attempt in the same genre, this one will not be exhaustive. Its thesis is that, so far from having to look around for things yet to do in the area of Christian initiation, so much remains to be done that we can hardly be said yet to have begun at all. Only about half of the Roman Catholic dioceses in this country, one notes, bothered to respond to a recent questionnaire from the Bishops' Committee on the Liturgy concerning implementations of the Rite of Christian Initiation of Adults [RCIA]; less than half of these indicated that some work on adult initiation was beginning; and only about half of these in turn expressed interest in taking part in a national study of the matter.[1]

One doubts that this is due merely to sloth. One suspects that a large reason for it is that the RCIA presents such a vastly strategic overhaul of almost every way we look at the gospel in the Church that many are simply at a loss concerning where first to begin translating this vision into practice. This is, most likely, a correct evaluation; it is also probably salutary. For to feed the RCIA piecemeal, so to speak, into the meatgrinder of conventional parochial practice will almost surely result in transmuting the document's challenges into neat little packets of a *status quo* that is becoming more problematic each year. Put another way, this process is an

[1] See T. Randolph, "Preliminary Survey on the Catechumenate in America Today," *Becoming a Catholic Christian* (New York 1978) 35.

alchemy that will turn the RCIA's precious metal of renewal into the cold and heavy lead of more mere reforms.

What seems needed in this case is the leavening of insight — insight into both the contents of the RCIA and its implications. At this point a lot of courage and some very deft diagnosis is required. What follows amounts to some few selective stabs in this direction, nothing more.

CATECHESIS

The problem of catechesis is of central concern. More specifically, I think the issue is not so much with conversion-therapy-catechesis versus religious education-catechesis, but with the general deritualization of catechesis which has been a long-term phenomenon in Western Christianity since the Middle Ages. Prior to that time, the Fathers understood catechesis to be a process the nature and form of which were determined entirely by its "final cause," namely, *sacramental* initiation. Catechesis was thus permeated from beginning to end with a rich and carefully calibrated sacramental ethos. It was a process of "enlightenment" consummated in the illumination *(photismos)* of baptism-in-its-fullness, that is, baptism, chrismation or consignation, and Eucharist. This was so because initiation was always into the Church, the Body of Christ and the locale of his lifegiving Spirit: it was an ecclesial process throughout, which means it was sacramental at every stage, for the Church itself is the primary sacramental entity in and after the Incarnate Word.

Catechesis was thus intrinsically sacramental from beginning to end, and the catechumenate was a sacramental structure in the Church. Catechumens were signed with the cross, and baptism was seen to begin in this. Catechumens were fed the "sacrament of salt," and the Eucharist was seen to begin in this. Catechumens, it seems, were even taught doctrine out of Scripture homiletically in an event that was much like a service of the word which concluded with prayer, hand-laying, and dismissal. On their election for baptism they were publicly scrutinized in the solemn presence of the local church in much the same manner.

The conclusion is inescapable that *being catechized and sacramentalized were not separate enterprises, but one and the same process in the catechumenate.* The pedagogical sophistication of this approach is worth a lot of thought in our own day when sacraments and catechetics have drifted so far apart, weakening both enterprises and introducing a certain schizophrenia into Christian life and pastoral endeavor.

More seriously even than this, however, is the matter of how a deritualized or desacramentalized catechesis shuts down perception of how evangelization before it and mystagogy after it are related. For catechesis as the premedieval Church understood it was the linchpin that gave evangelization its coherence and mystagogy its point of departure. Evangelization, catechesis, and mystagogy in this light are stages in a single grand program of Christian formation, a program that both leads to and contains within it initiation into the sacramental heart of ecclesial living in Christ. This being the case, an evangelization that does not lead to catechesis is as abortive as a catechesis that does not lead to sacramental initiation; as a sacramental initiation that initiates one into nothing; as a mystagogy that reflects and refers back to no remembered sacramental events of illumination. Evangelization, catechesis, sacramental initiation, and mystagogy are compenetrating functions of each other; a single economy within which an ecclesiology is born, a pastoral theology is generated, and the unity of the Church is secured in faith. To say less than this is to say too little.

THEOLOGY

The Roman Catholic theological establishment in this country has never yet addressed itself in any depth to the principles and results of reflection on baptism for a theology of sacraments, liturgy, ministry, church order, ethics, or the nature of the Church itself. Yet the baptismal implications of the Conciliar documents and the new rites of initiation bear on what it means to live a Christian life in a world such as we now occupy in a way that affects all our most significant issues. Not least of these is that of a pre-Augustinian view of original sin which, while granting the fallenness of the world, does not end in holding unbaptized infants personally culpable for sin before God. This view in no way diminishes the necessity of baptism for all: it does, however, make the *quamprimum* baptism of infants more a matter of sound pastoral judgment than one of theological necessity in all cases. This is especially true in view of the Council's repeated insistence on the theological reality of a catechumen's true communion with Christ in his Church even prior to baptism. This notion will inevitably alter how we view the relation of the unbaptized to God, the relation of a catechumen of whatever age to God in the Church, and the pastoral function of catechesis and the sacraments of initiation in the Church. The shift is also one that escapes many theologians and frightens everyone else, particularly bishops and pastors. Both it and its implications therefore need careful analysis and exposition.

Equally intimidating are the effects a restored baptismal theology and practice will have on our unconventional views of ministry. The new and all but unprecedented ability of Roman presbyters to confirm not by delegation but by law is only the tip of the iceberg. This change in historic Roman practice came about not in order to lighten the workload of bishops, but for strictly theological reasons enunciated in number 34 of the RCIA — namely, the close and *necessary* relation of confirmation to baptism in context of an orthodox understanding of how each Person of the Trinity comes upon the baptized. So salient is this alteration in the ministry of confirmation that it has produced a rare instance of a liturgical rubric changing canon law: canon 782, which defined the bishop as *ordinarius minister* of confirmation, is now altered to read *Confirmationis minister originarius est Episcopus.*[2]

This shift in the ministry of confirmation for theological rather than merely practical considerations points to an even deeper fundamental evolution in both the theory and practice of ministry in the Church of our day. Allow me to pursue this by moving to the overtly liturgical areas where more exploration is needed.

THE LITURGY

Odd as it may seem to many, I am convinced that we must study more deeply and work harder to restore significance to the anoint-

---

[2] *Rite of Confirmation,* no. 7.

ings after baptism. One is not baptized (as were John's disciples) only in water but in the Anointed One by his Holy Spirit as well. We forget that we still refer to ourselves corporately as The Anointed, that is, Christians. *Christos* was not Jesus' family name.

I say this because it seems necessary to insist that the Holy Spirit is intimately locked into baptism by the gospels, Paul, and tradition: it is never allowed to float free into extraordinary manifestations alone. There is more to the Holy Spirit's role in the Church than extraordinary charismatic gifts. There is thus more to baptismal anointing than a *beau geste* in hospitality toward the newly washed. The work of Leonel Mitchell, Sebastian Brock, Gabriele Winkler and others has made it clear that the earliest churches considered baptismal anointing neither as a secondary element added to water baptism, nor the effects of baptismal anointing as charismatically extraordinary, "vertical," or discrete. Traditionally, nothing is more clear than that anointing is intrinsic to Christian baptism. For it is here that one is marked or sealed with the messianic Spirit of prophecy, priesthood, and kingship — being thereby constituted *Christos*, a "Christ," in the fullest post-paschal sense. In East Syria, it seems, water baptism was the *result* of being thus anointed: in the Graeco-Latin west, it seems that water baptism *prepared* for this anointing. In both cases, adherence to the Anointed One who is now life-giving Spirit was consummated necessarily in a water bath for the forgiveness of sins *and* by an unction of messianic consecration. *It is this latter act which gives liturgical specificity to the paschal difference between Christian baptism and the baptism of John,* a difference which the synoptic gospels are at pains to point out.

Whatever one thinks about the baptism of Jesus at John's hands in the Jordan, it is unassailable that the first Christian generation was aware that it constituted uniquely Jesus' own manifestation to the world and his commissioning for public ministry. Further reflection by New Testament authors seems to detect in it a prolepsis with two dimensions for the future.

The first proleptic dimension had to do with the consummation of Jesus' public ministry on the cross. As Beasley-Murray points out, concern with the water baptism of John — which was not initiatory but prophetic and for the forgiveness of sins — fades in

Jesus' circle as his ministry enters the cities from the wilderness. Jesus increasingly begins to refer, in messianic accents, to an ominous baptism with which he is to be baptized, namely, a baptism in calamity unto death. His ultimate earthly "anointing" is to be in his own blood.

The accomplishment of this first proleptic dimension of his baptismal manifestation simultaneously opens onto the second such dimension. It is the postpaschal appropriation of his consummated messianic vocation by others — an appropriation which occurs in Christian baptism strictly so-called, as distinct and now quite separate from all the other baptisms which preceded it. In this light the manifestation of Jesus of Galilee as the anointed Holy One of God does not reach final term in his own brief ministry on the cross, but only in the genesis of a community, the Church, in which the Spirit of that same anointed Holy One of God is abroad for service, for ministry, working Its wonders as It will. While the Church can be said to have been "born" on the first Pentecost after a labor of fifty days, it was conceived on the banks of the Jordan years previously.

In these reflections of New Testament authors we are witnessing the first stirrings of a baptismal theology of the Church, one that is laced with a messianic christology. I take this to be the *Urgrund* upon which the Church's apostolic traditions of ministry and pneumatology are first raised. It may also be the context within which it is possible to account for the way in which water baptism and the outpouring of the Holy Spirit seem to be related in the earliest strata of evidence — not so much in a rigid chronological sequence as in a tandem-like relationship whose common center of gravity is the exalted *Messiah-Christos*. Both water baptism and the outpouring of the Spirit are necessary, but it is of less importance to determine which comes first than it is to understand that *both* events result from the exaltation on the cross and in the resurrection of the anointed Holy One of God. Proclamation of his Good News in evangelization, together with conversion, the water bath, and the outpouring of the Spirit constitute the integrity of entry into that community which is the table fellowship, the *communio*, of the Church.

The implications of all this for catechesis, sacramental practice, and theological reflection are, I think, as fundamental as they are yet hardly explored. Which leads me to the matter of methodology.

METHODOLOGY

We liturgical scholars are not all we ought to be when it comes to methodological adequacy. Were this not so, then one of the most widely read among us would not have said: "In the time of the Fathers . . . confirmation . . . was the moment in the rite of initiation when the Holy Spirit was given to the candidates." Despite the industry of this scholar, the method betrayed by such a statement is disturbingly anachronistic. He moves back through early sources looking for "confirmation" out of a pastoral concern which has polemical side-purposes. But this procedure is valid only back to about the ninth century, when the second postbaptismal anointing in the rite of Rome began to become definitively separated from baptism, and then only in western Europe. To go beyond that time and area is not unlike an East Syrian scholar looking for traces of the *rushma* anointing among American Methodists.

The point I wish to make is that it is not enough in this business to be able to find evidence: one must then know what to do with it. Heuristics are one thing, hermeneutics another — especially in the matter of Christian initiation. Text collectors apprise us of what the sources are and of what they contain. Then we must be very apt when it comes to interpreting the sources both in their original contexts and in what we ought to make out of them in theory and practice today.

The Scylla in this is that we do no more than expound the liturgy as tradition delivers it. The Charybdis is that we either reject the tradition or fatally relativize it. In neither of these alternatives is a real liturgiological hermeneutic necessary: it may not even be possible. The only exception to this may obtain in attempts to relativize the tradition, in which case a certain hermeneutic seems to be in evidence. But it is one that is controlled by factors other than those inherent in the liturgy itself. Such a hermeneutic is discernible in the passage on confirmation in the time of the Fathers just quoted. It is also discernible in some current discussions on who can be ordained. And one suspects it will arise also at some point touching initiation, when initiatory inconveniences begin to be perceived in practice. This relativizing hermeneutic is, however, both soft in procedure and fairly obvious in its intent. It also is often meant to intimidate in debate, resorting to *ad hominem* reductionisms and indictments of motives. In doing this, it fails to confront hard-core issues embedded in the evidence — a confrontation that must be induced and adequately resolved if the discussion is to result in healthy conclusions that will sustain a community of faith at worship.

Paramount in any such resolution of confrontations with hard data in our area of concern must be the recognition that the liturgy is not merely one *source* of theology among many others of equal value but that the liturgy is, rather, *the very condition* of doing theology itself. The Church, its acts, and its faith about which we theologize is a community at prayerful worship before God at all times. We must accept, and we must expound more adequately to others (especially to our theologian colleagues), that the old patristic maxim *legem credendi lex statuat supplicandi* means what it says.

This is especially crucial in matters of Christian initiation. For one who works in these matters quickly discovers that here the *lex supplicandi* has been vastly overlayered by various *leges credendi*, many of which received their final formulation and doctrinal value in the rage of polemics between, say, Augustine and Pelagius in the fifth century, or between Catholic and Protestant in the sixteenth. How one sorts out competing or even opposing laws of worship and belief in a *post factum* situation is both difficult and perilous. But there is no way around it unless we merely choose to succumb to reductionisms of one sort or another. The RCIA, to put it bluntly, has restored a *lex supplicandi* that occupies a definite primacy of place due to its fundamental content. It is thus a subordinating criterion for the *lex credendi*. We must not allow theologians or pastors to forget or ignore this. This means that we liturgical scholars must be more disciplined with ourselves than we have been. In illustration of which, allow me to conclude (as I hope, constructively) with some reflections on the matter of ministry.

BAPTISM AND THE QUESTION OF MINISTRY

A baptismal element needs to be introduced into our contemporary discussion of ministry. This baptismal element is a basic one that goes farther into the theological heart of the matter of ministry than revisionist history or the politics of liberation. It presumes that baptism is the prime enabler for ministry first by the Church and then in the Church. It suggests that a theology of holy orders is a function of our theology of baptism, and that disfunction in either will be manifest in both. And because rights follow needs in the Church as in any other human society, it asks whether a right to ordination can be demonstrated in terms not of some oblique ideology but in terms of baptism as the sustained genesis of the Church from era to era. It deals less with how the ordained "resemble" Christ than with how the baptized participate in his unending high priestly ministry before the Father for the world. It insists that the often cited text of Galatians 3:28 is not about ordination but about baptism — as the preceding verse makes clear: "For as many of you as were baptized into Christ have put on Christ." Indeed, the rest of the epistle is a commentary precisely on what this means, not for an equal-opportunity order of ministry but for a faithful Church.

Paul, it seems, saw clearly that a faithful church is the condition of faithful worship and faithful ministry. Worship and ministry are important only to the extent that they are functions of the Church, Christ's Body and the locale of his life-giving Spirit. As such, worship and the several ordained ministries both discover and actualize the Church to itself: which is to say that worship and the ordained ministries operate within the overarching sacramentality of the Church and as functions of it.

The end of both worship and the ordained ministries is the Church being faithful. The ground out of which worship and the ordained ministries arise is the Church being faithful. The Church begins and ends in fidelity to the gospel. Its life is a faithful life, and this fidelity consists in its remaining itself in Christ by his Holy Spirit. Anything that interferes with this or distracts from it — be it an oversacralized liturgy, too great an absorption with specific ideologies or social programs, or a too hieraticized or clericalized ministry — attacks the Church's fidelity to its own nature and purpose.

For to identify the Church with the liturgy as the "holiest" thing the Church does really profanes all else. To turn the Church into a set of social movements risks seeing the Church only as *in via*, forgetting that it is also already *in statu patriae* through Christ and in his Spirit. To equate the Church with its ordained ministries deministerializes the baptized faithful. To take only a part to the exclusion of the whole closes the open door to God the Church is meant to be.

One way to avoid this is to realize first that ministry is a Church-wide phenomenon, and thus a baptismal reality at base. But while one cannot discuss baptism without ministerial implications arising, it has unfortunately become usual to discuss ministries without ever feeling it necessary to enter into the implications of this discussion for baptism. That holy orders are rooted in baptism never seems to cross our minds. I suggest that it must, and I do so by emphasizing one quality tradition regularly associates with both ministry and baptism as incarnational realities in the life of the Church, namely, sacerdotality.

I stated in my book that the Church baptizes to priesthood: it ordains only to executive exercise of that priesthood in the major orders of ministry.[3] Indeed *Ordo Romanus XI* of the ninth century has the baptized and anointed neophytes vested in stole and chasuble as they are presented to the Bishop of Rome for consignation prior to the beginning of the Easter Eucharist. The point being that *sacerdotium* in orthodox Christianity is not plural but single. It is that of Christ, shared among those in solidarity with whom (*not* in substitution for whom) he was himself baptized in Jordan, and also in solidarity with whom he now stands as both sacrifice and sacrificer in heaven — a concept that has been central in the old Roman anaphora's *anamnesis* and oblation section at least since the fourth century.

Those to be ordained come bearing all this with them as they approach their "ordering" into colleges of service to this prophetic

---

[3] Aidan Kavanagh, *The Shape of Baptism: The Rite of Christian Initiation* (New York 1978) 187–188.

and royal priesthood, this holy nation. While every presbyter and bishop is therefore a sacerdotal person, not every sacerdotal person in the Church is a presbyter or bishop. Nor does sacerdotality come upon one for the first time, so to speak, at one's ordination. In constant genesis in the font, the Church is born there as a sacerdotal assembly by the Spirit of the Anointed One himself. *Laos* is a priestly name for a priestly person.

The sacerdotal community of the baptized needs ministers to serve its needs, but the presence of ministers exercising *sacerdotium* within it neither de-sacerdotalizes everyone else nor deprives the community at large of its corporate "ministry of reconciliation" in the world, nor does this reduce the baptized to the level of a proletariat composed of second-class citizens in the Church. Nothing could be more opposed to the deepest instincts of Catholic tradition than this.

Yet the association of priesthood with the presbyterate among the Western churches has presbyteralized not only the ministry but the very sacerdotality of the Church as well. This in turn has lent a certain ruthless logic to the pernicious perception of ordination to the presbyterate as the only way of achieving true Christian status, or even "first-class citizenship," in the Church. Our various seminaries are full of people seeking this apparent yet nonexistent "honor."

Once a single order of ministry, rather than baptism, comes to define sacerdotality in the Church, and then casts the whole of ministry into primarily political terms, several consequences occur:

First, the Church appears as a pyramid-like structure functioning by the delegation of power from the top. This model of the Church is aristocratic and elitist, no matter whether it is run by ecclesiastical princes or by a collegial Comintern of experts. Its base is essentially a baptized proletariat that has no powers and few rights, except to be led.

Second, pastoral theology and practice in such a milieu mutates into a process by which it is determined where the faithful are to be led and by what means — both ends and means being increasingly interpreted by sociology and political ideology rather than the gospels as traditionally received. All else alters to follow: worship becomes education, prayer becomes therapy, ministry leadership, polity becomes politics, and theology ideology. The community of faith becomes a community of works, the goodness or badness of which is measured by polls.

Third, ministry is separated into ordained, that is, leadership, functions of high political significance on one hand, and into unordained "case worker" functions of mutual affirmation and care according to the latest clerical or professional techniques on the other. But while separate, these two kinds of ministry are nonetheless symbiotic and complementary. Their prime analogue is found in the bureaucratic structure of the secular state. They both function according to a tight system of interlocking presumptions that has little if anything to do with the gospel, and this system they each share and draw upon to produce an implicitly totalitarian, univocal, and introverted society which is less open to the world's true needs than it is dependent on the world's favor. But unlike its secular analogue, this society is too riven with guilt to run the world: thus, the world runs it.

Needless to say, Catholic tradition stands over against all this. It does not define sacerdotality in presbyteral terms, but in terms that are first christic and ecclesial (that is, baptismal), and then episcopal. The Catholic concept of ministry, in particular, is sacerdotal and sacramental rather than socio-political. Its analogue is not that of political power delegated from some sanctioned bureau, but that of Israel's mediating role of service between God and humankind as manifested in the Temple liturgy of the atonement — a liturgy peculiarly consummated in Christ. This analogy, so elaborately traced out in the Epistle to the Hebrews, has penetrated the Roman tradition on sacerdotality and worship to an extent found, so far as I can tell, in no other historic Christian tradition East or West.

Speaking now of that tradition in particular, I find no evidence in it that entry into the mystery of sacerdotality consummated in Christ is had either exclusively or primarily in ordination. On the contrary, the Roman tradition holds that participation in the mystery begins with the very first stages of entering into communion with Christ's Church and is brought to full ecclesial term in baptism by water and Holy Spirit. At that point, one is anointed with as full a sacerdotality as the Church possesses in and by the

Anointed One himself. Ordination cannot make one more priestly than the Church, and without baptism ordination cannot make one a priest at all. Becoming a Christian and becoming a sacerdotal being are not merely correlative processes, they are one and the same. And the process is so radical and extensive that it overflows even the sacraments of initiation and holy orders. For if sacerdotality is essentially a function of mediating between God and people in Christ, this can begin even prior to baptism. Thus the RCIA, number 18, specifies that when two catechumens marry, or even when a catechumen marries a non-Christian, the appropriate marriage rite is to be used, just as for the baptized faithful. The conclusion seems to be that the catechumen mediates the sacramental grace of holy matrimony in this instance even prior to baptism — that is, engages in a sacerdotal act typical of a community that is a holy nation, a royal priesthood.

If this is true, then it is inescapable that the foundation upon which the communication of sacerdotality rests is primarily *communion with Christ in his Church* rather than the sacramental acts of baptism or holy orders taken in themselves and abstracted apart from this same communion. Put another way, sacerdotality, it seems, arises in direct ratio to the degree in which one enters ever more fully into faith in Jesus Christ the high priest among his priestly people.

Baptism by water and Holy Spirit functions as a sacramental sign with *this* as the reality of meaning it articulates and, in turn, causes. *Sacramenta significando efficiunt gratiam.* Baptism by water and Holy Spirit marks the point at which the faith of an individual and the faith of the community are locked into an irrevocable, incarnately public equilibrium of sustained mutuality. But in normal circumstances this faith-engagement begins to happen even prior to baptism. This incipient, even prebaptismal, communion is sacerdotal in nature from the first. Baptism stamps it with a public character which is then overtly and actively sacerdotal in function. In baptism one enters not just into passive membership in Christ's body, the Church, but into its own obligation to mediate God to people and people to God in a manner which is adamantly ecclesial in nature and scope. The Church, said Paul, is a ministry of reconciliation, of mediation, in and for the world. The baptized

Christian participates in this sacerdotal ministry by living in faithful witness (*martyria*) to the gospel in community. It is a life of faith from which good works flow; but good works alone do not justify such a life. Faith is not deepened by good works: good works are deepened and multiplied by growth in faith-communion. But the nature, powers, and gifts of communion in faith are complete and sufficient with illumination by water and Spirit — an event the Roman tradition understands to include water baptism, its pneumatic seal in consignation or chrismation, and the spiritual food of the Eucharist. To say that every Christian is a priestly being is to affirm that the Church is sacerdotal because of its inherence in Christ who is the high priest of God because he is Son of man.

It is in this baptismal perspective that ordinations must be seen in order to be grasped in their integrity. One thing this perspective throws into bold relief is that *ordination* is not to "priesthood" in general but to specific executive exercise of sacerdotality in service to the Church. Orthodox Christian tradition is more adamant on this matter than many realize. It insists that one be ordained not only to a specific type of ministry in the Church, but also to the regular exercise of that ministry only within the local church where the minister's communion in faith is actually lived out. Wandering bishops ordaining people at large for *in globo* ministry to the world in general is a phenomenon that goes so against Roman instinct as to be ruled out by canon law. The taproot of this prohibition is theological, having to do with that sacerdotal view of ministry which rests not exclusively on the validity of the orders of the ordaining one or on his intention, but on the state of communion with Christ in his Church on the part of all concerned. Because of this, the unbaptized can neither ordain nor be ordained. Because of this, while a merely irregular ordination is probably valid, a materially schismatic one is probably not valid, and a formally schismatic ordination is certainly invalid. Baptism makes everyone priests of God in Christ, but it makes no one a presbyter.

I have not even scratched the surface of what needs yet to be done concerning Christian initiation. Even so I have already gone on too long. I close with only a brief personal note, for whatever it may be worth.

I am becoming — not in spite of but, as I think, because of my work in Christian initiation — far more patient of what C. S. Lewis called "mere Christianity." Perhaps Christendom has been killed by an "un-mere Christianity" as much as by any other factor. The gospel demands that I affirm my belief in only Father, Son, and Holy Spirit: the gospel does nothing more than presume that I will discover my own way of living accordingly among others who believe likewise.

And I hope I do not disillusion anyone, or damage the faith of anyone, if I insist with you, my colleagues in faith, that *this is all there is to it.* For salvation comes by faith, not by works. And it is this *faith* which is the summit from which all the Church's power flows, the vortex to which all the Church's life returns. The Constitution on the Sacred Liturgy of the Second Vatican Council is badly misconstrued if it is thought to have said that the liturgy is this, alone and by itself. The liturgy is this only to the extent that the liturgy is defined as *the act by which the Church is most itself* — in prayerful worship before God in Christ become life-giving Spirit.

This brings me very low. Which is precisely where one must be as the great cosmic dance of the liturgy begins. My first step must be an odd one, for my shoes are filled with water, my hair drips chrism, and I discover to my consternation that I left my clothes at home. The gospel we proclaim, like him in whom and by whom we live at one, is peculiar indeed.

Laurence H. Stookey

15. Three New Initiation Rites

In the mid-1970s the liturgical attention of the sacramental churches appears to be focused upon baptism and related rites. Revised initiation liturgies have been produced recently by a variety of Christian bodies. The new formulations involve far more than rearranging commas, removing sexist language and changing "Thou art" to "You are." Indeed, the new liturgies require a radical reorientation of baptismal theology and practice. Publication of the new rites is but the beginning of a process of educating both clergy and laity concerning sacramental baptism.

The profound changes in the approach to baptism have resulted from a variety of influences. Biblical and patristic studies have emphasized the importance of the baptismal mystery in the life of the ancient Church. Reformation studies have demonstrated the centrality of baptism in the theology of Luther and, to a lesser extent, that of Calvin. These studies have clarified the issue of sacrament versus ordinance which separated these two reformers from Zwingli and the Anabaptists. Renewed seriousness about systematic theology has made us more aware of the dependence of liturgical theology upon the doctrines of creation, sin, redemption, the Church, and the kingdom of God.

That is only the beginning. European controversies about the validity of baptizing infants and concern for baptismal discipline have caused some of us on this side of the Atlantic to reexamine at least the basis of our own practices. Historical study has raised questions about a separable confirmation rite at the very time when studies in Christian education and psychology have challenged the usual practice of confirming persons in pre- or early adolescent years. And the social conscience of the Church has made it clear that the Christian life cannot be isolated and self-centered; hence neither can the rites of initiation be privatistic and focused solely upon the salvation of the individual.

It is not surprising therefore that revision of the traditional rites has become imperative. More striking than the fact of revision is the similarity found among the various new rites. The recent formulations resemble each other more closely than each resembles what preceded it in the respective denomination. Even where differences are obvious, those differences reflect struggles with a common set of issues.

Concrete examples of all this can be found by examining three services of initiation published by Protestant groups within less than two years of one another.[1]

STATUS AND SCOPE OF THE THREE LITURGIES

The joint Lutheran rites are for provisional use only, as a "first step toward the rite to be included in a more permanent inter-Lutheran service book." In the publication on baptism, a rationale for the new rite is set forth by examining in turn the historical

[1] The texts discussed here are those generally available at the time of writing: *Contemporary Worship 7: Holy Baptism* (1974); *Contemporary Worship 8: Affirmation of the Baptismal Covenant* (1975). Prepared by the Inter-Lutheran Commission on Worship, an agency of the Lutheran Church in America, The American Lutheran Church, The Evangelical Lutheran Church of Canada, and The Lutheran Church — Missouri Synod; published jointly by Augsburg Publishing House (Minneapolis), LCA Board of Publication (Philadelphia), and Concordia Publishing House (Saint Louis). *The Draft Proposed Book of Common Prayer and Administration of the Sacraments and Other Rites and Ceremonies of the Church* (1976). Prepared by the Standing Liturgical Commission of the Protestant Episcopal Church in the United States of America; published by The Church Hymnal Corporation, New York. *A Service of Baptism, Confirmation, and Renewal: An Alternate Text* (1976). Prepared by the Section on Worship of the Board of Discipleship of The United Methodist Church; published by The United Methodist Publishing House, Nashville.

It should be noted that the Inter-Lutheran Commission has prepared new drafts since *Contemporary Worship 7 and 8,* and that action of the 1976 General Convention has resulted in changes in the Episcopal rite; however, in neither case are published texts available as yet.

development of baptism, the current theological situation and the characteristics of the provisional service. Then follows a section of notes on the rite — detached rubrics. Finally, there is a baptismal rite itself in two forms: [1] a complete service including entrance rite and liturgies of the word, holy baptism and the Eucharist; [2] a shorter service subtitled, "For Use with Services Other than the Holy Communion." These services are to be used with candidates of any age and are sufficiently flexible to allow for the reception of an entire family when some members are to be baptized and others have been baptized previously.

The booklet concerning affirmation of the baptismal covenant has a similar format: introduction, notes, a rite of renewal when baptism is not celebrated, and a rite of renewal within the liturgy of baptism.

The Draft Proposed Book was prepared for consideration by the 1976 General Convention of The Episcopal Church in the process of permanent Prayer Book revision. This Convention amended and approved the Draft Book; that action must be ratified by the 1979 General Convention before the new rites are finally adopted. During the interim, the new rites may be used but the 1928 Prayer Book remains the only official liturgy of the denomination. Thus in the Episcopal process of revision things are further along than in the Lutheran process, but they are not yet complete.

The Draft Proposed Book contains the service of holy baptism preceded by a page of notes concerning the service and followed by two and one-half pages of additional directions. The service itself embodies the rites of baptism, episcopal confirmation, reception into communion (from other denominations), and reaffirmation of baptismal vows. Formulae for conditional and emergency baptism are included in the directions.[2]

---

[2] Portions of the full rite appear elsewhere in the book. Material related to confirmation is printed separately to facilitate the rite when baptisms are not being celebrated; and material related to renewal is included in the liturgy for the Easter Vigil. In both cases only necessary minor adjustments are made in the texts.

In March 1976, The United Methodist Church published A Service of Baptism, Confirmation, and Renewal: An Alternate Text. In one sense this is a completed rite. Unlike the Lutheran work, it is not a provisional draft; and unlike the Episcopal book it does not need further approval by a denominational body. But in another sense the United Methodist text is less final than either of the other rites is ultimately intended to be. The new material is an alternative to (not a replacement of) services in the 1964 Book of Worship. Selection between the two texts is a matter of local discretion.

The United Methodist rite provides for reception of members by transfer and on an affiliate or associate basis as well as for baptism, confirmation and renewal. A single liturgical text is adaptable for all occasions. An introduction, commentary and general instructions are provided in booklet form. The introduction discusses the nature of baptism and its relationship to confirmation and renewal. The commentary consists of systematic rubrical instruction for the minister; the general instructions deal with more general matters: baptismal discipline, emergency baptism, design and placement of the font, and optional acts.

Stapled into the center of each booklet is a separate eight-page folder which contains the actual text of the service. This folder is available in quantity for parish use and can be attached inside a hymnal cover.

BAPTISM AS COVENANT

The affinity between the three new rites is most clearly seen in their common emphasis on baptism as covenant. This covenant involves God the initiator, the individual in relation to a congregation of Christ's Church, and the whole Church in relation to all of God's creation.

God: The Initiator of the Covenant. The centrality of divine action in establishing the covenant is evident in all three rites. A comparison of the respective prayers of thanksgiving over the water reveals an impressive ecumenical understanding of God's historical and sacramental activity.

Inter-Lutheran

Holy God, mighty Lord, gracious Father: We give you thanks, for in the beginning your Spirit moved over the waters and you created heaven and earth. By the gift of water you nourish and sustain us and all living things.

By the waters of the flood you condemned the wicked and saved those whom you had chosen, Noah and his family. You led Israel by the pillar of cloud and fire through the sea, out of slavery into the freedom of the promised land. In the waters of the Jordan your Son was baptized by John and anointed with the Spirit. By the baptism of his own death and resurrection, your beloved Son has set us free from bondage to sin and death and has opened the way to the joy and freedom of everlasting life. He made water a sign of the kingdom and of cleansing and rebirth. In obedience to his command, we make disciples of all nations, baptizing them in the name of the Father, and of the Son, and of the Holy Spirit.

Pour out your Holy Spirit, gracious Father, to make this a water of cleansing. Wash away the sins of all those who enter it, and bring them forth as inheritors of your glorious kingdom.

To you be given praise and honor and worship through your Son, Jesus Christ our Lord, in the unity of the Holy Spirit, now and forever. *Amen.*

Episcopal

We thank you, Almighty God, for the gift of water. Over it the Holy Spirit moved in the beginning of creation. Through it you led the children of Israel out of their bondage in Egypt into the land of promise. In it your Son Jesus received the baptism of John and was anointed by the Holy Spirit as the Messiah, the Christ, to lead us, through his death and resurrection, from the bondage of sin into everlasting life.

We thank you, Father, for the water of Baptism. In it we are buried with Christ in his death. By it we share in his resurrection. Through it we are reborn by the Holy Spirit. Therefore in joyful obedience to your Son, we bring into his fellowship those who come to him in faith, baptizing them in the Name of the Father, and of the Son, and of the Holy Spirit.

Now sanctify this water, we pray you, by the power of your Holy Spirit, that those who here are cleansed from sin and born again may continue for ever in the risen life of Jesus Christ our Savior. To him, to you, and to the Holy Spirit, be all honor and glory, now and for ever. *Amen.*

United Methodist
Minister
Eternal God:
When nothing existed but chaos,
you swept across the dark waters
and brought forth light.
In the days of Noah
you saved those on the ark through water.
After the flood you set in the clouds a rainbow.
When you saw your people as slaves in Egypt,
you led them to freedom through the sea.
Their children you brought through the Jordan
to the land which you promised.

Congregation
Sing to the Lord all the earth.
Tell of his mercy each day.

Minister
In the fullness of time you sent Jesus,
nurtured in the water of a womb.
He was baptized by John
and anointed by your Spirit.
He called his disciples
to share in the baptism of his death and resurrection
and to make disciples of all nations.

Congregation
Declare his works to the nations,
his glory among all the people.

Minister
By the power of your Holy Spirit,
bless this gift of water

and those who receive it.
Wash away their sin
and clothe them in righteousness
as those who have died and been raised with Christ.

Minister and Congregation
All praise to you, Eternal Father,
through your Son, Jesus Christ,
who with you and the Holy Spirit
lives and reigns forever. Amen.

The central prayer of each rite makes it clear that God has initiated our salvation and that by grace we are brought into covenant with him. The Lutheran and United Methodist services both
include opening statements for the liturgy of baptism which stress
God's action in the sacrament. The Lutheran rite further emphasizes the fact that it is God who baptizes by including (as an option) the Eastern baptismal formula cast in the passive voice:
"(Name) is baptized in the Name of the Father/And of the
Son/And of the Holy Spirit."

Throughout the new services it is clear that baptism is more
than an ordinance or human profession of faith before God; baptism is a sacramental gift through which God declares his grace.

The Individual and Congregation in Covenant. It is equally apparent
in the revised rites that baptism is not a magical action thrust upon
passive recipients. The baptismal covenant involves the commitment
of the individual within the context of a Christian congregation.

In all three services the candidates are questioned concerning
their faith. The extent of the questions varies. The Lutheran rite is
the most concise: There is a single vow of renunciation (which
may be broken into three parts, if desired, in order to balance the
triple affirmation) followed by the recital of the Apostles' Creed in
three parts. The Episcopal rite is the most complex: There are
three renunciations followed by three affirmations. Then the
Apostles' Creed is used in three sections. Next come five questions related to commitment — a rather cumbersome total of four-
teen responses by the candidates, to say nothing of questions of
intent asked prior to the renunciations. The United Methodist rite

steers a middle course: four vows containing aspects both of rejection and profession, followed by the three creedal questions.

All three rites employ the ICET text of the Apostles' Creed used interrogatively; and in each rite the whole liturgical assembly joins in saying the affirmation.[3] This is an innovative feature in all three traditions. Lutherans have usually had candidates answer "I do" to three creedal questions. In the American Prayer Book the whole thing was streamlined as follows: "Dost thou believe all the Articles of the Christian Faith, as contained in the Apostles' Creed?" "I do." And Methodist rites in the recent past have been defective in making no use of the Creed at all at baptism — and sometimes not even requiring any trinitarian affirmation.

Use of the Apostles' Creed in its ancient baptismal form stresses the tie between the faith of the candidate and the faith of the holy catholic Church. But all three new rites also stress the relationship between the faith of the candidate and the faith of a particular congregation of that Church. Thus there is a clear preference for baptisms administered in the presence of the congregation.

Recommendations concerning the corporate nature of the service vary in their firmness but not in their intent. The Lutherans suggest that baptism is "normally" and "usually" celebrated at a regular Sunday morning service. The Episcopalians indicate that the sacrament "is appropriately administered" at the chief service on a Sunday or other feast. The United Methodists state rather bluntly that "the sacrament is to be administered in the presence of the congregation." They add that this should be the congregation of which the candidate is to be an active member; persons who request baptism in a local church to which they are not logically connected "should be referred to their own congregations and pastors." The once-familiar practice of private baptism is frowned upon by all.

[3] In the United Methodist rite use of the full creed is not mandatory. The alternate text was required to conform to the denomination's *Book of Discipline* which instructs simply that candidates shall "profess their faith in God, the Father Almighty, maker of heaven and earth, and in Jesus Christ his only Son, and in the Holy Spirit." Use of the full creed is strongly encouraged, however, as "a desirable expression of the historic and universal faith of the Christian Church."

The congregational aspect of the sacrament is also emphasized through stress on lay participation in the rite. For example, sponsors are no longer simply to be personal friends whom the candidate or family wishes to honor. The Lutherans note that sponsors are to be "practicing Christians, mature in faith and piety. The sponsor represents in a specific way the congregation's desire to nurture those to be born into the Christian family." Nor are sponsors merely a safeguard against an infant's loss of parents. In all rites, adult candidates may also have sponsors. The Lutherans note that such persons "can help integrate the new members into the various dimensions of the life of the parish." Both Lutherans and United Methodists suggest that sponsors for adults may be provided by the congregation (as distinct from personal choice by the candidates); this principle of selection emphasizes community responsibility.

In the Lutheran and Episcopal rites, sponsors present candidates by name near the beginning of the baptismal liturgy. In the United Methodist service this function is assigned to the officer of the congregation known as the lay leader, or to some other "representative of the congregation designated for this responsibility." The lay leader or representative joins in the laying on of hands and (when infants are baptized) may give a charge to sponsors later in the service. The Episcopalians suggest that sponsors act as lectors and lead the intercessions. Episcopalians and Lutherans indicate that when the Eucharist is celebrated the gifts of bread and wine might well be presented by the newly baptized or their sponsors.

In the United Methodist rite the laying on of hands may involve not only the minister and designated lay representative but also parents and other family members (including baptized children), sponsors, and others gathered at the font. This departure from the use of clerical hands exclusively is intended to symbolize both the corporate nature of the Church and the fact that through baptism we are made members of the laity. The United Methodists also provide that after the act of baptism (or renewal) opportunity may be given "for those who have received the rites to bear witness to their faith or experience in their own words."

The entire congregation is given significant new roles in each of the liturgies. The extent of congregational participation in the vows varies, but such participation is expected in each rite. In all three the people join in an act of welcome after baptism; this may be followed by the peace. Lutheran and Episcopal formulations include litanies; in the United Methodist service three congregational responses punctuate the prayer of thanksgiving over the water.

These and other functions assigned to the laity reveal in all three rites a strong determination to prevent clerical domination of the service. This determination is not the result of a vicious anticlericalism nor even of the necessary recognition that liturgy is the work of the whole people of God. Rather full participation is related to the fact that the individual's covenant in baptism is bound up inextricably with the congregational covenant.

The Covenant Community in Service to God's Creation. The covenant dimension of baptism extends beyond local congregational life. The new liturgies emphasize the conviction that the whole people of God are bound together in service to the total creation.

The Lutheran intercessions contain the petition that those about to be baptized may "always and everywhere witness to the Lord by word and life." Both the Episcopal and United Methodist services clearly state the implications of discipleship in social terms. In the Episcopal rite candidates are asked: "Will you seek and serve Christ in all persons, loving your neighbor as yourself?" and also, "Will you strive for justice and peace among all people, and respect the dignity of every human being?" The United Methodist service seeks "allegiance to the kingdom which [Christ] has opened to people of all ages, nations, and races"; it then goes on to ask, "Will you resist evil, injustice, and oppression in whatever guises they present themselves?" Finally, the candidate pledges "to serve as Christ's representative in the world."

Both the Episcopalians and the United Methodists address the newly baptized as those who share in Christ's priestly ministry. It is ironic in light of Luther's emphasis on the priesthood of believers that the Lutheran text is the only one which makes no direct reference to priestly service (though 1 Peter 2:4-10 is among the epistles appointed for use). Of the three rites the Lutheran is most apt to be open to privatistic interpretation; certainly this is not the intention of the authors, as their introduction makes clear. Perhaps this facet of the service will be strengthened in subsequent drafts of the rite.

In all of the services there is clear indication that baptism constitutes admission into the whole Church of Jesus Christ, not merely admission into a congregation or a denomination. Phrases such as "body of Christ," "household of God," "Christ's universal Church," and "the Lord's family" indicate the scope of the Christian community. In the United Methodist welcome, members of the congregation give this pledge to those being received: "Together with you and all Christians we seek the unity of the Spirit in the bond of peace, that in everything God may be glorified through Jesus Christ." Those who read the new liturgical texts carefully are in little danger of assuming that the covenant is one of individual privilege rather than responsibility and service to God's whole creation.

BAPTISMAL DISCIPLINE AND RENEWAL

The recent services make clear that the baptismal covenant is not to be entered into hastily nor forgotten readily. Both discipline at the point of entrance and the need for renewal are emphasized.

All three groups stress the importance of prebaptismal counseling. In addition to personal consultations with the pastor, the United Methodists encourage congregations to provide study groups and other corporate activities for those preparing for the sacrament. Indeed they suggest that "baptism may be justifiably deferred or declined when those seeking the rite will not participate in prebaptismal counseling, or when parents or other sponsors proposed for infants and children are not themselves committed members of Christ's Church."

The covenant is to be entered into only once — and all the publications in one way or another stress the uniqueness of the unrepeatable rite of baptism. Nor is Christian initiation to be confused with cultural rites of passage which can be engaged in once and then forgotten. The Lutherans speak of the "lifelong dynamic of Baptism" in which the symbolism of death and resurrection through the sacrament becomes a paradigm for "daily dying to sin and rising to new life." They stress the fact that Christians who witness the rite are thereby reminded of their own baptism.

Indeed all three denominational rites provide a specific form for the renewal of the baptismal covenant. The renewal rite may be congregational in nature or may be a special act of renewal by particular persons. In the Lutheran and Episcopal liturgies renewal is primarily verbal, centering upon the vows of the covenant. In the United Methodist service of renewal the thanksgiving over the water is included, and water may be sprinkled toward the people with the words, "Remember your baptism and be thankful." Renewal is not rebaptism, though the use of water in both rites may cause confusion on this point — a risk the United Methodists considered worth taking.

Both Lutherans and United Methodists emphasize the importance of preaching on baptism, though slightly different strategies are suggested. The Lutherans seem to prefer that at every baptismal festival "the sermon should present the church's teaching on Baptism in the light of the theme of the day." The United Methodists advise that "while it is not intended that the minister preach on the meaning of the rites each time they are administered, ample provision should be made in the preaching program to instruct congregations in the nature of baptism and its renewal."

Specific emphases on discipline and renewal differ in the denominational approaches, but it is evident that in all there is a rejection of familiar "easy come, easy go" practices. Once again baptism is being treated with the seriousness worthy of a sacrament.

BAPTISM IN RELATION TO CONFIRMATION
AND THE EUCHARIST

All three denominational publications reveal a desire to restore the unity of the ancient initiatory rite; all have done so with respect to the baptism of adults, at least. The baptism of infants in relation to confirmation and first communion remains a thorny issue, one by no means resolved.

In the Lutheran rite it is clear that when adults are baptized with the laying on of hands this constitutes full initiation, though these adults will later affirm their baptismal covenant from time to time. In the 1975 publication (Contemporary Worship 8) a three-facet pattern is suggested for those baptized as infants: first communion "in middle childhood"; catechetical studies which are offered to children and youth "through their first 15 or 16 years" and which may be particularly important "in middle adolescence"; and affirmation of the baptismal covenant at the latter end of this catechetical period. It is noted that "such a rite for Affirmation of the Baptismal Covenant would replace what has been known as the Order for Confirmation. The word 'confirmation' is better dropped from usage because the many and varied meanings it has acquired through the years cause confusion."

In two important respects Contemporary Worship 8 is more bold than the 1974 Contemporary Worship 7. The latter did not firmly advocate communion before an affirmation of baptism nor did it so positively discourage the term "confirmation." It should be noted that the most recent (unpublished) drafts of the renewal rite have restored the term. "Public opinion" within Lutheranism simply would not allow so abrupt a dismissal of the word, despite the confusion which it has engendered.

Among Episcopalians, Prayer Book Studies 18 created a furor by proposing in 1970 [1] that the laying on of hands formerly associated with confirmation be transferred to baptism even in the case of infants, [2] that no further confirmatory rite be used with those thus baptized, and [3] that, while the unitary rite ideally would be an episcopal function, for obvious practical reasons bishops could delegate this function to priests (as has been done by the Orthodox for centuries). The controversy which ensued is too detailed for discussion here.

Suffice it to say that the Draft Proposed Book has a kind of "have your cake and eat it too" compromise: While the bishop is the chief sacramental minister of the diocese, baptism by a priest is considered "full initiation" (as Eucharists celebrated by priests have long been considered full Eucharists). But Episcopal confirmation has been restored and is defined as the first occasion on which baptized Christians make a "mature public affirmation of their faith and commitment to the responsibilities of Baptism" and receive the laying on of hands by the bishop.

In the Draft Proposed Book confirmation is "expected" but apparently not required of those baptized at an early age; nothing is stated concerning episcopal confirmation of those baptized as youth or adults. The action of the 1976 General Convention has modified this position. Now the laying on of hands by a bishop is expected of youth and adults; but this is not specifically called "confirmation." Presumably some will regard the laying of episcopal hands upon youth and adults to be confirmation; but others will regard it simply as renewal of the baptismal covenant in the presence of the bishop (who uniquely represents the catholicity of the Church into which the person was baptized). Thus the laying on of hands by a bishop is reaffirmed as an expectation (if not an absolute necessity) in every case.

In the Draft Proposed Book nothing specific is said about admission to the Eucharist. Heretofore the Prayer Book included a rubric restricting communion to confirmed members. There is now no trace of such a rubric. One can only assume that silence gives consent — at least among those who are already disposed to allow communion before confirmation or without it altogether.

Things are simpler for the United Methodists. The term "confirmation" was not officially used for the service of reception until 1964 nor was the laying on of hands a mandatory action until then. The rite has never been reserved to bishops. Even so, the term "confirmation" is sufficiently ingrained to make its abolition impractical despite the preference of the committee which drafted the new liturgy. Confirmation is interpreted as "the first renewal of the baptismal faith made by those who received the sacrament during infancy or childhood." It is mandatory only in the sense that all baptized persons are expected to renew the baptismal covenant periodically.[4]

---

[4] This statement pertains to theology rather than polity. The United Methodist *Book Of Discipline* does require in youth or adulthood a personal profession of faith for full membership in the denomination. But the new liturgical text implies a distinction between membership in "Christ's universal Church" and membership in The United Methodist Church. The former is fully effected through baptism; the latter is not and the denomination is left to wrestle with this disparity.

No reference is made to the time of first communion, but the denomination has neither rules nor strong taboos forbidding early communion. The matter usually is left to parents in consultation with their pastor. In many parishes it is not uncommon for children to be communicated, though reception by infants is rare.

It is obvious that the three denominational groups have wrestled with a common problem. And while the solutions to that problem vary in detail, one thing is clear: In none of the three rites is there any disposition to view confirmation as a quasi-sacramental imparting of the Holy Spirit which somehow "completes" baptism. Rather, confirmation is one occasion among many on which the baptismal covenant is renewed; and the gift of the Spirit is associated with God's sacramental activity in baptism.

LITURGICAL CONTEXT AND ACTION

Festival Services. In the new rites the relation of initiation to the Christian year is emphasized. Lutherans in particular encourage baptismal festivals. In Contemporary Worship 7 they suggested the Third Sunday in Advent, the Baptism of our Lord (First Sunday after the Epiphany), the Easter Vigil (or Easter Day; or the Second Sunday of Easter), Pentecost, and All Saints' Day (or Sunday) as particularly appropriate occasions. In Contemporary Worship 8 a suggested calendar of "stated times" for parish baptisms is provided. The Third Sunday in Advent has been dropped as a recommended time; two other occasions have been added: a time in September, since this is often a time of renewed parish activity, and the Feast of Transfiguration (the Sunday prior to Lent).

The Episcopalians also deem certain occasions to be especially appropriate: Sunday of the Baptism of our Lord, Easter Eve, Pentecost, All Saints' Day (or the Sunday after), and the occasion of a visitation by the bishop who is normative as celebrant.

United Methodists specify no special times for baptism; but it is suggested that congregational renewal is particularly appropriate to the Sunday of the Baptism of the Lord and the Easter Vigil (or another time within the Easter season).

In all of the denominations a eucharistic setting for baptism is recommended with enthusiasm even though this runs counter to recent practice in all quarters. Lutherans and Episcopalians offer noneucharistic options as a concession to the reality that many parishes are not yet ready for full festival services. While the United Methodists do not provide a full order of service, they recommend that "when possible, the Lord's Supper should be part of the total service."[5]

Ceremonial. The new importance attached to baptism is accompanied by increased attention to the significance of the sacramental water. All suggest that the font may be filled as a part of the service. Lutherans discourage sprinkling as lacking "optimum symbolic effectiveness." The United Methodists retain it but suggest that "a generous amount of water" be used in the font. Episcopalians continue to prescribe only immersion or pouring. Lutherans and United Methodists also accept these two modes; both denominations single out immersion as a viable possibility and suggest that provision for it be taken into consideration by parishes planning building or renovation programs.

Signation is traditional for Episcopalians. The new Lutheran liturgy assumes its use; and it is an option for United Methodists who suggest using the sign of the cross, the sign of the fish, or both. All three groups add the use of chrism as an option.

In the Lutheran and United Methodist baptismal rites signation and the laying on of hands are two distinct acts. For Episcopalians the imposition of the hand accompanies signation, thus providing another point of ambiguity: Those who wish to see the ancient unity of baptism and the laying on of hands can find it in the new Episcopal rite; others who wish to stress the importance of a distinct imposition of hands by a bishop can view the use of the hand in baptism administered by a priest as an act incidental to signation.

If used in the Episcopal service, the chrism must have been blessed by a bishop though a priest may administer it in his absence. This provides a symbolic tie to the bishop as chief celebrant and may avert class distinction between those who in baptism

[5] A recommended full eucharistic order into which the new initiation rites may be incorporated is published separately under the title *Word and Table: A Basic Pattern of Sunday Worship for United Methodists* (Nashville 1976).

received the laying on of an episcopal hand and those who received the imposition of a presbyteral hand only.

The imposition of hands for acts of renewal other than confirmation varies among the new rites. In the United Methodist pattern, hands may be laid upon any individual renewing that baptismal covenant, whether at confirmation or some other time. The same was true in the 1975 Lutheran formulation; in a more recent (unpublished) draft, however, hands are imposed only at confirmation. In the Draft Proposed Book the format and style of typefaces employed left unclear which occasions were appropriate for the imposition of hands apart from confirmation. At the 1976 Minneapolis convention the matter was clarified: The bishop *may* lay hands upon those being received into membership from other denominations and upon those who have already been confirmed as Episcopalians and wish to make a reaffirmation of the baptismal covenant.

Lutherans and United Methodists suggest the presentation of new clothes and the baptismal candle with appropriate statements being provided to accompany each action. The Episcopal service suggests the use of the candle only, and no statement is prescribed.

The United Methodists add a note of caution concerning supplementary acts at baptism: "Care should be taken . . . not to obscure the act of administration itself. Always the use of oil, new clothes, and the baptismal candles is secondary to God's sign given in the water itself." The caution is characteristic of a concern which pervades the United Methodist document. Because Methodists do not stand in quite the same tradition of liturgical usage as Lutherans and Episcopalians, two dangers present themselves. On the one hand, many in the denomination may reject ceremonial as un-Methodist, un-Protestant, or even un-Christian! On the other hand there is the danger that some United Methodists, long starved for ritual acts, may overemphasize innovations and thus miss the uniqueness of the central sacramental act.

But in a larger sense, the United Methodist note of caution is characteristic of the spirit of all three publications. All of the revision committees have been sensitive to the problems involved in liturgical change. Pastoral discretion is urged; the rites are intended to be flexible throughout.

Symbolic of the new importance of baptism is a concern for the centrality of the font which, all publications note, should be visible when the rite is administered. Lutherans specify that "the font should be of a size to establish its symbolic significance." United Methodists (who frequently have substituted a small glass or brass bowl for a formal font) declare: "The font should always be present in the place of worship as a visible reminder of the centrality of this sacrament; it should not be stored in a closet or relegated to an obscure position at times when baptism is not being administered."

Such comments are representative of a new attitude. No longer is baptism something to be administered in private or as an appendage to public worship; nor is it to be ignored between the occasions of its administration. As the introduction to the Lutheran booklet on baptism observes, this sacrament of initiation, though administered only once to each person, has a continuing effectiveness for the whole community; it "remains a continuing call to repentance, faith, and obedience to Christ."

In their introduction the Lutherans also declare that "a new wave of [liturgical] renewal is in motion which centers in the Sacrament of Holy Baptism. This interest in baptismal renewal includes the liturgy but goes much further. It is concerned with Baptism's role in the piety and faith of the people of God. Baptism's significance for preaching and teaching, and for Holy Communion is being examined. The central place of Baptism in the development of a Christian ethic is being recovered. Baptismal renewal reaches into every aspect of the church's ministry." In this statement the Lutheran revisers speak not only for themselves but also for the Episcopal and United Methodist committees. It is hoped that indeed they speak for the whole Church, bound together as it is by one Lord, one faith, and one baptism.

Eugene L. Brand

16. New Rites of Initiation and Their Implications: in the Lutheran Churches

If one is to understand current Lutheran activity regarding initiation rites, one must have some understanding of the current Lutheran scene. Likewise, if one is to understand the current Lutheran scene, one must understand how it came to be. We cannot be content merely with liturgical descriptions; there must also be theological description, and both must be done within historical and cultural contexts. The cultural context is especially important when dealing with baptism and confirmation since they, far more than the Eucharist, reflect differences among cultures. For that reason it is doubtful that any single practice can be established that will apply equally to the various cultures in which a given confession may be represented.

The manner in which the Lutheran Reformation began and then spread through northern Europe does allow us to describe a common Lutheran tradition which exhibits characteristic liturgical and theological aspects. Having done that, we can deal with the modifications of this common tradition under the impact of varying cultural contexts.

THE COMMON LUTHERAN TRADITION
A. Because the Lutheran reformers saw themselves as confessors of the true biblical and patristic heritage within the Church, they did not deal radically with the liturgical tradition as they inherited it. Infant baptism had been the norm, and baptism and confirmation had been regarded as separate sacraments. The privilege of

the altar had been withheld from the baptized until they reached the age of discretion — the time when they were capable of their first confession. The question of infant communion was not, therefore, discussed by the reformers.

B. As chief prophet, Luther exercized a strong influence upon the fledgling movement. He accepted infant baptism, seeing in it full initiation into the community of Christ, the moment of ordination into the priesthood shared by all Christians:

"For a priest, especially in the New Testament, was not made but was born. He was created, not ordained, He was born not indeed of flesh, but through the birth of the Spirit in the washing of regeneration" (John 3:6f.; Titus 3:5f.).[1]

It is worth observing that neither the 1523 *Taufbüchlein* (prepared the same year as the treatise just quoted) nor the 1526 simplified baptismal rite contains any reference to this concept of baptismal priesthood.[2] Of major importance was Luther's understanding of baptism as the paradigm of prevenient grace in God's dealings with us.

Luther objected to confirmation being numbered among the sacraments because it lacks Scriptural warrant.[3] Somewhat mischievously he speculates that confirmation had been made a sacrament to give bishops something to do:

"For after they (bishops) relinquished to their inferiors those arduous sacraments (i.e. Baptism and Eucharist) together with the Word as being beneath their attention . . . it was no more than right that we should discover something easy and not too burdensome for such delicate and great heroes to do . . ."[4]

---

[1] Martin Luther, "Concerning the Ministry (1523)," *Luther's Works*, 40, American Edition (Philadelphia 1958), 19. Hereafter, LW.

[2] Both orders in LW, 53.

[3] This is the position of thc Apology to the Augsburg Confession: "Confirmation and extreme unction are rites received from the Fathers which even the church does not require as necessary for salvation since they do not have the command of God. Hence it is useful to distinguish these from the earlier ones which have an express command from God and a clear promise of grace." XIII, 6.

[4] "Babylonian Captivity of thc Church (1520)," LW, 36, 91.

No objections were raised to the link between the age of discretion and reception of the bread and wine nor to the parallel link between confession and communion.[5] Indeed, the passion for catechetics is one of the hallmarks of the Lutheran reformation. It grew out of the need to prepare people to receive the sacrament worthily.

C. In comparison with the preceding centuries of diversity, Lutheran initiation practice was consolidated: Baptism in infancy, confirmation (together with confession and absolution) as admission to the Lord's Table. In spite of Luther's opposition to confirmation as a sacrament, his great emphasis upon instruction was a major factor in the evolution of a new kind of confirmation.

Arthur Repp has distinguished six different major types of confirmation within the Lutheran churches: catechetical (as instructional preparation for Holy Communion, often without liturgical form), hierarchical (derived from Bucer; emphasis upon confession of faith and vow of obedience to the Church), sacramental (accents from Roman tradition retained; gift of the Spirit through laying on of hands, conferral of fuller membership), traditional (relating only to Baptism, not a rite of admission to the Eucharist), pietistic (moment for personal confession and witness; acceptance of obligation to lead the Christian life), and rationalistic (exaltation of confirmation over Baptism; declaration of allegience to a local congregation, a religious oath). The first four types emerged in the 16th century; the pietistic and rationalistic types emerged in the 17th and 18th centuries. Not until the 19th century was confirmation accepted in the Church of Sweden and only then "as the rite for the admission to the Lord's Supper."[6]

Following the 16th century, Lutheran baptismal rites were affected by a reductionistic process typical of churches dominated by theology, and by the shifting sands of sacramental theology. In

[5] Compare the prefaces to the Small and Large Catechisms of Luther and the Augsburg Confession (XXV, 1), and Apology (XXIV), the Large Catechism (V, 2).

[6] Details and documentation in A. Repp, *Confirmation in the Lutheran Church* (St Louis 1964), 21–83. Compare LWF Commission on Education, *Confirmation, a study document* (Minneapolis n.d.) 22–33.

spite of the great emphasis on the gift of the Spirit in baptism, the rites contained little expression of it. The biblical fulness characteristic of the so-called Flood Prayer in Luther's own rites was often severely diminished. Between 1523 and 1526 Luther himself had excised exsufflation, giving of salt, the longer exorcism, the *ephphatha*, chrismation, and the giving of the candle. The theological question about the essence of baptism came to be accepted as a liturgical program: only the water and the Word are needed; keep it simple.

THE THEOLOGICAL ISSUES

A. The characteristic feature about Lutherans and initiation has not been the shape of their rite but rather the substance of their theology. Mainstream Lutheran theology has stalwartly rejected any suggestion that baptized persons are anything less than full members of the Church. Though at the same time Lutherans have generally clung to confirmation, their theology of baptism has prevented seeing it as a sacrament or seeing in it the completion of baptism. They reject, therefore, both a "Dixian" view of the relationship of baptism and confirmation and a Pentecostalist concept of two baptisms. However one understands confirmation, one must exclude it from the *sacramental* process of initiation!

In Baptism God makes the candidates his children by adoption for the sake of the death and resurrection of Jesus Christ. Put another way, God incorporates candidates through baptism into Jesus' death and the promise made sure by his resurrection. As persons who are thus *en Christo* by baptism, they share Christ's relationship with the Father and they share Christ's mission in the world. As God's children they are bound together in the bond of divine love.

Baptism, then, marks the inception of the Christian life and determines its shape and direction. It is life in Christ, life in community, life under the cross (but with the sure hope of resurrection victory), life marked by service. Baptism is not a momentary event to be celebrated and then left behind; it is, in the words of Luther's Small Catechism, a *daily* drowning of the "old Adam" and the *daily* rising of the new person.[7]

[7] Small Catechism (IV, 12).

Until recently, no theology has exalted Baptism more than Lutheran theology. A Lutheran concept of ethics must derive from baptism. A concept of the Church which is not completely communal and incarnational cannot stand. A view of the clergy which relegates priesthood to them exclusively is a priori condemned.

B. I have no apologies for mainstream Lutheran baptismal theology; current biblical and patristic studies have, it seems to me, vindicated it. Baptismal practice is, however, something else again. It must be confessed that Lutherans have failed to realise in practice the implications of their theology.[8] Current studies have spotlighted this contradiction once again, and Lutherans are beginning to see it and act to resolve it. More about that later.

THE CULTURAL DIFFERENTIATION

A. At the beginning of this paper I set forth the importance of the cultural context for an accurate appraisal both of the problems of Christian initiation and their possible solutions. It is well known that world Lutheranism is bound together neither by a central teaching authority nor by a system of church order. In this respect it differs significantly from the Roman and Anglican communions and, to some degree, from the Reformed (Presbyterian) churches. Lutherans have their common bond in a theological perspective which is set forth in a series of confessional writings.

The obvious differences between the Lutheran churches are due more to their differing cultural contexts than to any other factor — of that I am more and more convinced. For purposes of this discussion, I shall group Lutheran churches under three headings: 1) the original Lutheran family concentrated in Germany and Scandinavia, 2) the emigrant churches of North America, Australia, and Latin America, 3) the churches born in missionary activity. I would relate the indigenous churches of Central Europe to the original family and would add to it also what the Germans call "diaspora churches." I would admit that the boundary between groups two and three is sometimes fluid.

---

[8] See E. Brand, "Baptism and Communion of Infants: A Lutheran View," *Worship* 50 (1976), 29-42, and my as yet unpublished address to the Canadian Liturgical Society, 1977, "Christian Initiation: Pastoral Considerations."

1. In addition to being the heirs of a longer and unbroken cultural development, the original family of Lutheran churches is, or recently was, state and/or folk churches. That mixes their life with their national culture in ways unparalleled elsewhere. In such a context, baptism and confirmation have cultural supports and sociological overtones unparalleled in the churches of groups two and three. Because of the territorial nature of the churches (where still intact), even the ecumenical aspects of these questions are perceived differently than in the other groups.

2. Most of the Lutheran churches of North America, Australia, and Latin America were established by groups of emigrant Lutherans from the original family of churches. So long as they retained the use of their native tongues, they remained isolated from the surrounding culture. When they adopted the language of their new country, the process of indigenization began. By now Lutherans in the United States are far enough along in this process that their thought and life is influenced only minimally by their European backgrounds. Lutherans in Canada and Australia are a generation or two closer to the roots. Those Latin American churches which do not have a missionary origin seem to be in the initial stages of indigenization.

The state/folk church mentality is not completely absent from the emigrant churches, but either it plays a minor role or, in recent emigrations, it functions to maintain separateness from the surrounding culture. Baptism and confirmation have few cultural supports or sociological overtones. Because American Lutherans live in a non-territorial situation completely, ecumenical questions can have an immediate relevance for contacts with other Christians. There tends to be, therefore, more crossfertilization of thought and practice between the churches than is usual, I believe, in Europe. Lutheranism in the United States certainly shows the influence of the dominant Anglo-American Protestant ethos.

3. The Lutheran churches born in missionary activity are found throughout the world but chiefly, of course, in Africa and Asia. Their transition from transplanted organisms to fully indigenous churches appears to be, at once, both more simple and vastly more complex than the transition of the emigrant churches. To gather adequate information on initiation from them and to inter-

pret it responsibly is a specialty in itself — one beyond my capabilities. Regretfully, then, this paper will deal only with groups one and two.

B. All groups of Lutherans have been involved in the ecumenical ferment of our times; they have heen influenced by such concomitant movements as the liturgical movement. My impression is that among the original family of Lutheran churches ecumenical involvement has tended to be theoretical and carried on at bureaucratic and academic levels. Where territorial separateness still prevails — e.g. 90% of the Swedish population is Lutheran, less than 1% is Roman Catholic; 87% of the German province of Schleswig-Holstein is Lutheran, while in lower Saxony (historically a Lutheran stronghold) the provincial Church of Hannover (Lutheran) numbers only 52% of its population; Denmark is 93% Lutheran; Norway 94%; Finland 92% — there could hardly be much ongoing parish-level involvement. The situation has changed, or is changing, however, owing to greater mobility of population. A concomitant of territorialism often is that the people are much less consciously Lutheran than in the emigrant churches.

In the emigrant family ecumenical involvement is, of course, also carried on at bureaucratic and academic levels. But because of the intermixture of the churches geographically, the possibility exists of regular activity at the parish level. The immediate Christian neighbors of a local Lutheran parish in America are more likely to be a Roman Catholic and a Methodist parish than other Lutheran parishes. In times of heightened awareness of the ecumenicity of the Church, then, Lutherans of group two are likely to be involved more pragmatically in the ecumenical ferment. The liturgical reforms of Vatican II have had more direct impact upon Lutheran parishes in the United States, I think, than has been the case in Germany or Scandinavia.

The only documentation I have for these observations about ecumenical involvement is a Lutheran World Federation project on lectionary reform. While much was accomplished, the ultimate goal proved elusive. The Lutherans of the original family — Germans and Scandinavians — adopted a revised one year lectionary supplemented by cycles of "preaching texts," while the emigrant

Lutherans (with the exception of Australia) have adopted a modified form of the Roman *Ordo Lectionum Missae*. It was deemed more important, in the second group, to have readings in harmony with immediate Christian neighbors (the Episcopalians and Presbyterians in the USA had already opted for the Roman plan) than to be in harmony with Lutheran churches overseas.

C. These cultural differences have also been influential in the work of liturgical revision. To do its work responsibly, the Inter-Lutheran Commission on Worship (North America) has worked out of and within its Lutheran heritage. But it has in no way felt confined by that heritage. In rather pragmatic fashion, the Commission has been open to mainstream developments in Western liturgy. Its theoretical defense has been that the definition of Lutheranism as a confessional movement and the Lutheran Confessions themselves do not mandate the perpetuation of Lutheran particularities. Quite the contrary![9]

For good or ill, the revised liturgical materials of the Roman Church, the Episcopal Church, and the Lutheran churches of North America exhibit a remarkable degree of commonality which is, I believe, unparalleled on the European side of the Atlantic.[10] For most people, emigration has made theoretical the historic ties with the bloody battles of the Reformation era and, while the emigrant churches may bear the name Lutheran more self-consciously, they do it without the historic memory that still looms, for example, between *evangelisch* and *katholisch* in Germany.

German and Scandinavian work on the rites of initiation must take full cognizance of the cultural and sociological aspects of baptism and confirmation. Law requires pastors in some places to baptize virtually any infant presented. The discussion about the occasional services hallowing the crises of personal and familial life is much more acute in the state/folk church milieu. In the emi-

[9] A sketch of the differences between German and American Lutheranism is in my *Kirche als Familie*, Reihe Gottesdienst 6, ed. von Schade & Schulz (Hamburg 1976).

[10] It supports my view that the relationship of the Episcopal Church to the Church of England exhibits some of the same tensions as that of North American Lutheranism to European Lutheranism.

grant churches which have become indigenized, that sort of problem intrudes less strongly: Initiation can be dealt with more exclusively as a church problem. In reality, of course, the birth- and puberty-rite aspects of initiation cannot be ignored completely. But neither the Church nor the clergy are perceived as part of the national establishment in the same way they are, by tradition, in Europe.

I apologize for laboring these introductory points, but I think them to be vital to an understanding of Lutheran work on initiation. Let me now report on work in progress. In most cases the liturgical point of departure has been a baptismal rite similar to Luther's 1526 *Taufbüchlein* and a confirmation rite which admitted one to communicant status.

REPORT ON INITIATION RITES

A. *Scandinavia.* For information on these churches, I am indebted to Dr. Helge Fehn.[11] The churches of Denmark, Finland, Norway and Sweden are state churches and their liturgical books have the force of law.

1. Baptism. Both Norway (1971) and Sweden (1977) have prepared recent draft revisions of their baptismal rites. They have the following characteristics in common: a) they are clearly congregational services rather than being mere ritual acts, b) in form they have a greater fulness than the present official orders, e.g. the congregational element is emphasized by presenting the candidate to the congregation (Norway) and by recalling their own baptism to the assembly; the second part of the service is shaped after the service of the Word in the Mass, but with other readings than Mark 10 and Matthew 28 and with obligatory sermon (brief); in the third part of the service there is a conscious marking of the water together with a brief verbal tracing of the line from the water in creation to Jesus' baptism in the Jordan; both rites allow for the use of a baptismal candle; the final part of the service contains an admonition and prayer (Norway) or intercessions (Sweden).

[11] From an unpublished paper of the Lutherische Liturgische Konferenz Deutschlands, R 219-77: "Ueberlegungen zur Revision der kirchlichen Amtshandlungen in den nordischen Kirchen," Lecture by Dr. Helge Fehn, 25 April 1977.

The congregational emphasis is significant as an antidote to the usual view of baptism as family celebration and public naming of the child. In certain Swedish circles, fixed times for Baptism have become established to enable courses of instruction in Baptism for parents and sponsors to take place prior to the appointed baptismal Sundays.

2. Confirmation. The variety of post-Reformation practice among Lutherans can be seen in Scandinavian practice. In all the countries young persons are confirmed between 14 and 16 years of age, and are thereby admitted to Holy Communion. As we noted earlier, confirmation came late to Sweden and is still almost identical with a rite of admission to communicant membership. Appropriate to their pietistic heritage, the Finns have thought of confirmation as a time for individuals to confess their faith openly and for themselves. A draft order of 1958 added a blessing of the candidate, a matter still under discussion. In Denmark and Norway, confirmation has been seen as a mutual confession of faith by the candidates and the congregation; in this century the concept of blessing has become dominant in Norway.

Just last year the Norwegians completed the draft of a new rite which no longer takes its impulse from the concept *confirmatio*. It is based on the following principles: a) baptism is the fundamental sacrament with which confirmation must not compete. As an ecclesial ceremony, confirmation is not required but, when it is used, it should be done in such a way that it best serves the life of the individual and the Church at the moment. b) *Didaskontes* (Matt. 28) implies a catechetical task, but even more it implies *training* in the Christian life through faith, worship, and the service of others. c) This learning and training is a lifelong process of which formal catechetical instruction is but one phase (the only one which applies to almost all Norwegian youth). d) What takes place in the *service* of confirmation which concludes this formal instruction is not of chief importance. "Confirmation is not a point in time with prayer and the laying on of hands, confirmation is a continuing thing."[12] Basic to this concept is repeated intercession for the confirmands throughout their period of instruction. What

12 Ibid., 6.

distinguishes the intercession in the service of confirmation is that it is done for each candidate individually.

3. First Communion. In all of Scandinavia, confirmation constitutes admission to Holy Communion. But this practice is beginning to give way. That Denmark was the first to admit children to the altar in ever increasing number is attributed by Professor Fehn to the influence of Grundtvigianism. In 1973 the Finnish Synod affirmed the admission of children to communion, but must work out the canonical details before the practice can be implemented. In 1970 the Swedish Synod was overwhelmingly in favor of admitting confirmands to communion during the period of their instruction. In 1975 the same Synod was sympathetic to the idea that children of practising families should be allowed to take communion with their parents. Since 1968 children above the age of 12 have been admitted under certain circumstances by the Church of Norway. A program to admit children at age 10–11 is under way. It would mark one phase of a life-long series of phases in Christian development.

B. *Germany.* Many of the same judgments regarding recent practice which stand behind the Scandinavian developments have been made also in Germany. That is evidenced by the discussions on confirmation preparatory to the report of the Commission on Education to the Fourth Assembly of the Lutheran World Federation (1963, Helsinki).[13] The two major thrusts propelling German Lutheran work on initiation rites would appear to be the theological debate on infant baptism (K. Barth, O. Cullmann, J. Jeremias, K. Aland) and dissatisfaction with present confirmation practice.

No official orders for baptism and confirmation have been published in Germany since the appearance of *Agende III* (1962), though experiments and studies have increased. The Lutheran Liturgical Conference of Germany is in the initial stages of revision. The prevailing orders assume the baptism of infants: "As a rule children are baptized during the public worship of the congregation," though they do provide for admission to the catechu-

---

[13] This report published in English as *Confirmation, a study document* (Minneapolis n.d.).

menate and for adult baptism.[14] The order for confirmation is clearly understood as admission to the Eucharist:

"Those baptized as infants (*im unmündigen Alter*), after they have received special pastoral instruction, are, through confirmation, admitted to the Sacrament of the Altar."[15]

What will emerge from the work of the German Commission remains to be seen. Voices have been raised in favor of admitting confirmands to the altar, and the new Lutheran Bishop of Bavaria (Henselmann) is reported to have said that in the Lutheran Church there are no theological grounds against the communion of children.[16] In 1964 the Synod of Kurhessen-Waldeck declared itself in favor of the admission of confirmands to the Eucharist. The Church of Saxony recently made possible the admission of children who have reached the age of ten.[17] Several experiments with admitting children could be enumerated. Is it not reasonable to expect that new drafts of initiation rites will break the link between confirmation and first communion in Germany?

A clearer baptismal emphasis has also emerged. In a paper on the Occasional Services (Amtshandlungen), Dr Frieder Schulz points to baptism as their theological basis:

"According to the baptismal command, the universal commission to proclaim the Gospel, the trinitarian prevenient grace of God, and the summons to discipleship are all bound up in an exemplary manner in the foundational churchly act of baptism. Accordingly, all the other churchly acts are to be understood as baptismal remembrances, blessings, and 'confirmations.' "[18]

Perhaps this emphasis will lead to a fuller liturgical development of the rite of baptism itself. The *Agende III* rite already took steps in that direction.

[14] *Agende für Evangelisch-Lutherische Kirchen und Gemeinden*, III, (Berlin 1962), 15 and 38.

[15] Ibid., 81.

[16] Heinr. Gerlach, "Abendmahl mit Kindern," *Quatember* (1976), 3-4, 6.

[17] Ibid., 3, 7.

[18] F. Schulz, *Theologische Begründung und inhaltliche Bestimmung der Amtshandlungen*, Unpublished paper, 11 March 1977, 3.b.

The German discussion of the entire initiation complex is marked by concern for the relationship of these rites to the lives of individuals and families. In a situation where only a small percentage of Christians attend services with any degree of regularity, the Occasional Services are seen increasingly as *the* opportunity for the Gospel to impact upon life at kairotic moments. That in addition to seeing them as help for persons in their struggle through these crises. Recent studies indicate that people understand their relationship to the Church primarily in terms of these Occasional Services.[19]

C. North America. Revision of liturgical materials for the churches of North America was the mandate given the Inter-Lutheran Commission on Worship in 1966. It is a joint agency of the Evangelical Lutheran Church of Canada, the Lutheran Church in America, the Lutheran Church — Missouri Synod, and The American Lutheran Church. A provisional rite for Holy Baptism was published in 1974 as *Contemporary Worship 7* (CW 7). A provisional rite for the Affirmation of the Baptismal Covenant appeared the following year as *Contemporary Worship 8* (CW 8).[20] In modified form, these rites are scheduled to appear in the forthcoming *Lutheran Book of Worship* (1978).

1. Baptism. In the *Lutheran Book of Worship,* the baptismal liturgy will be relocated from the collection of occasional services to a place beside the eucharistic liturgy as a testimony to its centrality in the life of the Church. Compared with its predecessors in the *Service Book and Hymnal (1958)* and the *Lutheran Agenda,* the new baptismal rite has two additions: a) a Thanksgiving solemnly introduced with Salutation and *Gratias agamus.* The Thanksgiving traces the biblical motif from the waters of creation through the Exodus to the Jordan in a manner reminiscent of Luther's Flood Prayer. Because of Lutheran theological sensitivity it is not a bless-

---

[19] Compare Hans-Völker Herntrich, "Kasualien und Lebensordnung," *Jahrbuch für Liturgik und Hymnologie,* 18 (1973/1974), 55–64; and Manfred Seitz, "Unsere Kasualpraxis — eine gottesdienstliche Gelegenheit?" (unpublished paper of the LLKD, R 208a–77).

[20] The baptismal rite is described in my *Baptism, a pastoral perspective* (Minneapolis 1975).

ing of the water; in the epiklesis the Holy Spirit is invoked upon the sacramental washing; b) The restoration of the prayer for the Spirit's gifts with the laying on of hands, and the sign of the cross historically associated with chrismation. The optional use of the baptismal candle and a welcome into the congregation complete the rite. Normally it is to be celebrated within the Sunday service. With appropriate modifications the single rite is used both for infants and adults. The practice of fixed times for Baptism in coordination with the church year is suggested.

The new rite marks an approach to primitive fulness, restoring the "confirmation elements" to the baptismal liturgy. It is fuller liturgically, in order to express the dignity accorded the sacrament in our theology but seldom evidenced in practice. It gives more explicit expression both to the sacramental activity of the Holy Spirit and to the gift of the Spirit to the baptized person. As such, it becomes a clearer reflection of the Lutheran insistence upon baptism as bestowal of the Holy Spirit. At its best, Lutheran teaching has always implied a rite such as this.

2. Confirmation. With such a baptismal rite as CW 7, confirmation makes even less sense than before. An unrepeated rite which contains the laying on of hands and admits to the Eucharist is experienced sacramentally whether it is called a sacrament or not. Inevitably it overshadows baptism in the person's life of experience. The provisional Affirmation of the Baptismal Covenant was offered as a *repeatable* rite, useful especially at the conclusion of formal catechetical instruction but also when receiving members from other church bodies, when receiving lapsed Christians, and to mark other appropriate occasions in one's life. CW 8 says nothing about admission to the altar.

There was little negative criticism of the provisional baptismal rite, but many criticized CW 8 for departing from the Lutheran tradition of confirmation. For a time it seemed that the name "confirmation" would have to be restored. Loss of confirmation was perceived as a threat to Lutheran identity. The initiatory phenomenon of "hazing" is clearly present in such criticism. It is related to the preceding course of special instruction — it cannot be done in our public schools — which the candidate must undergo. Parents say to their children, "I went through it; you

will go through it." From such a viewpoint, to remain unconfirmed is to remain less than complete as a Lutheran.

A compromise has been reached. The *Lutheran Book of Worship*
will contain a rite called Affirmation of Baptism. Its three uses will
be made clear through subheadings assigned to each form of
address to the candidates: confirmation, reception (of members),
restoration (of the lapsed). Rubrics will suggest not combining the
confirmation use with others on a given occasion. The laying on
of hands has been reserved for the confirmation use. Gone is the
fourth use of the provisional CW 8: for other appropriate occasions in life.

What has evolved is not completely consistent, but it marks a
step away from the overshadowing of baptism by confirmation;
confirmation is no longer the rite of admission to thc Lord's Table.
In some respects our experience as we have moved from provisional to permanent rite has been parallel to that of the Episcopal
Church/USA.

3. First Communion. As participants in the Lutheran World Federation confirmation study mentioned earlier, American Lutheran
educationists inaugurated a study of their own. A process was set
up whereby congregations could discuss the matter of confirmation and first communion.[21] Following completion of the study,
the Joint Commission on the Theology and Practice of Confirmation made its report to the presidents of the cooperating churches.
The report contains this definition:

"Confirmation is a pastoral and educational ministry of the
Church which helps the baptized child through Word and Sacrament to identify more deeply with the Christian community and
participate more fully in its mission."

Note the similarity to the principles underlying the Norwegian
reform. The report also broke the link between confirmation and
first communion by suggesting the latter at the level of the fifth
grade (about age 10), while extending the program of confirmation
ministry into the middle teens. The report was accepted and the
matter was left to congregations for implementation. Seven years

---

[21] See Frank Klos, *Confirmation and first Communion, a study book* (1968).

later it has enjoyed widespread implementation except in the Lutheran Church — Missouri Synod.

The admission link had thus been broken before the Inter-Lutheran Commission on Worship set about revising the initiation rites. At the present time it would seem that North American Lutherans have successfully moved "confirmation" beyond the scope of Christian initiation, making of it a rite to mark the conclusion of the confirmation ministry only. Technically, it is devoid of any sacramental overtones and of its former character as admission to the altar. I say "technically" because it will take much longer for Lutheran consciousness to make the adjustment.

The initiation rites of the *Lutheran Book of Worship*, then, will consist of baptism and first communion separated in most cases by the interval of a decade. There is a brief and simple instructional prelude to first communion, but no particular rite has been drafted. A word of welcome may be included in the sermon, and intercession for the new communicants is to be made. The new communicants simply join their parents at the altar for the first time. The initial sharing of bread and wine is, after all, the *proprium* of first communion! To surround it with public examinations and vows runs the definite risk of reintroducing what was objectionable about confirmation.

Theologically and liturgically the way is clear in North America for lowering the age of first communion to the baptismal eucharist itself. But our Lutherans are not yet ready for that. At least they now are able to discuss the concept and remain rational!

A similar development in initiation rites does not seem to have occurred in Australia, the other major emigrant church. The recent *Lutheran Hymnal* of the Lutheran Church of Australia (1973) follows the older practice of including neither baptism nor confirmation among its liturgical materials (it does contain a rite for emergency baptism).

CONCLUDING OBSERVATIONS

A. If the pattern of lowering the age of first communion and separating it from confirmation persists, and if "confirmation" is understood increasingly as the culmination of a period of formal instruction, it is reasonable to expect the restoration to Lutheran baptismal rites of the "confirmation elements": the laying on of hands and chrismation. I hope the North American rite is a harbinger of things to come both there and elsewhere.

B. The age of first communion can be lowered and the baptismal rite enriched so long as "confirmation" in some form remains. It seems that Lutheran self-consciousness is not yet able to tolerate the idea of an unconfirmed Lutheran. The tenacity of that seems due more to rites of passage at puberty with their attendant hazing than to theological convictions. The appropriateness of a public confession of faith from those baptized in infancy (beyond their participation in the Eucharist) must be admitted, of course. Whatever form confirmation takes, it must not be part of the initiation process which culminated earlier in first communion.

C. Gradually people must be helped to understand that baptism is connected with Easter, not with the birth of babies. In Europe that would require the overcoming of centuries of "Christendom-conditioning." Both in Europe and other Lutheran churches it would require seeing baptism as more than the antidote for original sin. After years of encouraging people to baptize their children soon after birth so that the stain of original sin might be washed away, it is not a simple task to persuade them that relating baptism to the church year is a better way.

In a perceptive article, Urban Holmes observes a shift in modern consciousness of God away from an individual sin-salvation relationship toward a more creational, communal relationship in which redemption is seen as restoration.

"There is a new root metaphor forming. The relationship between God and man is no longer that between a Tudor monarch and his subject. Rather this is the relationship: *God is the ideal subject or self, who needs relationship with subjects other than himself.* He is intentional; he has a vision for the future. Within this project there is a oneness of all creation, amid diversity. And like any ideal subject he loves and fully expects to be loved by all other subjects, you and me. The fruit of such love is cooperating in the fulfillment of his vision. He will never waver in his commitment to us, perhaps to the point of suffering with us in our sin and failure, although the explicit suggestion is never made. God is the perfect friend."[22]

There is much in that statement with which I take issue: it needs, I think, sharper Christological and eschatological expression. And yet I think that Holmes is on to something very basic which may support our efforts regarding baptism.

New beginnings have been made in Lutheran initiation practices. Only time will tell the results.

[22] Urban T. Holmes, "Ritual and the Social Drama," *Worship* 51 (1977) 211–212.

Bryan D. Spinks

17. Vivid Signs of the Gift of the Spirit? The Lima Text on Baptism and Some Recent English Language Baptismal Liturgies

Although Christian liturgy abounds with signs, symbols and ceremonies, liturgists have been slow to examine the nature of symbolism in relation to their own discipline. At the Society for Liturgical Study Conference at Harwarden, Wales in 1980, Christopher Walsh gave a brief evaluation of the work of Victor Turner and Mary Douglas, and attempted to draw out insights for Christian liturgy.[1] More recently, and more profoundly, David Power has grappled with the complexity of the whole spectrum of signs, signals and symbolism in relation to liturgy.[2] In this wide-ranging analysis and discussion, Power writes: "Symbols mediate between experience and reality, between the subjective and the objective, and between the cognitive and the affective. Through them human experience is brought to expression and so to discovery. . . . Because symbol systems grow and develop, their use needs to be regarded critically. They do not dispense one from thought, but give rise to it and demand it."[3]

Critical reflection on liturgical symbolism in the light of insights from anthropologists and philosophers, when applied to individual symbols and signs, would seem to endorse one of the conclu-

[1] Christopher Walsh, "Liturgy and Symbolism: A Map" in *Symbolism and the Liturgy I*, ed. Kenneth W. Stevenson, Grove Liturgical Study 23 (Bramcote, Notts. 1980) 17–26.

[2] David N. Power, *Unsearchable Riches: The Symbolic Nature of Liturgy* (New York 1984).

[3] Power, 172.

sions drawn by Walsh: "the first and absolute priority is to rescue from vacuity and inanition the basic primordial symbols of immersion, anointing, bread, eating and drinking. (As one American commentator has forcefully but rather indelicately said, our stylized and sanitized wafers, sprinklings, etc., are about as liminal and primordial as scented toilet paper.)"[4] Concern for allowing the symbol and signs of baptism to be as effective as possible is emphasized in the Lima document: "As was the case in the early centuries, the gift of the Spirit in baptism may be signified in additional ways; for example, by the sign of the laying on of hands, and by anointing or chrismation. The very sign of the cross recalls the promised gift of the Holy Spirit who is the instalment and pledge of what is yet to come when God has fully redeemed those whom he has made his own (Eph 1:13-14). The recovery of such vivid signs may be expected to enrich the liturgy."[5]

Whereas BEM 18 refers to the "symbolic" dimension of water, BEM 19 prefers the term "sign" when applied to the ceremonies of anointing, laying on of hands, and signing with the cross. It is generally agreed that there is an important distinction between a symbol and a sign, though there is a total lack of agreement on the precise meaning of these two terms.[6] The terminological confusion evidenced by *I simboli dell'iniziazione cristiana* (the proceedings of the International Liturgical Congress held at Rome in 1982)[7] is rightly noted by Michael Witczak.[8] Lima offers us no definition of these two terms but it may be assumed that they mark a distinction between the normally *sine qua non* ceremony with water, and the additional ceremonies which in some traditions are omitted, and in others may be omitted in cases of emergency without rendering the baptismal act invalid.[9] The concern of this paper, how-

---

[4] Walsh, 25.

[5] *Baptism, Eucharist and Ministry*, Faith and Order Paper No. 111 (Geneva: World Council of Churches 1982) art. 19. Hereafter BEM.

[6] See Nicholas Sagovsky, *Liturgy and Symbolism*, Grove Liturgical Study 16 (Bramcote, Notts. 1978).

[7] Analecta Liturgica 7, *Studia Anselmiana* 87 (Rome 1983).

[8] *Worship* 58 (1984) 476–477.

[9] E.g., S. P. Brock, "A Short Melkite Baptismal Service in Syriac" in *Parole de l'Orient* 3 (1972) 119–130; *Apostolic Constitutions* 7:22.

ever, is not with precise definition of "symbol" and "sign" as such, but with the advice that anointing and handlaying, where used, should be "vivid," which I take to mean clear and obvious, and the opposite of obscure and ambiguous. My purpose, therefore, is to reflect on the possible implications of this article, and at the same time, by way of comparison, to evaluate the signs of anointing and handlaying in the following English language liturgies:

The Roman Catholic Rite of Christian Initiation of Adults, 1972.	(RC)
The Alternative Services Book of the Church of England, 1980.	(ASB)
The Alternative Prayer Book, Church of Ireland, 1984.	(IPB)
The Book of Common Prayer, Episcopal Church, USA, 1979.	(APB)
The Methodist Service Book (Great Britain), 1975.	(Meth)
A Book of Services and Prayers, United Reformed Church, 1980.	(URC)
The Book of Common Order, Church of Scotland, 1979.	(BCO)
Reformed Book of Common Order, National Church Association, Scotland, 1977.	(RBCO)
Lutheran Book of Worship, USA, 1978.	(LBW)
Lutheran Worship, Missouri Synod, 1980.	(LW)

The consideration of these liturgies rests on the assumption that the problems, tensions and differences which they exhibit are representative of a wider comparison of denominational baptismal liturgies.

THE VIVID SIGN OF ANOINTING OR CHRISMATION

Anointing has a variety of associations in the Bible, particularly with regard to priests and kings, but also it is associated with God's *action* of conferring the Holy Spirit.[10] BEM 19 is concerned

[10] Leonel L. Mitchell, *Baptismal Anointing* (Notre Dame 1978); Nicola Bux, "L'olio Simbolo dello Spirito Santo," *Studia Anselmiana* 87, 123-135; Emmanuele Lanne, "L'acqua e L'unzione nelle chiese orientali," ibid., 137-156.

with anointing as a sign of the Spirit, and not with its use as a protective. The recommendation of a "recovery" of the sign of anointing as sign of the Holy Spirit would appear at first sight to be addressed to the churches of the Reformation and their derivatives, since anointing forms part of the Eastern and Roman Catholic baptismal rites. Anointing was, for example, dropped from Luther's Taufbüchlein of 1526, and from the early Reformed rites of Basle, Zurich and Berne, as well as from the later Anglican Prayer Books. Of the recent English rites under discussion, IPB, Meth, URC, BCO, RBCO and LW make no provision at all for anointing.

An initial objection to the inclusion of an anointing may be that in the West its significance is questionable. J. D. Crichton observes: "In spite of its rich symbolism in the Old and the New Testaments, it remains difficult for us to use. In industrial society it is thought of as a lubricant and those bold enough to examine the sumps of their cars know that it is a nasty black mess. It does not help very much to be told that Greek athletes anointed themselves with oil to give strength and suppleness to their limbs. For as soon as you have to be told that this 'signifies' that, you are being told at the same time that the symbol is dead."[11] In reply to Crichton it may be said that baptism presupposes belief — of the whole ecclesia, as well as the family of infants and the faith of mature candidates. With all that belief implies in terms of nurture and instruction, the community of the Anointed One ought not to need an explanation of the significance of anointing. If the ceremony needs explanation, then it will be because catechesis, preaching and Bible reading have been deficient. Baptismal anointing as a ceremony amongst the followers of the Anointed One ought to be a powerful sign with associations of priesthood, royalty and the Spirit (1 Pt 2:9; Is 61:1-3) though this will be made clear and obvious by the prayers and formula which accompany the action.

Looking at those liturgies under discussion which do include anointing at baptism, it is highly questionable as to whether any

[11] J. D. Crichton, *Christian Celebration: The Sacraments*, 2nd ed. (London 1980) 22.

can be viewed as making the sign "vivid." Probably the nearest to such a description is RC, where the postbaptismal anointing is accompanied by a prayer which draws upon biblical imagery to indicate before God and to the congregation the significance of the ceremony. There is, however, as Aidan Kavanagh has repeatedly pointed out, an unfortunate anomaly which rather confuses the significance of the sign.[12] In confirmation there is also an anointing, and when confirmation follows baptism directly, only the prayer and anointing of confirmation is used. If confirmation does not follow, the prayer and anointing of the baptismal rite is used. But the two prayers differ. Kavanagh writes: ". . . the prayer to be said at the postbaptismal chrismation speaks of the meaning of the act in terms of the neophyte's being anointed 'As Christ was anointed Priest, Prophet, and King,' so that he or she may always live as a member of his Body, the Church. The prayer said for the chrismation at confirmation speaks, instead, of the neophyte's being given the Holy Spirit and his sevenfold gifts. Thus when confirmation is celebrated *apart* from baptism, the chrismation after baptism is christic and messianic in character: when it is celebrated *with* baptism, the chrismation is pneumatic and charismatic. It could be argued that in this particular case a structural peculiarity in the Roman rite has been exchanged for a verbal anomaly."[13] It is difficult to see how this anomaly can be rectified without omitting the chrismation from the rite of confirmation. This verbal anomaly certainly confuses the meaning of the postbaptismal anointing. Unless the same sign is going to be duplicated and given different meanings, clarity will only be possible here if the christic and pneumatic dimensions are properly combined.

LBW gives provision for a postbaptismal consignation with oil. A psalm or hymn may be sung after the baptism, and the minister takes the candidate to the altar. There follows a prayer with the laying on of hands, and then the sign of the cross is made on the forehead, and the minister says: "N, child of God, you have been

---

[12] Aidan Kavanagh, "The New Roman Rites of Adult Initiation," *Studia Liturgica* 10 (1974) 35–47 (p. 43); *The Shape of Baptism: The Rite of Christian Initiation* (New York 1978) 140.

[13] *Shape of Baptism,* 140.

sealed by the Holy Spirit and marked with the cross of Christ for-ever." The rubric notes: "Oil prepared for this purpose may be used." *The Report and Recommendation of the Special Hymnal Review Committee* of the Lutheran Church-Missouri Synod objected that the anointing and sealing of the Spirit happened in *baptism*, through the washing of the water with the Word, and that oil obscures the importance of water.[14] This objection is rather an overkill, since the use of oil is optional, and adds nothing to the signing of the forehead, despite the explanation given in the Man-ual.[15] The same criticism may be leveled at APB. It provides an optional consecration of chrism, and this prayer indicates the sig-nificance of anointing. However, the chrismation itself is optional. It comes after the bishop or priest has prayed over the candidates, and like LBW, is connected with the marking of the forehead with the sign of the cross: "N, you are sealed by the Holy Spirit in Baptism and marked as Christ's own for ever." Since the anoint-ing is optional, it is the signing rather than the anointing which has any significance.

First prize for nonsensical use of signs must, however, be awarded to ASB. Influenced by the Ely Report and the arguments of Charles Whitaker, the Liturgical Commission intended to make no provision for anointing. The General Synod, however, inserted a prefatory rubric allowing its optional use with the sign of the cross either after the renunciations before baptism, or as an alter-native, with the signing after the baptism. It also allows the bishop to use oil at confirmation. However, there are no rubrics mentioning it within the rite, nor any prayer or statement which refers to it, and therefore its use has not the slightest significance. Why not daub on green paint, or put on party hats at these points in the service? Far from a "vivid" sign we have here an example of what the English Puritans called a "dumb ceremony." Any meaning has to be imported from historical liturgical usage, or the usage (and formulae) and theology of other denominations.

[14] *Report and Recommendations of the Special Hymnal Review Committee* (Saint Louis 1978) 27.
[15] Philip H. Pfatteicher and Carlos R. Messerli, *Manual on the Liturgy: Lutheran Book of Worship* (Minneapolis 1979) 185–186.

In the light of this confusion, Lima's call for the recovery of anointing as a vivid sign is refreshing. However, the churches look in vain for further guidance in the supporting documents as to what might constitute a vivid sign. The essay on chrismation by Cyrille Argenti in the collection described as giving fuller treatment of the technical issues, is woefully inadequate.[16] It is well known that oil was quickly ritualized in the baptismal rites, but the studies of Ratcliff, Mitchell, Brock and Winkler have served to emphasize that there was a variety of usages with a variety of associations.[17] The Old Syrian tradition, shared apparently by Armenia, and possibly parts of Egypt,[18] knew only one anointing with olive oil which *preceded* baptism. According to Brock, this was based upon the Jewish pattern of circumcision-lustration, the mark of Abraham being replaced by the mark (*rushma*) of the Messiah.[19] The anointing implied ownership, new life, sonship, and gift of the Spirit. In other areas — North Africa, Thmuis, Jerusalem and the region of Antioch — we find a postbaptismal anointing with *myron* which is associated with the odor of Christ, or the Holy Spirit.[20] At Rome we find two postbaptismal anointings. The reason for this diversity, as Mitchell and Kretschmar have suggested,

---

[16] Cyrille Argenti, "Chrismation" in *Ecumenical Perspectives on Baptism, Eucharist and Ministry*, Faith and Order Paper No. 116, Max Thurian, ed. (Geneva 1983) 46–67.

[17] E. C. Ratcliff, "The Old Syrian Baptismal Tradition and its Resettlement under the Influence of Jerusalem in the Fourth Century," *Studies in Church History* 2 (London 1956) 19–37 (= *Liturgical Studies* [London 1976] 135–155); Mitchell, *Anointing*; S. P. Brock, "Studies in the Early History of the Syrian Orthodox Baptismal Liturgy," *Journal of Theological Studies* NS 23 (1972) 16–64; "The Syrian Baptismal Ordines (with special reference to the anointings)," *Studia Liturgica* 12 (1977) 177–183; Gabriele Winkler, *Das armenische Initiationsrituale*, Orientalia Christiana Analecta 217 (Rome 1982).

[18] G. Kretschmar, "Beitrage zur Geschichte der Liturgie, insbesondere der Taufliturgie, in Agypten" in *Jahrbuch für Liturgik und Hymnologie 1963* (Kassel 1964) 1–54, esp. 43–50.

[19] S. P. Brock, "The Transition to a Post-Baptismal Anointing in the Antiochene Rite" in *The Sacrifice of Praise*, ed. Bryan D. Spinks, Bibliotheca Ephemerides Liturgicae, Subsidia 19 (Rome 1981) 215–225.

[20] E.g., the postbaptismal prayers in Sarapion and *Apostolic Constitutions* 7:44.

may stem from a ritualization of different bathing customs.[21] But the subsequent duplication as evidenced in the Syrian Orthodox and Maronite ordos indicates a synthesis of practice, and a growing confusion over significance. These findings are passed over in silence by Argenti, who argues mainly from Western Latin sources to conclude that the present Byzantine rite's chrismation constitutes a "vivid" sign. In fact, in contrast with many other Eastern rites, the Byzantine prayer of chrismation is rather obscure in its intentions, being concerned with the seal (*sphragis*) of the gift of the Spirit, rather than with exploring the rich biblical associations of anointing. The actual chrismation is accompanied only by the words "The seal of the gift of the Holy Spirit." I would urge that the term "seal," however venerable, is not obvious in its meaning; Schmemann's hint that it reveals the gift given in baptism is hardly obvious in this formula.[22]

Although by no means identical, the same criticism may be made of the present East Syrian rite, where the postbaptismal anointing[23] which was added to the rite is accomplished with the *qarna* rather than the *laqna*, but the rich, even if fanciful, associations of the *qarna* are left unexpressed.[24] It is to be regretted therefore that the formula of the Byzantine rite seems to be the basis for Max Thurian's formula in his *Example of an Ecumenical Baptismal Liturgy* which is left bereft of any accompanying prayer.[25]

[21] Mitchell, *Anointing*; G. Kretschmar, "Recent Research on Christian Initiation" in *Studia Liturgica* 12 (1977) 87–106.

[22] Alexander Schmemann, *Of Water and the Spirit: A Liturgical Study of Baptism* (New York 1974) 78.

[23] Mitchell, *Anointing*, 72, refers to the view of T. Thompson and Denzinger (shared by Assemani and Badger) that the rubric gives no indication that oil should be used at this point. However, F. F. Irving, *The Ceremonial Use of Oil among the East Syrians*, Occasional Paper of the Eastern Church Association (Oxford and London 1902) made careful inquiry among the Nestorians and manuscript service books, and demonstrated that there was an anointing directed at this point. Archdeacon Yonan Y. Yonan in a letter of 7 March 1985 confirms that this is the practice, and it is with the *qarna*.

[24] The legend is that the *qarna* originally consisted of water from Christ's baptism, water from his pierced side, to which oil was added after Pentecost, and each apostle took a horn of oil with this mixture in it.

[25] In Max Thurian and Geoffrey Wainwright, eds., *Baptism and Eucharist:*

However, there are Eastern rites, such as the Coptic and Armenian, where postbaptismal anointing is accompanied with words which give vivid meaning to the act of anointing, and perhaps these would provide a better guide as to what constitutes a vivid sign. Lima, I would submit, far from being addressed here solely to Protestant churches which omit any anointing, is apposite to many churches, East and West, where chrism is used, but its accompanying prayer or formula makes it an obscure or ambiguous sign. In place of Thurian's formula I would offer that used in the rite of the ecumenical Chapel at Churchill College, Cambridge, which combines the messianic, priestly and pneumatic associations of anointing: "Jesus the Anointed One anoints you with grace, and signs you as one of his flock. You are a member of a chosen race, a royal priesthood, a holy nation, God's own people. May the Holy Spirit which is poured out upon you sanctify and preserve you. N, you are signed with the oil of Anointing in the Name of the Father, and of the Son, and of the Holy Spirit. Amen."

THE LAYING ON OF HANDS

As a biblical sign, the laying on of hands signified a variety of things, though the two basic meanings in the Old Testament appear to be identification and transference.[26] In the New Testament it is associated with appointment to office, conferring a blessing, healing, and, in certain passages of Acts, a sign of the Spirit. Discussing this latter usage, David Daube concluded that the context implied that it was an instance of the Old Testament *samakh*, a leaning rather than a placing of the hands, signifying the pouring of something (usually one man's personality) into another.[27] Daube noted, however, that the precise significance has no real precursor in the Old Testament, and may be regarded as a distinc-

---

Ecumenical Convergence in Celebration (Geneva 1983; Grand Rapids, Michigan 1983).

[26] See a recent summary by Michael Sansom, "Laying On of Hands in the Old Testament," *Expository Times* 94:11 (1983) 323–326.

[27] David Daube, *The New Testament and Rabbinic Judaism* (London 1956; rpt New York 1973) 233–246 (p. 241).

tive and suggestive ceremony of early Christianity.[28] Lima accepts that this ceremony may still be a vivid sign of the Holy Spirit.

Since handlaying in the context of Christian initiation is associated with the rite which has come to be called confirmation, it is immediately apparent that this is a minefield; in different churches there is a variety of usages and meanings attached to confirmation, and to this ceremony. In the West from the fifth century the laying on of hands and anointing were increasingly interpreted as explicitly conferring the Holy Spirit.[29] There are those churches where the laying on of hands is a sign of strengthening, empowering, blessing, and admittance into full communicant membership. And there are those rites such as the Byzantine, Syrian Orthodox and Armenian, where there is no postbaptismal laying on of hands. These differing usages are all reflected in the recent English liturgies examined here.

An Explicit Sign of the Gift of the Spirit. RC retains the understanding of confirmation as a conferring of the Holy Spirit. When administered as a separate rite from baptism, in the homily the bishop says (or similar words), "Bishops are successors of the apostles and have this power of giving the Holy Spirit to the baptized, either personally or through the priests they appoint"; and, "The gift of the Holy Spirit which you are to receive. . . ." When celebrated immediately after baptism he says, "Now you are to share in the outpouring of the Holy Spirit." The celebrant prays that God will pour out the Holy Spirit on the baptized to strengthen them with abundant gifts and anoint them to be more like his Son. Then the celebrant and presbyters associated with him lay hands upon all who are to be confirmed, and he prays for the gift of the Holy Spirit. The chrismation is a sealing of the gift of the Spirit. So emphatic is this stress that the impression is given that before confirmation the baptized have been living a life completely devoid of any indwelling of the Spirit.

In LBW we find two handlaying ceremonies. The first is immediately after the baptism, whether for infants or adults, and is

[28] Ibid., 243.
[29] J.D.C. Fisher, *Christian Initiation: Baptism in the Medieval West* (London 1965).

accompanied by prayer for the Holy Spirit. At confirmation there is a further laying on of hands, with prayer asking for the stirring up of the gift of the Holy Spirit. The first handlaying, then, is associated with the conferring of the Holy Spirit, and the second is a sign of stirring up, confirming (whatever this might mean) and empowering. But most strange is LW. Here also we find a handlaying in baptism and one at confirmation. Since anointing was objected to on the grounds that the Spirit was sealed in water with the Word, it is ironical that the petition at baptismal handlaying is for "strength in grace," but that at confirmation is explicitly pneumatic: "N, God the Father of our Lord Jesus Christ, give you his Holy Spirit, the Spirit of wisdom and knowledge, of grace and prayer, of power and strength, of sanctification and the fear of God."

A Sign of "Confirming," Empowering, Admittance and Growth. The majority of the rites fall into this category (IPB has no service of confirmation included). Some are ambiguously worded, and some allow alternatives, resulting in an uncertain or ambiguous sign, or a sign which can mean many things.

ASB is an example of studied ambiguity. The bishop, who is the sole minister of confirmation, is directed to stretch out his hand toward the candidates. He prays a prayer indicating that the candidates have been given new birth in baptism by water and the Spirit. Petition is made: "Let your Holy Spirit rest upon them." The actual laying on of hands is accompanied by the formula: "Confirm, O Lord, your servant N with your Holy Spirit." Certainly the handlaying is a sign of the Spirit, but it is a sign of confirming, whatever this term actually means.

In APB there is no handlaying in the rite of baptism, which is regarded as admitting to full membership of the church. The rite of confirmation is presented as a mature confession of faith. The laying on of hands accompanies this, but according to the prayers, it is a sign of sending forth in power; strengthening, empowering and sustaining, or defending.

In Meth the laying on of hands is optional, but if it is used, it is clearly intended as a sign of the Spirit. It is preceded by a prayer asking God to establish the candidates in faith by the Holy Spirit, and increase in them the gifts of grace. Then either with or without the laying on of hands comes the formula: "Lord, confirm your servant N by your Holy Spirit that he may continue to be yours for ever." Once again, although here the handlaying is a sign of the Spirit, by using the word "confirm" there is an ambiguity; the whole problem is, what is "confirmation"?

In URC we find an anomaly between confirmation and reception at the baptism of believers, and confirmation of those already baptized. In the former the minister *may* lay hands on the head of each candidate in turn, or *may* raise his hand in blessing over each. In the latter service the rubric mentions only the possibility of handlaying on the heads of the candidates. The formula asks for confirming and strengthening by the Holy Spirit. This is followed by a statement of acceptance of the candidate into full membership of the church, and a welcome with the right hand of fellowship.[30] We may note that as with Meth the handlaying is an optional sign.

In BCO the laying on of hands is also optional. The minister may lay his hand upon the head of each candidate and give a blessing in the words of a sentence of Scripture (e.g., Rom 15:13; Eph 3:16-17) or a scriptural charge (e.g., 1 Cor 15:58; Jude 20), or one of three prayers may be used. The first asks God to "confirm you by his Spirit that you may be established in the Covenant" (surely at variance with Calvin's Convenantal baptismal theology?); the second is the prayer from the Anglican 1662 rite asking God to defend the candidates and increase in them the Holy Spirit; the third asks God to give the candidates grace. This is followed by a statement of admission, and the right hand of fellowship. Thus, depending upon which formula the minister chooses, the laying on of hands — if used — can be a sign of blessing, a charge, confirming, empowering, defending, or a prayer for grace.

The Absence of Handlaying. Since the laying on of hands is optional in Meth, URC and BCO, there may be occasions when the sign is entirely absent. However, the sign is deliberately excluded in RBCO. RBCO criticized BCO as interpreting confirmation in an

---

[30] Gal 2:9. The custom passed into the English Free Church tradition, probably from the Moravians via Methodism.

unscriptural, unreformed way, derived from Anglo-Catholic and Roman Catholic practice. Indeed, it regards the BCO rite as an example of Scoto-Catholicism. In the rite of admission to communicant membership, after a profession of faith the Aaronic blessing is given, and the right hand of fellowship. The Spirit is entirely associated with the rite of baptism, that is, the ceremony with water.

It becomes obvious, therefore, that although many rites have a ceremony of handlaying (though presumably not *samakh!*), it is a sign which signifies a wide variety of things. In many ways BCO encapsulates the confusion: there may or may not be handlaying, and if there is, it can mean confirming, increasing, strengthening, blessing, a solemn charge, or a prayer for defense or for grace. Now, while a sign might well trigger a variety of associations, it would seem that we have here a variation on Humpty Dumpty in Lewis Carroll's *Alice Through the Looking Glass:* " 'When *I* use a word,' Humpty Dumpty said in rather a scornful tone, 'it means just what I choose it to mean — neither more nor less.' " For "word" substitue "the laying on of hands." The question is (to paraphrase Carroll), can you make it mean so many different things? Does it not cease to have any real significance? Does it not result in the opposite of "vivid"?

Apart from David Holeton's excellent summary of the confusion over confirmation,[31] the supporting documents of Lima are singularly unhelpful. In his essay on chrismation, Cyrille Argenti treats the Byzantine postbaptismal chrismation as an equivalent to handlaying in the Western tradition, and Max Thurian in his experimental rite gives handlaying or anointing as alternatives. While the ecclesiological and pneumatological result of the Byzantine and Western ceremonies may be the same, that is not sufficient justification for regarding handlaying and anointing as alternatives, particularly when anointing is being used in a christic dimension. Furthermore, although the laying on of hands is attested first in the West with Turtullian in North Africa, and the *Apostolic Tradition* at Rome, the handlaying is not an alternative to chrismation, but in addition to it. Also, the Coptic, Ethiopic and East Syrian

[31] David R. Holeton, "Confirmation in the 1980s" in *Ecumenical Perspectives,* 68–89.

rites do have a laying on of hands. It may be argued that the first two of these derived the ceremony from North Africa, or from the influence of the *Apostolic Tradition*. However, the East Syrian rite has had a handlaying at least from the time of Iso'yahb III (though the silence of Narsai does not necessarily mean that it was unknown before[32]). In this rite it comes before the signing with the *qarna*, and its accompanying prayer suggests that it may have been some sort of dismissal ceremony rather than some sign of the Holy Spirit.[33]

It is very interesting that in a recent paper Aidan Kavanagh has suggested that *structurally* the laying on of hands by the bishop in *Apostolic Tradition* is an episcopal dismissal from baptism into full fellowship of the baptized community.[34] If this suggestion has substance, then handlaying was a sign of blessing and dismissal and not a conferring of the Spirit. This, surely, is not far short of G.W.H. Lampe's description of confirmation as "the blessing of the bishop to a new member of his flock, and a commission to take his place as an active partner in the Church's apostolic task."[35] Admittedly, however, it would seem difficult to sustain Kavanagh's suggestion in relation to the traditional Western prayer for the sevenfold gift of the Spirit.

It may be, therefore, that the laying on of hands cannot become a vivid sign before there is agreement on its significance. At present it is a sign which signifies very different things, and simply using the word "confirm" is to hide in ambiguity. Perhaps except where it is used immediately after baptism, it would be better to omit the sign. Certainly when it is used in connection with full membership or admission to communion, it is a sign in conflict with BEM 14.

[32] A. Raes, "Ou se trouve la confirmation dans le rite syro-orientale?" in *L'Orient Syrien* 1 (1956) 239–254.

[33] Mitchell, *Anointing,* 73, suggests that it is a final blessing.

[34] Aidan Kavanagh, "Confirmation: A Suggestion from Structure," *Worship* 58 (1984) 386–395.

[35] G.W.H. Lampe, *The Seal of the Spirit* (London 1951) 316.

Lima is both the culmination of many years' work and the beginning of a serious debate. This review of BEM 19 in relation to certain English postbaptismal rites is too limited to offer firm conclusions. Its findings can be no more than a prelude. From the discussion I would wish to offer a suggestion and a series of questions as an agenda for clarification.

A Suggestion on the Relationship of Postbaptismal Rites (Signs) to Salvation/Justification. One of the obvious problems regarding the ceremonies of water, anointing and handlaying is noted in BEM 14: "Different actions have become associated with the giving of the Spirit. For some it is the water rite itself. For others, it is the anointing with chrism and/or the imposition of hands, which many churches call confirmation." A rather longer explanation was given in Accra 15-18. Commenting on this latter document, Geoffrey Wainwright stated: "I suspect that some of the deepest divisions in the area of Christian initiation concern the anthropology and theology of *signs*. How far does the performance of signs *produce* the reality which they signify? How far is it spread over a future time-span? How far, on the other hand, does the performance of signs *presuppose* already the existence of the reality signified? In what measure must the reality be present before the signs are allowed to express it?"[36] It is to be regretted that these pertinent questions have apparently been left unanswered.

BEM 1 states that baptism is a gift of God. BEM 9 points out that baptism is related not only to momentary experience but to lifelong growth into Christ. There is, then, a present and a future dimension. But, as T. F. Torrance makes clear, baptism and faith are concerned with something that has already happened and has already been achieved in Christ: "Certainly ritual and ethical acts have their proper place in the administration of baptism, but baptism itself is focused beyond those acts upon the one saving act of God embodied in Jesus Christ in such a way that, when the Church baptizes in his name, it is actually Christ himself who is

[36] Geoffrey Wainwright, "Christian Initiation in the Ecumenical Movement," *Studia Liturgica* 12 (1977) 67–86 (p. 75).

savingly at work, pouring out his Spirit upon us and drawing us within the power of his vicarious life, death and resurrection."[37]

Insofar as baptism makes present the salvific work of God in Christ, baptism tells us what God has done, is doing, and will do for us, to us and in us. God has elected us and reconciled us to himself, and is refashioning us in the image of Christ. Baptism, therefore, is concerned with the past, present and future. Faith has to do with the recognition of the past, present and future action of God. Is it possible, therefore, to regard the symbol and signs and their accompanying prayers and formulae in this way? It is often forgotten that in the English language at least, the simple present tense can express a past, a present and a future, over against the continuous or progressive present tense which expresses only the present.[38] The liturgical symbol and signs, using the simple present, would reach back to the past, express the present, and declare the future.

Questions Which Need Clarification Regarding the Maximizing and Making Vivid. The following questions need a detailed and full answer:
— How far is a sign dependent upon accompanying prayers and formulae for its vividness?
— What things are intended to be signified in baptismal anointing?
— Can anointing be used intelligently without the necessity of a so-called theology of oil?
— In view of the confusion over the word "confirm," is handlaying a useful sign of the Spirit?
— Would the kiss of peace or the right hand of fellowship express better the meaning of confirmation (assuming that an episcopal

[37] T. F. Torrance, "The One Baptism Common to Christ and his Church," *Theology and Reconciliation* (London 1975) 83.

[38] W. Stannard Allen, *Living English Structure* (London 1959) 70; W. Davidson and J. C. Alcock, *English Grammar and Analysis* (London 1941) 50, 66. The use of the simple present to convey present and future is a well-established usage. The historic present is less common today, but grammatically the simple present is capable of this interpretation. One suspects that this is too simple for systematic theologians!

kiss or handshake is as efficacious as an episcopal hand on the head!)?

The work of anthropologists serves to underline the power of symbols and signs in the lives of human communities. If the community of the redeemed becomes careless about its symbols and signs, then, as Aidan Kavanagh has warned, they may begin to work in ways we may not wish.[39] It may be that they already have, and have thus become signs of confusion and disunity. One hopes that attention to these questions may result in vivid signs of postbaptismal rites which will reveal God's saving work and also the unity of his church.

[39] Aidan Kavanagh, "Symbolic Implications of Christian Initiation," *Studia Anselmiana* 87 (Rome 1983) 223–241 (p. 229).

Paul F. X. Covino

18. The Postconciliar Infant Baptism Debate in the American Catholic Church

The Second Vatican Council had no intention of abolishing the practice of infant baptism. While calling for revision in the rite of infant baptism, the Council clearly assumed that the practice would continue. The decision to restore the catechumenate for adults likewise gave no indication that the restored adult catechumenate would alter the practice of baptizing infants. These relatively innocent declarations of the Council did, however, give rise to a plethora of speculation about the advisability of infant baptism in the postconciliar Church. The phenomena of dechristianization and secularization in Western Europe prompted Catholic writers there to question seriously the custom of baptizing infants when the likelihood of the child ever being confirmed or receiving first Eucharist was minimal. Indeed, the pastoral situation of the European Church demanded that its baptismal policy be reevaluated.[1]

Prior to and during the Council, the question of infant baptism had not been a major issue in the American Catholic Church. The years immediately after Vatican II witnessed a slight increase in

[1] See, for example, J. C. Didier, *Faut-il baptiser les enfants?* (Paris 1967); C. Pape, "Problemática acerca del bautismo de párvulos," *Teologia y vida* 8 (1967) 291–299; B. Rey, "L'Eglise et le baptême des enfants," *Révue des Sciences Philosophiques et Théologiques* 52 (1968) 677–697; *Christsein ohne Entscheidung, oder Soll die Kirche Kinder taufen?* ed. W. Kasper (Verlag 1970); K. Aland, *Taufe und Kindertaufe* (1971); D. Grasso, *Dobiamo ancora battezare i bambini?* (Assisi 1972); R.-M. Roberge, "Un tournant dans la pastorale du baptéme," *Laval Théologique et Philosophique,* 31 (1975) 227–238 and 33 (1977) 3–22.

American Catholic concern with the question, although it by no means rivaled the discussions in France. It was not until the late sixties that American Catholic literature on the question of infant baptism even began to appear,[2] and it did not become a serious question of debate among Catholic writers in the United States until the early seventies.[3] This seems to reflect the fact that the Church in the United States did not face the same pastoral dilemma that the Church in France, for instance, faced. Indeed, the United States did not undergo the radical dechristianization that European countries underwent.[4]

This essay will examine the major arguments and thoughts on the advisability of the practice of infant baptism in the Roman Catholic Church in the United States, as expressed in the writings of American Catholics from 1965 to 1980. It will cover the fifteen year period from the end of the Second Vatican Council in 1965 to the publication of the instruction on infant baptism by the Congregation for the Doctrine of the Faith in late 1980.

It is evident from a review of American Catholic literature on infant baptism in this period that certain positions appeared repeatedly in the writings of different authors. This is not to say that individual presentations of these positions did not differ; indeed, authors tended to continually develop the arguments that had been previously presented. However, one can discern several key arguments that were basically constant throughout this period. Specifically, the important and unique contributions of the many writers involved in this debate can be reduced to four positions. Each one of these positions represents common perceptions of

[2] The earliest postconciliar American Catholic writings I could find that dealt directly with the question of infant baptism were from 1968: C. Kiesling, "Infant Baptism," *Worship* 42, 617–626; P. Sherwood, "Introduction," *Resonance*, no. 6 (1968) 5–8; "Pastoral Problem of Infant Baptism," *Resonance*, no. 6, 122–127.

[3] The sheer difference in numbers is representative of the relative seriousness of the issue: seven writings on the topic appeared in the seven years after the Council (1965–1971), whereas thirty-nine appeared in the nine subsequent years (1972–1980).

[4] Cf. R. Redmond, "Infant Baptism: History and Pastoral Problems," *Theological Studies* 30 (1969) 83.

ecclesiology, faith and baptism, while individual adherents to each position suggest various solutions and recommendations for future practice.

The first two positions which will be discussed were the two most thoroughly developed in this time period, and will be classified (borrowing the terms assigned them by Nathan Mitchell[5]) as the "mature adulthood school" and the "environmentalist school." The third position, which is less an argument for or against infant baptism than it is for rejoining the rites of initiation into one integral rite at whatever age, I shall call the "initiation unity school." The fourth position, which is the least developed since it appeared rather late in the period, recognized the importance of different initiatory practices to correspond with the different ways in which people come to Christianity. I shall refer to this fourth position as the "corresponding practice school."

The term "school" is used here not to imply a group of people involved in any formal exchange of ideas and strategy, but rather to classify various authors who shared similar viewpoints and positions. While proposing these categories, I acknowledge that there is a great amount of flexibility among individual representatives of each position. For example, some authors espoused the views of more than one school, as in the case of many from the mature adulthood and environmentalist schools who also argued for the reunification of the three now separated rites of initiation, a characteristic of the initiation unity school. Furthermore, some authors could not be considered in the "main line" of the school to which they were most closely associated. Recognizing these limitations, I propose these four categories as a summary of the most important positions developed in this period.

THE MATURE ADULTHOOD SCHOOL

The mature adulthood school[6] was present in varying degrees throughout the postconciliar years. Its foundations lay in the con-

[5] Cf. N. Mitchell, "The Once and Future Child: Towards A Theology of Childhood." *Living Light* 12 (1975) 428–430.

[6] I would list the following as representative of the mature adulthood school: Richard Guerrette, David Greye Perrey, Aidan Kavanagh, Ralph Keifer, Charles Gusmer, the recommendations of the 1973 meeting of the

cerns of the late sixties about the apparent incongruity of baptizing infants who were incapable of faith, and the proposals to
delay confirmation to a later age when those receiving the sacrament could be responsible for a commitment to a more mature
faith. In the very last months of 1980, tenets of this school drew
official criticism from the Congregation for the Doctrine of the
Faith, an action which indirectly served to acknowledge that this
had become a serious position in Catholic baptismal thought.

Essentially, the proposals of the mature adulthood school developed out of a dual concern with the quality of faith in communities and the manner of celebrating baptism. Thus, the question
which the authors were ultimately trying to answer was how to
improve the quality of faith and church life. Indiscriminate infant
baptism was criticized as a factor contributing to the existing
impoverishment of church life. Indeed, the criticisms of infant
baptism and the value placed on adult initiation by this school
were not concerned with the rituals themselves so much as with
the kind of Church that such changes in the baptismal policy
could create.

The initial impetus for this school was a view of faith and
Church which was presented in the documents of Vatican II. The
Church in the theology of Vatican II, as Richard Guerrette summarized it, is "a community of God's chosen people who, through
their faith-response to his call in Christ, are making their way as a
pilgrim people toward the kingdom."[7] Baptism in this view was
seen as a faith-commitment to Christian service (i.e., *diakonia*).
This view caused some initial concern over baptizing infants at all,
since infants could not make such a commitment,[8] but it soon
came to focus on the community into which one was baptized,
following the shift in focus from the individual to the community
in the revised rite of infant baptism of 1969. Viewed in light of the
definition of Church given above, many parish communities were
regarded as spiritually poor. Reflecting on this communal problem,

North American Academy of Liturgy, and the articles in *Resonance*, no. 6
(1968), and *Made, Not Born* (Notre Dame 1976).

[7] R. Guerrette, "Ecclesiology and Infant Baptism," *Worship* 44 (1970) 434.

[8] Cf. "Pastoral Problem of Infant Baptism," *Resonance*, no. 6 (1968) 122.

Aidan Kavanagh said that "we are, perhaps, just beginning to realize that our problem is not primarily liturgical, but social. The problem is with ourselves as a community of faith shared. Liturgical problems are mere symptoms of this more radical malaise."[9] Kavanagh's reference to "liturgical problems" also reflected a growing dissatisfaction with the existing private and often haphazard manner of celebrating the sacrament.

The apparent "shallowness" of faith in many Christians led most of the authors of this school to focus on an act of *mature* faith as the requisite for baptism. This not only ruled out infant baptism (as did any stress on the individual's prerequisite commitment to the faith), but it also emphasized that baptism implied much more than a simple verbal profession of faith. Evidence of Christian faith in one's life, arrived at through a process of conversion, was to be the hallmark of a Christian. Often, advocates of this position were working out of a frustration with what they saw to be Catholics "who had no more idea of what it means to be a Christian than the pastor's cat."[10] The perfunctory manner in which infants were baptized with little concern for their subsequent Christian formation was seen to be a major cause of this situation. The proposals to remedy the situation called for a far more discriminate practice of infant baptism (i.e., baptizing only the children of "mature, adult Christians") or a total abandonment of infant baptism in favor of baptism at the personal request of an adult. The only American Catholic author in this period who called for a total abandonment of infant baptism (writing under the name of David Greye Perrey) based his recommendation on this very reasoning.[11]

Another concern of the mature adulthood school involved the incongruity of infant baptism in the existing sociological situation. This concern had been voiced during the sixties by writers in Western European countries, with American writers reflecting it in

---

[9] A. Kavanagh, "Initiation: Baptism and Confirmation," *Worship* 46 (1972) 264.

[10] Cf. D. G. Perrey, *Baptism at 21* (New York 1973) 178–179.

[11] Cf. D. G. Perrey, and "Let's Stop Baptizing Babies," *U.S. Catholic* 37 (1972) 14–15.

the seventies. Such authors[12] felt that infant baptism was defensible when the cultural structures provided an environment for Christian development, and, conversely, indefensible when these structures no longer existed. In other words, Christianity and Western cultures had been essentially coterminous for centuries during the medieval and early modern eras in Europe, while the system of parochial schools and parish organizations provided a Catholic subculture in the United States. Such situations could be relied upon as developmental environments for those baptized in infancy. When these cultural situations began to degenerate and a plurality of values and customs abounded, this reliance was no longer feasible, thus calling infant baptism into question.

As mentioned above, only David Greye Perrey recommended the total abolition of infant baptism, while other authors of the mature adulthood school criticized particular problems in the existing practice of infant baptism. For example, following the initial emphasis on personal, mature faith after Vatican II, suggestions were made to delay confirmation to a more mature age.[13] The awareness of the adult nature of Christian faith was soon extended to baptism, resulting in the first questions about baptizing infants.[14] This discussion betrayed a problematic overemphasis on the individual being baptized, and subsequent discussions noted that the real focus is on the community into which one is baptized. This same focus was evident in the Rite of Baptism for Children. Thus, although Perrey maintained that only adults can make the response in faith demanded by God's call, the majority of the mature adulthood school respected the newly reenforced focus on community faith.

The shift in focus introduced a more fundamental concern with infant baptism, and that was indiscriminate baptism when the

[12] Cf. R. Keifer, "Christian Initiation: The State of the Question," *Worship* 47 (1974) 396–397; A. Kavanagh, "Christian Initiation in Post-Conciliar Roman Catholicism: A Brief Report," *Studia Liturgica*, 12 (1977) 110–111; "Editorial," in D. Power and L. Maldonado (eds.), *Liturgy and Human Passage, Concilium* 112 (New York 1978) vii–viii.

[13] Cf. F. J. Buckley, "What Age for Confirmation?" *Theological Studies* 27 (1966) 655–666.

[14] Cf. "Pastoral Problem of Infant Baptism," 122.

likelihood of the child's future formation in the faith was slim. Thus arose the question of the baptism of children of *"non satis credentes* parents."[15] Most authors of this school allowed for the possibility of infant baptism when there was an assurance of a future upbringing in the faith, but held that baptism should be delayed in other cases. Without such assurances of future Christian formation, the notion of God's grace and *ex opere operato* efficacy was felt to be reduced to a type of magic requiring little if anything on the part of the parents and community. While not denying the effect of divine action in baptism, such authors placed a stronger emphasis on mature, personal faith in the parents and community, and ultimately in the one being baptized.[16]

The criticism of particular problems associated with infant baptism developed into a more general view of infant baptism as benign but abnormal after the publication of the Rite of Christian Initiation of Adults in 1972. Quickly, authors of this school saw in this new rite the Church's desired norm of Christian initiation.[17] Noting the historical precedence for the conversion journey of the catechumenate resulting in full initation at the paschal vigil, this school proposed that this process must once again become normative. If this process were to be normative, then the initiates would normally be adults. The baptism of children, in which such a catechumenal process would follow the sacrament, would have to be considered "abnormal," though licit. Advocates of this position found further evidence to support it in the typographical placement of the Rite of Christian Initiation of Adults before the Rite of Baptism of Children and the Rite of Confirmation. The fact that the rite for adult initiation was the last of the three initiation rites to be published was also seen as an indication of its maturity and completeness. "This rite, emerging at the end of a long process of research, consultation and collating reactions to the previously issued rites of baptism for children and confirmation by bishops,

---

[15] Cf. Guerrette, 433–437 and P. Vanbergen, "Baptism of the Infants of *non satis credentes* Parents," *Studia Liturgica* 12 (1977) 195–200.

[16] Cf. Kavanagh, "Initiation: Baptism . . . ," 262–276.

[17] Cf. J. Gallen, "American Liturgy: A Theological Locus," *Theological Studies* 35 (1974) 307.

was thus the last and most mature outcome of the postconciliar subcommission's work."[18] The baptism of infants was further compared by Aidan Kavanagh to the low Mass — a permissible, yet unencouraged, option.[19]

⌈ The influence of the Rite of Christian Initiation of Adults cannot be overstated in discussing the mature adulthood school. Representative authors were not emphasizing the new rite simply for its ritual elements, although they certainly favored these. What they sought was the realization of the vision of the Church contained in the rite. The Church was seen as the communion of committed persons of faith. Thus, Aidan Kavanagh stated: ". . . a Christian is a person of faith in Jesus Christ dead and risen among his faithful people. This faith is no mere poetic thing but a way of living together: it is the bond which establishes that reciprocal mutuality of relationships we call communion, and it is this communion which constitutes the ecclesial presence of Jesus Christ in the world of grace, faith, hope, charity and character. This is what the eucharist celebrates, signifies and causes within the community of the faithful: it is the church. This is what initiation in the fullest sense disciplines one for: it is the church."[20]

Working, as they were, out of the rite for adult initiation, these authors assumed the corresponding view of the Church and the faith quality of its members. Such a Church of high-caliber, deeply committed persons required the "discipline" of the prerequisite catechumenate and this, in turn, implied a process adapted to adults. In other words, having assumed a vision of the Church, this school proposed as normative the initiatory policy that would produce such a Church. -Somewhat elitist

Baptism in the mature adulthood school thus meant something very different than it did in the environmentalist school. As initiation into the full sacramental life of the Church, baptism was, in a

[18] A. Kavanagh, *The Shape of Baptism: The Rite of Christian Initiation* (New York 1978) 105.
[19] Cf. A. Kavanagh, "The New Roman Rites of Adult Initiation," *Studia Liturgica* 10 (1974) 35.
[20] A. Kavanagh, "Christian Initiation of Adults: The Rites," *Worship* 48 (1974) 333.

sense, an accomplishment. Those interested in the faith would be admitted to the Church as catechumens to begin (or continue) their faith development. Only upon reaching a level of mature, adult faith, however, would these catechumenal Christians be baptized. Using the Rite of Christian Initiation of Adults as the basis for their procedure, the advocates of this position envisioned this initiation as consisting of the full initiatory rites (baptism, confirmation and Eucharist at once). Thus, although catechumens would be considered members of the Church, baptism and its admittance to the full sacramental life of the Church would signify the attainment of a certain maturity of faith as reason for full initiation.

While different reasons can be discerned for favoring this approach (e.g., frustration with baptizing the children of nonpracticing Catholics, the desire to improve the quality of faith and church life, admiration for historical precedent of adult initiation following the catechumenate), the authors of this school did not seriously differ in their arguments or proposals. All viewed the process involved in the Rite of Christian Initiation of Adults as normative, and were interested in a Church of actively committed Christians with a high level of personal faith. The extent to which infant baptism would be "tolerated" in this policy differed: David Greye Perrey called for its abolition, while the recommendations of the 1973 meeting of the North American Academy of Liturgy viewed it as derived from the adult form and proper for the children of "responsible Christian parents."[21] Either way, the emphasis on adult initiation was accompanied by a marked lack of enthusiasm for infant baptism, and Perrey's proposal could be seen as simply the logical conclusion of the school's main line of thought.

THE ENVIRONMENTALIST SCHOOL

The arguments and proposals of authors representing the environmentalist school[22] of infant baptism were very similar. The number

[21] Cf. Gallen, 307.
[22] Representatives of this school would include Christopher Kiesling, William Allen, Norbert Rigali, Charles Keating, James Challancin, Eugene Maly and Francis Buckley.

of concerns and suggested alternatives to practice was far less
than in the mature adulthood school. Essentially, the arguments of
this school were strongly ecclesiological in reaction to what was
perceived to be a theological poverty and pastoral inadequacy in
the preconciliar practice of indiscriminate and private infant baptism. It may be noted that some of the basic concerns of the
environmentalist school were the same as those of the mature
adulthood school. Other concerns differed, as did the proposals
for future practice.

Arguments in favor of infant baptism were reoriented in the
early postconciliar years. Whereas the Augustinian concept of
original sin had been the standard argument for infant baptism
before Vatican II, the arguments of the environmentalist school
became prevalent after the Council. This is certainly attributable in
part to the lack of reference to original sin and the emphasis on
the role of faith in the Constitution on the Sacred Liturgy. "The
purpose of the sacraments is to sanctify men, to build up the
Body of Christ, and, finally, to give worship to God. Because they
are signs they also instruct. They not only presuppose faith, but
by words and objects they also nourish, strengthen, and express
it."[23] The mature adulthood school interpreted this passage to
mean that baptism presupposes faith on the part of the person
being baptized. Certainly, this emphasis on faith could not be
ignored, and the intepretation of it by this school presented a real
challenge to the practice of infant baptism.

Early authors of the environmentalist school noted this problem
and said that the social dimension must be taken into account
more when discussing infant baptism. Christopher Kiesling stated:
"The problem with infant baptism, I suggest, stems from our
thinking of baptism too much in terms of the individual and his
expression of faith. . . . Although there is much talk today about
the Christian community and its necessity for the individual in the
divine plan of salvation, we have not yet gone as far as possible
in applying this talk to baptism. . . . We still think of baptism as
offered by the church for the individual to express his subjective

[23] Constitution on the Sacred Liturgy 59; ed. A. Flannery, *Vatican Council II*
(Collegeville, Minn. 1975) 20.

faith. The baptism of infants is still embarrassing, for although baptism of an infant expresses the subjective faith of the Christian community, this is no help to the infant for his salvation through *his* faith, as long as the subjective faith of the baptized person is of primary importance in baptism."[24]

Indeed, it was difficult, if not impossible, to explain original sin and the positive effects of baptism if attention were focused exclusively on the infant. Kiesling also noted that postconciliar thinking about original sin stressed its interpersonal nature. "That condition of mankind which is referred to by the term 'original sin' has been analyzed in terms of interpersonal relationships which are essential to human nature. Man is not an isolated being; he is essentially a social being. Man becomes a person through encounter with other persons."[25] The grace that is imparted in baptism is not some kind of magic metaphysical change in the infant, but the acceptance into a community of people living in reversal of the sinful orientation which constitutes original sin.

This understanding of infant baptism and the important role of the Christian community were reflected in the Rite of Baptism for Children issued in 1969. The introduction to the rite stated that the true meaning of infant baptism was fulfilled only if the child were later formed in the faith in which he or she was baptized.[26] In addition, the role of the parents in the preparation of the baptismal celebration was stressed. Parents were encouraged to contact the parish priest even before the child was born so that they might be given suitable instruction and "for planning the actual celebration to bring out its paschal character."[27] When parents were not prepared to undertake the Christian formation of their child or to profess the faith themselves, the time of baptism could be delayed beyond the normal time, which was stated to be a few weeks after birth.

Citing the Rite of Baptism for Children which recognized that children cannot have or profess personal faith, but instead are

---

[24] Kiesling, 617–619.
[25] *Ibid.*, 619.
[26] Rite of Baptism for Children 3; in *The Rites* (New York 1976) 188.
[27] *Ibid.*, no. 8, p. 190.

baptized "in the faith of the Church,"[28] advocates of the environmentalist school distinguished three dimensions of the faith involved in infant baptism: "the incipient faith of the child, the
matured faith of the parent, and the corporate faith of the community."[29] All three aspects of the faith were seen as essential to the
meaning of infant baptism. Indeed, such authors[30] justified infant
baptism on the premise of an environment of Christian faith in
which the child would be raised. Baptism thus implied a commitment by the parents and community to form the children in the
faith in which they were baptized, the goal of this formation being
ultimately the personal acceptance of the faith by those baptized
in infancy.

The term "environmentalist" should not be confused with a
mere sociological meaning. The tenets of this school were fundamentally theological, stressing the work of the Spirit in the actions
of the Christian community, the corporate nature of sin and grace,
and a "high" sense of ecclesiology in which the Church or Christian community was seen as the environment in and through
which an individual is formed in the Christian faith. Participation
and membership in this community were the means to eventually
making a mature commitment to the faith. "The community assumes the responsibility to provide both the instruction and the
environment which will make [a later act of personal faith] a real
possibility for this child."[31] Authors of this school argued that this
was not really a new aspect of baptism, but a facet of the
Church's baptismal policy that had been understressed in the
past, while the emphasis was placed on the *quam primum* aspect.[32]

As in the mature adulthood school, some authors in the environmentalist school suggested that catechesis be revised to stress

[28] *Ibid.*, nos. 1-4, pp. 188-189.
[29] Cf. J. A. Upton, "A Solution to the Infant Baptism Problem," *Living Light* 16 (1979) 487.
[30] Cf. A. Leystan, "New Rite of Infant Baptism," *The Priest* 26 (1970) 52-57; C. J. Keating, "Baptism Sets Our Boundaries," *New Catholic World*, 217 (1974) 100-104; J. Challancin, "Infant Baptism: More Difficult Requirements?" *Homiletic and Pastoral Review* 77 (1977) 61-68.
[31] F. Krause, "Infant Baptism and the Domestic Church," *The Priest* 33 (1977) 26-27.
[32] Cf. Challancin, 63.

Christian formation, development in the faith, and service (i.e., *diakonia*). Infant baptism was not seen as preventing such catechesis; those baptized in infancy could indeed be expected to pursue a catechumenal-type journey of conversion as they grew up.[33] The Directory on Children's Masses of 1973 stressed the Church's continuing responsibility to those baptized in infancy, to "make sure that they grow in communion with Christ and with the Christian community."[34] A format for such growth was perceived by many parishes in the seventies to be an adaptation of the formation process of the catechumenate for those already baptized.[35]

In addition to the emphasis on the child's future formation and the environment for such formation, some authors stressed the importance of a child born into a Christian marriage. For example, William Allen noted that in infant baptism the child is perceived as already somebody vis-à-vis the People of God. "The child is not just any creature but a *special* creature, antecedently intended by God to be within the redemptive sphere of Christ Jesus."[36] Norbert Rigali expressed this same sentiment in an ecclesiological perspective. Since the marital union of Christians is a Christian community in its relation to the universal Church, Rigali explained that a child born to such a marital union is born into the Christian community.[37] Yet, even these explanations revealed an underlying concern with the most important unit of the Christian community in infant baptism: the family. It was the parents' commitment to the faith that was seen to justify the baptism of a child, and this commitment was perceived as a sign from God. "The Church can only baptize those who are sent to her by the Spirit. If the parents are living a life marked by obedience to the Spirit of God, then the Church will unhesitatingly and joyfully embrace the child as, literally, a Godsend."[38]

---

[33] Cf. M. Hellwig, *The Meaning of the Sacraments* (Dayton, Ohio 1972) 12.

[34] Directory on Children's Masses 8; Flannery, 256.

[35] Cf. T. Randolph, "The American Catechumenate: A Preliminary Report," Bishops' Committee on the Liturgy, *Newsletter* 14 (1978) 121–122.

[36] W. F. Allen, "Baptism of Infants," *The Priest* 29 (1973) 21.

[37] Cf. N. Rigali, "New Theology and Infant Baptism," *The Priest* 30 (1974) 16.

[38] M. Searle, *Christening. The Making of Christians* (Collegeville, Minn. 1980) 49.

The arguments of the environmentalist school were applied in varying degrees. Some authors used the arguments simply as a justification of infant baptism while still regarding the practice as an exception to the rule of adult initiation.[39] Others believed that, for children of practicing Catholics, infant baptism was the more natural and effective practice. "Adherents to this position stress the principle that people learn how to think, judge and behave most effectively as Christians through regular participation in the life of the community during all the stages of development between infancy and mature adulthood. To withhold access to the church's worship from children is to deny them the most effective and most widely available means for becoming convinced adult believers."[40] Essentially, this position advocated *discriminate* infant baptism, followed by a process of faith development culminating in the person's adult commitment to the faith. One can see that many authors of both the mature adulthood and environmentalist schools were in agreement here: the basic problem was indiscriminate infant baptism. Where they differed, of course, was in the mature adulthood school's view that adult initiation was the norm, and the view of many in the environmentalist school that infant baptism was by no means "abnormal" (i.e., a deviation from the norm) in the proper circumstances.

Underlying these arguments in favor of the baptism of children of Christian parents was a view of the Church as a community of people at different levels of faith. This community provided the environment in which all members could come to a mature, adult faith. It was thus not expected that every Christian would be of a high spiritual caliber. "The church, this school contends, is more than a community of transformed adults. It is also a nurturing environment that encourages gradual growth in faith for individuals and groups of all conditions, including children."[41]

Baptism in the environmentalist school was thus not regarded as an accomplishment upon reaching adult faith (as it was in the

---

[39] Cf. J. Gallen. "The Pastoral Celebration of Initiation," *New Catholic World* 222 (1979) 150.

[40] Mitchell, 429–430.

[41] *Ibid.,* 430.

mature adulthood school), but rather as "a valid and complete sign of the *beginnings,* the initiation of a Christian life which *ultimately begins to be fulfilled* in the sacraments of Confirmation, Matrimony, and Holy Orders."[42] These authors did not feel that adult faith subsequent to a conversion experience was a prerequisite to full sacramental life in the Church, but assumed that such faith could follow admittance to the Church's sacramental life in the case of children of practicing Catholics. Thus, while some proposed enrolling infants into a catechumenate as an option for children of nonpracticing Catholics,[43] advocates of this school were predominantly in favor of initiating children into the Church's full sacramental and worship life as the most effective environment.

As mentioned above, authors of the environmentalist school were basically defending infant baptism as a normal practice. We saw that some, however, continued to view adult initiation as the norm. At the other extreme, two authors during this period also argued for essentially indiscriminate infant baptism as the Church's norm. The arguments of Paul Donlan and Rockford Peterson[44] can be seen to be quite different from the standard environmentalist school arguments. Their understanding of baptism was that it is basically the means by which to remove original sin and through which God saves individuals. Stating that the Church has always taught that "all who die in original sin will not see God after death,"[45] these authors bemoaned the fact that current practice often delayed baptism "for the sake of everyone but the infant — who has to wait to become a child of God until everyone else is accommodated: priests, parents, godparents and the 'faith community.' "[46] These authors represented the only resurgence of such baptismal mentality in the American Catholic literature of this period. They are included in the discussion of the environmentalist school only by extension of the school's principles. In

[42] R. Peterson, "Let's Baptize Babies of Non-Practicing Catholics," *U.S. Catholic* 42 (1977) 15.

[43] Cf. Gallen, "American Liturgy . . . ," 307.

[44] P. A. Donlan, "Second Thoughts on Delaying the Baptism of Infants," *The Priest* 33 (1977) 31–33; Peterson, 14–15.

[45] Donlan, 37.

[46] *Ibid.,* 38, note 5.

other words, Donlan's view that salvation is attainable only in the Church and Peterson's stress on the future formation of the child baptized in infancy are related to the arguments of this school, although their main points are presented in a radically different way and their understanding of baptism is unlike that of the other authors of this school. These two authors represent an extreme of pro-infant baptism literature in this debate, just as David Greye Perrey represents an extreme of anti-infant baptism literature.

Finally, I would note that the arguments of this school are essentially concerned with justifying infant baptism as an ecclesial act. In so doing, they suggest improvements in both the understanding of baptism and its sacramental celebration by emphasizing the role of the community, especially the parents. Faith is stressed in relation to the community of faith and the subsequent personal faith of the child.

THE INITIATION UNITY SCHOOL

As noted above, the third position or school that was operative in the postconciliar debate on infant baptism was not primarily an argument for or against the practice. It was, rather, a position which advocated the celebration of the three now separated rites of initiation (baptism, confirmation, Eucharist) in one unified rite. Many authors from both the mature adulthood and environmentalist schools also espoused the positions of this school.

The question of the proper age for confirmation seems to have been the initial impetus for this line of thought. Proposals to delay confirmation to a more mature age, as represented by Francis Buckley in the early postconciliar years,[47] quickly led to questions of the meaning of confirmation. Richard Ling, for example, observed that there had been two very different meanings of confirmation in the Church's history. Up until A.D. 1300, Ling said, confirmation was seen as a part and completion of baptism, whereas the practice since then had viewed it as a rite of its own, signifying the completion of an individual's spiritual growth.[48]

[47] Cf. Buckley, 655–666.
[48] Cf. R. Ling, "A Catechist's Vote for Infant Confirmation," *Living Light* 7 (1970) 49.

Concurrently, confirmation had become a rite of adolescence and social majority, imparting strength for the challenges of adulthood. In this light, the further delay of confirmation to a later age only reenforced this trend. Acting on these observations, Ling advanced the first proposal by an American Catholic author in this period to confirm infants.[49] It should be noted, however, that this early proposal saw such confirmation of infants as a rite separate from baptism.

The publication of the revised Rite of Confirmation in 1971 was clear evidence that the Roman Church's norm for those baptized in infancy would continue to be confirmation at later age of maturity. The Rite of Christian Initiation of Adults, however, which was published in the following year, set forth the baptism, confirmation and first Eucharist of adult initiands in the same ceremony. The introduction to the rite noted that the ancient practice of the Roman liturgy maintained that "an adult is not to be baptized unless he receives confirmation immediately afterward."[50]

The unification of the three initiatory rites in adult initiation was quickly followed by numerous theological and historical examinations of the relation of the three sacraments of initiation. Aidan Kavanagh's first contribution to the infant baptism debate suggested that "if infant baptism is proper then there seems no compelling reason why its immediate completion in confirmation should be improper."[51] After recalling Richard Ling's observation that physical age became significant for confirmation only in the Middle Ages,[52] Kavanagh went on to say that "although no person has a *ius* or right to baptism, the baptized *do* possess rights to confirmation and the eucharist."[53]

Later in the decade, Tad Guzie espoused similar sentiments in arguing that "Confirmation does not have a separate meaning from Baptism,"[54] but is simply the completion of the baptismal ac-

---

[49] *Ibid.*, 42–56.
[50] Rite of Christian Initiation of Adults 34; *The Rites*, 30.
[51] Kavanagh, "Initiation: Baptism . . . ," 274.
[52] Cf. Ling, 49.
[53] Kavanagh, "Initiation: Baptism . . . ," 274.
[54] T. Guzie, "Should We Cancel Confirmation?" *U.S. Catholic* 44 (1979) 19.

tion, and therefore has no theological reason to stand alone as a sacrament unto itself. In fact, its separation from baptism causes it to lose — not gain — theological significance. Furthermore, initiation into the Christian community loses its significance if the new initiand is not allowed to share in the Eucharist until a later time. In the same year, Julia Ann Upton noted, as one of the five main pastoral problems associated with the current understanding of infant baptism, that "a separation of the sacraments of initiation implies that there are different degrees of membership in the community."[55]

Liturgical research into the evolution of Christian initiatory practices revealed that what came to be three individual sacraments was originally celebrated in the early Church as one rite of initiation. While the revised rite of adult initiation had reunited these sacraments in one rite, it was argued that such a reunification should be effected for infant initiation, since this, too, had been the practice of the early Church. In addition, the connection that had been drawn between the separated sacraments of initiation and life-cycle events was seen as untenable in a "post-Christian" era.[56] Indeed, it was generally recognized that the popular understanding of confirmation as a rite of maturity and adulthood overshadowed the sacrament's relation to baptism. The continued separation of the sacraments of initiation was seen to reenforce this misunderstanding. The general agreement among professional liturgists to reuniting the rites of initiation can be discerned from the recommendations of the 1973 meeting of the North American Academy of Liturgy. The very first of these recommendations stated that "the rite of Christian initiation should normally consist of the unified sacramental event in which the three now separated moments (baptism, confirmation, Eucharist) are integrated. The full rite is to be used at any age when a person is initiated."[57]

After 1972, advocates of the mature adulthood school were able to note that, in addition to all its other advantages, the rite of adult initiation had realized the reunification of the three initiatory

[55] Upton, 489.

[56] Cf. "Editorial," in D. Power and L. Maldonado (eds.), *Structures of Initiation in Crisis, Concilium* 122 (New York 1979), vii–viii.

[57] Gallen, "American Liturgy . . . ," 307.

rites. Adult initiation was thus further argued to be normative since it resulted in initiation to the full life of the Church, whereas infant baptism had to be completed later in confirmation and Eucharist. Only later in the debate did authors of the environmentalist school argue that the unification of the initiatory rites did not necessarily rule out infant baptism. The practice of the Orthodox Churches provided an example of initiating children using the integrated rite of baptism, confirmation and Eucharist. A consensus then began to develop in relation to reintegrating the rites of initiation. Just as authors of the mature adulthood and environmentalist schools agreed on the fundamental problem of indiscriminate baptism, so they also came to agree on reintegrating the rites of initiation. In fact, no direct opposition to this point appeared during this period.

THE CORRESPONDING PRACTICE SCHOOL

The fourth major position in the postconciliar American Catholic debate on infant baptism appeared relatively late in this period and remains the least developed. Thus, the rather brief treatment of it in this essay in not an indication of its being unimportant, but simply a result of the fact that the theory and some initial arguments for it appear only rather late in the literature of this period. It may be presumed that this school will further develop in the coming years, especially since the practices suggested by this position do not conflict in any serious manner with the directives of the Vatican's instruction on infant baptism of late 1980.

This fourth position, which I have called the corresponding practice school, essentially holds that individuals come to Christian faith in different ways, depending on various circumstances, and that correspondingly different practices of initiation should be employed. In other words, such authors argued that the three new rites of Christian initiation *together* represent Catholic initiatory policy, and that the rite which corresponds to the initiand's circumstances is the one that is "normal" for him or her. This would take into consideration not only family circumstances (such as practicing or nonpracticing parents), but also the sociological situation: that is, if Christians were such a minority in a certain culture that the Christian upbringing of children might be very difficult, adult initiation might be the more appropriate practice in that context.

The first indication of such reasoning in American Catholic literature accompanied the speculations about the revised initiatory rites in the years immediately following the Second Vatican Council. Noting that there was a general consensus among theologians and church leaders of the relation between baptism and faith, Polycarp Sherwood went on to explain that such consensus did not imply any single practice of initiation. ". . . baptismal practice must vary both liturgically and pastorally. Liturgically, in that appropriate rites must be devised for the baptism of infants, recognizing their true condition, that the unseparated sequence, baptism-confirmation-eucharist, be preserved or restored where possible, that the catechumenate be restored; pastorally, in that flexibility of rite be allowed according to needs of persons, places, and times."[58]

Even though such a varied policy did come into effect in the following years with the publication of the revised rites of infant baptism and adult initiation, the acknowledgement of such variety of practice did not play a major part in the infant baptism debate until the late seventies. Instead, the debate was primarily concerned with justifying or advocating one of the two practices.

The first American references to the positions of the corresponding practice school after the publication of the revised rites were in relation to remarks by European authors. Pièrre-Marie Gy, for example, was quoted: ". . . if we look at the Roman ritual for baptism, it has two parts: infant baptism and adult baptism. These two sections of ritual were prepared by the same people and they build together one unity. Adult baptism, I think, should by no means be thought of as a kind of abolition of infant baptism or something that would have to take its place. . . . the importance of adult baptism in the various Western, civilized countries will depend on the present crisis of faith in our countries. If this crisis develops, probably the number of infant baptisms will not be so

---

[58] P. Sherwood, "Introduction," *Resonance*, no. 6 (1968) 5.

great as now and it would become more difficult for Christian parents to raise their children to mature Christian faith.[59] An American Episcopalian representative of this school, Daniel Stevick, observed that an exclusive focus on one type of baptismal spirituality or practice would result in a defective initiatory policy.[60]

Among American Catholic authors, it seems that the proposals to delay the baptism of children of nonpracticing parents and the concerns with baptizing infants in a sociological and cultural situation that was not conducive to their future faith development were two factors that led to a greater awareness of the different ways in which people come to the Christian faith. A statement by the American Bishops' Committee on the Liturgy in 1978, for example, noted the uniqueness of God's call and its context in a particular situation or circumstance.[61]

At the same time, it was becoming generally recognized that an exclusive use of either adult initiation or infant baptism would result in inadequacies and oversights. Aidan Kavanagh observed that the present situation of the Church required the existence of two sets of initiatory theory and practice.[62] He further remarked that "the diversity of initiatory practices in the various churches remained the rule for centuries,"[63] and that a single normative practice probably never existed. The 1979 liturgy issue of *Concilium* was more explicit in indicating suggestions for the future direction of this school. "It is highly important to look to the varied ways in which belonging to a community can be expressed, and to the meaning of rituals as practised, rather than to their theoretical meanings. . . . The question of the age at which to celebrate them, may be solved in several ways. It could be argued that not one of these ways has of necessity to be preferred to the others.

---

[59] P.-M. Gy, quoted in R. Reichert, "A Catechist's Response to the Rite of Christian Initiation for Adults," *Living Light* 14 (1977) 142; cf. also P. A. Liégé, "Le baptême des enfants dans le debat pastoral et théologique," *La Maison-Dieu*, 107 (1971) 27.

[60] Cf. D. B. Stevick, "Types of Baptismal Spirituality," *Worship* 47 (1973) 24.

[61] Bishops' Committee on the Liturgy, "Christian Commitment," *Newsletter* 14 (1978) 109.

[62] Cf. Kavanagh, "Christian Initiation in Post-Conciliar . . . ," 109.

[63] Kavanagh, *The Shape of Baptism* . . . 115–116.

In other words, different and differing pastoral approaches can be simultaneously theologically sound . . . in face of any proposal to celebrate the sacraments of initiation in any particular way, the important question is that of the meaning which such a celebration might have, given all the individual, community and social factors involved."[64]

Thus, this school would propose that no one initiatory practice is *normative*, but that different practices corresponding to the circumstances are *normal* in the respective situation. The Church's provision of rites for infant baptism, adult initiation and various other circumstances is seen as further indication that this school is essentially presenting a valid interpretation of the Church's revised baptismal policy. ". . . the fact that we now have a rite of infant baptism as well as accommodated versions of the rite for the Christian initiation of adults for use with other children does point to the inescapable fact that God works with people as they are; or, in the language of the theologians, grace builds on nature. Being baptized at six days or six weeks is not the same as being baptized at six years or sixteen years of age."[65]

What, then, does the examination of these four positions reveal about the postconciliar infant baptism debate in the American Catholic Church? Essentially, I would say, it reveals that the debate has progressed from a basically unquestioned acceptance of the practice of infant baptism, through pastoral and theological concerns about the practice, to a new and reoriented understanding of the place of infant baptism in the Church's total initiatory praxis. Major influences in the debate seem to have been Vatican documents, literature from non-American/non-Catholic sources, theological reflection (especially varying ecclesiologies and perceptions of faith), historical evidence, and pastoral experience.

Recognizing just what was influencing the thoughts and recommendations of the authors contributing to this discussion can now reveal the assumptions that were operative and which often led to disagreement with other authors. In other words, we now have

---

[64] Editorial in L. Maldonado and D. Power (eds.), *Structures of Initiation in Crisis*, *Concilium* 122 (New York 1979) viii–ix.

[65] Searle, 50.

the chronological and critical distance to see that agreement was virtually impossible between certain authors because they were operating under different meanings of baptism or faith, or were reacting to different influences. For example, the idea that adult initiation is normative developed out of a view of the Church as a community of converted, convinced believers, while those who defended infant baptism assumed that the Church is made up of convinced believers as well as those whose faith is still undeveloped. The former view would obviously hold infant baptism to be a deviation, while the latter would find infant baptism quite normal. Indeed, the question of infant baptism merely scratched the surface of far more fundamental attitudes to initiation, faith and the Church.

Eugene L. Brand

19. Baptism and Communion of Infants: A Lutheran View

The ancient tradition of infant baptism has continued in the West, but the ancient tradition of infant communion has not. Full participation in the eucharist before one has reached "the age of discretion" has been opposed on differing grounds in the Roman Communion and the Churches of the Reformation. Attempts to defend it theologically, however, have tended to be similar: an emphasis on the objectivity of sacramental grace.

That emphasis has always been inadequate; today it is largely irrelevant. If it is true that the question of today is the question of identity, and if the Christian expression of that quest has surfaced in the ecclesial question, then a defense of infant communion needs to root in baptism and the nature of the Church, the ecclesial community.

Christians have been preoccupied with "community" in a manner unprecedented in Christian experience. The ecumenical question is a community question, and so is the liturgical question. At the root of it all is the question, What is the Church? And, What is the Church? leads inevitably to the questions about the eucharist and Christian initiation which have loomed so large recently. Christians are seeking to understand their identity in terms of relationships in Christ rather than as subjects of a hierarchical or theological system. It is this quest which makes the emphasis on objective sacramental grace irrelevant and which has, in part, led to change in the Church's life.

Effective change in the Church comes in an all-pervasive manner. It doesn't come from the top down (a former fallacy), nor from the bottom up (the present "grass roots" fallacy). Effective change comes from both directions at once. It comes in response to a climate of need perceived. Its articulation may come from the top down, but that articulation requires a climate of need to make it effective.

Where they have met the needs people have about identity — and thus about community and their relationship to God — the ecumenical and liturgical movements have made a significant impact. Where they have gotten sidetracked or gone beyond where the majority of people feel their need, they have become the plaything of the *afficionados*.

Recent attention to the worship plight of children has emerged, has it not, from a new sensitivity to the communal nature of the Church, especially as it is ritualized in the eucharist? If that is so, then a theology relevant to the situation must be cast in terms of the communal nature of the Church.

People who still regard their communion as a private matter between themselves and God will continue to see the privilege on the altar as an "adult privilege." For them the sacrament tends to be related to understanding, or faith, or contrition. But where people have caught the vision of the eucharist as a corporate meal, the question must eventually arise, Why can't the children participate?

It is, of course, inappropriate to divorce the sacraments from the Church, though systematic theology often does. But the question of the participation of children in the eucharist must be answered not in terms of the theology of the sacraments (narrowly conceived), but of the theology of the Church. This essay attempts to do that in Lutheran terms which, it is hoped, have some echoes in other ecclesial communions.

BAPTISM

If infants were not baptized, their role in corporate worship would be of minimal concern. But mainstream tradition reaching back into earliest times still prevails. It is likely that infants are baptized today for the same reason the early Church began baptizing them, even though our theological defense of the practice may differ from theirs.

The usual theological defense for infant baptism could benefit from more candor, especially where biblical materials are concerned and where insights into human nature are involved. Let us be frank to admit that nowhere in the New Testament is infant baptism clearly reflected. When accounts mention the baptism of households, that probably includes children, but it is not certain. The New Testament picture of baptism assumes the sequence which always applies in a mission situation: gospel proclamation → response of faith and repentance → baptism with the laying on of hands → membership in the community of faith. The accounts in Acts indicate that the sequence was not uniform everywhere, but these elements are almost always present.

What about the Great Commission (Mt 28:18-20)? It is a very important passage: [a] it indicates that the Church of Saint Matthew's day clearly understood its baptismal practice to derive from the command of the risen Lord; [b] it indicates the universal scope of the gospel and the Church. But it can hardly be the actual words of Jesus, also for at least two reasons: [a] if the universal scope of the Church's mission had been so clear from the ascension onward, why did the Holy Spirit resort to so many signs to persuade Saint Peter that it was kosher to baptize Cornelius and company (Acts 10)? and [b] if baptism in the name of the Holy Trinity was part of Jesus' command, why do all the accounts in Acts speak of baptism in[to] the name of Jesus only? The authority of the matthean passage is not being questioned, only an oversimple basing of baptism on that passage alone. New Testament scholars these days tend to connect Christian baptism with the baptism of Jesus, seeing that as the link with John the Baptist's preparatory work and as the paradigm of Christian baptism.

The baptismal rite for infants in the *Lutheran Agenda* has a wondrous example of the kind of biblical footwork which should be avoided now. The initial address emphasizes the Great Commission and speaks about original sin (optional section), and then proceeds to this conclusion: ". . . and also hath given promise in the last chapter of Mark: He that believeth and is baptized shall be saved; Forasmuch, also, as the holy Apostles of the Lord have written: The promise is unto you and to your children (Acts 2:39), and again: Baptism doth also now save us (1 Peter 3:21): it is meet and right that, in obedience *to His command* and trusting in His promise, you should bring this child to be baptized in His name."[1] Infant baptism cannot be built directly upon dominical authority; it is a modification of baptismal practice responsibly undertaken by the Church.

The problem of infant baptism is, fundamentally, the problem of baptism and faith — of "biology" and the Spirit. *Baptisma*, the term the New Testament either invented for baptism or at least reserves for it, refers to more than a rite using water — to more than the entire ritual procedure. It refers to the whole complex meaning of becoming a Christian, a meaning which is focused in the ritual action.[2] As Neville Clark has written, the rite is like the visible top of the iceberg of *baptisma*.[3] Properly, then, baptism refers to the rite *and* the life of faith to follow. Luther certainly championed that view in teaching that the life in Christ is a daily baptism.

In baptism, a gracious God acts to make the candidate his son or daughter. If that is understood in the Johannine terms of new birth (or, birth from above), the act of grace has an analogue in biological birth. Any person — any infant — becomes God's child because of God's "parental" act. One is *born anew* of water and the Holy Spirit. Upon this basis the case for infant baptism often rests: it must be valid because it is God's act.

True enough. But there's more to sonship than biology. If a dispute arose over custody of a ten-year old adopted at infancy, the relationship with the biological father would not be regarded as significant as the interpersonal relationship with the adoptive father. Translated into theological terms: baptism is not just the establishing of a relationship in a momentary ritual act; baptism, if it is to function as God intends, must result in a relationship of faith. The two cannot be separated except for purposes of discussion. Both are implied in the claims made for baptism.

[1] *Lutheran Agenda* (St Louis n.d.) 2. Italics added.

[2] Cf. Kittel, *Theological Dictionary of the New Testament* 1, 545.

[3] Neville Clark, "Baptism and Redemption," *Crisis for Baptism* (London 1965).

It is because of the relationship of the rite of baptism and the baptismal life of faith that adults have not been baptized without prior evidence of faith. Indeed, it was to begin the shaping and molding of such a life that the catechumenate was developed. On similar grounds, such a catechumenate is being restored to the disciplines of baptism — not primarily to make theologians out of neophytes, but to make them truly baptismal people.

The first clear reference to infant baptism is in Irenaeus, writing at the end of the second century.[4] Half a century later, in his commentary on Romans, Origen could write, "The church received a tradition from the apostles to administer baptism, even to infants." Infant baptism, in some areas at least, doubtless antedates the references in Irenaeus. While theologians may have dealt with infant baptism in documents lost to us, it is important to remember that the early theologizing still extant supports a practice already in existence. It is interpretation after the fact; it is not done to introduce a new practice.

The supporting argument which held center stage for centuries bore the stamp of Saint Augustine and the Pelagian controversy: infants are born in sin; no such person can enter the kingdom of heaven; baptism "obliterates original sin in infants,"[5] therefore, infant baptism is not only desirable, it is obligatory.[6] In its condemnation of Pelagius the Synod of Carthage (418) made the Augustinian view official.

So long as the argument from original sin has a biblical view thereof, and so long as it is not thought that God must damn any unbaptized infant, the argument still stands today in support of the grace/"biology" side of the equation, for God "obliterates" original sin by making the infant a member of his kingdom. Forgiveness of sin is reconciliation with God.

This stress on the objectivity of grace in the sacrament, however, did lead the Church to neglect the life-of-faith side of things. The Lutheran fathers were conscious of this and it led them to speak of infant faith. Gerhard: "Baptism is the washing of regeneration; but regeneration cannot take place without

---

[4] *Adv. Haer.* II.22.4.
[5] *Pecc. orig.* 19.21.
[6] Cf. J. Pelikan, *The Christian Tradition* 1 (Chicago 1971) 317-318.

faith. . . . We are not solicitous about the mode of this faith, but we simply acquiesce in the fact that infants believe."[7] Here, too, an existing tradition which it was unthinkable to repudiate was being defended — now, however, in the arena of faith rather than grace. That the theologians were reaching is all but admitted by Gerhard and is further indicated by Chemnitz: "When we say that infants believe or have faith, it must not be imagined that infants understand or perceive the movements of faith; but the error of those is rejected who imagine that baptized infants please God and are saved, without any action, within them, of the Holy Spirit . . . since . . . it is certain that the Holy Spirit is efficacious within them, and that, too, in such a way that they can receive the kingdom of heaven. . . . Although we neither understand nor can explain in words of what nature is that action or operation of the Holy Spirit in infants who are baptized, nevertheless from the Word of God it is certain that this occurs. This action or operation of the Holy Spirit in infants *we call faith, and say that infants believe.*"[8]

The intention of the Lutheran fathers to balance "biology" with the Holy Spirit is crucial and laudable. Their manner of argument may be more problematical today. While it is true that faith is worked by the Holy Spirit, is it really satisfactory to speak of the presence of faith in someone who can make no conscious response? Would it not be better to say that infants are baptized *unto* faith, i.e., we risk baptizing them because we trust that given the environment of a Christian home and the fellowship of the Church, faith will grow and mature? And would that not, in turn, imply a selective practice of infant baptism? To guard against the same overemphasis on objective sacramental grace which bothered Chemnitz, and to give proper emphasis to faith, should one not speak only of baptizing infants born into viable Christian families?

This distinction is worth making. In its polemics against Abrahamic guarantees, the New Testament makes it clear that one is not a member of the fellowship by natural birth, but only by water and the Spirit. It is, therefore, unnatural to keep the children even partially outside the larger Christian family in which

[7] Cited from Schmidt, *The Doctrinal Theology of the Evangelical Lutheran Church* (Minneapolis 1961) 549.

[8] *Ibid.*, 550.

the parents share. They should be sealed by the same Holy Spirit and thus marked for the kingdom as were their parents. To do this wholesale, however, without any assurance of the growth of faith in response to exposure to the word in its myriad forms, is just as suspect as to herd adults together and baptize them indiscriminately with a fire hose. It reflects a mechanistic concept of grace which is unacceptable. One is tempted to draw the analogy of the indiscriminate fathering of children.

The life of faith is life in the Spirit. Thus, we are baptized in water and the Holy Spirit. This latter emphasis is marked both in the New Testament and in early baptismal rites by chrismation with the laying on of hands. These actions and the water bath comprise the focal points of the rites of initiation into kingdom fellowship.

With the increase of infant baptisms a separation grew, leading to two rites separated in time: baptism with its water bath and confirmation with its laying on of hands. By the early twelfth century, Hugo of Saint Victor is speaking of confirmation as a sacrament. In 1439 it was declared a sacrament by the Council of Florence. The Council of Trent fixed it doctrinally in the sacramental system.

Luther's problems with confirmation as a sacrament are expressed in the *Babylonian Captivity:* there is no convincing scriptural warrant. But one cannot escape the impression that, for Luther, confirmation conflicts improperly with baptism. From his day on, Lutheran theology has testified to baptism as full initiation into the fellowship of believers, and as granting the Holy Spirit. Theologically, Lutherans affirm the position of the early Church.

But Lutheran liturgical conservatism and the Lutheran pedagogical ethos got in the way. Confirmation was reintroduced, though not as a sacrament. One can affirm that all baptized persons live in the Holy Spirit. But if there is a later rite which children consciously experience which includes the dramatic gesture of the laying on of hands and the prayer for the Spirit's gifts — that will create an experiential conflict with the theological assertion. Further, one can say that all baptized persons are full members of the Church. But if children are not allowed to participate in the eucharist until after confirmation, then confirmation — again experiontially — becomes the gateway to *real* Church membership. Luther's fears were not groundless. Not only has confirmation achieved sacramental status among Lutherans (it feels like one even while we say it isn't), it has tended to overshadow baptism in importance. We have suffered from a proper theology which has been contradicted by faulty practice.

The provisional rite for baptism prepared by the Inter-Lutheran Commission on Worship is the proper ritual consequence of an earlier decision taken in many Lutheran circles to divorce first communion from confirmation.[9] It restores to baptism the laying on of hands and the prayer for the Spirit's gifts, and it removes any subsequent rite of passage blocking the path to the altar. A complementary rite for the Affirmation of the Baptismal Covenant is proposed for use at the end of more intensive catechetical work *and* other times in one's life when it is appropriate publicly to affirm one's baptismal status.[10] Occurring after one is already communing, and not being a once-for-all rite removes the liturgy for Affirmation — or should do — from the sacramental rites of passage. Now we must be on guard lest first communion itself take on the trappings of a rite of passage.

Loading first communion with paraliturgical baggage formerly associated with confirmation is a real hazard because of the extent to which confirmation is engraved in Lutheran folk-consciousness. It may take decades of patient instruction and practice before Lutherans really feel at home with baptism as *the* rite of initiation — before they are comfortable with a practice which conforms to their theology. The thing that will help, however, is the heightened consciousness of how the eucharist and Christian community are intertwined. This conspires to raise the question of earlier communion. And that, in turn, reinforces the concept reflected in the provisional rites of initiation.

The same sort of instinct which did not allow children born into the community to remain unbaptized is now raising the question: If children are full members of the household of God by virtue of baptism, why can they not join us in the family meal given for

[9] Contemporary Worship 7: *Holy Baptism* (1974).
[10] Contemporary Worship 8 (1975).

our spiritual nourishment and for the intensification of our fellow-ship? In this question can be seen the kind of convergence of theological understanding and cultural need mentioned earlier. Where these sensitivities have not developed, not only does the question not arise; people strongly resist the changes implied.

FIRST COMMUNION

The classical pattern of initiation in the early Church culminated in first communion. The neophyte was baptized in semi-seclusion, then brought before the bishop for the laying on of hands, then admitted into the circle around the altar. With slight modifications, Lutheran liturgies follow the same sequence for adult candidates. But what about infants and young children?

The evidence is clear that until the eleventh century baptism was not usually administered without first communion following. The documentation has been collected by J.D.C. Fischer in his book for the Alcuin Club.[11] Infants received the species at baptism indicating that the pattern developed with adults was applied to them as well. The practice was defended on the same Augustinian base which undergirded infant baptism: because of sin, no one should be allowed to die without communion. Two things should be noted especially: [a] even in the West the communion of infants was considered normal and natural for ten centuries; [b] the theological rationale was the same for *both* sacraments: If infant baptism (or, *because* infant baptism), then infant communion.

During the eleventh century, however, the accelerating victory of sacramental realism over Augustinian symbolism caused the Church to develop questions about infant communion. The concern was not with worthy participation; the questions related to the increasing scrupulosity regarding the consecrated bread and wine. Infants often were not completely successful in swallowing the host, and that raised questions of mind-blowing proportions for sacramental literalists.

The doctrine of concomitance, however, offered a temporary reprieve, permitting the tradition of infant communion to be defended and continued. Twelfth century theologians continued to

[11] *Christian Initiation: Baptism in the Medieval West* (London: 1965).

point out that one needed both baptism and viaticum for heaven. If, therefore, infants cannot swallow the host, give them the wine only. They still receive the whole Christ. Rubrics directed the use of a leaf or the priest's finger to administer the wine, pointing out the natural ability of infants to suck. Small children received both species by intinction.

But the doctrine of concomitance also buttressed the practice which finally spelled the end to infant communion. Scrupulosity over the consecrated elements led in the thirteenth century to withholding the cup from the laity — a practice which soon pervaded the West. With it went infant communion since, by this time, it was wedded by the same concomitance to the chalice. There is an interesting footnote which indicates the tenacity of infant communion: after they were denied the consecrated wine, infants in some places were given ablution wine from the chalice.[12] It is also worthy of note that the Council of Trent still found it necessary explicitly to deny that infant communion is necessary for salvation, but also to dispute those who contend that infant communion is useless and not efficacious.[13]

In 1215, the Fourth Lateran Council made its landmark decision that confession must precede communion, and that first confession should occur at the age of discretion. First communion, then, was associated with confession rather than with baptism. The tridentine *Rituale Romanum* of Paul V forbade the communion of children. As could be expected, the "age of discretion" has been variously interpreted in the Roman Communion.

At the time of the Reformation, then, infant baptism as soon as possible after birth was the rule. At about age seven children went to confession for the first time and made their first communion. Infant communion and the communion of young children were not, therefore, discussed in Reformation sacramental polemics; they had already disappeared.

What the Reformation did latch on to, however, was the medieval connection between confession and communion. Later, when confirmation had become part of the normal Lutheran pattern, it

[12] *Die Religion in Geschichte und Gegenwart* [R.S.S.] 3 (Tübingen 3/1958) 1284.
[13] *Sess.* 21, 4.

was understood, at least in part, as preparation for first communion: "The theological significance of confirmation, too, was still rather obscure in the 17th century. . . . Bucer had first introduced it in Hesse in 1539. From there it spread in all directions and found its way into various church constitutions, though there was no unanimity as to its essence and form. Yet it shared one basic purpose in large measure: that of catechetical examination previous to the first communion.[14] Via confirmation, Lutherans perpetuated the medieval ethos regarding first communion. Before receiving it, one must "understand it" and be able to confess one's sin — i.e., to be able to examine one's self. From that day to yesterday, 1 Corinthians 11:28-29 has been intoned in support of the confirmation-first communion link: "Let a man examine himself, and so eat of the bread and drink of the cup. For anyone who eats and drinks without discerning the body eats and drinks judgment upon himself." The two crucial things are penitential self-examination and the "ability" to discern the body, by which Lutherans have meant the ability to understand the real presence — a perfect continuation of medieval insistence that confession precede first communion and that the age of discretion be interpreted to mean the ability to distinguish between divine and normal food! Still something cannot be condemned just because it perpetuates a medieval practice. Comments are thus necessary on what has changed since the tenth century.

The link between baptism and first communion for those baptized in infancy has been broken both by the fragmentation of initiation rites and by the new linking of first communion with confession. Access to the altar, therefore, is not based upon the privilege of the baptized to participate fully in the family rites; it is now based upon the capability of the baptized — after instruction — to examine themselves and to "understand" the theology of the eucharist, at least in its essentials.

Of course, it is possible to say that the link between baptism and first communion has not been broken, that it has only been lengthened to include instruction and confession which always

[14] Friedrich Kalb, *Theology of Worship in 17th Century Lutheranism* (St Louis 1965) 133.

were part of initiation and which have been delayed only because of the altered situation posed by infant baptism.

At its best, Lutheran theology would understand catechetical instruction, confirmation and penitential self-examination all as part of *baptisma,* and therefore as ways of strengthening the link between baptism and first communion. Purely on the theological plane, that is hard to dispute. But experience does not seem to preserve that theological unity. Actual experience has made confirmation overshadow baptism. Actual experience, where the emphasis is upon theological understanding and self-examination, has subtly perverted the concept of "worthy participation" in the eucharist into something the individual achieves. It is on the level of experience that recent practice must be questioned.

A second thing has also changed. Since the medieval period, the theology which undergirds infant baptism is no longer *also* applied to the Lord's Supper. And that has led Lutherans to curious situations. In his *Kinderkommunion,* the R. G. G. writer notes that the communion of infants had not been the problem in the Reformation, but then proceeds to show that had it come up, Lutherans would have had problems with it theologically: "It is, of course, true that the faith of the recipient does not constitute the Lord's Supper; but Christ can only be received in faith. According to the New Testament this faith is the 'acceptance of the kerygma about Christ' (Rom 10:14-17). And that assumes a thorough instruction which is not possible with children in their minority [*unmündigen Kinder*]. The same thing goes for early communion."[15]

In the light of earlier comments on baptism and faith, could not this same argument be used against infant baptism? If the Lutheran fathers got around it in baptism by virtually equating faith with the gift of the Holy Spirit, and if that, then, enabled them to maintain the point: Christ can only be received in faith, could not the same theological gymnastics be applied to holy communion for newly baptized infants? Does the fact that this was not done indicate that theologically they were really supporting practices already in effect? If so, does that not suggest — especially in the light of ten centuries of a different practice in the West and

[15] R.G.G. 3, 1285. Writer's translation.

twenty centuries in the East — that ultimately the problem actually is not theological?

Since the Church wishes to baptize infants born into its midst, it has shown how grace and faith can responsibly be related to support that practice. If the Church wishes to practice the communion of newly baptized infants, grace and faith can responsibly be related in support of that. It is not that theology can be used to support any practice; e.g., grace and faith cannot responsibly be related to support the indiscriminate baptism of all infants.

Others have noted this discrepancy between acceptance of infant baptism and denial of infant communion. In an analytical postscript to his study of baptism up to the Reformation, the Munich church historian Georg Kretschmar asks rhetorically whether the separation of baptism and first communion did not promote the curious idea that one must judge differently the relationship between faith and sacramental reception in baptism and the eucharist? And has not that led to regarding baptized young Christians *not* as full participants in the fellowship of believers (*Kirchengemeinschaft*)? In other words, how can one be said to be fully a member of the Church, yet have the altar be off limits?[16]

But what about 1 Corinthians 11:28-29? Recent commentaries lead one to conclude that "discernment of the body" does not mean the ability to articulate the doctrine of the real presence. It means rather to see how the reception in common of the *sacramental* body of Christ relates to one's behavior within the *ecclesial* body of Christ. You cannot claim to care about the one while disregarding the other. To do so, as some of the Corinthian Christians apparently were, is to eat and drink judgment upon yourself and, not only that, but also to undermine the very health of people in the ecclesial body — "that is why many of you are weak and ill, and some have died" (1 Cor 11:30).

Self-examination, in the Corinthian context, then, meant to see to it that one's relationships with other members of the congregation did not break the fellowship of love in Christ's body which we both are and which we receive. It is the Corinthian correspon-

---

[16] Georg Kretschmar, "Die Geschichte des Taufgottesdienstes in der alten Kirche," *Leiturgia* 5 (Kassel 1970) 342.

dence which underlines so dramatically the corporate nature of the eucharist and its implications for the common life.

If the passage is applied to children, therefore, it must mean their ability to understand themselves as interrelated with a community — a relationship like their family. That perception comes — at least in its most basic form — early in childhood. But the question should at least be entertained: Should one apply universally a passage dealing with an essentially adult situation? Is that responsible hermeneutically? One could further ask why this passage did not prevent infant communion for ten centuries, and why it still doesn't in the East. One could even wonder whether the passage was "co-opted" because it fit the situation of the Church on the eve of the Reformation. If there is any truth to that, one could wonder whether our own climate of need suggests a new approach.

Does not all this lead to the conclusion that there is no *theological* reason for withholding the species of the eucharist from any baptized person in good standing, including infants, assuming, of course, that infants are not indiscriminately baptized? To base infant communion on a concept of objective sacramental grace alone easily leads to a mechanistic, grace-factory view of the eucharist; growth in the environment of faith must also be given full significance.

It is one thing to commune an infant/young child who regularly comes with its parents to the altar and who, thus, more and more consciously will "understand" the connections between the gospel, the bread and wine, the biological family relationship and the relationship within the ecclesial family under the Spirit. Teaching about the eucharist would, from the beginning, have an experiential referent. It is quite another thing to baptize and give communion indiscriminately to infants unattached to the local congregation, merely in the name of objective grace. While such sacraments are doubtless valid, that's not the point. The administration of them has put into question the quality of life in the Spirit; it has reduced the Church to mere "biological" and juridical relationships.

Having concluded that no theological barrier exists to infant communion, the pastoral question of strategy remains. So long as no rite of passage separates first communion from baptism, defense of deferring full eucharistic participation until there is a dawning perception of life in community is possible. Or there is a mediating compromise: administering the species to newly baptized infants in the baptismal eucharist, thus clearly demonstrating their right of access to the altar and completing the initiation rites in one motion, but then delaying the next communion for a few (very few!) years.

CONCLUSION

Infant baptism places a heavy educational and formational obligation both on the family and the parish. There is a growing awareness that this effort must be more than instructional; it must not falter at spiritual formation and sensitizing to human need. It must relate to the contexts of worship and life "in the world." On the other hand, it must not hesitate to instruct. Biblical literacy, for example, is part of Christian maturity.

In the final analysis, however, it all hinges on the Church, the Church which is corporate and familial, where the personal is valued, but where there is no place for the individualist. This ecclesial family springs from the womb of the font, out of the waters of baptism, by the action of the Holy Spirit. To understand it, our best analogue is the vitally functioning family. The family analogue has two great advantages for children: [a] in most cases it relates directly to their ongoing experience, [b] it has infinite degrees of maturity and perception.

We must see baptism as "biologically" as we see natural birth. And we must see the resultant relationships eucharistically in the context of love and obedience and service. The communion of infants rests on such foundations.

Mark Searle

20. Infant Baptism Reconsidered

"What the value of baptizing infants might be is an extremely
obscure question. But one must believe there is some value in it"
(St Augustine. *De quantitate animae*, XXXVI, 80).

During the past twenty or thirty years sacramental theology has
undergone an enormous transformation. Undoubtedly the leading
indicator if not the cause of this transformation is the abandonment of the questions and vocabulary of Scholasticism in favor of
more existentialist and personalist approaches to understanding
what sacraments are and how they function in the Christian life.
What began as a recovery of the ecclesial dimension of the sacraments quickly led to further shifts: from speaking of sacraments as
"means of grace" to speaking of them as encounters with Christ
himself; from thinking of them primarily as acts of God to thinking of them mainly as celebrations of the faith community; from
seeing sacraments as momentary incursions from another world to
seeing them as manifestations of the graced character of all human
life; from interpreting them as remedies for sin and weakness to
seeing them as promoting growth in Christ.

Such shifts have been prompted in part by theological developments but also by the influence, both on theology and pastoral
practice, of a growing awareness of the radically altered sociocul-
tural circumstances in which the Christian life is lived in the second half of the twentieth century. Yet while the practice of infant
baptism has been particularly challenged in this "post-Christian"
era, it has remained strangely neglected in the work of theological
reconstruction. Instead, theological discussion of infant baptism re-

mains largely dominated by the inherited methodologies of historical study and deductive arguments from doctrinal first principles.

Yet infant initiation is deserving of more imaginative reconsideration. It remains an issue close to the experience of every believing family. But even from the theologian's perspective, if most of
the issues of current theological interest come together in the
sacraments,[1] most sacramental questions come together in a particularly concentrated way in the issue of the sacramental initiation
of infants. Here converge such problems as how to speak of God,
the relationship between the order of grace and the order of history, the relationship between grace and freedom, the nature and
role of the Church as mediating the mystery of salvation, and the
relationship between the language of faith and the basic experiences of human life. Conversely, of course, one's personal and
denominational position on such issues as these will invariably
color one's understanding of what, if anything, is transpiring
when an infant is baptized.

The focus of this essay, however, will be considerably more
modest. Less than a theology of infant initiation, this will be more
of a prolegomenon for such a theology, looking at how the question of infant baptism has been raised in the past, how it poses itself today, and how it might be approached differently in order to
break out of the stalemate to which traditional arguments have led.

NOTES FOR A HISTORY OF THE QUESTION

History shows for the most part that where the sacraments are
concerned, practice is invariably a step or two ahead of theology.
With the exception of the Reformation, the practice of baptism
gives rise to theological reflection rather than being shaped by a
priori theological principles. Thus it is necessary to distinguish between the practice of infant baptism and theological attempts
either to justify it, to undermine it, or to influence the shape of its
practice. Similarly there are two distinct if related histories: the
history of the practice of infant baptism and the history of its theology. Here it is clearly impossible to give an adequate account of

---

[1] Stephen W. Sykes, "The Sacraments," in *Christian Theology*, eds. Peter C.
Hodgson and Robert H. King, rev. ed. (Philadelphia 1985) 274–301.

either history, so we shall be content to make some observations on each with a view to demonstrating the need for a fresh look at the whole matter.

On the History of Baptism. In most accounts of the history of infant initiation, too little consideration has been given to the relationship between infant baptism and clinical or deathbed baptism. The question of whether the early Church baptized has been debated to a standstill.[2] The evidence is insufficient to draw any firm conclusions either way, though in the final analysis what we know about familial unity and patriarchal authority in the ancient world makes it less than likely that the children of Christian parents would have been left to make a decision for themselves. The apparently fairly widespread practice of deferring baptism until rather late in life would seem to be a secondary development of the fourth century associated with the discipline of once-in-a-lifetime penance. What we do know with complete certitude, however, is that infants who were baptized (and the evidence becomes universal after the year 200) were initiated along with adult converts in the paschal sacraments of water, chrism, and altar.

The fact that infants and young children were wholly initiated needs to be underlined, because the subsequent breakup of Christian initiation into distinct celebrations of infant baptism, delayed confirmation, and separate "first Communion" was never something deliberately chosen or decided by the Church. It just happened. It happened despite the best efforts of Church authorities from late antiquity to the High Middle Ages to prevent it happening and to mitigate its effects. The ideal of unified sacramental initiation for infants and young children remains in place in the East and in some parts of Hispanic Catholicism. In most of the West,

[2] Among a very extensive literature, the following must be accounted the most significant works: Oscar Cullmann, *Baptism in the New Testament* (London 1950); Karl Barth, *The Teaching of the Church Concerning Baptism* (London 1948); Karl Barth, *Church Dogmatics*, IV:4 (Edinburgh 1969); Markus Barth, *Die Taufe ein Sakrament?* (Zollikon-Zurich 1951); Kurt Aland, *Did the Early Church Baptize Infants?* (Philadelphia 1960); Joachim Jeremias, *Infant Baptism in the First Four Centuries* (Philadelphia 1960). More recently see Paul Jewett, *Infant Baptism and the Covenant of Grace* (Grand Rapids 1978) and Geoffrey W. Bromiley, *Children of Promise* (Grand Rapids 1979).

however, the postponement of episcopal confirmation lasted so long, despite efforts to avoid it, that it came to be accepted first as inevitable and eventually as desirable. Apparently resigning themselves to the disintegration of the rites of initiation, the Churches of the West came increasingly to endorse the separation of confirmation and first Communion from baptism, though it only became a universal policy after the Council of Trent.[3]

The root causes of this drift towards separation are to be found as far back as the third century in provisions made for the baptizing of catechumens in danger of death. The fourth-century Church historian Eusebius cites the comments of Pope Cornelius († 253) on the sad history of the heretic Novatian. The pope ascribed Novatian's defection from the unity of the Church of Rome to the fact that he had been baptized in an emergency when he had fallen seriously ill and was thought to be near death. When subsequently he recovered, he allegedly never went to the bishop for the completion of the rites of initiation: "Without receiving these, how could he receive the Holy Spirit?"[4]

Whatever the facts of Novatian's case, the practice of baptizing catechumens thought to be on the point of death and the subsequent completion of their initiation by the bishop if they recovered are clearly attested in the following period. Thus the Council of Elvira, Spain, in 305 ordained as follows:

"Canon 38: *That in cases of necessity even laypersons* [fideles] *may baptize.* It was agreed that a faithful man who has held fast to his baptism and is not bigamous may baptize a sick catechumen at sea, or wherever there is no church at hand, provided that if he survives he shall bring him to a bishop so that he may be confirmed [perfici] through the laying-on of a hand."[5]

Presumably the same held true for infants who were born sickly and considered unlikely to survive. Normally children would be

[3] J. D. C. Fisher, *Christian Initiation. Baptism in the Medieval West. A Study in the Disintegration of the Primitive Rite of Initiation*, Alcuin Club, n. 47 (London 1965). See *Catechism of the Council of Trent*, II, iii, 17 (Dublin 1829) 183.

[4] Eusebius, *The History of the Church*, VI, 43:20, trans. G. A. Williamson (Minneapolis 1975) 283.

[5] E. C. Whitaker, *Documents of the Baptismal Liturgy*, Alcuin Club, n. 42 (London 1970) 222–223.

kept for baptism at Easter, to be initiated along with the rest of the catechumens, but if their life was in danger they would, like any other catechumen in danger of death, be baptized without delay and would have their initiation completed by the bishop if and when they recovered.

But what had at first been the exceptional case eventually became commonplace as an increasing percentage of the candidates for baptism came in fact to be children in a period where infancy was itself so precarious a condition that to be newborn was ipso facto to be in a life-threatening situation. Even without the additional encouragement of the Augustinian doctrine of the damnation of unbaptized infants, it is hard to imagine that emergency baptisms would not have been more common in the fifth and sixth centuries simply because baptismal candidates were predominantly children and because of the high incidence of infant mortality. Surviving documentary evidence would seem to support this hypothesis. Although the eighth-century supplement to the *Hadrianum* contained a form of catechumenate and initiation liturgy suitably abbreviated for infants, it is significant that this did not apparently catch on. Instead, infant baptism was increasingly celebrated using the much older Gelasian *Order for the Making of a Catechumen or for Baptizing*. But this rite was nothing other than a rite for baptizing the dying! So common did its use become in the Middle Ages that it eventually came to serve as the basis for the rite of infant baptism in the Roman Ritual of 1614.[6]

Thus it seems obvious that *quamprimum* infant baptism was simply a form of clinical baptism. Much later on, the Council of Florence implicitly admitted as much in its decree of 1442:

"Concerning children: because of the danger of death, which occurs frequently enough, since nothing else can be done for them except to baptize them, whereby they are snatched from the power of the devil and adopted as children of God, the Council admonishes that holy baptism is not to be delayed for 40 or 80 days or for some other period of time, as some are wont to do,

[6] Cfr. M. Righetti, *Storia liturgica*, IV (Milan 1953) 82–83; P. de Puniet, *Le sacramentaire romain de Gellone*. Bibliotheca Ephemerides Liturgicae, IV (Rome 1938) 90–91.

but they should be baptized as soon as conveniently possible [quamprimum commode fieri potest]. Therefore, in imminent danger of death, let them be baptized in the form of the Church even by a layman or woman, if no priest is at hand, quickly and without delay."[7]

What came to differentiate the situation of infants from that of unbaptized adults who fell gravely ill was that in the course of time, beginning in the late thirteenth century, the subsequent completion of their initiation came deliberately to be postponed until they had reached the "age of discretion," if indeed they lived that long.[8] Slowly and imperceptibly the Church had completed a volte-face, gradually abandoning its insistence that surviving children be brought to the bishop as soon as possible after baptism and suggesting instead that confirmation be "prudently" delayed until the children were old enough to need the sacrament.

The facts of the story are well enough known. What is not always recognized is that with this unwitting change of policy, the Western Church gave up trying to initiate infants. Once infant baptism is recognized as a form of clinical baptism — an emergency measure — it has to be acknowledged that, with the move to defer confirmation and first Communion, Christian initiation was in fact deferred until the child was old enough to be catechized. Instead of initiating infants, as had been the universal policy of the first millennium or more, the Church now put them on hold — baptizing them as a precautionary measure — until they came of age. The Catechism of the Council of Trent endorsed this deferred initiation for the Roman Church when it described the administration of confirmation to children under seven as "inexpedient" and went on to say: "Wherefore, if not to be postponed to the age of twelve, it is most proper to defer this sacrament at least to that of seven."[9]

What made this change of direction thinkable, of course, was the new theology of confirmation as a distinct sacrament, which

[7] DS 1349.

[8] P.-M. Gy, "Quamprimum. Note sur le baptême des enfants," La Maison Dieu 32 (1952) 124–129.

[9] See note 3 above.

the early medieval theologians had elaborated in an effort to persuade parents to bring their children to the bishop for the completion of their initiation. As it happens, the rationale for receiving the sacrament eventually became a rationale for delaying it until the age of seven, the age at which for many purposes a child ceased to be regarded as a child and was numbered among the company of adults.[10] The net result is that, beginning in the late thirteenth century and universally from the sixteenth, the Roman Catholic Church has really only initiated "adults," even though it continued to baptize the newborn as a precautionary measure within a few hours or days of birth. There is an irony here not often remarked upon: Roman Catholics and Anabaptists were actually closer together in their positions on infant baptism than they thought. Recognizing the precautionary and emergency character of infant baptism in the Roman Church does go a long way towards accounting for the largely remedial attitude towards baptism in post-Tridentine theology, as well as for the emphasis on catechesis as a necessary precondition for being confirmed and for making one's first confession and first Communion.

Since it is only in the twentieth century that the full history of the practice of initiation in the West has become available, such developments as we have described occurred without much sense of anyone introducing radical change. With that history now available, however, the Church is for the first time in a position to ask the question of whether the "accidental" reversal of her original policy with regard to the initiation of children is something she still wants to endorse. But since there is no virtue in returning to

[10] Interest in the history of childhood is relatively recent, largely inaugurated by Philippe Ariès' benchmark study, *Centuries of Childhood* (New York 1962). For a reassessment of Ariès' claims, see *The History of Childhood*, Lloyd de Mausse, ed. (New York 1974) and David Hunt, *Parents and Children in History. The Psychology of Family Life in Early Modern France* (New York 1970). It is now clear that the "age of reason" or "age of discretion," typically identified in Roman Catholic sources as around the age of seven to ten years, is less a determinate stage of psychological maturity than a juridical-social convention. Thus under Anglo-Saxon law a child who reached the age of seven could no longer be sold into slavery, while under Roman Law a child of that age became liable for criminal acts. In general it was the age at about which children began to mix with adults in medieval life and work.

an earlier practice simply because it was earlier, such a decision will require serious reflection on the place of the child in the economy of grace.

On the History of Baptismal Theology. Here again we shall confine ourselves to some remarks about the way the question of infant baptism has been posed at certain key moments in its history, with a particular eye to seeing whether the child as such was ever taken into account.

THE NEW TESTAMENT AND THE SUBAPOSTOLIC CHURCH. There is little or no evidence that infant baptism was ever posed as a question, unless Luke 18:15-17 be read that way.[11] Though some, such as Kurt Aland,[12] would take the silence of the first two centuries as indicating that the Church did not baptize infants, it is more likely, for the reason mentioned above, that the inclusion of infants and small children among the ranks of the baptizands was simply taken for granted. Moreover it should also be noted that children are among the beneficiaries of Jesus' miraculous cures in the Gospels, and that when they are mentioned at all in the teaching of Jesus it is to hold them up as paradigms of those who receive or are received into the Kingdom of God (see Mark 10:14-15; Luke 9:47-48; 18:15-17; Matt 18:1-5; 19:13-15). Thus while there is nothing directly excluding the baptism of children, children are put in a very positive light where the appropriation of salvation is concerned, a fact all the more remarkable in view of the predominantly negative view of children which subsequently came to prevail in the West. ~ *This needs to be more attended to. Anyone on later trad.*

TERTULLIAN (NORTH AFRICA, C. 150–220). Tertullian is the first writer known to have challenged the practice of baptizing infants and children.[13] It is notable that he neither challenges the validity of such baptisms nor questions the authenticity of the practice as an apostolic tradition. Instead he is content merely to argue that it

---

[11] So Cullmann, *Baptism in the New Testament* 72–78 and Joachim Jeremias, *Infant Baptism* 48–55. For an opposing viewpoint see G. R. Beasley-Murray, *Baptism in the New Testament* (Grand Rapids 1973) 320–329.

[12] Kurt Aland, *Did the Early Church Baptize Infants?*

[13] *de baptismo*, 18. (ET: *Tertullian's Homily on Baptism*, trans. E. Evans [London 1964] 36–38.)

is unnecessary and unwise. It is unnecessary, he says, because children have committed no sins — "why should innocent infancy come with haste to the remission of sins?" Yet elsewhere Tertullian seems firmly convinced that every child born into this world is born as a child of Adam and subject to Satan's dominion.[14] The baptism of children is also unwise, for it involves a double jeopardy: jeopardy for the baptized themselves, if they grow up unfaithful to their baptism, and jeopardy for their sponsors, who may be prevented by death from fulfilling their commitment or may be thwarted by the child growing up with "an evil disposition." It is far wiser, Tertullian argues, to "let them be made Christians when they have become competent to know Christ." That competence means more than attaining catechizable age is clear from his advice in the same context that the unmarried should also defer baptism until such time as they have settled down either to marriage or to a life of continence.

/ What seems to be operative behind these suggestions is Tertullian's view of the *sacramentum* as a sacred oath of commitment and of the Church as a community of the vowed.[15] "All who understand what a burden baptism is will have more fear of obtaining it than of its postponement."[16] Thus for Tertullian baptism is a covenantal relationship in which both God and the baptized have reciprocal responsibilities, responsibilities which a child should not assume (apart presumably from imminent danger of death), because the risk of postbaptismal sin is too great. While Tertullian is the only author on record to have stated this position so clearly, the tendency to defer baptism, which becomes widespread in the fourth century, indicates that his views came to be widely shared.

AUGUSTINE (NORTH AFRICA, 354–430). The major contributor to a theology of sacraments in the West was Augustine, and nowhere was his influence more keenly felt than in the area of infant baptism. At a time when Christian parents frequently enrolled their children as catechumens but postponed their baptism indefinitely while their children were healthy, Augustine provided a major

[14] *de animta* 39–40, C.S.L., II, 842–843.
[15] D. Michaélides, *Sacramentum chez Tertullien* (Paris 1970).
[16] *de baptismo*, 19.

impetus towards *quamprimum* baptism.[17] Against the Pelagian emphasis on human responsibility in the work of salvation, Augustine stressed the absolute necessity of the grace of Christ. What was at issue was not the baptism of infants as such but the significance of the redemptive work of Christ in human history and in the life of each individual. Infants became a test case, and Augustine was able to point to the Church's traditional practice of baptizing even newborn children with the "one baptism for the forgiveness of sins" as evidence that they, too, were in sin and in need of Christ's saving grace.

Yet Augustine's autobiographical *Confessions* reveal a profound ambivalence in his attitude towards children and childhood.[18] On the one hand there is his extraordinary journey back into his own childhood, where he finds the roots of his later sins in the anxious grasping of the child, which he identifies as concupiscence. On the other hand when he begins to speak of his conversion, it is to childhood that he again returns for images of the truly converted experience. Margaret Miles summarizes Augustine as follows:

"The imagery with which he introduces the conversion experience is that of the child just learning to walk: 'Throw yourself on him. Do not fear. He will not pull away and let you fall. Throw yourself without fear and he will receive you and heal you' (*Confessions*, VIII:1). This strong imagery suggests, as do several other elements in the account, that what is necessary is a return to the earliest psychic condition of anxiety, a stripping of the cumulative object-orientation which, in adulthood, has become ingrained behavior."[19]

The ambivalence of Augustine's imagery is reflective of the ambivalence of the child. On the one hand childhood is the primordial experience of the dialectic between dependence and autonomy, grasping and letting go, to which true conversion must return and

[17] The most celebrated instance of the deferment of baptism is St Augustine himself. See *The Confessions of St Augustine*, Bk. I, ch. 11, trans. John K. Ryan (Garden City, N.Y. 1960) 53–54.

[18] See Margaret Miles, "Infancy, Parenting and Nourishment in St Augustine's Confessions," *Journal of the American Academy of Religion* 50 (1982) 3, 349–364.

[19] *Ibid.*, 355.

which it must redeem through reliving this dialectic under the influence of grace. In that sense childhood is an ideal state to be recovered, not just a past to be left behind. On the other hand since the child unconsciously seeks to resolve its anxiety by reaching and grasping and demanding, the root of all sin, concupiscence, is vividly displayed in its crying and its orality. As such the child represents all that is wrong with fallen humanity: "Who would not tremble and wish rather to die than to be an infant again if the choice were put before him?"[20]

In subsequent Western theology it was the darker side of the child, accentuated in Augustine's anti-Pelagian writings, which seems to have come to dominate. In the ninth century Walafrid Strabo reversed Augustine's argument: "Since all who are not delivered by God's grace will perish in original sin, including those who have not added to it by their own personal sin, it is necessary to baptize infants."[21] Thereafter the practice of infant baptism will be justified on the basis of the doctrine of original sin, not vice versa, and the negative view of childhood will prevail until modern times.

THE HIGH MIDDLE AGES: THE ELEVENTH TO THE THIRTEENTH CENTURIES. This period witnessed a resurgence of Manichean dualism, which saw the world of material creation as diametrically opposed to the world of the spirit and as the creation of the Evil One. This resurgence, occurring in the context of demands for Church reform and a return to the simplicity and purity of the Gospel, was often marked by a literal interpretation of the Scriptures. One such instance was the repudiation by the Cathars of infant baptism. As part of their argument, they cited Mark 16:16: "Whosoever believes and is baptized shall be saved and whosoever refuses belief shall be condemned." This challenged orthodox theologians to find ways of justifying the traditional doctrine that infants were saved by baptism even though they were clearly incapable of believing.

---

[20] St Augustine, *The City of God*, XXI, 4.

[21] *De ecclesiasticarum rerum exordiis et incrementis*, c. 27, text in J.-Ch. Didier, *Faut-il baptiser les enfants? La réponse de la tradition* (Paris), 239–240.

One answer was to distinguish between faith as an act of belief and faith as the habitual capacity for making such acts. "The infant," wrote Peter of Poitiers, "can neither believe, nor hope, nor love; yet it has faith, hope and love, just as it is endowed with reason even though it cannot yet reason and has the capacity for laughter even though it cannot yet laugh."[22] St Thomas Aquinas would make the same point, while adopting Plato's dubious analogy with the sleeping adult: "The inability of the child to act results not from the lack of the *habitus*, but from bodily incapacity, just as people who are asleep are prevented by sleep from exercising the virtues even though they do have the *habitus* of the virtues."[23] So infants are suitable subjects for baptism, the sacrament of faith, because despite their natural incapacity they receive the infused virtue of faith — together with hope and love — through the sacrament itself. Here, clearly, the Augustinian view of the child as equipped with an active if perverted will is temporarily eclipsed by a view of childhood centered on its dormant rationality. The child is the passive recipient of the ministrations of the Church as it is the passive recipient of the ministrations of its own parents, at least until its latent rational powers begin to stir.

THE SIXTEENTH-CENTURY REFORMATION. Since the key issue of the Reformation was justification, and since the Reformers generally accentuated the role of faith in the Christian life, it was hardly surprising that infant baptism became an issue. For Martin Luther the sacraments were quite secondary to faith in the divine promises, of whose reality they were tangible evidence, but it was a relatively small faction of the Reformers who took this doctrine to its logical conclusion. The Anabaptists, who derived their nickname from their refusal to recognize the validity of infant baptism and their insistence on rebaptizing those baptized in infancy, held that God's grace came through his Word and that baptism only had value for someone who submitted to baptism as an act of submission to the Gospel.

While the Anabaptists represented a number of divergent views, they were generally of one mind in seeing baptism as a personal

[22] *Sentences*, V:6, text in Didier, *Faut-il baptiser les enfants?* 256.
[23] *Summa Theologiae*, Pars III, q. 69, art. 6.

response to the Word of God, whereby a person covenants with other converted Christians to become the Church, the witnessing community. Since children are inherently incapable of such response or responsibility, they are incapable of baptism. The problem of original sin was resolved largely by ignoring it, since it was not clearly taught in Scripture.

Behind this Anabaptist approach to baptism, as behind much of the reforming program of both the Protestant Reformation and the Catholic Reformation, was the emerging modern concept of the person as an autonomous individual.[24] Whereas earlier and non-Western concepts of the person tended to identify the person in terms of his or her place in the community, the modern concept of the autonomous individual makes the individual self the source of its values and its own identity. Hence we have the emphasis on individual conversion and commitment and on the education which would shape each individual to take his place in the Church or in society. Through diligent training of intellect and will, Catholics and Protestants alike believed, a new generation of committed individuals could be formed. The Anabaptists in a sense set the pace for the other Churches in the sixteenth century by taking the logical step of deferring baptism until the child's education — the training of intellect, will, and conscience — had been completed, and a full, conscious, and deliberate act of obedience to the Gospel could be made. "This emphasis on personal, individually-sought baptism, exclusive of the religious community into which one entered at birth, earmarked Swiss, Dutch and German Anabaptists alike."[25]

Both Martin Luther and John Calvin rejected the Anabaptist position and retained the practice of baptizing infants, each of them for reasons that had little to do with baptism as such and still less to do with any sympathetic understanding of childhood.[26]

[24] See Louis Dumont, "A Modified View of Our Origins: The Christian Beginnings of Modern Individualism," *Religion* 12 (1982) 1–27.

[25] H. Schwartz, "Early Anabaptist Ideas about the Nature of Children," *The Mennonite Quarterly Review* 47 (1973) 2, 104. See also James McClendon, "Why Baptists Do Not Baptize Children," *Concilium* 24 (1967) 7–14.

[26] For a summary of Luther's and Calvin's views on infant baptism, see E. Schlink, *The Doctrine of Baptism*, trans. H. J. A. Bouman (St Louis 1972) 130–170.

Yet the same trend, symptomatic of the new humanism of the age, manifested itself in these other Churches as well, even though for various reasons its complete logical expression, denial of baptism to children, was inhibited. In a direct response to the dilemma raised by the Anabaptists, the other Protestant Churches reinterpreted confirmation — which they regarded not as a sacrament but as an ecclesiastical institution — as a rite of personal profession (confirmation) of faith which concluded the catechizing of those baptized in infancy.

The conservative defensiveness of the Roman Church towards everything suggested or promoted by the Reformers strongly mitigated the influence of this focus on the individual, but one symptom of it that does appear is the definitive move to postpone confirmation and first Communion, if not until the age of twelve then at least until the child reached the age of intellectual and moral discretion. The child might continue to be baptized in the faith of the Church, but the fullness of sacramental initiation would have to wait until the child was old enough to profess its own faith.

Implicit in this position is the identification of Christian life with adult life and with *individual* adult life. Until such time as they develop such adult capacities as intellect, will, and conscience, children can have no real place in the Church; they are barred from the sacraments. Childhood is seen merely as a period between birth and personhood. Not much more can be said for it than that it will pass.

THE TWENTIETH CENTURY. Modern discussions of infant baptism have been largely stimulated by a growing sense of the fragility of Christianity in the modern Western world and by the perceived need for a more credible witness to the Gospel in contemporary society. At first the discussion tended to focus among Protestants on whether the New Testament and the historical tradition offered any legitimation for the practice of infant baptism, but soon the argument shifted to more explicitly doctrinal positions.[27] What was ultimately at stake was less the salvation of infants (for the doc-

---

[27] For the main literature see note 2 above.

trine of original sin in its Augustinian formulation had been considerably diluted in the course of the nineteenth century) than the salvation of the Church as a witnessing community. The indiscriminate practice of baptizing any child presented at the font was agreed by all to be detrimental. What was at issue was whether infant baptism as such was an apostolic practice compatible with the Gospel or whether it was a later practice symptomatic of a loss of evangelical consciousness.

Among Roman Catholics the legitimacy and validity of infant baptism was never called into question, but in the de-Christianized conditions of postwar Europe, the Catholic Church faced the problems of a vast nominal membership and few deeply committed Catholics. Moves to curtail indiscriminate baptism were accompanied on the one hand by a recovery of the rich patristic teachings on sacramental initiation and on the other hand by the first steps towards a restoration of the ancient catechumenate.[28] In America these issues were taken up after the Second Vatican Council and especially in the wake of the promulgation of the *Rite for the Christian Initiation of Adults*.[29] As the name indicates, this was not exactly a full restoration of the baptismal discipline of the patristic Church, since it was now reserved for adults and for children of catechizable age. Younger children, who had taken their place alongside their elders in the original catechumenate, were henceforth excluded. For them a separate rite was provided, the *Ordo Baptizandi Parvulos* (1969).

This two-fold economy of sacramental initiation has not taken care of the issue of infant baptism, however. In fact it has served to raise new theological problems about what we are doing in baptizing small children.[30] Nor are these problems confined to discussions among academic theologians, for the contrast between the extensiveness and symbolic richness of the adult rite and the

[28] Henri Bourgeois, "The Catechumenate in France Today," in *Becoming a Catholic Christian*, ed. W. J. Reedy (New York 1979) 10–21.

[29] *Ordo initiationis christianae adultorum*, 1972 (ET: 1974, 1985).

[30] Aidan Kavanagh, *The Shape of Baptism* (New York 1978) 109–114, 196–197. For an overview of Roman Catholic discussions of infant baptism, see Paul F. X. Covino, "The Postconciliar Infant Baptism Debate in the American Catholic Church," *Worship* 56 (1982) 240–260.

relatively perfunctory character of the children's rite, both witnessed in the same parishes, has raised questions for pastors and faithful as well. Since this is where matters currently stand, it is worth identifying some of the challenges posed to infant baptism by the RCIA more closely.

Infant Baptism in the Shadow of the RCIA. There has been a tendency since the elaboration of the scholastic synthesis of sacramental theology in the thirteenth century to focus on the individual minister and recipient at the expense of the ecclesial context, on the sacramental moment at the expense of the initiatory process, on the efficacy of the sacramental act at the expense of the role of faith, and on the remedial value of baptism at the expense of the rich symbolism of the unified rites of baptism, confirmation, and Eucharist. On all these counts the RCIA brings welcome redress, but in doing so it calls into question the strategy of infant baptism whose ritual remains comparatively impoverished. The newly restored practice of adult initiation serves to highlight precisely those aspects of baptismal theology which the new rite of infant baptism continues to obscure. We shall identify four such elements, four elements with which any rethinking of infant baptism will require us to come to terms.

THE FAITH OF THE CANDIDATE. In contrast to the passivity of the infant, the adult coming to baptism is capable of faith and of all that faith implies. He or she can play a full, conscious, and active role in responding to the call of God's Word and submitting to the power of God's grace.

This powerful event of adult conversion has traditionally been envisaged in America in one of two ways. First, there is the early Anabaptist tradition, maintained by present-day Mennonites and some Baptists, for which this coming to faith is essentially cognitive and the product of conviction: a submission to the judgment of God's Word upon one's life and upon the world. It issues in a life-style which takes the Gospel seriously and glories in its countercultural challenge. Such conversion is radical, evangelical, and ethical. But there is another more widespread and certainly more recent tradition among American Protestant fundamentalists, in which conversion is less a matter of conviction than of experience.

Here baptism itself is subordinated to the "amazing grace" of discovering Jesus as one's personal savior.

These two traditions of adult conversion — the one issuing in a common life of evangelical discipleship, the other in a more individualistic, feeling experience of "being saved" — have both had some influence on American Roman Catholics as they adopt the RCIA. The effect of both is to render infant baptism an anomaly, and if Roman Catholics have shown themselves hesitant to rule out infant baptism altogether, they have certainly begun to raise questions about its value. These two native American conceptions of conversion come together with a traditional Catholic emphasis on faith as belief, to make conversion a highly personal decision and the celebration of baptism the occasion of a maturely considered faith commitment. It thereby achieves successfully what Catholics have been trying to do with confirmation with far less effect. The problem of "what to do with confirmation" is itself a trailing symptom, some would argue, of the problem created by infant baptism: membership in the Church without any guarantee that those so baptized will ever come to own their baptismal faith.

THE ECCLESIOLOGICAL FACTOR. As in the past, so too in the present, a preference for adult over infant baptism is closely tied to a particular ecclesiology. This connection is sometimes explicit, as with the Anabaptists and Mennonites, but it often lurks behind the screen of other arguments, as was the case with Tertullian. Today in the Roman Catholic Church, as in previous eras of reform, there is something of a reaction against the Church's perceived cultural compromises and the dream of a more faithful if smaller Church. Instead of the security and blandness of the *Volkskirche,* some hope for a believers' Church: a Church of small base communities whose members are committed to working in the world with uncompromising fidelity to Gospel values. Since Karl Rahner, Catholics have been accustomed to refer to this as the "diaspora Church." It envisages a fully active membership, gathered in small congregations, which will be fully participatory in their polity and marked by an evangelical life-style. Priority will be given to local congregations and to their self-discipline within the larger communion of the Church as a whole, rather than to the large, amorphous entities represented by national and international religious denominations. The dream of many contemporary Catholics could be summed up as "solidarity without legalism and pastoral responsibility without clericalism."

Among Avery Dulles' five models of Church,[31] this one obviously corresponds most closely to the "Herald" model, with strong overtones of the "Servant" model, but it is interesting to note that Catholics often appeal in support of such a vision to conciliar texts such as *Sacrosanctum Concilium* #41 and *Lumen Gentium* #26. Here the Church is said to manifest itself most adequately and visibly in the local assembly, where the faithful gather under the presidency of the bishop for the celebration of the liturgy. In appealing to these texts, it is not always recognized that two quite different models of Church are being fused. While this is of itself quite legitimate, the debate over infant baptism is muddied by the failure to acknowledge the new hybrid ecclesiology and to work out the implications of clinging to the sacramental model of Church while opting to develop a form of Church organization on the herald model. The Anabaptists in adopting the herald model rejected sacramentalism. Catholics appear as yet unwilling to face the issue: can a congregational model of Church with its emphasis upon the Word of God and on the need for adult decision be reconciled with the Catholic sacramental tradition, with its faith in the power of grace to work below the level of consciousness, even in the baptism of a child?

NEW UNDERSTANDING OF SACRAMENTALITY. One of the major contributions of the RCIA to Catholic life and to sacramental theology is the way in which it has forced us to break with an almost magical understanding of the sacraments as discrete moments of divine intervention and to adopt a more flexible understanding of sacramentality as a process admitting of degrees. In this latter perspective the temporal duration of the catechumenal process, the various stages in the journey of faith undertaken by the candidates, the various ritual celebrations that mark the way culminat-

---

[31] Avery Dulles, *Models of the Church* (New York 1974).

ing in the solemn Easter rites of baptism, confirmation, and Eucharist are all sacramental in varying degrees. The liturgy of Easter night is less the setting for three discrete sacramental "moments" than it is the climax of a process which is sacramental in its entirety.

The concept of a gradual growth in faith, marked by a succession of rites and stages which are themselves sacramental in a broad sense, offers an obviously attractive solution to the problem of infant baptism.[32] By enrolling infants in the catechumenate, we can give them something, whether their parents are committed Christians or not, while still withholding baptism until the children are old enough to ask for it themselves and to make a lasting commitment. There is obviously a precedent for such an arrangement in the Church of the fourth and fifth centuries.

What is remarkable in most of the discussion of the proposed infant catechumenate, however, is that two points are rarely, if ever, addressed. First, the rite of enrollment in the catechumenate requires of candidates that they already have manifested some initial conversion and that they be prepared to make their intentions known to the Church.[33] Second, the issue of when a child would be old enough to be elected for baptism is rarely indicated. Would it be at the age of three, as Gregory Nazianzen suggested in the fourth century, when the child is old enough to remember its baptism? Would it be a year or two after the child is old enough to be catechized? Or would baptism be witheld until the child is old enough to make a mature personal decision? Any solution but the latter — which would perhaps delay baptism until the child was of marriageable age — is vulnerable to at least some of the objections raised against infant baptism and would thus constitute only a partial solution.

In actual fact while enrolling the child in the catechumenate is often promoted on the grounds that the rite of enrollment is itself

---

[32] R.-M. Roberge, "Un tournant dans la pastorale du baptême," *Laval Theologique et Philosophique* 31 (1975) 227–238 and 33 (1977) 3–22.

[33] *Rite for the Christian Initiation of Adults* (Washington 1985) n. 41. See also Congregation for the Doctrine of the Faith, *Instruction on Infant Baptism* (Oct. 20, 1980) nn. 30–31. English text in *Origins* 10:30 (January 8, 1981) 479.

a kind of sacrament, the desire to delay the baptism of children until they are old enough to take part actively in their own initiation is itself associated with a "low" view of sacraments. The deferment of the sacrament makes sense because sacraments are seen more in terms of their nature as human actions than in terms of their nature as acts of God. There is, in other words, a possible inconsistency in subjecting the helpless infant to the "sacramentality" of enrollment in the catechumenate but refusing to submit it to the "sacramentality" of the complete rite of initiation.

THE MEANING OF BAPTISM. For centuries, as we saw, popular Catholic understanding of baptism was dominated by Augustine's teaching that children dying in original sin would be excluded forever from the vision of God. Conciliar teaching on the Christian life and the renewed rites of Christian initiation have shifted attention to the more positive aspects of baptism and especially to the paschal character of the Christian life as a sharing in the death and resurrection of Christ. This is an immense gain, but the paschal character of baptism is sometimes propounded in such a way as to seem to preclude the baptism of infants. When Aidan Kavanagh, for example, describes baptism as "a transitus from shame to celebration, from the conviction of sin to the appropriation of one's complete forgiveness in Christ"[34] little room appears left for the baptizing of preconscious infants.

With respect to this emphasis on the radical discontinuity between the "before" and "after" of baptism, two points need to be made. The first is that studies on the meaning of *pascha* in Christian usage have shown that it was used in three distinct if related senses and that the translation *pascha* = *transitus* (transition, journey) is relatively late and only became widespread with Augustine.[35] The popularity of the *transitus* meaning and its eclipse of the earlier meanings (which interpreted the term as referring

[34] Kavanagh, *The Shape of Baptism*, 199. For a trenchant review of Kavanagh's position, see T. A. Droege, "The Formation of Faith in Christian Initiation," *The Cresset* 66 (1983) 6, 16–23.

[35] Antonius Scheer, "Is the Easter Vigil a Rite of Passage?" in *Liturgy and Human Passage*, eds. David N. Power and Luis Maldonado (Concilium, 112) (New York 1979) 50–61.

either to God passing over the children of Israel and sparing their lives or to the lamb — Christ — by whose blood they were spared) was largely due to the association of adult baptism (passage through the waters) with the Easter Vigil. Thus it is somewhat tautologous to argue that the paschal character of baptism requires the kind of break with the past which characterizes adult conversion, when it was precisely that sort of conversion which led to pascha being identified with the people's passage through the Red Sea rather than with God's merciful sparing of his children.

Secondly, research on the early history of Christian baptism, especially in East Syria, has made it abundantly clear that not everything in Christian life can be reduced to the death/resurrection motif and that this was not quite the root metaphor for baptism either in the New Testament or in early Christianity that some have supposed it to be. In fact, for reasons which no one has yet been able to explain, the Pauline doctrine on baptism as a participation in the death and resurrection of Christ was totally without influence in the first three centuries of the Church.[36] Instead, the dominant image, especially in Syria, was not Calvary but the Jordan, not the death of Jesus, but his baptism and manifestation as Son.[37] Around the image of the baptism of Jesus and his messianic anointing being shared by those being baptized, there clustered a whole range of images much more congenial to the baptism of infants: adoption, divinization, sanctification, gift of the Spirit, indwelling, glory, power, wisdom, rebirth, restoration, mission, and so forth. These, it should be noted, are as much part of the traditional meaning of baptism as the death and resurrection imagery. But this is not to suggest that we retain one set of meanings for adult initiation and another set for infant initiation. On the contrary, both sets of images are properly activated in any baptism, which means that adult initiation needs to be thought of in terms of rebirth and return to infancy, while infants, if they are

---

[36] André Benoit, *Le baptême chretien au 2e siècle* (Paris 19).

[37] On the Syrian baptismal tradition see S. Brock, "Studies in the Early History of the Syrian Orthodox Baptismal Liturgy," *Journal of Theological Studies* n.s. 23 (1972) 16–64; Gabriele Winkler, "The Original Meaning of the Prebaptismal Anointing and Its Implications," *Worship* 42 (1978) 24–45; S. J. Beggiani, *Early Syriac Theology* (Lanham, Md 1983) 101–124.

to be baptized, must be capable in some way of dying and rising with Christ.

Conclusion. Having selectively reviewed some aspects of the history of baptismal practice and baptismal theology and looked at some of the challenges to infant initiation posed by the restored adult rite, it is now time to try to pull together what we have learned from this review which might suggest that a rethinking of infant initiation is both timely and necessary. Traditional ways of thinking appear inadequate for the following four reasons.

First, it is striking that past and present discussions about infant baptism are rarely about baptism alone or about infants at all. Usually the subject of infant baptism is raised in the context of another argument, whether it be about the nature of the Church as a community of witness or about the relationship of God's grace to human works. John Calvin's position on the baptism of the children of believers, for example, is entirely derived from his conviction concerning the essential unity of the Old and New Covenants, so that what was said of circumcision for the Jews may be said of baptism for Christian children. The traditional arguments for or against infant baptism, then, are characteristically deductive arguments from a priori doctrinal principles in which the nature of childhood itself is rarely made the subject of theological reflection.

Second, the necessity, legitimacy, and advisability of infant baptism have been addressed from many different angles. The question has been posed in historical terms (did the primitive Church baptize infants?), in pastoral terms (is baptizing people in infancy the best way to socialize them?), in ecclesiological terms (is the Church intended by Christ one that requires adult commitment?) and in sacramental terms (are the sacraments such that they can be effective without the free and knowing cooperation of the recipient?). But the question has rarely if ever been posed theologically (is there any place in the divine economy for the child as child?) or Christologically (what soteriological value is to be ascribed to the infancy and childhood of Jesus?).

Third, infant baptism tends to be favored by those who see the sacraments primarily in terms of the work of God and to be opposed by those who see the sacraments primarily as divinely instituted ways of responding to God's Word. Thus pedobaptists characteristically justify infant initiation on the grounds that it is prime evidence of God's initiative in human salvation; antipedobaptists see God's merciful initiative as located in his intelligible Word, to which only a conscious and informed mind can offer adequate submission. Thus the arguments for or against infant baptism at a doctrinal level appear to be *au fond* arguments about the relative value of Word and sacrament. Does the Word merely prepare for the sacrament? Does the sacrament merely seal our acceptance of the Word in faith? Is baptism the beginning and precondition of further Christian socialization, or is it its crowning moment? Once again, though, the problem with posing the question in this way is that it still neglects to pay any serious attention to the condition of the child as child. Neither the view of the child as not-yet-adult, nor the view that baptism "infuses" a supernatural habitus of faith, hope, and love into the infant, takes seriously the possibility that the infant might live a life of faith, hope, and love precisely as a child and precisely as a child-in-relationship within the context of its own *ecclesia*, the Christian family.

Fourth, the history of the theology of baptism would seem to corroborate the thesis first put forward by Philippe Ariès, namely that the characteristic attitude of adults towards children until modern times was one of indifference. In his classic work *Centuries of Childhood*, published in 1962, Ariès sets out to refute those pundits who idealize the family life of previous generations while decrying the degeneration of family life in the contemporary world. In this mission Ariès admirably succeeds, painting what must seem to us a shocking portrait of neglect and abuse in the raising of children in the medieval and early modern periods. He concludes that adults, including mothers, were generally ignorant of the inner life of the child and, what is more, indifferent to it. Children under the age of six or seven were not really considered as persons but as subrational and thus subhuman. Ariès, of course, is talking about cultural attitudes and about a culture in which the concepts of childhood and family as we understand them had not yet emerged. This cultural mindset does not preclude genuine instances of love for children, of course, any more than our culture's high valuing of children is able to prevent the continuing abuse and exploitation of children in our own society.

Ariès' study on the medieval and early modern periods finds an echo in Robert Pattison's survey of the place of the child in the literature of classical and late antiquity. He writes:

"Certainly the most striking feature of classical literature's attitude towards children is the thunderous silence that envelopes the idea of childhood, especially when compared to the outpouring of concern and attention recent centuries have produced on the same subject."

"The classical silence does not necessarily indicate indifference," he argues; yet he admits that "Roman infants were largely neglected before they came to a reasonable age. . . . Childhood raised few questions and evoked only the slenderest train of associations. The child may have contained the possibility of perfection, but until the possibility actually bore fruit, he remained subrational and therefore subliterary."[38]

It is really only in the seventeenth and eighteenth centuries that Pattison begins to find the child coming to play a role in English literature, a finding which matches Ariès' claim that it was only at this period that the concept of childhood began to emerge. Before that time and to a very large extent for a long while afterwards, children were usually regarded as defective adults. Infancy and young childhood represented a precarious and insignificant introduction to life which properly began somewhere between the ages of four and seven, when the child — now able to speak, understand, and act — was given more or less complete admission to adult life.

In a more recent study of childrearing in seventeenth-century France, David Hunt has introduced an important qualification to Ariès' thesis. He writes:

"Far from viewing the unfolding of infantile potentials with benign indifference, grownups in that period were deeply disturbed by some aspects of the orality, the obstinacy, and the sexu-

[38] Robert Pattison, *The Child Figure in English Literature* (Athens, Ga. 1978) 5–6.

ality of their offspring and made determined efforts to mold or thwart altogether such inclinations."[39]

What this correction to Ariès seems to suggest is what the history of the doctrine of original sin would also seem to indicate: children have either been dismissed as subhuman because subrational and thus ignored, or their wilfulness has been recognized and has come to serve as a hook for the projection of adult fears and fantasies. As we remarked before, it is the latter attitude which seems largely to have prevailed in the West until relatively recent times, making children bear the brunt of adult anxieties about sin and salvation.[40] It is only in the twentieth century that serious studies of childhood have come into their own, but even so serious theological reflection on the matter has hardly begun.[41]

A NEW APPROACH TO INFANT INITIATION

There are at least three different angles from which a fresh evaluation of the practice of initiating infants to the Christian life might be approached.

From the perspective of the Church itself, which has to be concerned with the effective socialization of each new generation if it is to survive, the whole issue of what constitutes an effective way of socializing needs to be looked at and the place of sacramental celebrations within such a process needs to be considered.[42] It re-

[39] David Hunt, *Parents and Children in History*, 190.

[40] Nineteenth-century changes in cultural attitudes towards children and in corresponding approaches to childrearing appear to have been reflected in a gradual abandonment of the classical Augustinian teaching on original sin. See Bernard Wishy, *The Child and the Republic. The Dawn of Modern American Child Nurture* (Philadelphia 1968); H. Sheldon Smith, *Changing Conceptions of Original Sin. A Study in American Theology since 1750* (New York 1955).

[41] Karl Rahner, "Ideas for a Theology of Childhood," *Theological Investigations*, vol. VIII (New York 1971) 33–50; Randolph C. Miller, "Theology and the Understanding of Children," *The Nature of Man in Theological and Psychological Perspective* ed. Simon Doniger (New York 1962) 142–150; Nathan Mitchell, "The Parable of Childhood," *Liturgy* 1 (1981) 3, 7–12; Guy Bédouelle, "Reflections on the Place of the Child in the Church," *Communio* 12 (1985) 4, 349–367.

[42] See P. M. Zulehner, "Religionssoziologie und Kindertaufe" in *Christsein Ohne Entscheidung, oder Soll die Kirche Kinder Taufen?* ed., Walter Kasper (Mainz 1970) 188–206.

mains the case that because such socialization is presumed to be parish-based, it is only undertaken with preschoolers at the earliest. The Church apparently has nothing to say to or about young children from the time they are baptized shortly after birth until the time when they are old enough to be enrolled in preschool religious education programs. Thus pastoral practice is at odds with the rhetoric of the Second Vatican Council and of the baptismal liturgy, which speaks of the parents and the family as "the first and foremost educators of their children."[43] Any worthwhile rethinking of the Christian formation of the children of believers will therefore have to take both the children and the family more seriously as active participants in the life of the Church.

This would mean, in turn, that the perspective of the family itself needs to be considered and its experience taken into account. More specifically the Christian family is called to understand the events of its life — especially something as significant as pregnancy and childbirth — in the light of faith and to recognize the birth of each new child not only as a gift of God in some generic sense but as a specific word-event of God addressed to them.

Finally the event of baptism needs to be reflected upon from the child's point of view, once it is admitted that there is such a thing as a child's point of view. This would mean exploring how it can be said that the child as child can be said to be delivered from sin, adopted by God, incorporated into Christ, and made a dwelling-place of the Holy Spirit.

Here we shall leave the ecclesiastical angle aside to focus more closely on the family and the child. We shall first explore the implications of a theology of the family as a "domestic church" and then look at the possibility of regarding the child as an active participant in the sacramental process.

The Family as Church. The key to a new understanding of infant baptism is the vision of the family as a domestic church, *ecclesiola in ecclesia,* in virtue both of baptism and of the sacrament of marriage.[44] This means that the family, a communion of life in Christ

---

[43] See *Rite for the Baptism of Children*, n. 70. See also nn. 5, 39, 56, 64.

[44] Second Vatican Council *Dogmatic Constitution on the Church*, n. 11; *Pastoral Constitution on the Church in the Modern World*, n. 48; *Decree on the Apostolate of*

within the larger communion of the local and universal Church, participates in the mystery of the one Church as a sacrament of Christ and in the threefold operation of the Church's priestly, prophetic, and royal mission. Indeed whatever can be said of the Church as a whole can be said, *mutatis mutandis*, of the Christian family. Where the arrival of a new child and the decision for baptism are concerned, this ecclesial identity of the family suggests the following observations.

a. The family, exercising its prophetic function, has to discern the meaning of pregnancy, childbirth, and parenting, not in general but in terms of the birth of this particular child at this particular time. As Herbert Anderson points out, this is not a cue for mindless romanticizing.[45] Very often feelings about the child are ambivalent, while the emotional and physical costs involved in pregnancy, birth, and childrearing are high, and future prospects may appear daunting. It is, in any case, from the specifics of the event and the actual history of its occurrence that faith will seek to read the merciful will of God, so that the event becomes itself a moment of revelation, a Word of God expressed in the contingencies of family life.

b. The events of conception, pregnancy, birth, and parenthood, read in faith, evoke in turn the priestly function of the domestic church: a priesthood exercised in thanksgiving and intercession certainly but also in the rituals and "sacraments" of family life which include everything from prenatal diet and exercise to the most mundane aspects of caring for the newborn.

c. The word and sacrament encountered and lived in the domestic setting find their fulfillment and their touchstone in the liturgical proclamation and celebration of the local Church, especially in

---

the Laity, n. 11; *Decree on Christian Education*, n. 3. The reference to the sacrament of marriage is not intended to preclude the possibility that single parent families or irregular marriages might not de facto be microchurches in virtue of the quality of the faith life and public witness of such families, but merely to underline the sacramental and ecclesial dimension formally established by a marriage witnessed by the Church.

[45] Herbert Anderson, "Pastoral Care in the Process of Initiation" in Mark Searle, ed., *Alternative Futures for Worship*, vol. 2: *Baptism and Confirmation* (Collegeville 1987) 103–136.

the sacraments of the bath, the oil, and the table. Here the old axiom *sacramenta propter homines* (sacraments are for people) needs to be complemented with the corresponding axiom *sacramenta propter ecclesiam* (sacraments are for the Church). In contrast to the scholastic identification of the purpose of the sacraments as two-fold — forgiveness and sanctification — the Second Vatican Council teaches that the sacraments have a triple purpose: to sanctify, to build up the Church, to glorify God (SC, 59). Thus baptism is to be understood as celebrated not only for the recipient but for the benefit of the whole community of faith. Realistically this means that baptism is celebrated not only for the infant but for the parents and siblings and for the parish. This is not to suggest, as sometimes seems to be suggested, that the baptism is *really* for the parents or that infant baptism justifies itself as a "teachable moment" in the life of the parents. In a more profound sense the liturgy of baptism depends for its ability to "translate" the child from outside to inside the Church upon the reconstituting of that Church in the liturgical assembly and particularly upon the reconstituting of the family in its organic unity as an *ecclesiola in ecclesia*. If the child is baptized in the faith of the Church, then the identity of the family as constituted by faith, as itself a sacrament of faith, must be "confected" anew in the process and event of sacramental initiation. In short, the family is part of the sacramental sign of baptism and will be confirmed as such by taking its part in the enactment of the rites themselves.[46]

d. The family-as-Church is probably the best context, too, in which to address the issue of what it means to say that baptism is for the forgiveness of sins, or that baptism "washes away" origi-

[46] The willingness of the Church in the past to baptize dying infants without even consulting the parents is simply one aspect of the diminished sign value of emergency baptism. Other aspects would include the absence of an ecclesial community, the celebration of baptism outside the Easter season, the lack of a full ritual setting, and the omission of confirmation and Eucharist. Unfortunately scholastic theology of the sacraments took such extreme cases as the starting point for a theology of baptism. The Second Vatican Council repudiated this approach by making the fullness of the sacramental sign, in all its communitarian and ritual dimensions, normative. See *Constitution on the Liturgy*, nn. 26, 27, 67.

nal sin. A major problem with much discussion of the doctrine of original sin is that it is not always sufficiently acknowledged that the concept of original sin is derived by way of contrast to the prior concept of the new life of Christ made available in baptism, and is thus to be understood in contrast to the life of the Spirit lived in the communion of the Church. If St Augustine led us to think of this contrast in terms of natural generation versus sacramental regeneration, a way of resolving the embarrassments provoked by some of the formulations deriving from this contrast (for example, on the inherent sinfulness of sexual activity even within a sacramental marriage) would be to highlight the mystery of the Church — and thus of the Christian family — as the embodied mystery of grace. Such an embodiment of God's eschatologically victorious grace in Jesus Christ is never totally unambiguous: we see now only as in a glass darkly. But the ambivalence of marriage and of the family is matched by the ambivalence of the Church itself as a social and historical institution, pointing beyond itself only more or less adequately, both being natural institutions as well as sacraments of life in Christ.

Just as the Church has consistently to remind herself and others of her otherworldly inner nature, so too must the family. This being so, the celebration of baptism for the forgiveness of sins, for the overcoming of alienation from God, would serve to reinforce the intentionality of the family in its specific role as a community of Christ's holiness and grace in the world. The dual nature of the Christian family requires a "double birth" for each new child: the one in the delivery room and the one in the baptistery.

Were the child of Christian parents not baptized, the opportunity of re-presenting its vocation to holiness would be passed up and the ambivalence of the family would be rendered all the more ambiguous. Correspondingly if a family merely "goes through the motions" of having its child baptized without at the same time taking stock of its own vocation to be a sacrament of grace and holiness, the child would be validly baptized as a member of the institutional Church, but the reality signified by membership of the Church — participation in the very life of God, which is for-giveness of sin — would be unlikely to be realized, and the shadow of original sin would still linger over the child precisely because that shadow would be cast by members of the family. The overcoming of original sin by the grace of Christ is not magic. It happens sacramentally, that is through signs. It happens because the rite is a sacrament of the faith of the Church which, where a small child is concerned, is in effect the faith of the family. Where the family does not consciously live the life of faith and grace, it is hard to see how baptism can then and there be fruitful for the forgiveness of sin. The child will have to await the effective intervention of some other representative of the faithful Church for its baptism to "revive" and to become fruitful in the life of grace and faith.[47]

The Child as Subject of Sacramental Initiation. For the historical reasons suggested above, children, especially the newborn, have traditionally been regarded as passive recipients of adult ministrations: clean tablets to be written on, clay to be molded by parental hands. Or else they were seen as active only in manifesting the signs of concupiscence, the fallen will. As Robert Pattison observes: "In the Augustinian view, the child is perhaps subrational, but this is of no importance and properly the business of philosophy, not religion. More important, the child is a creature of will, a sinner *ab ovo* and in this no different from adults."[48]

Such primitive psychotheologizing can no longer be entertained in the wake of the immense amount of research done in this century into the world of the child. Andrew Thompson has brought together an impressive array of insights into the child's experience of the world, especially in terms of the child's relationship to its parents and siblings.[49] We shall be content here to highlight some aspects of this recovery of childhood which relate to the capacity of the child for sacramental initiation.

[47] This view is consistent with that of Augustine (Ep. 98, 10) that the child unlike the adult cannot place an obstacle to the grace of the sacraments. Recognizing the mediation of the family in the sacramental process also necessitates recognizing that the family itself may constitute an obstacle to the child's life of grace.

[48] Pattison, *The Child Figure*, 18.

[49] Andrew D. Thompson, "Infant Baptism in the Light of the Human Sciences" in Mark Searle, ed., *Alternative Futures for Worship*, vol. 2: *Baptism and Confirmation* (Collegeville 1987) 55–102.

Before that can be done, however, there is a preliminary step to be taken. Unless there are good reasons for thinking that the child *as child* has some part in the economy of grace and may be called, precisely as a small child, to witness as part of the sacramentality of the whole Church which is "a sacrament or sign of intimate union with God and of the unity of all mankind" (LG, 1), there is a danger of romanticizing childhood and of reading into the life of the child salvific realities which are in fact suspended until such time as the child gradually acquires those adult characteristics of intellect, will, and which are the preconditions for their realization. But, as Karl Rahner has demonstrated, there is every reason to believe that childhood not only falls within the compass of God's grace, but that

"childhood itself has a direct relationship with God. It touches upon the absolute divinity of God not only as maturity, adulthood and the later phases of life touch upon this, but rather in a special way of its own. . . . The fact that it contributes to the later stages of life is not the sole criterion of its own intrinsic rightness."[50]

Not the least of our grounds for believing that this is the case is to be found in the Incarnation itself. "What was not assumed is not redeemed," is the old patristic axiom, but childhood was assumed. Irenaeus put this best:

"Christ came to save all [human beings] by himself: all, I say, who through him are reborn in God: infants and children, youths and adults, and the elderly. For this it was that he lived through every age [of life]: made an infant for the sake of infants; a child for the children, sanctifying those of that age and setting them an example of devotion, fairness and obedience; a youth for the sake of young people, becoming an example for them and sanctifying them for God. . . ."[51]

Thus infants and young children are sanctified in principle insofar as the Son of God became a child and lived through childhood's experiences in total union with the will of the Father, thereby

[50] Rahner, "Ideas for a Theology of Childhood" 36–37.
[51] *Adversus haereses*, II, 22.4. Text in Didier, *Faut-il baptiser les enfants?* 95.

redeeming infancy and childhood. Thereafter, childhood lived in the Spirit of Christ — albeit necessarily in a preconscious and prereflective way — is sanctified and may be seen as a sign of the glory of God and of the unity of the redeemed human family.

Let us briefly spell out the implications of this with reference particularly to those aspects of the baptismal event which infant baptism might be supposed to obscure.

FAITH AND THE SACRAMENT OF FAITH. While all the sacraments of the Church are sacraments of faith, the term applies particularly to baptism, which, from the New Testament onwards, has always included the candidate's profession of faith. It was for this reason that the Anabaptists and their successors have denied the validity of infant baptism, and that some modern Catholics have been led to question its value. There is no denying that the practice of having parents or godparents answer the faith interrogation on behalf of the child was inappropriate at best and a subterfuge at worst.[52] It was simply a way of getting around the fact that the candidate was *in statu infantis*. What helped compound the problem was the increasing tendency to consider faith primarily in cognitive terms.

It is not clear that St Augustine had a conceptual understanding of faith in mind when he spoke of the child being baptized in the faith of the Church,[53] but this understanding was certainly operative in the twelfth and thirteenth centuries when the issue arose again.[54] Recognizing that a child cannot "believe" in the sense of making an active submission of the intellect, St Thomas Aquinas taught that in baptism faith was infused as a 'habitus,' which he defined as "a quality not easily removed, whereby one may act

[52] It is to be noted that in the Roman Catholic *Rite for the Baptism of Children*, the parents and godparents profess their own faith and do not presume to speak for the child. See nn. 2 (Latin text) and 56.

[53] St Augustine uses *fides* and *credere* in several different if related ways. On the meaning of faith for Augustine, see among others: J. M. Egan, " 'I believe in God': I. The Doctrine of St Augustine," *Irish Ecclesiastical Record* 53 (1939), 630–36; R. Aubert, *Le probleme de l'acte de la foi* (Louvain 1945) 21–30; M. Loehrer, *Der Glaubensbegriff des hl. Augustinus* (Einsiedeln 1955); Chr. Mohrmann, "Credere deo, credere deum, credere in deum," in *Melanges J. de Ghellink*. Gembloux: Eds. J. Duculot, 1951, vol. I, 277–285.

[54] See note 10 above.

easily and pleasantly."[55] It is hard to see what sense can be made of the idea of "infusing" a child with the capacity for acts of faith, especially when the analogy is drawn, for the purposes of distinguishing between the virtue of faith and its exercise, between a child and a sleeping adult.

Instead of redefining faith to fit in with one's preconceived notions of infancy, however, it might be more fruitful to reconsider the child and its capacity for some kind of life of faith even in its status as an infant. Clearly an infant is prerational. If faith is conceived of simply as an act of grace-enlightened reason, then the child has nothing to do but wait until its rational capacities are sufficiently developed as to be able to cooperate with grace. Its Christian life, like its adult life, remains a thing of the future. But the Second Vatican Council moved to counter an excessively cognitive view of faith with a return to the Pauline concept of faith as an "obedience of faith," which it went on to define as that obedience "whereby a person entrusts his whole self freely to God."[56] For an older child or an adult this will surely mean, as the council says, "offering full submission of intellect and will to God who reveals, and freely assenting to the truth revealed by him."[57] But this second part of the definition is a specification of what it means to entrust one's whole self freely to God, a specification which undoubtedly applies to all who have attained the use of reason, but which does not preclude the possibility that those such as infants and retarded adults might not also live a life of total dependence upon God. Indeed it is the infant and the "youngest child" who constantly bring the subversive message of the Gospel as salvation by obedience of faith to a Church constantly prone to place too much confidence in its intellectual respectability.[58]

James Fowler has proposed a view of faith which corresponds closely to the conciliar understanding of theological faith. In

[55] *Summa Theologiae*, Pars III, q. 69, art. 4. See also III, q. 68, art. 9 and q. 69, art. 3. On the meaning of "faith" for St Thomas, see Wilfrid Cantwell Smith, *Faith and Belief* (Princeton 1979) 78–91. See also *Ibid.* 70–78 on faith/*credo* in relation to baptism.

[56] *Dogmatic Constitution on Divine Revelation*, n. 5.

[57] *Ibid.*

[58] See R. Haughton, *Tales from Eternity* (New York 1973) 19–49.

Fowler's view, faith need not be necessarily thought of as an exclusively religious phenomenon. "Rather," he suggests, "faith becomes the designation for a way of leaning into life. It points to a way of making sense of one's existence. It denotes a way of giving order and coherence to the force-field of life. It speaks of the investment of life-grounding trust and life-orienting commitment."[59]

As he goes on to point out, this understanding of faith "means to imply that it is a human universal." He traces its development through infancy and early childhood and argues that the development of faith of some kind, some sort of making sense of the world, some sense of what one may base one's trust on and what makes life worthwhile, is an inevitable development in every child. Even before it becomes articulate — if indeed it ever becomes articulate about its faith, for this "leaning into life" is rarely brought to full consciousness — the child comes to faith. The question then is less one of whether a child can "have" faith than it is a question of the kind of faith it comes in fact to exercise in the first weeks and months of life. There is no need to have recourse to St Thomas Aquinas' distinction between *habitus* and *actus*, tailored as it is to a cognitive understanding of faith. With a precognitive understanding of faith, the child is seen, from the moment of its birth, to be enacting its developing faith as it encounters its human environment, experiences dependency and separation, shared meanings and ritual patterns, provision for its bodily needs, and a sense of its own social and sexual identity.[60] Faith is a holistic, prerational sense of who we are and of the kind of world we live in, an integrated vision of how things are and what it all means. From a theological perspective, then, what is at issue in the celebration of the sacraments is not so much whether the candidates have faith, but of whether their faith is faith in the God who raised Jesus from the dead. For adults this means that evangelizing is a matter of uprooting false faith as well as a matter of communicating true faith, a realization that has enormous im-

[59] James Fowler, "Perspectives on the Family from the Standpoint of Faith Development Theory," *Perkins Journal*, Fall 1979, 7.

[60] Erik Erikson. *Toys and Reasons. Stages in the Ritualization of Experience* (New York 1977) esp. 85–92.

plications for the catechumenate. For the children of the Church, it means forming them in right faith from infancy. To wait until they attain the use of reason is already to wait too long and to leave their faith to chance.

For Christians right faith is baptismal faith and baptismal faith is paschal faith. But how can infants be said to be baptized into such faith?

Paschal faith is the faith which was Christ's, the faith whereby he was made perfect through suffering and consistently surrendered his life into the hands of the God who alone could save him out of death (see Heb 5:7-8). Such a pattern, as something lived out by the community of the baptized, is what constitutes the faith of the Church. By baptism we have been fitted into a pattern of surrender and exaltation, of self-abandonment and deliverance, of dying and being raised. But such a pattern, far from being alien to the life of the child, is intrinsic to it. Having experienced the trauma of separation from the womb, the child is confronted with the task of learning to live as both autonomous and yet dependent, caught between the desire for communion and the need to accept separation, instinctively struggling to satisfy its own immediate needs yet learning to wait in trust for what it really needs. "The nerve to separate," says Fowler of the many experiences of separation and nonfulfillment in the infant's life, "depends upon the assured return to communion."[61]

Now this is clearly not the same as adult conversion (though it would seem to be something that would condition the very possibility of genuine adult conversion), but neither is it merely an illustration of some aspect of the paschal mystery. Is it not rather the paschal mystery as lived by every child that is born into this world? Or perhaps we should turn that around and say that Christ, in assuming our human condition, assumed the pattern which constitutes one of the most basic tasks of every human life and redeemed it. Unless we wish to withold the life of the small child altogether from the drama of redemption, must we not see here, *in statu infantis,* the primordial and universal pattern of human life which Christ assumed and redeemed? Is it not because

[61] Fowler, "Perspectives on the Family," 3.

of false faith, trust in false gods and false values, that sin has such an obvious hold upon the world? Sin cannot be reduced simply to individual, conscious, wilful acts. Similarly the redemptive gift of paschal faith, the Christlike way of "leaning into life," is not necessarily anything which has to await our conscious decision or deliberate choice. It is rather something which we discover to be already operative in us by the grace of God by the time we become aware of it.

This grace, this gift of faith, comes through hearing, through the Word of God addressed to the child. But the Word here is not the written Word, as yet unavailable to the infant, so much as the biblical *dabar*, mediated in this instance by the community of faith and especially the believing family. Thus it is not so much that baptism infuses faith into a child as that baptism is the deliberate and conscious insertion of the child into the environment of faith, which faith is the faith of the Church, which in turn is the faith of Christ himself. If the Church did not continue to live by the pattern of Christ's own faith in its dying and being raised to life, it would cease to be Church. Such existential faith constitutes the identity of the Church and the identity of the family as domestic church. It is into this faith that the child is baptized when it is baptized in the faith of the Church.

INTEGRATION INTO THE CHURCH. A major stumbling block to Anabaptist recognition of the validity of infant baptism is the view of the Church as a participative community of faith and mutual correction. Though situated at the opposite end of the baptismal spectrum, Roman Catholics seem to share the view that infants, being purely passive, are incapable of actively engaging in the life of the faith community. Believers' Churches apparently consider that the child has nothing to contribute to the faith life and witness of the local congregation, while Catholics, by neglecting small children between *quamprimum* baptism and the age of reason, seem to regard the child as unfit for active participation in community life. Why else should children, alone of all the baptized, be barred from confirmation and Eucharist?

In fact, however, as Andrew Thompson amply demonstrates, a newborn infant alters the configuration of family relationships from the day of its birth, if not sooner, having a major impact on the lives of its parents and siblings. Nor should this impact be seen as merely financial or psychological. The Second Vatican Council spoke perhaps more truly than it knew when it said: "As living members of the family, children contribute in their own way to making their parents holy" (GS, 48). Stanley Hauerwas puts the point more strongly when he writes that

"a good deal of sentimental drivel is written about children. Sentimentality not only belies the hard reality of caring for children, but worse, it avoids the challenge with which they confront us. Generally our children challenge the kind of self-image that finds its most intense expression in the expectations we have for them. If we are lucky, these expectations are modified by our children's refusal to be what we want them to be. . . . Children train us not only to be parents, but sometimes even better parents."[62]

Translating this into the terms of Christian theology, we might say that children bring both joy and the Cross. Children will test the sacrificial self-commitment, the self-delusions, and the spurious faith of those with whom they come in contact for any length of time. They summon parents particularly to a deeper understanding of the mystery of grace and of the limitations of human abilities. They probe the ambivalences of their "way of leaning into life." But they also evoke a spirit of wonder and benediction and become messengers of unsolicited consolation. All this is merely to suggest that in their own way children in fact play an extremely active, even prophetic, role in the household of faith. The obstacle lies not in the child but in the faithlessness of the adult believers. If there is any reason for not admitting an infant to faith and baptismal life in the communion of the Church, it may only be that the child's own God-given household is not faithful.

THEOLOGY OF BAPTISM. We have already noted that one of the most significant effects of the introduction of the adult catechumenate and a unified rite of sacramental initiation for adults has

[62] Stanley Hauerwas, "Learning Morality from Handicapped Children," *The Hastings Center Report*, October 1980, 45.

been the recovery of a fuller and richer understanding of baptism. In comparison with the rich heritage of patristic teaching on baptism, most modern Christians have inherited a drastically impoverished understanding of the wealth and wonder of the baptismal life. As we also noted, there is sometimes a tendency to blame this impoverishment on infant baptism, though it would probably be more accurate to say that it is the result of the institutionalization of *emergency* baptism. Conversely, the recovery of the paschal dimensions of baptism is sometimes promoted in such a way as to challenge, if not to preclude altogether, the practice of infant initiation. We attempted to suggest that this conclusion need not necessarily follow, since while some aspects of a positive theology of baptism (for example, adoption) are very much congruent with the baptizing of small children, other aspects (for example, dying and rising) can be seen to be viable even for infants, provided the state of infancy is carefully considered. But besides the questions of faith and participation in the paschal mystery already touched on, there are other important dimensions of sacramental initiation which are actually highlighted by the baptism of a small child.

A newly baptized infant is not merely one who is delivered from sin and from the threat of damnation, but one claimed by the irrescindable Word of God to be an adopted child of God, a living member of Christ, a temple of the Holy Spirit. The child in baptism enters into a new set of relationships with God, with the Church, and — we have argued — with its own family. In this instance, at least, water is thicker than blood! From early in our tradition comes the story of the father of the great Alexandrian theologian, Origen. The historian Eusebius reports: "It is said that often when the boy was asleep, he would bend over him and bare his breast and, as if it were the temple of the Spirit of God, would kiss it reverently and count himself blessed in his promising child."[63]

St John Chrysostom reflects the same sort of sentiment in an Easter sermon:

[63] Eusebius, *History of the Church*, VI, 2:15. Ed. cit., 241.

"Those who were prisoners yesterday are free men and citizens of the Church. Those who so recently were in sin and shame now enjoy righteousness and security. They are not only free, but holy; not only holy, but righteous; not only righteous, but children; not only children, but heirs; not only heirs, but brothers and sisters of Christ; not only brothers and sisters of Christ, but co-heirs with him; not only co-heirs with Christ, but members of him; not only members of Christ, but temples; not only temples, but instruments of the Holy Spirit.

"Blessed be God, for he has done wonders! (Ps 72:18) Do you realize how manifold are the blessings of baptism? While many believe that the remission of sins is the sole benefit of baptism, we have counted ten. That is why we baptize even tiny children, even though they have no sins, that they might gain righteousness, filiation, inheritance, and the grace of being brother and sisters and members of Christ and the grace of being the dwelling-place of the Holy Spirit."[64]

Furthermore one must agree with Karl Barth that "too little attention has been paid to baptism as a glorifying of God, that is, as a moment of his self-revelation. . . . While baptism does its cognitive work . . . the far greater and primary thing occurs: God receives glory in that he himself, as man recognizes him in truth, once more secures his just due here on earth."[65]

Admittedly Barth is thinking here of believers' baptism, but his words apply equally well, it would seem, to infant baptism as an act of thanksgiving and glorification of God. But it is important to draw a clear distinction between infant baptism and various forms that exist for giving thanks for the birth of a child. While childbirth is itself a striking moment of religious disclosure — one sufficiently powerful to have lent itself and its terminology as a metaphor even for adult initiation — and while it is properly a moment for the blessing of God, baptism cannot be reduced to a celebration of birth. A service of thanksgiving for the safe delivery of a child should be an option for those whose faith extends so

[64] St John Chrysostom, *Baptismal Homily III*, 5–6, text in Didier, *Faut-il baptiser les enfants?* 111–112.
[65] Karl Barth, *The Teaching of the Church Concerning Baptism*, 31.

far, but who are uncertain as to the meaning of the order of redemption and of Christian baptism, and whose allegiance to the community of faith is consequently less than firm. But it should be clear to believers and unbelievers alike that baptism is more than a celebration of birth. It is, as we have already stressed, a celebration and sacrament of rebirth: it is incorporation into the Body of Christ and into the pattern of his death and exaltation; it is a divine act of adoption, whereby a child is claimed by God for his own kind purposes; it is a consecration and sanctification effected by the outpouring of the Holy Spirit of Christ; it is an anointing with the Spirit of holiness for life and mission in this world and for the sanctification of the divine Name, in this world and in the world to come.

All this belongs to a child in principle, as surely and as undeservedly as the kingdom belongs to the heir apparent. Like many an heir apparent, the Christian child may be defrauded of its birthright, may even grow up knowing nothing of it. But, for all that, baptism remains a performative act with certain ineluctable entailments which, even though they be frustrated by the faithlessness of the family or parish, remain nevertheless eternally valid.

Since the practice of infant baptism predates the Augustinian doctrine of original sin, and since that doctrine has not played the major role in the East that it has in the West, one must assume that it is these positive benefits of baptism which have long underlain the Church's instinct to admit infants and small children to the font and the altar. In any case the practice of baptizing infants does not depend for its legitimacy upon the belief that without baptism infants are excluded forever from the vision of God. But it does suppose the possibility that infants *as infants* might be called to share the divine life in the Body of Christ, a possibility which, as we have argued, derives substantial support both from the fact that the Church has always baptized infants and from the insights into the nature of childhood gained from the research of the human sciences.

But while every human being is called to share the life of God, it is obvious that not every human being is called to live as a member of the Church. In the case of an infant born into a believing family, however, there is an a priori assumption that the fact of its being born into an ecclesial community constitutes a reasonable indication that this child is called by God to grace and to glory within the communion of the visible Church. This has nothing to do with John Calvin's assertion that the Old Testament precept concerning circumcision continues to operate under the new covenant. On the contrary, the distinctions we have made between first birth and second birth, between baptism and a celebration of thanksgiving, clearly indicate that Christian identity is precisely not inherited from Christian parents, but that the "accident" of being born into a practicing Christian household is rather an indication of the child's vocation, which it is the duty of the Church to affirm, ratify, and nurture. Consequently whenever a child is presented for baptism, it will be the responsibility of the local community to discern whether this child is certainly called to the life of faith by looking at the faith life of the family. More positively, those with pastoral responsibilities will take seriously the ecclesial character of the family as a household of faith and seek to raise the community's awareness of the sacramentality of the family.

INFANT BAPTISM AS A SACRAMENT FOR THE CHURCH. There was a time when the definition of a sacrament tended to focus on the matter and form of each sacrament, thus tending to depersonalize the sacraments. The twentieth-century renewal of sacramental theology has overcome this narrow and static understanding by seeing the sacraments more dynamically as an interaction between the recipient and the minister who, representing the Church, represents Christ. More recently the public and ecclesial dimension of the sacraments has been recovered, enabling us to recognize that sacraments, when properly celebrated, are meant to redound to the benefit not only of the recipient but of the whole ecclesial community. Such an understanding finds authoritative expression, for example, in the General Introduction to the Order of Penance which goes so far as to say that "the faithful Christian, as he experiences and proclaims the mercy of God in his life, celebrates with the priest *the liturgy with which the Church continually renews itself*" (par. 11, emphasis added).

The truth of this axiom is, of course, even more apparent in the experience of the RCIA, which is teaching us that the initiation of new members not only affects their own lives, but calls for new configurations of relationships within the host community itself.

In infant baptism, we have argued, the ecclesial ramifications of the rite have immediate importance for the family, which is reconstituted by the liturgy of baptism in its God-given identity as a household of faith, a domestic church. Thus the importance of the renewal of baptismal promises (for the parents no longer speak in the name of the child, but in their own name) consists in the fact that the making of the promises is a sacramental act as well as a moral commitment: it is the family actualizing itself as a domestic household of faith within the communion of the local assembly. The formulae of renunciation and profession of faith are, as it were, words of consecration whereby the local Church confects itself as a living sacrament of faith. This perspective on the family-as-ecclesial-sacrament enables us then to grasp more profoundly what is meant by speaking of the parents in particular as the child's "first teachers of the faith." Stanley Hauerwas makes this point more broadly applicable when he says that the Church does not *do* religious education, but *is* a form of education that is religious.

"Religious education is not . . . something that is done to make us Christians, or something that is done after we have become Christians; rather it is the ongoing training in those skills necessary for us to live faithful to God's Kingdom that has been initiated in Jesus. For that Kingdom is constituted by a story that one never possesses, but rather constantly challenges us to be what we have not yet become."[66]

Consequently, parents do not so much promise at their children's baptism to teach them merely what they know. Instead, they commit themselves anew to learning the story by living it, and it is chiefly by the parents living the Christian story that their children will come to pick it up and to develop the skills necessary to be faithful to it. The story and the skills are only partially con-

[66] Stanley Hauerwas, "The Gesture of a Truthful Story: The Church and Religious Education," *Encounter* 43 (1982) 319-329.

veyed in explicit lessons. Christianity, it has been said, is more caught than taught, and the model for learning it is closer to that of an apprenticeship than that of a classroom. In this apprenticeship the accent is on doing the things that Christians do, which makes the practice of withholding from small children the anointing of the Spirit and regular participation at the Eucharistic table all the more unfortunate.[67] It suggests that these sacraments are rewards for lessons learned or markers in the child's growth to maturity, instead of being what they are, namely, the means of our continuing formation in Christian fidelity.

But besides the immediate liturgical sacramental dimensions of infant baptism for the family and the local church, there is also the question of whether, when the sacraments of initiation are made accessible to small children, something important is not gained for the Church's own self-understanding. This is not the place to discuss whether and in what sense adult initiation might be said to be "normative," but even if this were to be admitted, it could not be used to disparage the practice of infant initiation as such, except at the cost of departing from the Catholic tradition or at least sacrificing significant elements of that tradition. N. P. Williams in *The Ideas of the Fall and Original Sin*[68] identifies two sets of conflicting ideas in the theology of redemption: those associated with what he calls the image of the "once born" and those associated with the image of being "twice born." The former gives rise to a theology which stresses continuity and growth in human life, the latter to a theology which highlights conversion and discontinuity. While we would resist, for reasons given earlier, any attempt to describe infants who are baptized as "once born," the

[67] While the Churches have begun to give more consideration to the presence of pre-school children at the liturgy (see, for example, R.C.D. Jasper [ed.] *Worship and the Child*. Essays by the Joint Liturgical Group [London 1975]), serious attention to the issue of infant Communion is mainly confined to the Anglican churches. See, *Communion Before Confirmation?* Church Information Office (London 1985) and *Nurturing Children in Communion*, Grove Liturgical Studies, n. 44 (Bramcote, Notts. 1985). See also, David Holeton, *Infant Communion Then and Now*. Grove Liturgical Studies, n. 27 (Bramcote, Notts. 1981).

[68] N. P. Williams, *The Ideas of the Fall and Original Sin* (London and New York 1927).

contrast between a theology of continuity and a theology of discontinuity accurately summarizes the differences between those who support infant baptism and those who see it as difficult to reconcile with the evangelical values manifest in adult conversion and adult initiation.

Adult baptism, the economy of the "twice born," tends to draw to itself the vocabulary of regeneration as opposed to generation; of brothers and sisters rather than sons and daughters; of voluntary decision rather than divine vocation; of change rather than faithfulness; of breaking with the past rather than growth towards the future; of death and resurrection rather than adoption and filiation. The language of infant initiation, on the other hand, is inclined to speak in terms of the womb rather than the tomb, of election rather than choice, of loyalty rather than commitment, of the preconscious operations of grace rather than of personal convictions, of nurturing the life of faith rather than of passing from unbelief to belief. In Jungian terms, a regime which attaches importance to infant initiation gives a larger role to the "feminine" aspects of Christianity, while adult initiation displays the more "masculine" elements of Christian imagery.

While there are many other and stronger reasons for upholding the baptism of infants, this would seem a further argument for retaining it. At a time when the Church is so intent on rescuing the humane values of Christianity and is concerned to do greater justice to the role of the family and to the Christian vision of sexuality, and at a time when the role of the nonrational and prerational dimensions of the life of faith is being recovered,[69] perhaps infant initiation ought to be seen less as a problem to be grappled with than as an opportunity to be grasped. Far from barring children

[69] Vatican II retains the definition of faith given at Vatican I ("the full submission of intellect and will to God who reveals") but subordinates it to the broader concept of an "obedience of faith," thus making submission of intellect and will the form that such obedience will take for those already endowed with intellect and will, but leaving open the possibility that those not so endowed — infants, young children, and the retarded — might still be said to be capable of faith. In any case, intellective and voluntary capacities vary enormously from person to person and of themselves do not adequately describe the full scope of personal life that is being claimed by the grace of God.

from the font, the chrism, and the altar, the Church should welcome their participation in these sacraments as a reminder both of the catholicity of the Church and of the fact that, no matter how informed or committed we might be as adults, when we take part in the sacramental liturgies of the Church we are taking part in more than we know.

CONCLUSION

Historically speaking, the practice of infant baptism always seems to have preceded and in some ways eluded attempts to justify it theologically. It seems to have been more a matter of the Church's instinct than the putting into effect of a clearly thought out strategy, while attempts to make sense of it have always fallen short of success. Similarly with this essay. It would be foolish to claim that the argument is now settled, but it may legitimately be claimed, if the arguments advanced here hold water, that the grounds of the discussion need to be changed. This in turn will influence practice, since a fresh grasp of what is involved in baptizing an infant will suggest ways of assessing when baptism may properly be celebrated for infants, how it may be prepared for, and most importantly how it may be lived in a process of ongoing initiation to the life of faith in the context of family and parish. Central to this reconsideration of baptism, however, will be theological reflection on the data of the human sciences concerning the child-in-relationship.

Acknowledgments

The essays in this collection were originally published in the following periodicals and books:

Aidan Kavanagh, "Christian Initiation in Post-Conciliar Catholicism: A Brief Report," *Studia Liturgica* 12 (1977) 107–115.

Georg Kretschmar, "Recent Research on Christian Initiation," *Studia Liturgica* 12 (1977) 87–106.

Adela Yarbro Collins, "The Origin of Christian Baptism," *Studia Liturgica* 19 (1989) 28–46.

Gabriele Winkler, "The Original Meaning of the Prebaptismal Anointing and its Implications," *Worship* 52 (1978) 24–45.

Paul F. Bradshaw, "Baptismal Practice in the Alexandrian Tradition: Eastern or Western?" in Paul F. Bradshaw, ed., *Essays in Early Eastern Initiation*, Alcuin/GROW Liturgical Study 8 (Bramcote/ Notts. 1989) 5–17; appearing here through the generous permission of the editors of Grove Books, Ltd.

Jean Laporte, "Models from Philo in Origen's Teaching on Original Sin," *Laval théologique et philosophique* 44, 2 (1988) 191–203.

Maxwell E. Johnson, "From Three Weeks to Forty Days: Baptismal Preparation and the Origins of Lent," *Studia Liturgica* 20 (1990) 185–200.

Paul F. Bradshaw, " 'Diem baptismo sollemniorem': Initiation and Easter in Christian Antiquity" appears also in E. Carr, S. Parenti, and A.-A. Thiermeyer, (eds.), Εὐλόγημα: *Studies in Honor of Robert*

Taft, S.J., (*Studia Anselmiana* 110, Analecta liturgica 17; Rome 1993) 41–51. It appears here thanks to the generous permission of Stefano Parenti.

Aidan Kavanagh, "Confirmation: A Suggestion from Structure," *Worship* 58 (1984) 386–395.

Joseph L. Levesque, "The Theology of the Postbaptismal Rites in the Seventh and Eighth Century Gallican Church," *Ephemerides Liturgicae* 95 (1981) 3–43.

Gabriele Winkler, "Confirmation or Chrismation? A Study in Comparative Liturgy," *Worship* 58 (1984) 2–17.

Frank C. Quinn, "Confirmation Reconsidered: Rite and Meaning," *Worship* 59 (1985) 354–370.

Paul Turner, "The Origins of Confirmation: An Analysis of Aidan Kavanagh's Hypothesis," *Worship* 65 (1991) 320–336.

Aidan Kavanagh, "Response," *Worship* 65 (1991) 337–338.

Aidan Kavanagh, "Unfinished and Unbegun Revisited: The Rite of Christian Initiation of Adults," *Worship* 53 (1979) 327–340.

Laurence H. Stookey, "Three New Initiation Rites," *Worship* 51 (1977) 33–49.

Eugene L. Brand, "New Rites of Initiation and their Implications: in the Lutheran Churches," *Studia Liturgica* 12 (1977) 151–165.

Bryan D. Spinks, "Vivid Signs of the Gift of the Spirit? The Lima Text on Baptism and Some Recent English Language Baptismal Liturgies," *Worship* 60 (1986) 232–246.

Paul F. X. Covino, "The Postconciliar Infant Baptism Debate in the American Catholic Church," *Worship* 56 (1982) 240–260.

Eugene L. Brand, "Baptism and Communion of Infants: A Lutheran View," *Worship* 50 (1976) 29–42.

Mark Searle, "Infant Baptism Reconsidered," in Mark Searle, ed., *Alternative Futures for Worship*, vol. 2: *Baptism and Confirmation* (Collegeville 1987) 15–54; appearing here through the generous permission of The Liturgical Press, Collegeville, Minnesota.

Subject Index

Childhood, theology of, 371, 374–375, 377, 378, 387–390, 394–396, 401, 404–405

Chrism, 61, 73, 96–97, 155, 163ff., 173, 210ff., 224, 229, 289, 315, 318, 324, 367

    consecration of, 87, 89, 163ff., 178, 213, 289

Chrismation, xix, 148, 154, 155, 157, 162, 173, 178, 180–181, 187, 190, 198, 218, 220, 228, 230–232, 235–236, 295, 306, 311–312, 316, 319, 322, 356 (*See also* Confirmation, Consignation)

Christ-Messiah, xiv, 64ff., 71, 155–157, 189, 200, 219, 235, 264

Christendom, xiii, 5, 273, 308

Chrysostom, John, 4, 16–19, 59, 64, 73ff., 91, 145, 249, 402

Church, 3, 4, 7, 24, 29–30, 152, 260, 262, 264, 267, 271–272, 284, 291, 296, 330, 334, 349–350, 366, 382, 386, 389–394, 405–409 (*See also* Ecclesia)

Clausum Paschae, 190ff.

Clement of Alexandria, 89

Communion (*See also* Eucharist)

    as completion of initiation, xiii, 225, 228, 252–253, 270, 335

    first, xi, 12, 285, 288, 302, 306–307, 327, 357–364, 367–368, 378

    infant, xix, 13, 293, 308, 350, 358–364, 409

Competentes, 134

Concomitance, 358–359

Confession, First, 359–360

Confirmation, xi, xvi–xviii, 2, 12, 14, 148ff., 158–159, 209–210, 212–258, 262, 265, 286–288, 292, 295, 302, 305, 314, 323, 327, 330, 341, 343, 356, 359, 368, 370–371 (*See also* Hand laying)

    affirmation of Baptism as, 276, 284–285, 287, 301, 305–306, 357

    as completion or perfection of initiation, 149, 156, 158, 201, 220, 222, 224, 226, 228, 288

    age for, 342, 378

    baptism and, 148, 155, 158, 215, 219, 234, 255, 342

    before first communion, 294, 301, 302–303, 306, 360

    bishops and, xvi, xviii, 7, 12, 149ff., 201, 211ff., 217, 219ff., 293, 319 (*See also* Bishop[s], *and* Hand laying)

    catechetics and, 256, 294, 301, 305 (*See also* Catechesis)

    chrismation and, 202, 217, 219ff., 308, 314 (*See also* Anointing[s], postbaptismal, *and* Chrismation)

    connection to Baptism, 2, 3, 148, 158, 217, 305

    development of, 148–158, 219–237, 238–258 (*See also* Hand laying)

    episcopal ratification as, 212, 227, 255

    essential rite of, 202, 224 (*See also* Chrismation, *and* Hand laying)

    eucharist and, 148, 234, 255, 294, 303, 342 (*See also* Communion, first, *and* Eucharist)

    Holy Spirit and, xvi, 141, 202, 215, 217, 222, 224, 227, 230–234, 252, 294, 314, 319–321, 324 (*See also* Anointing, postbaptismal; Chrismation; Bishop[s]; Hand laying; *and* Holy Spirit)

    ordinary and original minister of, 262

    Protestant Reformers and, 225–226

    Scholastic theology of, 215, 229, 234, 356

    Seal of, 224

Consignation, xiii, 15, 19, 151, 153, 156, 220, 224, 229, 230, 231, 237, 289, 314

Constantinople, 97, 132, 133, 145, 146, 147
Constitution on the Church (Lumen Gentium), 382
Constitution on the Sacred Liturgy (Sacrosanctum Concilium), 336, 382
Conversion, 3–5, 264, 380–381, 399
Coptic, 83, 94, 96, 318, 322
Cornelius, pope, 368
Councils and Synods
  Agde, 250
  Arles III, 199, 209–210, 213, 217, 246
  Barcelona II, 208
  Braga II, 131
  Carthage II, 245, 354
  Elvira, 226, 368
  Florence, 356, 369
  Laodicea, 150, 153, 240–241
  Lateran IV, 359
  Milevis, 250
  Nicea, xv, 135, 142
  Orange I, xvii–xviii, 199, 209, 210, 212–213, 217, 227
  Riez, 199, 209, 217, 227
  Toledo I, 208
  Trent, 356, 359, 368, 370
  Vaison, 212
  Vatican II, 8–9, 262, 298, 327–328, 330, 332, 379, 390, 397
Creed, 28, 95–96, 128–130, 280–281 (See also Profession of Faith)
Cross, sign of, 171, 226, 311, 315 (See also Consignation)
Cyprian of Carthage, 222
Cyril of Alexandria, 92
Cyril of Jerusalem, 4, 20, 59, 64, 93ff., 126ff.

D
Damasus, pope, 245
Decentius of Gubbio, 224
Decretum of Gratian, 215
Didache, 22–25, 32

Didascalia Apostolorum, 26, 59, 66, 70, 117
Didymus the Blind, 92
Dismissal(s) (See Missa)
Divinae Consortium Naturae (Apostolic Constitution of Paul VI), xvi, 203
Duns Scotus, 11

E
Easter vigil, 138, 145, 182, 185, 288 (See also Paschal Vigil)
Ecclesia, Ecclesiology, xiii, xix, 5, 7, 152, 329, 334, 336, 338–339, 350, 362, 365, 381–382, 389–394, 405 (See also Church)
Egeria, 91, 149, 242–243, 253
Egypt, xiv, 17, 20, 22, 82ff., 113ff., 316
Ephrem, 59, 67–68
episcopal, xvii–xviii, 10, 157 (See also Bishop[s])
Episcopal Church (U.S.A.), xviii, 274–291, 298, 306
Essenes (See Qumran)
Eucharist, xi, xx, 6, 13–14, 32, 99–100, 149, 151–152, 156–157, 238, 282, 351, 362–363 (See also Communion)
Eutychius, 83
Evangelization, 1, 4, 260–261, 264, 398
Exorcism, 28–29, 75ff., 91–92, 138, 144, 173, 329, 241, 255, 295 (See also Anointing[s], exorcistic)

F
Faith, 272–273 (See also Baptism, faith and)
Faustus of Riez, 179, 197–199, 214ff., 227–229, 233–234
First communion (See Communion, first)
Font, 181, 186–187, 197, 207, 288, 291

Foot-washing, 20, 173, 204, 206, 209
Forehead, 171, 224, 253, 258 (*See also*
Anointing[s], forehead)

G
Gallican (Gaul), xvii, 135, 141,
159–202, 212, 214, 221, 226, 228, 257
Garment, baptismal, 173f., 188, 190,
205, 290
Gelasian Sacramentary (Gelasianum),
118ff., 123, 125, 130, 132, 133, 134,
175, 224, 369
Georgian Lectionary, 127–128
German(y), 176, 229, 257, 296,
298–299, 302–304
Gnostic(ism), 26, 30
Good Friday, 17–18, 85, 87, 128, 169
Great Week (*See* Holy Week)
Gregory I, pope, 250
Gregory Nazianzen, 145, 383

H
Hadrianum, 369
Hand laying, xvi, xvii, xix, 12, 14,
26, 30–33, 149ff., 157, 199, 208, 212,
214, 219–222, 224–232, 235–258,
285–286, 289–290, 306, 308, 311–312,
318–319, 356–357, 368 (*See also*
Confirmation)
Ḥatmā, (Hatmah), 61ff.
Head, xiv, 64ff.
Himerius, 143, 145
Hippolytus of Rome (*See Apostolic
Tradition*)
Historia Ecclesiastica (*See* Socrates
and Sozomen)
Holy Orders (*See* Orders,
Ordination)
Holy Saturday, 128, 146
Holy Spirit, xvi–xvii, xix, 139, 143,
154–156, 163ff., 167–168, 170, 172,
176–177, 182, 184–188, 190, 192,
195–197, 200, 207, 216, 220, 222,
224, 226, 229–230, 232–233, 235, 238,

262–264, 271, 316, 353, 355–356, 368
(*See also* Anointing[s], Holy Spirit
and; Chrismation; Confirmation,
Holy Spirit and; *and* Hand laying)
Holy Thursday, 189
Holy Week, 89, 122–124, 127, 130–135

I
Immersion, 13, 30–32, 289
Indiscriminate Baptism, 330, 332,
336, 340–341, 362, 363, 379
Imposition of Hands (*See* Hand
laying)
Infant(s)
baptism of (*See* Baptism,
infants and)
communion of, xix, 303, 293,
350, 358–364, 409 (*See also*
Communion, first)
full initiation of, 341, 343–344,
358–364, 400, 408–409
Innocent I, pope, 145, 224, 257
Inter-Lutheran Commission on
Worship (ILCW), 275, 278, 299,
304, 357
Irenaeus of Lyon, 354, 395
Iso'yahb III, 323

J
Jerome, 120
Jerusalem, 16, 18, 20, 92, 122ff.,
133–134, 149, 152, 242, 316
Jesus
baptism of, by John, 19, 35ff.,
47ff., 69, 231, 263, 385
and institution of Christian
baptism, 35ff., 49ff., 231
John the Baptist, xiii, 32, 35ff., 69, 79
Judaism, 27, 30–32, 36, 103, 232

K
Kiss, 16, 152ff., 221, 252–253

Pedilavium (See Footwashing)
Pelagius, Pelagianism, 101, 198–199, 234, 354
Pentecost, 89, 138–139, 143–145, 184–185, 191, 214, 216 (See also Baptism, Pentecost and)
Peter of Alexandria, 83, 90
Philo of Alexandria, xx, 101–117
Photizomenoi, 134
Pontificals, Roman, 229–230
Prayerbook Studies, 286
Priesthood of all believers, 268ff., 283, 293, 296, 391
Profession of Faith, 27, 95–96 (See also Creed)

Q

Quam primum, 9, 262, 338, 369–370, 400
Qumran, xiii, 30, 32, 38ff.
Quodvultdeus of Carthage, 129–130

R

Rabanus Maurus, 198, 228, 234
Reformation, 12, 225, 292f., 313, 359, 361, 366, 377
Reformed Book of Common Order, National Church Association, Scotland (1977), 312–313, 321
Renunciation of Satan, 27–29, 75f., 114, 280
Rite of Baptism for Children (RBC), 332–333, 337, 339
Rite of Christian Initiation of Adults (RCIA), xviii–xix, 155, 237, 259–273, 312, 364, 333–335, 344, 348, 379–381, 406
Rite of Confirmation, 333, 343
Rite, Roman, xvi, xvii, 5, 14, 95, 148, 221, 314
Rituale Romanum, 359, 369
Roman (Rome), xi, xiv–xv, 1, 8, 20, 97, 118–125, 133–134, 136, 139, 144, 145, 147, 160, 208, 221–223, 371

Rule of St. Benedict, 248–249
Rule of the Master, 248
Rušmā (Rushma), 61ff., 265, 316

S

Sacrament(s), Sacramental, 1–2, 7, 144, 159, 260, 293, 295, 305, 336, 351, 362, 365, 373, 382–384, 386, 396–400, 405
Salt, 131, 295
Sarapion of Thmuis, 92, 98
Scandanavia(n), 294, 296, 298–302
Scrutiny, 91, 125, 130, 132–133, 136
Seal, xvi, 13, 17, 68, 188, 224, 263, 315, 317, 356
Sentences of Peter Lombard, 215
Severus of El Asmunein, 83, 85
Sin, xv, 338
  Original, xv, 101–117, 261, 308, 336ff., 352, 358, 374–375, 379, 393–394, 404
Sign(s), 17, 61–63, 310–326, 336 (See also Rushma)
Siricius, pope, 143–145
Socrates, 118, 125, 136
Sozomen, 245
Spain, 21, 130–132, 144, 160, 208–209, 221, 257
Sphragis, 317
Spirit (See Holy Spirit)
Sponsors, 282
Syntaxis, 28, 95 (See also Creed, and Profession of Faith)
Syria(n), xiv–xv, xvii, 15–16, 26, 28–30, 33, 55ff., 64ff., 71ff., 75, 92–94, 133, 205, 208–209, 316, 319, 385
  East, 17, 19, 24, 60, 69, 75, 263, 317, 322–323
  West, 60, 63, 76ff.

T

Teaching of St. Gregory, 59, 67, 69
Tertullian, 4–5, 26–27, 74, 133,

138–139, 146, 214, 222, 253–254, 322, 372–373
Testamentum Domini, 93
Theodore of Mopsuestia, 18–19, 59, 75
Theophilus of Alexandria, 84, 88, 97, 99
Timothy of Alexandria, 87
Typicon, 132, 146

V
Vita S. Hilarii, 246

W
Washing(s), xii, 46f.
Water, blessing of, 29, 84, 222, 278–280, 304–305
World Council of Churches, xix, 311
Würzburg Capitulary, 121, 125

Z
Zwingli, Ulrich, 274